Thoreau's Sense of Place

The American Land and Life Series

Edited by Wayne Franklin

Thoreau's Sense of Place

Essays in American Environmental Writing

Edited by RICHARD J. SCHNEIDER

Foreword by Lawrence Buell

UNIVERSITY OF IOWA PRESS ᴪ Iowa City

University of Iowa Press, Iowa City 52242
Copyright © 2000 by the University of Iowa Press
All rights reserved
Printed in the United States of America
http://www.uiowa.edu/~uipress

The publication of this book was generously supported by the
University of Iowa Foundation.

Printed on acid-free paper

Library of Congress Cataloging-in-Publication Data
Thoreau's sense of place: essays in American environmental writing/
edited by Richard J. Schneider; foreword by Lawrence Buell.
        p.   cm. — (The American land and life series)
    Includes bibliographical references and index.
    ISBN 0-87745-708-5, ISBN 0-87745-720-4 (pbk.)
    1. Thoreau, Henry David, 1817–1862 — Knowledge — Natural
History.   2. Thoreau, Henry David, 1817–1862 — Views on
environmental protection.   3. Environmental protection —
United States — History.   4. Thoreau, Henry David, 1817–
1862 — Influence.   5. American literature — History and
criticism.   6. Natural history — United States — History.
7. Environmental protection in literature.   8. Place (Philosophy) in literature.   9. Nature in literature.   10. Setting
(Literature).   I. Schneider, Richard J.   II. Series.
    PS3057.N3 T46   2000
    818'.309 — dc21
                                                99-058112

00   01   02   03   04   C   5   4   3   2   1
00   01   02   03   04   P   5   4   3   2   1

CONTENTS

ACKNOWLEDGMENTS

Thanks are due to Lawrence Buell, who gave me encouragement in developing this book and who put me in touch with Wayne Franklin, editor of the American Land and Life series, to whom thanks are also due for his wisdom and persistence, which gave focus to the project. The Internet listserves provided by both the Thoreau Society and the Association for the Study of Literature and the Environment did much to facilitate choosing and organizing the contributors to the project. Thanks to all in those two organizations who contributed either essays or suggestions. The compilation of the book was facilitated by Olivia Coil of the Wartburg College Humanities Office and her staff of reliable students. The extra time needed to coordinate a large project such as this was made possible through the release time provided by the Slife Professorship in the Humanities at Wartburg College. Finally, I owe thanks, as always, to my wife, Mary, and to my children, Eric, Heidi, and Rick, for their ongoing personal support.

Lawrence Buell

These essays teach a lesson Henry David Thoreau knew but even good teachers often forget: the enlightenment that comes with discovery worthy of the name means complication more often than consensus.

During the past decade, literary scholarship has discovered the environmental(ist) Thoreau. This dimension of his life and work had for more than a century strongly attracted creative writers and thinkers of environmentalist persuasion, but until quite recently academic Thoreauvians of literary bent took relatively little interest in it. All who have become so should take satisfaction in the fact that the chief fruit to date of this new attention to the green Thoreau has been a vigorous question-raising, not a laying of matters to rest. Was transcendentalism a roadblock to Thoreau's natural history interests, or did it inspire them? What did Thoreau know of nineteenth-century life science—or rather sciences, plural, for this was a field in a state of intense ferment. To what extent was Thoreau biocentric, to what extent anthropocentric? Did Thoreau's commitment to nature, existentially and as an object of study, interfere with his development as a writer or quicken it? These are only a few of the questions explored by the new environmentally valenced inquiry into Thoreau's life and writing, and small wonder that individual scholars disagree about them. They are big issues, and Thoreau was a complex and irrepressibly contrarian thinker.

Among the contested issues of this kind, the matter of Thoreau's sense of place looms up as especially knotty, partly because the concept of place itself is luminous but indeterminate (it can be relatively large or small, relatively tangible or abstract, etc.) and partly also, perhaps, because there is a deceptive self-evidence both to Thoreau's biographical lococentrism as a lifelong Concordian and to his insistent self-marginalization as a critic of his community. This makes for an analytical discourse of strong opinions and chronic stumbling blocks. When Thoreau identified with Concord, with precisely what did he identify? What was the mix of community and biotic affiliation? What sort of sense of place is implied by Thoreau's repeated exoticization of his Concord surroundings and by his literal and discursive sorties on day trips and more extended trips to the north country?

The trickiness of such questions, together with the awareness that Thoreauvian placiality takes the form of discursive moves that he both absorbed from precursors and transmitted with new inventiveness, also makes it logical and valuable for a number of the contributors to this volume to situate Thoreau in the company of a number of other place-oriented writers. Here too the same caveat applies: Thoreau is hard to fix precisely in literary and cultural history, being an omnivorous but finicky reader and a writer who liked to take extreme positions and who tends to provoke similarly mixed feelings. Although it seems obvious—perhaps too obvious—that Thoreau was a giant in the "nature writing" tradition (among other traditions), it is hard to identify a first-rate successor who has felt for him the same worshipful admiration that, say, Dante felt for Virgil and Pope for Milton. To feel "close" to Thoreau is probably bound to mean, for a thinking person, experiencing both a sense of rejection and the will to be nobody's disciple.

That, however, may be a further reason why setting Thoreau in place is a potentially attractive project, as well as a timely one given the contemporary resurgence of place theory throughout the human sciences. Surely a situated Thoreau makes for a more attractive as well as a truer version of him than a freestanding Thoreau. However we understand Thoreau's sense of place, the process of so doing, if done faithfully, sets him on some sort of common ground while honoring the intractable idiosyncrasies—"place" by definition occupying a middle ground between solipsism and objectivity. I fancy that Thoreau himself would have liked this. For whatever he sometimes said to the contrary, he was happiest when he wasn't thinking about his own freestanding apartness but instead feeling part of something.

No scholar can do it all. Not even nineteen of them. But this is a book at once diverse and thoughtfully coordinated, from which, to my pleasure and humility, I've learned much about things I supposed I already understood. Whether or not we can dare hope Thoreau himself would have valued it, Thoreauvians should.

Thoreau's Sense of Place

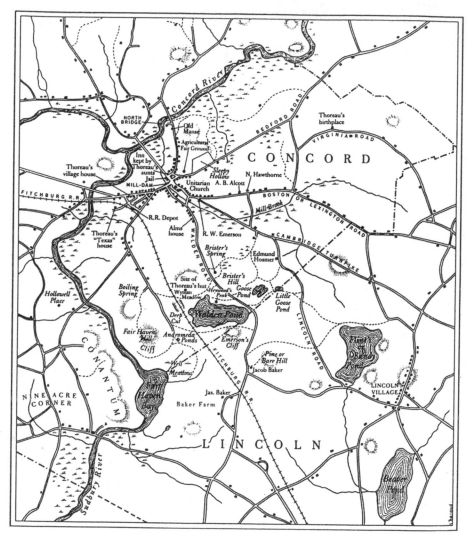

Walden Pond Area in 1845, from Walden *by Henry David Thoreau. Adapted from a map of Concord, Massachusetts, compiled by Herbert W. Gleason in 1906. Annotations copyright © 1995 by Walter Harding. Reprinted by permission of Houghton Mifflin Company. All rights reserved.*

INTRODUCTION

In a Journal entry for December 6, 1856, Henry David Thoreau observes that he was "born into the most estimable place in all the world, and in the very nick of time, too."[1] Taken out of context, this passage appears to be Thoreau's praise for the special qualities of Concord and its environs. In context, however, it turns out to be just the opposite, an argument for the ordinariness of Concord and an example of Thoreau's own ambivalence about place.

In the Journal passage in which the above quotation appears, Thoreau comments at some length about the virtues of deprivation in winter, such as how being unable to take his boat out on the frozen river will make him appreciate all the more being able to go boating in the spring. Any place or time, no matter how restricted, he suggests, has its advantage to the person wise enough to recognize it. In that context, Thoreau's Concord is "the most estimable place" because, despite its smallness and relative isolation, it is still a source of "homely every-day phenomena and adventures" (*J* IX:160). Since "it is the greatest advantage to enjoy no advantage at all" (*J* IX:160), Concord is as good as any other place. Place is of no concern to a wise man, and voyaging to other places is "only great-circle sailing."[2] The greatest wisdom is to accept whatever place one is given, wherever that is.

If, on the one hand, place is nothing to Thoreau, on the other hand it is everything to him. Concord might be just another site no better than any other for everyday adventures, but elsewhere in the Journal he describes it as having an aesthetic appeal special to river towns: "I think that a river-valley town is much the handsomest & largest-featured. Like Concord & Lancaster for instance. Natural centers."[3] Later that year (1850) he describes Concord and its environs as especially good for walking, because "I can easily walk 10 15 20 any number of miles commencing at my own door without going by any house — without crossing a road except where the fox & the mink do" (*PJ* 3:102). Such passages, together with the great detail in which Thoreau chronicles the special qualities of Walden Pond in *Walden*, make it obvious that for him place does make a crucial difference in how one perceives one's experience in nature.

To recognize the ambivalence about place in Thoreau's thinking is

1

certainly nothing new. It is simply the epistemological split between subject and object that scholars have long made a central issue in Thoreau studies and that Thoreau himself emphatically recognizes. "Who placed us with eyes between a microscopic and a telescopic world?" he asks in bewilderment in the Journal (J VI:133). Formalist critics have tended to emphasize the "telescopic," the transcendentally idealistic and mystical, side of this split — as Thoreau himself says, "the idealist views things in the large" (J VI:129). In this view, Thoreau is a literary artist and philosopher whose interest in nature provided him with a set of symbols for dealing with human concerns; Thoreau, in writing about nature, is really writing about the human mind. If that is so, then his concern for the "microscopic" and scientific and for peculiarities of place, if not kept properly in check, was a distraction from his literary goals. As Thoreau himself admits, "the habit of looking at things microscopically, as the lichens on the trees and rocks, really prevents my seeing aught else in a walk" (J III:336–37).

But as Thoreau himself also realized, the more distant and idealized view could also be flawed. By focusing his sight on a distant mountain, he finds that he cannot see the "farmhouses, the lonely mills, wooded vales, wild rocky pastures. . . . All these, and how much more, I *overlook.* I see the very peak, — there can be no mistake, — but how much I do not see, that is between me and it!" (J IV:366, Thoreau's emphasis). How to see what is "between me and it," how to understand and image his relation with nature, that is the essence of Thoreau's dilemma. "With regard to . . . objects," he says, "I find that it is not they themselves (with which the men of science deal) that concern me; the point of interest is somewhere *between* me and them (i.e. the objects)" (J X:165, Thoreau's emphasis). "The thing that really concerns me," he says in the same Journal entry, "is not there, but in my relation to that" (J X:164). He was searching for a way to bridge the epistemological gap between the observer and the observed, between the perceiver and the place.

What is most interesting about recent Thoreau studies is their emphasis on this relation between Thoreau and the places he writes about and a new willingness to take that relation seriously as a central concern in understanding Thoreau. This shift in critical perspective has led, as Lawrence Buell has chronicled in *The Environmental Imagination* (see esp. 362–69)[4] to a new emphasis on the "green" Thoreau, on Thoreau the environmentalist, a Thoreau rooted firmly in particular places and interacting with particular objects. From this point of view, Thoreau's interest in science is no longer seen merely as a distraction from his larger philosophical interests but as an integral part of them. His science and his interest in place, particularly his pioneering efforts in ecology, are now seen as his artistic and scientific effort to save the natural environment, both at large and in particular places, from destruction.

But as Buell also points out, "not all contemporary environmental historians, ecophilosophers, and environmentalist activists worship at Thoreau's shrine" (366). And rightly so, for the ecocritical emphasis on a green Thoreau in some ways simply recasts the old epistemological split into a new split between anthropocentric (or homocentric) and ecocentric (or biocentric) views of nature, and Thoreau ends up on both sides of this newly defined split as well. As I point out in my own essay for this volume, for instance, Thoreau's essay "Walking," the essay whose praise of the wild has been adopted as a rallying cry by environmentalists, contains not only an apparently ecocentric plea for preserving wilderness places but also Thoreau's explicit endorsement of an overtly anthropocentric view of place and history derived partly from Humboldtian comparative geography. It may well be that, as Buell claims, "appearances of self-contradiction notwithstanding, the development of Thoreau's thinking about nature seems pretty clearly to move along a path from homocentrism toward biocentrism" (138), but those self-contradictions and that development still seem very much open to discussion.

One way to continue the discussion is to compare Thoreau to a twentieth-century nature writer such as Aldo Leopold, an exercise which reveals both the prescience and the limitations of Thoreau's biocentrism. Central to Leopold's thinking, for instance, is his concept of "home range," the distance which an animal will travel in its daily activities and the variations in that distance due to seasons and weather conditions. By following deer tracks in the snow both backward to their beds in a thicket and forward to their feeding grounds in a cornfield, Leopold finds that the range of the deer's nightly activity "from bed to breakfast is a mile."[5] By observing the behavior of a rabbit when chased by a dog, keeping track of how far from their feeder chickadees are sighted, and examining the contents of the droppings of grouse, Leopold is able to make similar estimates of the home range of these animals (83–85).

Such close observation of animal behavior can be found also in the "Winter Animals" chapter of *Walden* in Thoreau's description of the behavior of foxes when being chased by hunters and of partridges which "will come regularly every evening to particular trees" (276). His Journal is also filled with such observations of animal behavior, for, as he says, "I spend a considerable portion of my time observing the habits of the wild animals, my brute neighbors. By their various movements and migrations they fetch the year about to me. Very significant are the flight of geese and the migration of suckers, etc., etc." (*J* VIII:220). Both Thoreau and Leopold understand that, as Thoreau puts it, "a history of animated nature must itself be animated" because "as soon as I begin to be aware of the life of any creature, I at once forget its name" (*J* XIII:154, 155). Here Thoreau clearly exemplifies the shift in scientific emphasis from taxonomy toward ecology, a shift which Leopold articulates most effectively in the twentieth century: "Every farm is a textbook on animal ecology; woodsmanship is the translation of the book" (86).

Leopold articulates the ecological approach to nature in terms of "the A-B cleavage," in which people in group A see "the land as soil, and its function as commodity production," while people in group B see "the land as a biota, and its function as something broader" (258–59). There are plenty of group A people in Thoreau's writing: farmer Flint of Flint's Pond in the chapter on "The Ponds" in *Walden*, "the unclean and stupid farmer, whose farm abutted on this sky water, whose shores he has ruthlessly laid bare . . . who loved better the reflecting surface of a dollar" (195); or the misguided proprietors of woodlots who fail to understand that letting cattle, who have a habit of butting down pine trees, into a pasture where pine trees are just beginning to grow will make the land productive for neither crops nor wood. The farmer, with an eye on a fast buck, ignorantly defeats his own purpose.[6] Such farmers are like Leopold's group A forest managers who want to "grow trees like cabbages" (259). Thoreau and Leopold are both clearly in group B, defenders of nature trying to persuade the group A majority to see in nature something more than commodity.

Two of the most famous expressions of this concern for seeing higher laws in nature are Leopold's poignant description of a dying wolf and Thoreau's description of his participation in the killing of a moose. Neither man is against hunting at first. Leopold, trained in the "wise use" theories of forest management, had once conducted an aggressive campaign against predators during which he vowed to kill "the last wolf or lion in New Mexico."[7] Thoreau accompanied moose hunters in the Maine woods because although he "felt some compunction about accompanying the hunters," he "wished to see a moose near at hand, and was not sorry to learn how the Indian managed to kill one."[8] He describes his position as that of "chaplain to the hunters" but adds that "the chaplain has been known to carry a gun himself" (99).

The result of both hunting experiences, however, is an epiphany and a conversion. Leopold describes his youthful participation in the shooting of a small pack of wolves, an action based on the erroneous assumption that "because fewer wolves meant more deer, . . . no wolves would mean hunters' paradise" (138). On witnessing the last breaths of one of these wolves and seeing "a fierce green fire dying in her eyes" (138), however, Leopold discovers "something new to me in those eyes — something known only to her and to the mountain" (138). This incident becomes his conversion to an ecological perspective, to the recognition that the wolf, the deer, and the vegetation on the mountain are all part of an interdependent system which cannot spare one of its components without severely damaging, perhaps even destroying, the rest. This, Leopold says, is "thinking like a mountain" (137). Thoreau witnesses the shooting of a female moose and at first takes only a scientific interest in its corpse, measuring its dimensions so that he would not "be obliged to say merely that the moose was very large" (*MW* 113). But when his guide begins to skin the moose, Thoreau reacts with revulsion at seeing "that still warm and palpitating body pierced with a knife, then see the warm milk stream from the rent udder, and the ghastly naked red carcass appearing from within its seemly robe" (115). After that, he says, "I had had enough of moose-hunting" (118).

The difference in these two antihunting conversions is a difference both in kind and in permanence. Leopold's conversion is both profoundly ethical and profoundly ecological. He makes us feel that he will never again seek to exterminate wolves; he has been initiated permanently into the ranks of group B thinkers. Thoreau's conversion is essentially an aesthetic one: the skinning of the moose is an ugly spectacle. His objection is similar to that against eating animal food, which he expresses in *Walden*: "there is something essentially unclean about this diet and all flesh, and I began to see where housework commences, and whence the endeavor, which costs so much, to wear a tidy and respectable appearance each day, to keep the house sweet and free from all ill odors and sights" (214). In addition to its ugliness, Thoreau objects only to the purpose of hunting the moose "merely for the satisfaction of killing him — not even for the sake of his hide" (*MW* 119). To hunt for subsistence would be another matter: "I think I could spend a year in the woods fishing and hunting just enough to sustain myself, with satisfaction. This would be next to living like a philosopher on the fruits of the earth which you had raised" (119). He recognizes that the hunting of the moose could lead to its extinction, but rather than calling for its preservation, he observes with some satisfaction that after its extinction, future cultures will be compelled to create a mythological creature to take its place: "The moose will perhaps one day become extinct, but how naturally then, when it exists only as a fossil relic, and unseen as that, may the poet or sculptor invent a fabulous animal with similar branching and leafy horns . . . to be the inhabitant of such a forest as this" (115). To Thoreau, the moose is an aesthetic but not an ecological necessity in the Maine woods.

There is, then, a crucial difference in urgency in the attitudes toward nature in Leopold and Thoreau. Leopold, as an expert in forest management, has seen the disastrous effects of an overpopulation of deer on the plant life of a mountain and realizes that the extermination of the wolf as predator can rapidly destroy a mountain's ecosystem: "just as a deer herd lives in mortal fear of its wolves, so does a mountain live in mortal fear of its deer" (140). Thoreau, too, is aware that the extermination of predators and other animals can significantly affect a place such as the Concord woods, but to him that effect is local and aesthetic only; he does not see it as part of a formula for more widespread ecological disaster, for if the larger animals no longer dwell in the Concord woods, they still exist in abundance further west. "When I consider that the nobler animals have been exterminated here," he says, "the cougar, panther, lynx, wolverene [sic], wolf, bear, moose, deer, the beaver, the turkey, etc., etc., — I cannot but feel as if I lived in a tamed, and, as it were, emasculated country" (J VIII: 220). He feels the absence of these animals primarily in aesthetic terms: for him, "The forest and the meadow now lack expression" without these animals (J VIII: 221); "I listen to a concert," he says, "in which so many parts are wanting" (J VIII: 221); and, "I take infinite pains to know all the phenomena of the spring . . . thinking that I have here the entire poem, and then, to my chagrin, I hear that it is but an imperfect copy that I possess and have read, that my ancestors have torn out many of the first leaves and grandest passages" (J VIII: 221). Thoreau expresses his sense of loss only in artistic terms; the absence of these animals diminishes the number of artistic symbols available to him in the Concord woods, but it does not jeopardize the very existence of the woods.

It is, of course, unfair to expect the same sense of urgency about ecological matters in Thoreau in the middle of the nineteenth century as one finds in Leopold in the middle of the twentieth. True, extinctions of entire species such as the great auk had occurred even before Thoreau's time, and, as David Foster observes, "Thoreau lived at an unfortunately opportune time to document the historical decline and eventual extinction of the passenger pigeon."⁹ Despite his awareness of the decline in pigeon population through his reading and his own observation, however, Thoreau's Journal entries show no significant concern about the fate of the pigeons. It would not be until the middle of the twentieth century that Aldo Leopold would speak at a dedication for a monument to the extinct passenger pigeon and observe that "For one species to mourn the death of another is a new thing under the sun" (117).

Such extinctions could be accepted in Thoreau's day as part of a larger divine plan. The sense that human intervention in nature could be contrary to a divine or natural order on a national or global scale would not fully arrive until the twentieth century. Donald Worster, for instance, defines the beginning of the "Age of Ecology" as the sense of environmental urgency created by the invention of the atom bomb during World War II (339–40). Soon thereafter, Rachel Carson would sound the alarm about the pollution of our national waterways by pesticides. The closest thing to an urgent environmental problem in Thoreau's day was perhaps the destruction of the eastern forests. As Foster reminds us, "By 1845, when Thoreau set up temporary residence in the cabin . . . at Walden Pond, the New England landscape was near its peak of deforestation" (12). But on this issue, like so many others, one finds Thoreau on both sides — surveying the woodlots around Concord so that farmers could cut them down to sell as firewood, while also doing extensive replanting of trees at Walden Pond and making pioneering studies of forest succession.

Karl Kroeber, in a recent review-essay, suggests that twentieth-century ecological writers such as Leopold and Carson are actually quite "un-Thoreauvian,"¹⁰ that "Leopold and Carson treat nature in a fashion radically different from the way Thoreau does" and that "*pace* Buell, the best contemporary ecological writers follow their lead" (311). These writers, he argues, are in a tradition deriving more from William Bartram than from Thoreau (315), one that is based in the objectivity of science and that leads toward "deep ecology," which Kroeber defines as an approach that "regards human beings as a not extraordinarily important element in a total environment that has in the past, and will in the future, flourish without the presence of humans" (311). This deep ecology tradition is essentially antianthropocentric. Kroeber sees Thoreau, however, as essentially anthropocentric and at best a practitioner of "shallow ecology," a view of nature "which seeks to improve and sustain an environment healthy for human endeavors, for instance by correcting inefficient land-use practices, saving wilderness areas, or preventing pollution" (311).

As the essays in this volume will suggest, however, Kroeber's understanding of Thoreau's attitude toward and use of science does not fully acknowledge the complexity of Thoreau's science. See, for instance, the essays by Walls and Rossi. Kroeber also neglects Thoreau's animism, which occasionally makes Thoreau sound very much like a deep ecologist: "It is as immortal as I am," Thoreau says of a pine tree, "and perchance will go to as high a heaven, there to tower above me still" (*MW* 123). Kroeber is surely correct, however, in suggesting that Thoreau's originality lies in his awareness of the basic problem of "the gap between immediate sensual experience and the verbal structure that conveys it" (325). Indeed, Thoreau's strength lies in his awareness of and participation in a whole range of problems in the interaction among the individual (usually the writer), American culture, and nature. As Laura Dassow Walls puts it in her essay in this volume: Thoreau "maps a range of conflicts and potentials in environmental thought," and it is this breadth in his encounter with nature and with specific places in it, together with the depth of his exploration of sometimes contradictory points of view about these places, that might best qualify him as the founder of American environmentalism.

This volume is organized into chapters focusing on four of these basic conflicts, expressed below as sets of questions, which both Thoreau and subsequent writers in the American environmental tradition must necessarily confront:

I. RELATING TO PLACE: "BETWEEN ME AND IT"

How do Thoreau and his successors attempt to cope with the basic epistemological split between perceiver and place inherent in writing about nature? Where in his writing does Thoreau move toward biocentrism, and which writers among his successors make the most effort to be biocentric?

In this section, Laura Dassow Walls and William Rossi argue that the perceived split between Thoreau's anthropocentric transcendentalism and his more biocentric interest in science is a misconception, with Walls arguing that Thoreau was able to incorporate a protoecological Humboldtian science into his anthropocentric transcendentalism. Rossi comes to a similar conclusion that Thoreau was able successfully to merge his interests in transcendentalism and science, but he approaches the issue from the opposite starting point, arguing that Thoreau's science derived from, rather than in opposition to, his transcendentalism. My own essay shows that Thoreau's science and his anthropocentrism could nevertheless sometimes be at odds with each other, by showing how his acceptance of Arnold Guyot's Humboldtian geography leads to his affirmation of Manifest Destiny rather than to a defense of wilderness. All three of these essays emphasize the importance of understanding how nineteenth-century scientific theories informed American ideas of place, nature, and culture.

The essays by Ted Olson and Jim Papa follow the conflict between anthropocentric and biocentric approaches into the twentieth-century by comparing Thoreau with two of the best-known contemporary environmental writers, Wendell Berry and Annie Dillard. Olson shows that Berry's increasingly anthropocentric approach based in his interest in farming leads him to reject Thoreau's less social approach to the value of nature, while Papa argues that Dillard is less interested than Thoreau in making things in the natural world "mean anything beyond what they are."

II. IMAGING PLACE: FINDING A DISCOURSE TO MATCH DISCOVERY

What kind of discourse is most effective for writing about place? Are the genres that Thoreau uses frequently, such as the excursion and the journal, effective tools for depicting nature? How are verbal depictions of place different from visual ones? How do anthropocentric and ecocentric approaches to place require different forms of discourse?

David Robinson addresses the first and last of these questions by exploring how the excursion genre allowed Thoreau to connect his interest in nature with his sense of social alienation and ethics. Isaiah Smithson contrasts Thoreau's verbal landscapes to the visual landscapes of painters Thomas Cole and Asher Durand to argue that Thoreau's verbal renderings of nature are more original and less conventionally nationalistic and religious than the visual renderings of Cole and Durand.

Peter Blakemore explores how Thoreau used his Journal as a means of sharpening his own awareness of place and of inhabiting the particular environment of Concord, and he shows how this emphasis on local inhabitation continues in turn-of-the-century nature writers such as John Muir, Mary Austin, and Sarah Orne Jewett. J. Scott Bryson returns us to the split between anthropocentric and biocentric stances by discussing how twentieth-century "ecological" poets, while obviously more biocentric in their responses toward nature, nevertheless address issues which Thoreau addressed with some frustration in his own poetry.

III. SOCIALLY CONSTRUCTING PLACE: CULTURE AND NATURE

To what extent are images of place culturally constructed in Thoreau's writing and in American nature writing in general, and how do those images in turn affect culture? For instance, what is the impact on Thoreau and his successors of cultural assumptions deriving from economics, gender, literary conventions, or nationality?

In this section, James McGrath places Thoreau's various approaches to nature in the context of modern geographer D. W. Meinig's ten ways of viewing a landscape. McGrath emphasizes how Thoreau's use of many of these ten viewpoints enables him to know the Concord woods fully as a specific and unique locality. Bernard Quetchenbach then demonstrates how views of the Maine woods by "spiritual saunterers" and "industrial saunterers" simultaneously conflict and coexist both in Thoreau's writing and in the writing of other chroniclers of the Maine woods.

Rochelle Johnson compares Thoreau to his contemporary, Susan Fenimore Cooper, to explore the relation between gender and the written representation of place. Johnson suggests that Thoreau's fame as a nature writer and Cooper's relative obscurity reflect our culture's privileging of metaphorical masculine and subjective views of nature over more literal feminine and objective views. Greg Garrard focuses on matters of literary genre, showing how Thoreau and William Wordsworth use conventions of the literary pastoral to move in opposite directions in their views of nature: Thoreau moving toward a more biocentric perspective and Wordsworth toward a more anthropocentric perspective. Matters of nationality also enter the discussion through Aimin Cheng's essay; although geographer Yi-Fu Tuan has argued that there is a basic difference between the American sense of "space" and the Chinese sense of "place,"[11] Cheng argues that Thoreau's view of nature has much in common with the Chinese sense of place.

IV. SAVING PLACE: WRITING AS APPROPRIATION
OR PRESERVATION OF NATURE

*Does writing about nature necessarily involve the writer's appropriation
or even exploitation of the places and objects being described? Was
writing about Walden Pond an act of exploitation or of preservation
for Thoreau's most beloved place? If intended as a defense of nature,
is writing a more adequate or a less adequate defense than more
physically aggressive action, such as taking a crowbar to the Billerica
Dam (which Thoreau threatens to do in* A Week*) or Edward Abbey's
"monkey wrenching" of construction equipment?*

To begin this section, Nancy Simmons uses passages from Thoreau's
Journal to argue that he did indeed speak a word for nature in his nature
writing and that his perspective is truly biocentric. Robert Sattelmeyer,
on the other hand, argues that Thoreau did appropriate Walden Pond
for his own literary ends, using the pond as "less Thoreau's home than
his home page." Walden Pond as a place, Sattelmeyer reminds us, was
actually quite different in Thoreau's day from the way that Thoreau depicts it. Stephen Germic also sees Thoreau as imposing his own view on
the landscape by presenting an idyllic view of the Concord and Merrimack Rivers, but only by ignoring the textile industry which had become so strong a presence along New England's rivers.

Barbara "Barney" Nelson shifts the discussion from Thoreau's appropriation of nature to twentieth-century appropriation of Thoreau
by demonstrating how a current environmental writer, Roderick Nash,
has used and sometimes distorted Thoreau's words to support his own
environmental agenda. Susan Lucas concludes with a comparison of
Thoreau to Edward Abbey, arguing that both Thoreau and Abbey are
often viewed as environmental activists but that in both cases their defense of place was rooted more in language than in physical activism.

Among these four sections, the reader should watch for crosscurrents.
For instance, if the first two essays by Walls and Rossi explore the tension
between Thoreau's transcendentalism and his science, so does Simmons's
essay in the last section. The question of how Thoreau depicts a particular
place is raised not only in Papa's essay on Thoreau and Dillard, but also
by Blakemore in section II, by Johnson in section III, and by Sattelmeyer
in section IV. The extent to which Thoreau supported (either implicitly
or explicitly) or opposed a national political agenda is explored not only

in my own essay in section I, but also in Quetchenbach's essay in section III and in Germic's and Lucas's essays in section IV.

Also among these essays the reader will find some interesting shifts in emphasis in our perceptions of Thoreau. There is, for instance, a noticeable shift away from the focus on just one of his books, Walden, and toward an interest in other works, such as his Journal, his late essay "Walking," and his notes on seed dispersion. The recent shift toward seeing Thoreau's science as central to his writing rather than as peripheral or antagonistic to it continues in these essays, but there is new emphasis on geography as a companion science to ecology. And, as suggested earlier, one will find here some healthy disagreement about Thoreau's engagement with specific places and with nature in general.

No single volume, no matter how varied its contents, can capture the full complexity of Thoreau's interest in place or the wide range of his influence on later writers. But the hope is that this volume will point toward some fascinating new directions in our reading of Thoreau and of his many "sons and daughters" in the tradition of American environmental writing.

NOTES

1. Thoreau, *Journal of Henry David Thoreau*, ed. Torrey and Allen, vol. 9, 160. Subsequent page references are cited parenthetically in the text with *J* and the volume number.

2. Thoreau, *Walden*, 320. Subsequent page references are cited parenthetically in the text.

3. Thoreau, *Journal, Vol. 3: 1848–1851*, 79. Subsequent page references are cited parenthetically in the text with *PJ*.

4. Buell, *The Environmental Imagination*. Subsequent page references are cited parenthetically in the text.

5. Leopold, *Sand County Almanac*, 84. Subsequent page references are cited parenthetically in the text.

6. Thoreau, *Faith in a Seed*, 172–73.

7. Qtd. in Worster, *Nature's Economy*, 273. Subsequent page references are cited parenthetically in the text.

8. Thoreau, *Maine Woods*, 99. Subsequent page references are cited parenthetically in the text with *MW*.

9. David R. Foster, *Thoreau's Country*, 167. Subsequent page references are cited parenthetically in the text.

10. Kroeber, "Ecology and American Literature," 309. Subsequent page numbers are cited parenthetically in the text.

11. Tuan, "American Space, Chinese Place," 8.

I. RELATING TO PLACE

"Between Me and It"

Believing in Nature

Wilderness and Wildness in Thoreauvian Science

LAURA DASSOW WALLS

"In Wildness is the preservation of the World" — so runs the oft mis-quoted line from Thoreau's essay "Walking."[1] Why "Wildness" and not "Wilderness," as the line so often appears? What does the difference sig nify? In context, Thoreau clearly identifies "wildness" not as a distant place but as a quality, something ineffable and strange and raw at the heart of the most common experience: "Life consists with wildness."[2] It need not, then, be housed in a "wilderness" — yet it is hard to dissociate the two concepts, to accept one without the other.

The history of their entanglements leads us into nineteenth-century natural science, the domain that by asserting control over all things sought to transform the wild into the tame. Science, it is commonly as-sumed, can perpetrate such conceptual violence because it doesn't "be-lieve" in nature — has reduced the world of nature into objects and forces, on which science acts with impunity and without conscience. In "Walking," Thoreau counters such assumptions with an avowal: "I be-lieve in the forest, and in the meadow, and in the night in which the corn grows."[3] In an age of science, is it still possible to "believe" in forest and meadow and corn-growing night? — in a nature that grounds moral val-ues, lifts us into spiritual transcendence, promises personal and social redemption?

Only, it is often implied, to the extent that one repudiates science, which is said to be at war with belief, with faith. This assumption makes Thoreau's involvement with science difficult to accept as integral to his poetic and spiritual self. Yet in the nineteenth century, it was entirely possible and even necessary to "believe" in "Nature," an affirmation in-separable from Nature's source in a Christian God and from science as the appointed interpreter of God's meaning. This answer, though, raises further and more difficult questions: In which nature shall Thoreau believe? For he had a number of choices. In Baconian nature, so crucial to nineteenth-century America and romantic science, the forest and meadow and corn-growing night were agents of God, intended to contribute to the use and improvement of humanity so long as humanity should in turn serve as nature's servant and interpreter. In an even older trope of natural theology, forest and meadow and corn-growing night would be hieroglyphs, words in God's "Book of Nature," the symbolic key to the Book of Revelation: one would believe in them less for themselves than for the divine message they carried. However, a newer romantic natural theology, finding this system too static, sought to animate it such that forest and meadow and night would be thoughts of God, billowing through the evanescent material world; to believe in them was to believe in God's power and in the stark fullness of the Law that surged and sorted the particles of matter. In various ways, all these modes presumed that forest and meadow were to be believed in not for themselves alone but for something higher, something they served or translated or embodied. Yet it was also possible in nineteenth-century America to claim nature was its own reason for being — that the dark forest and the dank meadow and the mysterious forces of the night were the powers and presences of a self-generating and self-directing material nature not immediately responsible to God and perhaps, therefore, not immediately responsive to human will — a willed nature, a wild nature, a nature unpredictable and even a little frightening.

None of these choices was innocent. Belief in Bacon's nature allied one with imperialist nation-building, and reading the traditional book of nature meant reading the world as theological doctrine. Romantic nature updated the theology but enforced the hierarchical social organization, naturalizing it in often bitter or anguished reaction to the radical threat posed by subversive Continental materialists, who by taking God out of nature apparently reduced man to the level of the beasts. Thus, to "believe in nature" was not to escape from the domain of society and politics but to declare one's own political allegiances, one's ideology. The romantics were right: there is no way to see nature apart from the idea by which nature is made visible to the mind — there is no innocent eye. And in modern Western industrial society, the ideas which mediated visions of nature were inseparable from science, the embodiment of those ideas in the physical world and the organizing center for notions about nature, self, and society.

Thoreau's belief in nature has, in a process detailed recently by Lawrence Buell, led to his installation as the founding father of environmental thought in America.[4] I would add that Thoreau's participation in science maps a range of conflicts and potentials in environmental thought. In brief, I argue that Thoreau arrived at a radical view of nature as a self-generating, creative agent by incorporating Humboldtian protoecological science into traditional and romantic forms of natural theology.[5] The protoecology of Alexander von Humboldt showed Thoreau ways of valuing "wildness," while the ideology of the more mainstream natural theologies made "wilderness" a cultural necessity; rather than sacrifice either one, Thoreau saw the two working in concert, each completing the other. The concept of "environment," which emerged during Thoreau's lifetime, is the site at which these distinctions are intensified into contradictions: is humanity a part of nature, intervening and participating in an ecological system? Or is it exempt from nature, which is pure only in the absence of human will, design, and desire? These questions are related to the construction of modern science, occurring also during Thoreau's lifetime: was science to be democratic and participatory, or a specialized province restricted to the virtuous few? How is the two-culture split between literature and science related to the disappearance of science from a common shared culture, and the emergence of a form of literature recognized as "nature writing"? The following can only sketch some speculative answers, directed first to the bifurcation of science, then to some implications for the concept of "environment," which was for some brief period the common ground for both literary and scientific writers.

The bifurcation of science can be traced to Kant, who had declared that natural history, which "systematically ordered" the facts of nature, was separate from true natural "philosophy," which revealed the "primal, internal principle" by which facts were constituted.[6] Post-Kantian natural historians sought to elevate their field of knowledge to the level of a true science by discovering the necessary self-evident and self-constitutional principles according to which all objects in nature were formed, making sublunary nature just as "Newtonian" as the stars. Yet a self-evident nature can reflect only truths of the self. The environmental tradition insists on the otherness of nature, in a newer, "empirical" tradition which deliberately countered romantic rationalism. This tradition can be traced back to a road suggested, but not taken, by Kant. In teasing science apart from natural history, Kant did raise the possibility of an empirical, historical natural science, and although he excluded it from science proper, not all of his followers agreed. Alexander von Humboldt took the alternative pathway, not to replace but to complete the kinds of knowledge being developed by the "rational" sciences, and so developed an "empirical" alternative which appealed strongly to Thoreau.

Humboldt offered an empirical science analogous to a narrative "Civil History," a composition which would show the "simultaneous action" and "connecting links" of all the forces which pervade the universe, including deep space and all of geological deep time (since the description of what *is* could hardly be separated from what *was*), as well as, most surprisingly, the agency of the perceiving mind as well, since without the mind the external world has "no real existence for us."[7] Humboldt leaves no doubt that nature, from remotest nebulae to arctic lichens, from the primal cooling earth to the weather of the hour, exists entirely apart from us; yet that relation is radically asymmetrical: our mental existence is inseparable from our existence as beings in and of nature. The dualism that splits mind from nature, ME from NOT ME, collapses into a subtle interplay of mind, emotion, sensation, force, life, matter, and history, in a field of almost infinite density and complexity.

The kind of science Humboldt advocated — exact, detailed, holistic, and interactive field studies which gathered and collated a dazzling array of data from all points of the globe — is now in retrospect identified as protoecological. For although Humboldtian science never dominated the Anglo-European mainstream, one of its most visible legacies has been the study of the interaction between animals, plants, and their physical environment which emerged in the 1890s under the name of *ecology*.[8] In adapting Humboldt's global program to his own localized field studies, Thoreau too was pioneering this as-yet-unnamed science; and although his work did not directly influence its creation, Thoreau was part of its founding. Indeed, later generations of professional ecologists honored Thoreau's scientific work by citing it and incorporating it into their own, even as it was ignored or slighted by literary critics.[9]

What made Humboldt's ideals difficult to accept on his own terms was the implication that nature was not the product of divine design but self-generating. Hence, order was not dictated rationally from above but emerged cooperatively from below, from the collective interactions of constituent individuals. This implied that nature was not just analogous to, but actually was, a historical process subject to chance and contingency, hence inherently unpredictable and non-Newtonian. Thoreau's Journal becomes a massive gloss on this basic concept. Darwin, after first redefining evolution in *Origin of Species* (1859) as a historical rather than a progressive process, went on in *The Descent of Man* (1871) to propose even more radically that natural organisms actually made themselves through their own aesthetic choices. If wild meant "willed," as Thoreau proposed, Darwin's was a wild nature indeed. What inspired all three was the conviction that the natural world was real on its own terms, and mattered, both for itself and for the cultivation of human self-identity, culture, and civilization.

Debates over science, then, were really debates over broader historical, cultural, and philosophical issues. The strongest connection between science and general culture was through religious belief. In the centuries before Darwin, science was that realm of knowledge which sought to understand the workings of God's creation, making it a powerful way to affirm and extend religious doctrine. Francis Bacon, virtually the patron saint of nineteenth-century Anglo-America, had called science the "faithful handmaid" of religion, and the goal of Baconian science was to show how humanity could acquire the power of God and apply such power to human purpose, "to command nature" through obedience to her laws.[10] Bacon's pronouncement that knowledge was power became the watchword of nineteenth-century natural philosophers from Coleridge to Humboldt, Herschel to Emerson. Indeed, Emerson ends *Nature* with a ringing Baconian declaration: "The kingdom of man over nature, which cometh not with observation, — a dominion such as now is beyond his dream of God, — he shall enter without more wonder than the blind man feels who is gradually restored to perfect sight."[11]

Such language is troubling today. The power to command nature obviously implies the ability to alter nature in wide-ranging and catastrophic ways, but the danger seems curiously invisible to nineteenth-century eyes, even as they looked out on the ravages of an industrializing and urbanizing global economy. What did they see, that they could be so blind? I would submit that only when the power of humanity to alter nature becomes evident is the modern concept of "the environment" possible. A number of intellectuals, scientific and nonscientific alike, recognized at least as early as the 1830s that humanity was indeed remaking nature in fundamental ways.[12] Yet why not sooner? And why was it decades before those with the ability to "remake" acknowledged the potential to "destroy"?

The answers grow out of the fundamental assumption that God had designed a harmoniously functioning universe, an "economy of nature" composed of a balanced exchange among various species and their environment. It might seem that the undeniable fact of extinction showed that the "balanced" economy had already suffered devastating change, both in the geological past and in recent human history, but eighteenth- and early nineteenth-century writers had several ways to dismiss evidence of extinction, evidence they might have taken as proof that humanity's impact on nature is permanent: extinction is, as they say, forever. John Playfair, for example, notes in 1802 that species, even whole genera, of animals "are extinguished." Yet he adds, "It is not unnatural to consider some part of this change as the operation of man. The extension of his power would necessarily subvert the balance that had before been estab- lished between the inhabitants of the earth, and the means of their sub- sistence." Humanity "subverts" the balance of nature — yet the destruc- tiveness of human impact is absorbed as another "natural" force. Playfair concludes that "a change in the animal kingdom seems to be a part of the order of nature"; even the shells and corals of the former world don't resemble those of the present.[13] Human agency, even catastrophic hu- man agency, is swallowed up by the balancing power of nature. The con- clusion is built into the premise: humanity, which commands nature by obedience to its laws, can hardly step outside of nature's grand, cyclic, self-correcting, and continually regenerative economy.

The current usage of the word "environment" was introduced into the language by Thomas Carlyle, who in *Sartor Resartus* (1836) parodied both the "economy of nature" and those who espoused it.[14] Given that the evidence of humanity's power to radically reshape the global environ- ment was increasingly hard to dismiss, Carlyle's rhetorical reform in- verted the relationship of man to nature. From a small part of a greater whole, humanity became the greater whole of which nature was but a part. Carlyle had noted in 1829 as a "Sign of the Times" that "We remove mountains, and make seas our smooth highway; nothing can resist us. We war with rude Nature; and, by our resistless engines, come off always victorious, and loaded with spoils."[15] The dynamic equilibrium of pow- ers which characterized Humboldt's thought is taken up and intensified in Carlyle's parody into a play of "Force" which dissolves all matter and bears it forward in its resistless path. Humanity must become the agent, not the victim, of such forces: "Earth's mountains are leveled, and her seas filled up, in our passage: can the Earth, which is but dead and a vision, resist Spirits which have reality and are alive?"[16] Humanity is no longer merely the pinnacle of a stable and cyclical creation, but its con- tinuation and completion. The directionality of historical change has de- stabilized the circular dynamic, and humanity appears instead as the cul- mination of an essentially linear narrative.

As Carlyle shows, a new vision of global imperialism was emerging. Scientists like Lyell and Darwin were beginning to investigate the extent of human alterations of the face of nature, but the insight was not limited to scientists. Wordsworth's *Guide to the Lakes* narrates a fundamentally environmental history of a natural region by documenting, as Lee Sterrenburg shows, a nature profoundly affected by humans. By Wordsworth's day, many of the Lake District's aboriginal mammals were already listed as extirpated species. Wordsworth's historical review makes clear that "Because of these human-induced extirpations, we can never again return to nature's primaeval or original state — even in theory. . . . No romantic cognitive apocalypse will ever bring back the wolf, the boar, wild bull, the leigh and the forest ecosystems that supported them at the time of early Celtic settlement." Instead Wordsworth narrates an *environmental* history, which relies on "feedback between human-affected ecosystems and Wordsworth's views of nature."[17] This attention to the feedback between human activity and the natural ecosystem generates a startling new insight into a historical nature. Sterrenburg notes three ways in which the Wordsworth of *Guide to the Lakes* moved beyond the Wordsworth of the 1802 "Preface." First, humanity operates not through a remote "science" but as an immediate agent in nature's history, through "everyday social activities like mining, woodlot enclosures, and cattle grazing." Second, a greater degree of feedback among conceptual categories such as "poetry," "nature," "science," and "man" means that such categories are no longer isolated from one another; furthermore, "instead of an organism endowed with presence, 'nature' becomes more of an invisible system endowed with constraints and possibilities," which receives and emits a continual stream of messages as forests are cut down and non-native species introduced. Third, "Wordsworth speaks as an activist and a preservationist," arguing that "land should be managed in an ecologically responsible way" in order, as Wordsworth says, "to 'preserve the native beauty of this delightful district.'" One consequence of these insights is the new role Wordsworth sees for poetry, which now "evaluates and adjudicates human changes in the landscape," no longer declaring veiled or absolute presences but mediating "ecological trade-offs."[18]

The point of this comparison between Wordsworth and Thoreau is not to open nominations for the "real" father of environmental thinking, nor to suggest that Thoreau took his program from Wordsworth (although Thoreau apparently did read Wordsworth's *Guide*).[19] Rather, I wish to suggest what is distinctive about the move that some writers were making, beginning in the 1830s, toward nature as an interactive system incorporating human agency. Such a move precludes dualism and insists on an "ecological" interactiveness; it also defines complementary, rather than oppositional, roles for both the poet who seeks to articulate the messages sent by a changing nature, and the scientist who seeks to understand their causes and consequences for all participants, human and nonhuman. Both poet and scientist speak not to a cadre of specialists but to the ordinary human beings whose daily actions are altering the landscape: cutting, clearing, fencing, farming, grazing cattle, damming, channeling, walking, building. This entails a conceptual revolution: art and technology are not, after all, *un*natural, alienated, and oppositional, the tools by which nature would be conquered and subdued, but quite natural and, as a part of nature, able to help nature heal and grow back.

This direction in Thoreau's work is most explicit in the long-unpublished manuscript "The Dispersion of Seeds," where he offers his audience practical lessons in forest management and proposes that the town appoint "forest wardens" to oversee its "poor husbandmen," giving us Thoreau as America's first forest ranger, leading educational walks through the Concord woodlots and teaching the citizenry to recognize oak seedlings, to fence out cattle, and to refrain from shooting the squirrels and jays.[20] Thoreau became a classic exemplar of the Humboldtian spiral from love of nature's beauty to knowledge of nature's processes, knowledge which enhances love and leads to the desire to educate and enlighten others: from the self alone in nature to a social ecology in which the ethical self does not center and command, but decenters, negotiates, constructs, and defends alliances. Science becomes not the enemy but the key to this ethical system, because it is the method of science which teaches students how to listen to otherness, how to test their fine speculations against the resistances of nature — how to give nature a line-item veto. Leading natural scientists were well aware that no eye is innocent, that the mind will find in nature the mirror of its desire; hence the process of knowing must build in a way for nature to resist — in Thoreau's terms, for the pines to "push back." Yet poetry is also key because such negotiations occur only through the agency of language, the mediation of art. Thoreau's gift was in seeing how close the two, poetry and science, can be to each other. For if science writing aspired to be really about nature, to conduct to the mind information about the external world, poetry would turn inward to examine the workings of mind and language. Ideally, both genres would converge in recreating within the mind of the reader the experience and vision of the writer, a consummation

Thoreau addressed in the language of reproduction: "wet" versus "dry," "fertile" versus "sterile."

Yet there were pulls across the grain of this fruitful marriage of poetry and science. The very notion of a "marriage" presumes an already well matured dualism, which Thoreau was unable to reject entirely: only a purified nature, free of human contaminants, could open so exhilarating a space for liberation from human limitation. Only a purely nonhuman nature could become the site of spiritual renewal, the source of the necessary hard granitic core of truth and eternal, higher law. The clarity of the boundary between humanity and nature was a requirement for nature to be a stable resource for spiritual growth. As George Cheever, Congregationalist minister and an early Coleridge enthusiast, asked: "What, indeed, is universal nature, but a world of external occasions, to awaken consciousness of the powers of the spiritual world within us?"[21] The discipline of purifying the soul of "worldly" distractions enabled a classic form of hierarchical empowerment, the religious state of freedom through submission to the whole; for a time, the burdensome self is dissolved, the obstructive self free-flowing. Such a site must be set apart from the daily vexations of family and work, and unclaimed by the system of private property so that anyone could enter without trespass. Such a space offered a theater for experimentation with the identity of the self apart from society, enabling escape, regeneration, growth, and return. This may be the plot of *Walden*, but it is also the plot of the scientific laboratory, in which the disciplined and independent self enters a sacred space purified of social encumbrances and prepared to be the clear channel for the voice of truth as spoken by God himself. Science as a "discipline" becomes a priesthood of the few who have the independence, talent, and ability to withdraw from the world in pursuit of Truth.

But if dualism was too seductive to be refused, how could Thoreau have refused its pluralistic alternative? Extravagance has its attractions too: every object, every fact, is welcomed; every particle counts for itself and none are dissolved or reduced to another; nature is saved from the imperialism of mind, released into the freedom of its own being. Another kind of discipline, daily action in the world, replaced alienation with engagement, the dissociation of mind and body with their productive union. Once we are engrossed in the fields of nature, the act of perception draws us ever deeper into the absorbing complexities of natural phenomena, and the self, now fully embodied, acts not as an agent of transcendence but as the independent site for experience in the world. Such a self mediates not between God and humanity as a priest, but between earth and humanity as a guide and companion who models the good way of life in this place, at this time. Success leads one not ever higher into the lonely sublime Alpine heights of discovery, but ever deeper into the inhabited hills and valleys where teacher and student cooperate in a democratic project, wherein knowledge of the world is constructed and exchanged not in the province of the few but in the community of the many.

While such a commitment characterizes Thoreau's final decade, it does exact a cost. Romantic ecstasies are exchanged for coarsening contact with the "dry" science of guides and handbooks and the mediocrities of local natural history. The teacher descends from priestly elite to village schoolmaster, engaged not in the rigorous pursuit of Truth but in the gentle education of women and children, those for whom the mild and pacifying demands of natural history were thought to be best suited. Or at the other extreme, those field naturalists who *were* conducting original research were generally employed by the state and federal governments to collect and transfer data from the coasts, plains, rivers, and mountains of America's growing empire, making them little better than clerks conducting a resource inventory for the imperial masters of Manifest Destiny. Perhaps most difficult of all — worse than sacrificing ecstasy, masculine romantic heroics, and elite social status — was the ultimate loss of Truth. Dualism stabilized nature as a certain source of eternal knowledge; at the farthest reach of participatory social ecology was the troubling implication that truth could be forged only through disputation and imperfect consensus.

American culture in the nineteenth century could sacrifice neither dualism nor pluralism. Each provided a resource for the other: from romantic dualism, "wilderness"; from romantic pluralism, "wildness." The wilderness ideal set aside sacred spaces — sanctuaries, temples, and cathedrals — to serve both as private spaces for the ecstatic development of the self and as shared public stages for the performance of the drama of American self-making, preserving the original paradise from which America can measure its declension and to which it can always look for its ideals. The Thoreauvian wild relocated the regenerative life principle from a remote place lost in primal origins to an ongoing process occurring underfoot. Nature is not elsewhere, but everywhere, and all the land is holy, not just a few last best places.

Both formations are needed because neither is complete. If everywhere is holy, then nowhere is. Yet the wilderness is holy only insofar as you are nowhere in it. By definition, it is that place where you cannot live. As Emerson wrote to Muir in 1872, the solitude of the wilderness "is a sublime mistress, but an intolerable wife."[22] Or as William Cronon puts it, memorably, "if nature dies because we enter it, then the only way to save nature is to kill ourselves."[23] Ironically, this paradox confirms the deep connection of wilderness with that ideology of scientific knowing in which the price of truth is the death of the self, total objectivity. Critiques of wilderness have proliferated recently: it perpetuates the very dichotomy it was meant to correct; by pricing a few places out of the market it devalues the many places in which we do live, and by an odd backlash permits us to treat the common with contempt even while we love the sacred to death; the arbitrary, ruler-straight boundaries of wilderness and park lands reflect ethnocentric aesthetics not ecocentric requirements; wilderness values the monumental over the living, stasis over change, popular entertainment over natural otherness, scenic wonders over ecological management.[24] The fundamentally ecological concept of the "wild" offers a solution to such critiques by returning our focus to the unconstructed otherness of nonhuman nature, yet it offers up problems of its own: instead of believing in nature, we merely manage it. How can the yard we plant and mow and weed be worthy of worship? If all nature consists with "wildness," why value any particular place or being over another? It seems we cannot do without wilderness, for we need it to help us see the wild.

Hence, Thoreau's vision of forest management and daily engagement with nature produced a complementary vision of wilderness, open space that cannot, like his beloved woodlots, be owned, posted, and abused for private gain. Not only should the town appoint a forest warden to oversee its husbandmen, but each town "should have a park, or rather a primitive forest, of five hundred or a thousand acres . . . [to] stand and decay for higher uses — a common possession forever, for instruction and recreation."[25] Without wilderness, how would anyone be able to believe in nature? Without the wild, how would wilderness become a part of life?

Thus the two, wilderness and wildness, coevolved to compensate for each other's exclusions; and the pairings that result — laboratory and field, rational and empirical, transcendence and immanence, dual and multiple, pure and compromised, holy and homely — generate Thoreau's double aesthetic of withdrawal and engagement. Each side creates a necessary resource for the other, each a supplement for the other's absences. If, as I suspect, the construction of romantic subjectivity and modern social institutions is complexly intertwined with the scientific imagination, then the dilemmas created by the duality of wilderness and wildness are one legacy of the contests over nature being waged by nineteenth-century scientists. Does science, then, ground or betray the environmental imagination? My conclusion is that science, being irreducibly social, has been and remains a player on all sides of the issue, leaving us, in this post–Cold War era, without innocence and without villains.[26] No side is inherently hegemonic or inherently subversive. The ethos of wilderness can underwrite powerful acts of subversion or a static hierarchy of wealth and leisure; likewise, while the protoecology of Alexander von Humboldt emerged from a radical political underground, ecology as a science and as an ideology has been co-opted in service to the state in the name of purity, holism, and resource efficiency. Less balefully, both "sides" in this heuristic and porous binary include an aesthetic of the "cultivated" self, whose engagement with nonhuman nature helps create a truly "cultured" civilization.

As the nineteenth century wore on, and science withdrew from common culture to become a culture in itself, the literature of nature which followed Thoreau continued to develop the cultural space opened, then abandoned, by science. Hence an excursion into the forgotten conflicts buried in the prehistory of our contemporary concepts of wildness, environment, and ecology can serve as a reminder that there did, once, exist a viable form of science which underwrote environmental understanding and activism by connecting local knowledges with a global dialogue. Thoreau explored and practiced this science because it showed him how believing in nature might mean believing in humanity as well.

NOTES

1. Thoreau, *Natural History Essays*, 112.

2. Ibid., 114.

3. Ibid., 113.

4. Buell, *Environmental Imagination*.

5. This argument is more fully detailed in my *Seeing New Worlds*.

6. Kant, *Metaphysical Foundations of Natural Science*, 3–4.

7. Humboldt, *Cosmos*, I: 49–50, 55, 76.

8. See Peter Bowler, *The Norton History of the Environmental Sciences*, esp. 361–78.

9. Egerton and Walls, "Rethinking Thoreau and the History of American Ecology," 4–20.

10. Bacon, *The Great Instauration*, 8: 41.

11. Emerson, *Collected Works*, 1:45.

12. I am indebted here to Lee Sterrenburg, particularly to his essay "A Narrative Overview: The Making of the Concept of the Global 'Environment' in Literature and Science."

13. Playfair, *Illustrations of the Huttonian Theory of the Earth*, 469.

14. Sterrenburg, "Narrative Overview," 10.

15. Carlyle, "Signs of the Times," in *Works of Thomas Carlyle*, 27:60.

16. Carlyle, *Sartor Resartus*, 200.

17. Sterrenburg, "Romanticism, Technology, and the Ecology of Knowledge," 8.

18. Ibid., 24–27.

19. See Moldenhauer, "*Walden* and Wordsworth's *Guide to the Lake District*," 261–92.

20. Thoreau, "Dispersion of Seeds," in *Faith in a Seed*, 173.

21. Cheever, "Coleridge," 338.

22. Qtd. in Nash, *Wilderness and the American Mind*, 126.

23. Cronon, "The Trouble with Wilderness," in *Uncommon Ground*, ed. Cronon, 83.

24. For an interesting recent critique, see R. Edward Grumbine, "Image and Reality: Culture and Biology in the National Parks," 16–23.

25. Thoreau, *Natural History Essays*, 259.

26. Karl Kroeber makes a similar point in *Ecological Literary Criticism: Romantic Imagining and the Biology of Mind*, 3.

Thoreau's Transcendental Ecocentrism

WILLIAM ROSSI

As a number of recent critics have argued, while an ecocentric shift in
Thoreau's thinking and writing may have begun during his two-year stay
at Walden Pond, the deeper process of environmental bonding and the
literary effects of it did not become evident before the early 1850s.[1] The
first fruit, and in many ways the means of sustaining this bond, was
Thoreau's Journal — "the record of my love" and "affection for any aspect of the world" — which burgeons at this time into a voluminous,
open-ended account of his environmental and intellectual explorations
around Concord.[2] But ecocritical interest in Thoreau's greening has also
brought into sharper focus an abiding contradiction at work in this process, namely, the contradiction between Thoreau's growing tendency to
root his affection in place and the anthropocentric inclinations of his
persistent transcendentalism. The tension between these two tendencies
is especially conspicuous in the early 1850s. For the very moment when,
as Stephen Adams and Donald Ross have noted, Thoreau begins self-
consciously to refer to himself as a "transcendentalist" is the same moment that his scientific interest in Concord environs starts to intensify
and the ongoing Journal account of his "affection" deepens.[3] And far
from fading, this tension persists, as, ten years later, Thoreau continues
to identify himself, even in an essay concerned with a "purely scientific
subject," as "a transcendentalist."[4]

So long as this tension has been construed in epistemological terms,
it has posed little problem. Now that the once-potent critical myth of
Thoreau's post-*Walden* decline has died out, most critics have come to
appreciate how "Thoreau's interest in scientific approaches to nature . . .
merged with rather than replaced his transcendentalist approach," even
if that merger also entailed a keen awareness of the "limitations of scientific knowledge" in the face of "the full and ultimately mystical rich-

ness of nature."[5] Most recently, Laura Dassow Walls has persuasively argued that the major shift in Thoreau's career beginning in the early 1850s is better understood not as the transformation of "an Emersonian transcendental poet to a fragmented empirical scientist, but from a transcendental holist to something new which combined transcendentalism with empiricism," a methodology Walls refers to as "empirical holism," which Thoreau derived from Alexander von Humboldt.[6] But when the focus changes to include the ontological and ethical dimensions of Thoreau's transcendentalism in relation to nonhuman nature, the contradictory aspect of the tension is apt to reappear.

So far, with the exception of Lawrence Buell, those interested in Thoreau's ecocentrism have tended to resolve this contradiction by minimizing and even denying it, most often by representing Thoreau as eventually outgrowing this aspect of his Emersonian heritage.[7] Buell's analysis of Thoreau's "ragged progress" toward ecocentrism, on the other hand, brackets the question, preferring to focus on Thoreau's journey toward a recognizably modern ecoconsciousness and representation, noting that finally Thoreau "could not get past the Emersonian" vision "of the natural realm as symbolically significant of the human estate." But while the "idea that natural phenomena had spiritual as well as material significance appealed strongly to Thoreau throughout his life," it does not necessarily follow that this idea impeded Thoreau's ecocentric shift or that his transcendentalism remained unmodified.[8] As I will argue, situating Thoreau's environmental writing in the context of mid-nineteenth-century debates over evolution (or "development," in the contemporary idiom) suggests that his peculiar transcendentalist commitment may actually have fostered rather than retarded his ecocentrism, a connection that invites us to reconceive both.

Transcendental Correspondence Revisited

To do so we must first note that the belief underlying Emersonian correspondence, that "natural phenomena had spiritual as well as material significance," was hardly confined to transcendentalist circles. Emerson's habit of pointing to the eighteenth-century scientist and mystic Emanuel Swedenborg may well be an instance of what Buell has described as Emerson's rhetoric of "citational provocation," "gestur[ing] toward foreign [rather than Anglo-American] sources . . . when discussing the key cultural influences of his age . . . despite or because he knew it would affront" particularly his Bostonian audience; for, as Buell has noted elsewhere, the idea of correspondence was "generally in the air."[9] Thus, according to Walls, Swedenborg may have only confirmed what Emerson had already learned from a "far less fashionable source": the Scottish "common sense" philosopher Dugald Stewart.[10] Indeed, while it was not elaborated in the aesthetic and epistemological senses that Emerson developed with assists from Swedenborg and Coleridge, correspondence was integral to a broad heterogeneous discourse of natural theology that pervaded nineteenth-century Anglo-American science and culture.[11] Central to this discourse was the assumption, best known in the argument from design, that the natural order had been harmoniously designed by a benevolent Creator. In biological and geological theory, this assumption informed the belief that through a long series of geological transformations, plants, animals, and eventually humans had been perfectly adapted to the environments in which they lived. According to historian Dov Ospovat, until Darwin's alternative theory of relative adaptation appeared in *On the Origin of Species*, perfect adaptation "served as a complete explanation of organic phenomena." In Anglo-American natural science, this doctrine had "the status not of a postulate of natural theology, nor of an element in a particular ideology," but rather of "a *fact* apparent to all who took the trouble to observe organisms."[12] In much the same way, for those such as Emerson who contemplated what Thomas Henry Huxley later referred to as the question of "man's place in nature," the "fact" that humanity was perfectly adapted to nature was equally self-evident, if imperfectly realized. Consequently, the idea that (in a phrase Emerson found in the *Edinburgh Review*) a "subtle and mysterious analogy . . . exists between the physical and moral world" was virtually a cliché in the literary culture of this period.[13]

As a naturalist and environmental writer in this discursive setting, correspondence offered Thoreau, even more than it had Emerson, a means both of articulating and of more specifically investigating relations between "moral" and physical nature, human and natural history. Thus, while studying Harvard botanist Asa Gray's *Manual of the Botany of the Northern United States* in May 1851, Thoreau seized on an image of plant development as evidence that "There is no doubt a perfect analogy between the life of the human being and that of the vegetable — both of the body & the mind."

The botanist, Gray, says,

"The organs of plants are of two sorts: — 1. those of *Vegetation*, which are concerned in growth, — by which the plant takes in the aerial and earthy matters on which it lives, and elaborates them into the materials of its own organized substance; 2. those of *Fructification*, or *Reproduction*, which are concerned in the propagation of the species."

So it is with the human being — I am concerned first to come to my *Growth* intellectually & morally; . . . and, then to bear my *Fruit* — do my Work — *Propagate* my kind, not only physically but morally — not only in body but in mind. (*PJ* 3:224–25)

This passage marks the beginning of an extended point-by-point response to Gray's text in which, guided by the idea of correspondence, Thoreau refashions Gray's physiology into a master image of human physical, intellectual, and spiritual development in relation to nature. A textbook example of transcendental hermeneutics in action, Thoreau appears almost to be reading Gray's *Manual* by the light of Emerson's *Nature*, interpreting the "occult relation" existing "between man and the vegetable" through an explication of "particular natural facts" as "symbols of particular spiritual facts," exactly as Emerson had said.[14] Yet Thoreau's exuberance, his sense of discovery, and the particularity of his explication suggests that more is at stake here than a confirmation of early Emersonian transcendentalism or even of Thoreau's own hope, stated in his first published essay, that scientific "fact" would "one day flower" into a transcendentalist "truth" coextensive with science.[15]

We get closer to the source of Thoreau's excitement by noting that this particular fact of seed "expansion," or embryogenesis, had long been a favorite among transcendentalists for figuring the process of self-culture, a spiritual discipline of "unfolding" the self that the Journal was, in fact, initially conceived to serve.[16] In this respect, Thoreau's image of plant development represents precisely the kind of "work" that the Journal itself not only reflected but "propagate[d]" or performed.[17] What especially intrigues him, however, is how "the human being" or "the growing man" is implicated in a larger process, a "law" of development that Gray describes in the *Manual* as "a kind of polarity" defined by the "centripetal and centrifugal modes of [plant] evolution." As Thoreau quotes Gray, the plant "developes from the first in two opposite directions — upwards to expand in the light & air; & downwards avoiding the light to form the root. One half is aerial the other subterranean."[18] "So," Thoreau replies, "the mind develops from the first in two opposite directions — upwards to expand in the light & air" yet "[o]ne half of [its] development must still be root — in the embryonic state — in the womb of nature — more unborn than at first." To Gray's observation that roots may develop at any point on the stem, under the right conditions, "that is to say, in darkness and moisture, as when covered by the soil," Thoreau adds, "I.e. the most clear & etherial ideas (Antaeus like) readily ally themselves to the earth — to the primal womb of things — They put forth roots as soon as branches[,] they are eager to be *soiled*." [19]

As Walls has shown, the effort to identify such laws was a hallmark of the holism that pervaded romantic science. Thus, while in their new professional capacity scientists were strictly concerned with physical nature, those who styled themselves "philosophical naturalists" and sought to describe general laws thereby gestured toward the wider implications of their discoveries, as Darwin did by virtue of his own analogy between human ("artificial") selection and natural selection in *On the Origin of Species*.[20] If Thoreau's "discovery" indicates the sort of "science" he sought to practice at this time, one that, contrary to the positivist trend gaining ground in professional science, persisted in referring "phenomena to the human situation" (in Albert von Frank's phrase), his keen interest in Gray's law also marks the tenor of his engagement in contemporary evolutionary debates over how far such laws might apply to "the human situation."[21] Oddly enough, Thoreau's twin commitment to the metaphysics of correspondence and to a densely empirical knowledge of nature positioned him at the flashpoint of attempts to radically reconceive relations between physical and "moral" nature.

Although, as we will see, Gray's sense of the term "evolution" in the *Manual* is a distinctly pre-Darwinian one, his effort to theorize laws of "development" reflects his own cautious involvement in the ferment of evolutionary theorizing that followed the publication of Robert Chambers's anonymous evolutionary tract, *Vestiges of the Natural History of Creation* in 1844. For, as Gray knew well, embryogenesis was an especially contested site in the evolutionary debates. While Thoreau was not yet prepared, as he would be later, to participate in the technical dimensions of the debate, he had been deeply interested in the public controversy since it broke. Because of its intertwined transcendentalist and evolutionary resonance, Thoreau's roots and leaves image provides a unique window on the complexity of his developing ecocentricism. To appreciate that complexity, it will be worthwhile to briefly review the role of embryogenesis in the debate. We will then be in a better position to understand what was at stake in Thoreau's exuberant response to Gray's *Manual*, and to interpret the seemingly peculiar gender dynamics at work in his evocative image, in which "The growing man penetrates yet deeper by his roots into the womb of things."

Progressionists, Transmutationists,
and the "Universal Gestation of Nature"

Continental interpretations of vertebrate embryogenesis were first introduced to a large Anglo-American audience in Peter Mark Roget's *Animal and Vegetable Physiology*, one of eight Bridgewater Treatises published in the 1830s, most of them written by prominent Oxbridge scientists commissioned to demonstrate the "Power, Wisdom, and Goodness of God, as manifested in the Creation."[22] In concluding his treatise, Roget generalized two "laws" or "principles" that would afford his readers "enlarged views of [the] multitude of important facts" his dense, two-volume work had detailed. The first of these, the "principle of analogy," accounted for morphological resemblances "amidst endless modifications of details" in both plant and animal kingdoms, resemblances that allowed taxonomists to classify organisms simply by following "the footsteps of Nature herself." The presence of so many resemblances seemed to point to an overall, archetypal design or "ideal standard," what Darwin (employing contemporary usage) would refer to as a "general plan," underlying the organization of organisms in each kingdom and, possibly, in both.[23] This possibility, that nature was ultimately one, was strengthened by Roget's second principle, the "law of gradation," according to which every major modification of "the original type" received "some additional extension of its faculties and endowments by the graduated developement of elements . . . which are evolved in succession, as nature advances [upward] in her course."[24] For "further corroboration" of these laws, Roget offered a vivid picture of this process of "evolving" (i.e., in the root sense, "unfolding") in what Philip Rehbock describes as "one of the most appealing and long-lived doctrines" of the study variously known as "transcendental" or "philosophical anatomy" and "transcendental morphology": the phenomenon of embryonic repetition, later codified by Ernst Haeckel as the biogenetic law that "ontogeny recapitulates phylogeny."[25] Here, Roget suggested, the transformation or "progressive metamorphoses" of the fundamental type could actually be witnessed, at least in higher vertebrates, where the embryo appeared to traverse the entire vertebrate series, from fish through "reptile" and "quadruped" to its present form.[26]

Beheld in the context of romantic assumptions about nature as an organic whole, embryogenesis proved central to evolutionary theorizing because, as Roget's summary indicates, it seemed to epitomize the entire history of nature. Roget's own interpretation of this phenomenon, however, was not evolutionary in the material but only in the ideal sense of the term. Where Darwin and other transmutationists accounted for the "general [structural] plan" of animal and plant morphology as a product of genealogical descent with modification, progressionists like Roget saw the unfolding of a "unity of design" or "type" leading "up" to humanity. In this respect, as Evelleen Richards has said, progressionism was at best "evolution without physical continuity," since "the continuity exists only in the mind of God." [27] Hence, although he had devoted several pages to a cogent summary of the transmutation hypothesis, Roget took pains to disclaim as "unwarrantable and extravagant" this conclusion to which "many continental physiologists" and other "disciples of this transcendental school" were being led, confident that the "essential characters of each species . . . remain ever constant and immutable." [28]

Studies of the production and reception of the Bridgewater Treatises have shown that while neither the authors nor the publisher anticipated the phenomenal success and longevity of the series, most of the writers aimed at a broad, generally educated audience, with established scientists like Roget, William Buckland, and William Whewell also attempting to reach specialist readers. [29] Thus, while the topic may seem rather rarified now, in holding the line against transmutation, Roget was not arguing over some arcane phenomenon known only to specialists. Ultimately, he was guiding his readers' interpretation of what was becoming a powerful metaphor in Anglo-American nature discourse. As Richards has argued, because of its ambiguity, the metaphor of "the gestation of nature," in which "the history of nature [was] construed as one long gestation analogous to a normal human pregnancy," effectively "encapsulated the organicism, the uncompromising developmentalism, anthropocentrism, and insistence on the fundamental unity of all nature." This ambiguity not only contributed to its currency among generally educated readers of volumes like the Bridgewater Treatises but also "gave the metaphor of gestation its explanatory power and led to its wide deployment in nineteenth-century biology." [30]

That explanatory power and the broad public responsiveness to the metaphor played importantly in the fifteen-year controversy that raged over Chambers's *Vestiges* and his sequel, *Explanations*. Piecing together "hints" from recent research in various mainstream and marginal scientific disciplines in Britain and the Continent, Chambers argued that life on earth had developed from a simple monad, or "globule," "up" to the complexity of higher mammals, including humanity, a process which might yet result in an even "higher" human state under the right conditions. In explaining the mechanism for this "natural history of creation," Chambers appealed directly to "the living picture" provided by embryonic repetition at the same time that he literalized the metaphor of gestation.[31] Thus, he wrote, the reality of species mutability, "the production of new forms, as strewn in the pages of the geological record," has "never been anything more than a new stage of progress in gestation, an event as simply natural, and attended as little by any circumstance of a wonderful or startling [i.e., miraculous] kind, as the silent advance of an ordinary mother from one week to another of her pregnancy."[32] By making gestation the mechanism of the entire development process, a process he called "the universal gestation of Nature," Chambers effectively domesticated transmutation, as James Secord has noted, a hypothesis that Roget and many others had associated with French materialism and German metaphysical excess.[33] Domesticated or not, however, numerous reviewers and popular authors, incensed by Chambers's claim that he had "annulled" the "distinction . . . between physical and moral" spheres and alarmed by the popularity of *Vestiges*, invoked precisely these associations in attempting to discredit the unknown author.[34] This tactic is typified by Hugh Miller's enormously popular *Footprints of the Creator*, a work publicly endorsed by well-established professionals like Adam Sedgwick and Louis Agassiz, in which Miller represented Chambers's book as an excessively theoretical work heavily dependent upon the Naturphilosophie of Lorenz Oken, and thus, Miller insinuated, both unscientific and un-British.[35]

So notorious, current, and all-embracing was Chambers's hypothesis that few Anglo-American writers on nature in the late 1840s and 1850s, whether popular or professional, failed to stake out a position on it. Like other scientific reviewers of *Vestiges* and *Explanations*, Asa Gray had been at least as concerned with the regard of "unprofessional readers" for scientific authority as he was with the theoretical merit of Chambers's hypothesis.[36] In writing his *Manual of Botany* and *Botanical Text-Book* for "unprofessional" as well as preprofessional readers like Thoreau, Gray therefore took pains not only to present the most up-to-date account of plant taxonomy and physiology but also to reassert the validity of progressionist "unity of type" over transmutationist interpretations of plant development. In the *Manual*'s introduction, to which Thoreau responded in the Journal, Gray provided a condensed version of the extensive and more theoretically explicit treatment of plant physiology and morphological theory available in the *Botanical Text-Book*, to which Gray referred his reader.[37] Acknowledging a debt in the *Text-Book* to Goethe's "curious and really scientific treatise," *The Metamorphosis of Plants*, Gray considered the most complex among the "Phaenogamous" or flowering plants as the "highest grade of vegetation," "the perfected type" from which the "ideal plan" of the plant could be constructed.[38] This enabled the "philosophical botanist" to "trac[e], as it were, the biography of the vegetable through the successive states of its existence," effectively reading the phylogenetic "history" of the plant kingdom through the ontogenetic "biography" of its most highly developed species, an interpretation meant to reveal the entire "general scheme of the vegetable kingdom, and the unity of plan which runs through the manifold diversities it displays."[39]

Gray was careful to make clear that by describing "the floral organs" as "modified or metamorphosed leaves" after Goethe, and thus by speaking of "the progressive evolution of the plant," he was not endorsing the "more hypothetical or transcendental forms" in which the "theory of vegetable morphology may be expressed." Such metamorphoses, Gray stressed, do not represent transmutations of material forms from which the present plant has descended. We are not to suppose "that a petal has ever actually been a green leaf . . . or that stamens and pistils have previously existed in the state of foliage." Moreover, just as its "essential identity" is already present in the embryo, so "when the individual organ has once fairly begun to develope, its destiny is fixed."[40]

Toward a Transcendental Ecocentrism

While he accepts Gray's polar model of embryogenesis, Thoreau's refashioning of Gray's description into an evolutionary metaphor of universal gestation ("the womb of nature") suggests that, whatever else he meant by it, in identifying himself as a "transcendentalist" Thoreau was hardly oblivious to the current illicitly transmutationist and pantheistic connotations of the term. In the months ahead, he would explore transmutation as both a veiled "fact" of human history and a hint of human potential, opening up the possibility that human identity was no more "essential" and stable, in Gray's words, than its "destiny" was "fixed." This willingness to think with Chambers's hypothesis, which Chambers was updating and strengthening with every new edition, allied Thoreau to radical intellectuals such as Harriet Martineau and Henry George Atkinson, whose *Letters on the Laws of Man's Nature and Development* he read three months later,[41] and also with other naturalists, on whom Chambers's work, despite vigorous professional and lay campaigns against it, exerted a kind of subterranean influence. As Chambers himself noted bitterly in the preface to the tenth edition of his book (1853), while "obloquy has been poured upon the nameless author from a score of sources . . . his leading idea, in subdued form, finds its way into books of science, and gives a direction to research."[42] Consequently, as historians have begun to find, the path Darwin took to evolution, "along the route that led to natural selection," was not the only one. For "there were a number of paths that ran along side and sometimes intersected with Darwinism."[43]

Of course, to claim that Thoreau's image approximates anything we might want to call either "evolution" or "theory" would be ludicrous. Although it does contain the germ of Thoreau's later description of "the development theory" (made after reading Darwin's *Origin*) as implying "a greater vital force in Nature" and "a sort of constant new creation,"[44] this Journal passage is fascinating not because it is recognizably proto-evolutionary in a Darwinian sense. Rather, it is striking because it reveals Thoreau assimilating on his own transcendentalist ground the debate refracted through Gray's "philosophical" description, and thus engaging the ferment of contemporary evolutionary theorizing in the context of his own incipient ecocentrism. If his transcendentalist ontology seems here to be undergoing a kind of ideological transmutation itself, Thoreau's imaginative act nonetheless occurs very much within his "home" ideology rather than outside it. Thus, apparently with no sense of contradiction or struggle, in the very next day's Journal entry, the imperial and decidedly anthropocentric dimensions of transcendentalist ideology come out as Thoreau celebrates "Man the crowning fact — the god we know," in terms hardly distinguishable from the idealist progressionism of Gray's Harvard colleague, Louis Agassiz. When "from nature we turn astonished to this near but supernatural fact," he says, we "understand the importance of man's existence — its bearing on the other phenomena of life. . . . Man made in the image of God!" (*PJ* 3:229, 230). No doubt, too, Thoreau's reading of the growth of "the human being" is enabled by the racialist ideology everywhere present in contemporary biology and anthropology.[45] Just as Gray reads the phylogenetic history of the plant kingdom through its most "highly developed" species, Thoreau reads the unfolding of the "type" or universal "growing man" through his own ontogeny, a universal insight conferred by his own "higher" phylogenetic position as an Anglo-European man.

At the same time, in its bidirectionality Thoreau's model is strikingly unlike both the conventionally progressionist models of human evolutionary development and Chambers's model of transmutationist development, which is also unidirectional. Indeed, judging from the number of times he reiterates and reformulates it, this is what excites Thoreau most about the "law" Gray identifies: the simultaneous development "from the first in two opposite directions." Whereas the linear, unidirectionalist emphasis of nineteenth-century progressionism carried over into many models of evolutionary development, effectively privileging *Homo sapiens* as the "end," Thoreau articulates an interdependent model in which ideal development is both bidirectional and reciprocal.[46] The ideal or whole person, "body and mind," is not only one whose thought is strengthened by Antaean contact with the earth (in contrast to "the mere reasoner who weaves his arguments as a tree its branches in the sky — not being equally developed in the roots"), but one whose self-culture is simultaneously "soiled" and "soar[ing]" (*PJ* 3:226).

No doubt one reason this model appealed so immediately to Thoreau was that he had been groping toward it (had, in fact, already partly imagined it) himself, although neither in the precisely polar form derived from Gray nor with the evolutionary depth and scope provided by Chambers. Nonetheless, particularly in "Friday" of *A Week on the Concord and Merrimack Rivers*, where he urges that "Man . . . needs not only to be spiritualized, but naturalized on the soil of the earth," Thoreau imagines the prospect of a transcendental fidelity to place.[47] Readers of "Friday" could hardly be blamed for dismissing this notion as mere paradox, since it is developed in a travel narrative that, as Steven Fink aptly characterizes it, strains the conventional form of the genre "almost to the breaking point."[48] Here, Thoreau's narrative of the brothers' journey homeward under full sail strains against his expository flights into the symbolic significance of astronomical discoveries and other "faint reflections of the Real" (*A Week* 385). The point, however, seems to be that as the brothers get closer to home they realize the true significance of "that OTHER WORLD which the instinct of mankind has so long predicted": namely, that "Here or nowhere is our heaven" (*A Week* 380). The image of bidirectional growth that Thoreau appropriated from Gray, then, served further to embody this vision of humanity as simultaneously naturalized and spiritualized, by situating it not only "on" but *in* "the soil of earth." Moreover, the tensive unity of Gray's polar model enabled Thoreau to redefine the "centrifugal," aspiring tendency of his transcendentalism and the centripetal, rooting tendency of his incipient ecocentrism as opposite yet dual manifestations of one ontology, such that "The mind flashes not so far on one side — but its rootlets its spongelets find their way instantly on the other side into a moist darkness. uterine" (*PJ* 3:227); or, more epigrammatically, "No thought soars so high that it sunders these apron strings of its mother" (*PJ* 3:226).

But what *sort* of relation is figured to this "mother," this "womb of nature"? Coming from a naturalist, Thoreau's rhetoric of "the growing man" "penetrat[ing] yet deeper by his roots" into "the womb of things" unmistakably echoes the androcentric Baconian stance, which since the scientific revolution had functioned effectively as a means of technical and scientific domination of female nature.[49] In Thoreau's day, this stance was particularly visible in the effort to combat the threat posed by *Vestiges*, where it underpinned rhetorically what was often represented as the official philosophy of Anglo-American science. Cambridge geologist Adam Sedgwick's lengthy excoriation of Chambers's book in the *Edinburgh Review* provides a pure, almost self-parodic, example. While attempting to discredit *Vestiges* as a work of feminized, merely literary imagination, characteristic of "the trash of literature," Sedgwick draws heavily on Baconian rhetoric to represent science as a bastion of masculine privilege and "lawful" intellect.[50] Through "inductive reasoning," the natural philosopher makes his laborious "ascent up the hill of science," transcending both nature and body. Just as the "abstract language of man" provides the means by which humans are enabled to "soar far above" the "objects of sense" and the "material wants" of the "brute" (creating an "immeasurable interval" between us and them), so the "high truths of th[e] new [mathematical] language [of science] are based on conceptions of our own, stripped off from matter." By means of the experimental method, men of science can "test our conclusions," as Bacon said, by "put[ting] nature to the torture, and wring[ing] new secrets from her," and in this way "rise to an apprehension of general and eternal truths above all material nature."[51] As I have noted, insofar as Thoreau's image conflates physical and "moral" being with body and mind, it embodies an ontology, even an ethics, as much as an epistemology. Yet focusing on the latter dimension makes clear how, next to Sedgwick's official version, Thoreau's rhetoric appears to redirect rather than to endorse the Enlightenment project of extracting the secrets of nature. In his bidirectional countermyth, the relation is notably dynamic and reciprocal rather than extractive and progressive. While he shares Sedgwick's idealism to the point of figuring "the most clear & etherial ideas" as "soaring," Thoreau imagines them "Antaeus like," simultaneously "ally[ing] themselves to the earth — to the primal womb of things," "eager to be *soiled.*" Moreover, the ethic or open-ended goal imaged here is less one of power and masculine domination than of a nurturing contact and deepening intimacy, one that resonates faintly with nineteenth-century sentimental ideology and yet also incorporates distinctive elements of what Thoreau had begun to call "the Wild." Like the "womb of nature," a primary quality of "the Wild" is the fertile source of life "in search" of which "every tree sends its fibres forth," the same source toward which the walker unaccountably gravitates in "Walking," and contact with which assures him "that I am growing apace and rankly."[52]

Finally, Thoreau's self-consciousness in this period about the distinctive character of the Journal as "a record" of his "affection for any aspect of the world" may prompt us to read this passage self-reflexively. For however much Thoreau's exhilaration and the assumed teleology of the process he unfolds imply that he is unpacking the germ of a "perfect analogy" and thus "discovering" the correspondent human, or "moral," significance of Gray's image, as a writer he is equally conscious of making it an image. In this way, Thoreau's remarkably multivalent image may be seen to suggest not only the writer-naturalist's meditation on the character of his own "growth," the evolutionary natural history of creation in which he is embedded, and the correlative deepening of his knowledge of Concord environs. It may also represent the journal practice — the medium — in which Thoreau's knowing affection for this place was rooting and being brought to light. If in A Week Thoreau brought his exploration narrative home to the idea of a transcendental fidelity to place, in the 1850s he effectively planted that promise in the Journal, as the daily renewed and renewing practice of exploratory inhabitation.

NOTES

I would like to acknowledge research support for this essay from the National Endowment for the Humanities.

1. Buell, Environmental Imagination, 115–39; McGregor, Wider View of the Universe, 87–120.

2. Thoreau, Journal, Vol. 3: 1848–1851, 143. Subsequent volume and page references to the Princeton edition of the Journal are cited parenthetically in the text with PJ. Recent ecocritical studies of the Journal include H. Daniel Peck, "Better Mythology: Perception and Emergence in Thoreau's Journal"; Don Scheese, "Thoreau's Journal: The Creation of a Sacred Place"; and Robert Kuhn McGregor, A Wider View of the Universe, 104–11, 121–74. See also the essay by Peter Blakemore in this collection.

3. Adams and Ross, Revising Mythologies, 155–64. Robert D. Richardson Jr. de-

scribes Thoreau's effort to balance empiricism and transcendentalism at this time as his "practical transcendentalism," in *Henry Thoreau: A Life of the Mind*, 245–48.

4. Thoreau, *Natural History Essays*, 72, 73.

5. Schneider, *Henry David Thoreau*, 148; Hildebidle, *Thoreau, A Naturalist's Liberty*, 97.

6. Walls, *Seeing New Worlds*, 5.

7. This is the view developed, for example, in Robert Kuhn McGregor's *A Wider View of the Universe* and in Robert Milder's *Reimagining Thoreau*.

8. Buell, *Environmental Imagination*, 139, 125, 117.

9. Buell, "Emerson in His Cultural Context," 53; *Literary Transcendentalism*, 149–50.

10. Walls, *Seeing New Worlds*, 20.

11. See Robert M. Young, *Darwin's Metaphor: Nature's Place in Victorian Culture*, 126–63; John Hedley Brooke, *Science and Religion: Some Historical Perspectives*, 192–225; and William Rossi, "Emerson, Nature, and Natural Science."

12. Ospovat, *Development of Darwin's Theory*, 33, 36. Ospovat's analysis of Darwin's manuscripts shows that, through its various reworkings, Darwin's theory retained some version of perfect adaptation through the 1840s and into the 1850s.

13. For the debate on "man's place in nature," see James G. Paradis, *T. H. Huxley: Man's Place in Nature*, 115–63, and Robert M. Young, *Darwin's Metaphor: Nature's Place in Victorian Culture*, 164–247.

The review to which Emerson alludes was written by Francis Jeffrey; see *Journals and Miscellaneous Notebooks of Ralph Waldo Emerson*, vol. 4, 11.

14. Emerson, *Nature, Addresses, and Lectures*, 10, 17.

15. Thoreau, *Natural History Essays*, 28.

16. As Margaret Fuller put it, for instance, "Human beings are not so constituted that they can live without expansion, and if they do not get it one way, must another, or perish." Thus what "woman needs is not as a woman to act or rule, but as a nature to grow, as an intellect to discern, as a soul to live freely, and unimpeded to unfold such powers as were given her when we left our common home" (Fuller, *Woman in the Nineteenth Century*, 25, 27).

On Emerson's development of the doctrine of self-culture from Unitarian sources, see David M. Robinson, *Apostle of Culture: Emerson as Preacher and Lecturer*; and on Fuller and self-culture, see Robinson, "Margaret Fuller and the Transcendental Ethos: *Woman in the Nineteenth Century*."

17. On Thoreau and transcendentalist journal-keeping, see Thoreau, *Journal, Vol. 1: 1837–1844*, and William Rossi, "The Journal, Self-Culture, and the Genesis of 'Walking.'"

18. Gray, *Manual of Botany*, xii, xxiv; Thoreau, *Journal, Vol. 3*, 225.

19. Gray, *Manual*, xiii; Thoreau, *Journal, Vol. 3*, 226.

20. Walls, *Seeing New Worlds*; Rehbock, *The Philosophical Naturalists*. On Darwin's use of analogy, see Gillian Beer, *Darwin's Plots: Evolutionary Narrative in Darwin, George Eliot, and Nineteenth-Century Fiction*, 79–103.

21. Albert J. von Frank, "Composition of *Nature*," 22n. 18. Robert Sattelmeyer examines this passage as a provocative instance of Thoreau's speculation on unconscious intellectual and creative activity in "The Remaking of Walden," 167–68.

22. Roget, *Animal and Vegetable Physiology*, 1:xv.

23. Ibid., 2:625, 626; Darwin, *On the Origin of Species*, 434.

24. Roget, *Animal and Vegetable Physiology*, 2:629.

25. Rehbock, "Transcendental Anatomy," 147. On the complex history of nineteenth-century theories of evolutionary recapitulation, including Haeckel's version, see Robert J. Richards, *The Meaning of Evolution: The Morphological Construction and Ideological Reconstruction of Darwin's Theory*, and Stephen J. Gould, *Ontogeny and Phylogeny*, 33–85.

26. Roget, *Animal and Vegetable Physiology*, 2:631, 634.

27. Evelleen Richards, "'Metaphorical Mystifications,'" 136.

28. Roget, *Animal and Vegetable Physiology*, 2:636, 637.

29. Topham, "Beyond the 'Common Context,'" 237–39.

30. Evelleen Richards, "'Metaphorical Mystifications,'" 131.

31. [Chambers], *Explanations*, in *Vestiges*, ed. Secord, 109–10.

32. [Chambers], *Vestiges of the Natural History of Creation*, 2nd ed., 170. According to Walter Harding's *Emerson's Library*, this is the edition Emerson owned and thus one that Thoreau is likely to have used. The evidence for Thoreau's having read Chambers's book is described in William Rossi, "Thoreau and the *Vestiges* Controversy."

33. [Chambers], *Explanations*, 72; Secord, "Behind the Veil," 185–86.

34. *Vestiges*, 232.

35. Miller, *Foot-Prints of the Creator*, 36–47, 277–302.

36. [Gray], "Explanations of *Vestiges*," 506. On scientific reviews of Chambers's book, see Richard Yeo, "Science and Intellectual Authority in Mid-Nineteenth-Century Britain: Robert Chambers and *Vestiges of the Natural History of Creation*," 1–27. For an extended account of Gray's response to *Vestiges*, derived from annotations in his copy of the book, see A. Hunter Dupree, *Asa Gray, 1810–1888*, 143–48.

37. Thoreau later bought a copy of the fourth edition of *The Botanical Text-Book*, from which all quotations are taken.

38. Gray, *Botanical Text-Book*, 238, 240.

For a discussion of the influence on Gray of philosophical anatomy and "the new morphological ideas emanating from Europe," see Toby A. Appel, "Jefferies Wyman, Philosophical Anatomy, and the Scientific Reception of Darwin in America." As Appel notes, although Gray "has been described as an empiricist deeply opposed to the idealism of Agassiz," at this point, like his other Harvard colleague, Wyman, Gray "was also an idealist, if by this term we mean someone who sees a plan of creation in the morphology of organisms" (80).

39. Gray, *Botanical Text-Book*, 17, 79, 80.

40. Ibid., 237.

41. Sattelmeyer, *Thoreau's Reading*, 232.

42. [Chambers], *Vestiges*, ed. Secord, 206.

43. Evelleen Richards, "A Question of Property Rights," 168.

44. Thoreau, *Faith in a Seed*, 102.

45. Stocking, *Victorian Anthropology*; Bowler, *Theories of Human Evolution*, 41–58; and Bowler, *Invention of Progress*, 75–128.

46. On the "essentially non-Darwinian conceptual framework" to which Darwin's theory was accommodated in the nineteenth century, one that stressed "the orderly, goal-directed, and usually progressive character of evolution," see Peter J. Bowler, *The Non-Darwinian Revolution: Reinterpreting a Historical Myth* and *Life's Splendid Drama: Evolutionary Biology and the Reconstruction of Life's Ancestry, 1860–1940*, 1–96.

47. Thoreau, *A Week*, 379. Subsequent page references are cited parenthetically in the text.

48. Fink, *Prophet in the Marketplace*, 216.

49. Leiss, *Domination of Nature*; Merchant, *Death of Nature*. For a cogent eco-feminist reading of this Journal passage and related images in *Walden*, see Louise H. Westling, *The Green Breast of the New World: Landscape, Gender, and American Fiction*, 39–53.

50. [Sedgwick], review, 6, 3–4.

51. Ibid., 4, 6, 16, 17.

52. Thoreau, *Natural History Essays*, 112, 129. For an analysis of "fertility" and of the polar structure of "Walking," see William Rossi, "'The Limits of an Afternoon Walk': Coleridgean Polarity in Thoreau's 'Walking.'"

"Climate Does Thus React on Man"

Wildness and Geographic Determinism in
Thoreau's "Walking"

RICHARD J. SCHNEIDER

In his essay "Walking," Henry David Thoreau begins by stating his intention to "speak a word for nature, for absolute freedom and wildness" and
to make "an extreme statement . . . an emphatic one," because, he asserts,
"there are enough champions of civilization."[1] This opening is so rhetorically forceful that readers are immediately inclined to assume that he
will carry out this intention in the essay that follows. The opening alone
serves to establish Thoreau as a champion of nature against civilization.
However, I would like to make "an extreme statement" of my own in
this essay by questioning both how much Thoreau really champions nature rather than civilization in "Walking" and how extreme a statement
he really makes. I will do so by reading "Walking" in the context of
Thoreau's own reading of one of the most popular scientific documents
of his time.

"Walking" has often been read as a defense of nature, an ecological
manifesto. Roderick Nash says, for instance, that Thoreau's comments
on wildness in "Walking" "cut the channels in which a large portion of
thought about wilderness subsequently flowed."[2] James McIntosh takes
Thoreau's famous pronouncement in "Walking" that "in Wildness is the
preservation of the World" (224), the same passage that interests Nash,
to be the "obvious and central message" of Thoreau's essay.[3] More recently H. Daniel Peck has argued that "Walking" is an implicit call to
modern humanity "to develop a cosmology, to perform a 'worlding,'
that would fundamentally alter our relation to nature."[4] This focus on
Thoreau's interest in wildness and on changing our relation to nature is

one of the main reasons why Thoreau has become, as Lawrence Buell dubs him, "the patron saint of American environmental writing." [5]

Other critics, however, have noticed another theme in "Walking" that might be seen as undercutting Thoreau's apparent defense of the wild and of wilderness. As early as 1961, Walter Harding noticed that "Walking" "becomes almost chauvinistic in boasting the superiority of the American landscape." [6] In 1977, Frederick Garber observed that in "Walking" "Thoreau follows current patterns of chauvinistic myth" about the westward movement.[7] A contrast between Thoreau's comments on Indians in *A Week on the Concord and Merrimack Rivers* and in "Walking" suggests to Garber "the basic tensions between Thoreau's twin desires — one for radical wildness and another for reclamation — and the paradoxes and contradictions to which the tensions will lead him." [8] More recently David Robinson has emphasized this paradoxical element in "Walking" in suggesting that Thoreau's concept of wildness "is inextricably bound up with the historical tragedy of the American West and the continuing ecological tension, particularly acute in the West, between the desire to preserve the wild and the desire to make use of it." [9] Robert D. Richardson, on the other hand, deemphasizes this ecological tension and argues that in "Walking" Thoreau is not following contemporary myths about the West and wildness but is instead undercutting them. "Thoreau's idea of the West," Richardson says, "is not an affirmation of the westward march of civilization" but instead a recognition of "what is wild within us." [10] In this essay, I will argue that in "Walking" Thoreau attempts to affirm both what is wild within us *and* the westward march of civilization, and that this attempt leads to the ecological tension noted by Garber and Robinson. This tension can best be understood by reading "Walking" in the context of the geographical determinism popular in Thoreau's time.

In 1851, Thoreau was reading a book by the Swiss geographer Arnold Guyot entitled *The Earth and Man.*[11] Guyot's book contained his 1849 series of lectures on geography and history, which was so popular in book form that the 1851 edition that Thoreau borrowed from Emerson was already the fourth edition. *The Earth and Man* quickly became the main scientific underpinning for the political idea of Manifest Destiny, the idea that the westward movement was part of a divine plan which Americans were obligated to implement by settling and plowing America's forests and prairies. This heroic process of settling the wilderness would create a new civilization, said Guyot. By 1890, historian Frederick Jackson Turner seemed to prove that Guyot was right when Turner concluded that the process of settling the West had been completed and that "the existence of an area of free land, its continuous recession, and the advance of American settlement westward, explain American development." [12]

While he was reading Guyot, Thoreau was writing "Walking," which he was splicing together from two lectures, one on "Walking" and one on "The Wild." He found Guyot's ideas quite interesting and took a number of notes from *The Earth and Man*, some of which he quotes in "Walking." Indeed, Guyot's theories of science and history are at the heart of "Walking" in ways that have not previously been recognized. To read "Walking" in the context of Guyot's theories reveals the irony in the Sierra Club's choice of "In Wildness is the preservation of the world" as a rallying slogan for preserving the wilderness, for to walk westward into the wild with Thoreau and Guyot is to endanger the wilderness, not to preserve it. To begin to understand why that is so, let us first meet Arnold Guyot.

Arnold Guyot had been recruited from Switzerland by Louis Agassiz to give a series of lectures at Harvard in 1849 on "comparative physical geography," a holistic Humboldtian geography which was to take geography out of the lowly realm of dry facts — "drier than the remainder biscuit after a voyage," as one reviewer bluntly put it (in Guyot, front matter reviews) — and into the higher realm of philosophy. Its goal was nothing less than "to comprehend the purposes of God, as to the destinies of nations, by examining with care the theatre, seemingly arranged by Him for the realization of the new social order, towards which humanity is tending with hope. For the order of nature is a foreshadowing of that which is to be" (33). Nature's purpose, as Guyot saw it, was to fulfill the needs of humanity, and the main hypothesis of physical geography was that "the forms, the arrangement, and the distribution of the terrestrial masses on the surface of the globe . . . reveal a plan" whereby specific continents are designed by God "to perform a special part corresponding to the wants of humanity" (34). To demonstrate that plan, Guyot marshals an impressive array of Humboldtian-style data: statistics, graphs, charts, comparative drawings of human facial types, and maps regarding land elevations, ocean depths, distribution of land forms, relative dryness and humidity, average rainfalls, wind and ocean currents, and types of vegetation and animal life.

The historical narrative which Guyot derives from all of this data is nothing less than God's plan for humanity, by which "the civilizations representing the highest degree of culture ever attained by man, at the different periods of his history, do not succeed each other in the same places, but pass from one country to another, from one continent to another, following a certain order. This order may be called *the geographical march of history"* (300, Guyot's emphasis). Guyot accepts, reluctantly at times, the common origin of all humanity — an idea much disputed in his day — and speculates that the place of origin was probably western Asia because of "its gigantic proportions, the almost infinite diversity of its soil, its central situation," all of which "render it suitable to be the continent of *germs* [i.e., seeds]" for humanity (30, Guyot's emphasis). The progress he then describes in detail is a movement of civilization, of what he calls the "historical" (i.e., white) races west and north: from western Asia (i.e., the Middle East) to Greece to Europe and eventually to America.

This movement is toward the temperate climates, which are most suited to the development of complex civilizations because "in the temperate climates all is activity, movement. The alterations of heat and cold, the changes of the seasons, a fresher and more bracing air, incite man to a constant struggle, to forethought, to the vigorous employment of all his faculties" (269). In such a climate, nature grants man "ease and leisure, which give him scope to cultivate all the lofty faculties of his higher nature. Here physical nature is not a tyrant, but a useful helper; the active faculties, the understanding and the reason, rule over the instincts and the passive faculties; the soul over the body; man over nature" (269–70). Movements out of western Asia in other directions prove to be false starts for humanity. Moving eastward into Asia, people find resources to achieve a relatively high level of civilization but are then prevented from any further advance by the sheer gigantic scale of nature, which they eventually despair of ever conquering further, and by their isolation from each other. Movements south also fail, because the tropical heat and humidity are too enervating and deter people from making the effort necessary to create a higher civilization.

Guyot's teleological view of history is based not only on the superiority of temperate climates, but also on two other scientific principles: that the basic formula of all life is in a *"mutual exchange of relations"* (95, Guyot's emphasis) and that all organisms tend to progress from homogeneity to diversity. The former principle he illustrates with the chemical example of a zinc plate and copper plate being placed near each other to produce electricity. This reaction demonstrates how "everywhere a simple difference, be it of matter, be it of condition, be it of position, excites a manifestation of vital forces, a mutual exchange between the bodies, each giving to the other what the other does not possess" (95). "To multiply these differences," he says, "is to extend and to intensify life" (95). This principle of mutual exchange, of duality, explains why God did not create just one climate and one race. God's plan uses diversity of climate and cultures to extend and intensify human life.

Progress thereby becomes a process of increasing human complexity: "progress . . . is *diversification*; it is the variety of organs and of functions" (97, Guyot's emphasis). Civilization and specialization become synonymous: "the almost infinite *specialization* of the functions corresponding to the various talents bestowed on every man by Providence . . . [is] the sign of a social state arrived at a high degree of improvement" (97, Guyot's emphasis). Guyot's argument here is explicitly directed against Rousseau's ideas of the simplicity of life in nature and of the noble savage. "Could we hope to see the wonders of architecture unfolded among a people [the Indians of the Rocky Mountains] who have no public edifices but the overhanging foliage of their forests?" he asks (98). What "a false philosophy [Rousseau's] has called the simplicity of nature" is in reality "opposed to the true nature of man" (98). The highest civilizations are, in short, the most complex; God's plan moves humanity from simplicity to increasing complexity, from primitive and simple cultures to civilized and complex cultures.

The climate and geography most conducive to complexity, according to Guyot, are those of Europe. Not only does Europe have the requisite temperate climate, but it is the continent "whose forms of contour are most varied" (45–46), a variety which encourages the development of human diversity: "No continent is more fitted, by the multiplicity of the physical regions it presents, to bring into being, and to raise up so many different nations and peoples" (296–97). It also has a central location in relation to other continents, a location crucial to its historical role: "it is the continent most open to the sea, for foreign connections, at the same time that it is the most individualized, and the richest in local and independent districts" (46). Europe is the seedbed of civilization where complex cultures have been nurtured and developed. "Nowhere on the surface of our planet," Guyot asserts, "has the mind of man risen to a sublimer height; nowhere has man known so well how to subdue nature, and to make her the instrument of intelligence" as in Europe (31).

Europe has historically played its role well, Guyot argues, but by the nineteenth century it has reached its fullest potential and has no room for further development: "historical ties of every kind, ancient customs, acquired rights, as much to be respected as any other rights of man, and, above all, the want of resources and of room for an ever-increasing population, are almost insurmountable difficulties, seeming to indicate that the work begun upon her soil is to be finished elsewhere" (320). Civilization now must transfer a vanguard of its people to a new, more spacious continent with a similar temperate climate: "And to what continent? The geographical march of civilization tells us, to a new continent west of the Old World — to America" (321). In America lie vast untapped resources passively waiting to be put to use by civilization on the march: "America lies glutted with its vegetable wealth, unworked, solitary. Its immense forests, its savannas, every year cover its soil with their remains, which, accumulated during the long ages of the world, form that deep bed of vegetable mould, that precious soil, awaiting only the hand of man to work out all the wealth of its inexhaustible fertility" (231).

This idea of America's special destiny in human history is central to Thoreau's theme in "Walking." By expressing his agreement with it throughout the essay, he allies himself with Guyot and thereby champions civilization as much as wildness. Or perhaps it is more accurate to say that he champions civilization *by* championing wildness.

As described in "Walking," for instance, a walk in the woods for Thoreau is not a rejection of civilization but a religious exercise by which the walker is enabled to return to society. Sauntering, Thoreau says, is "going *à la Sainte Terre*" — to the spiritual Holy Land within each person (205). Because its goal is spiritual, it is an attempt to make place irrelevant, "to be equally at home everywhere. For that is the secret of successful sauntering" (205). Thoreau's sauntering is as much a state of mind as a physical exercise; the physical act itself cannot foster the freedom or wildness necessary for spiritual renewal, for "Our expeditions are but tours and come round again at evening to the old hearth-side from which we set out. Half the walk is but retracing our steps" (206). Although he says that the ideal would be to set out on a walk with the idea of never coming back to civilization, he himself never does so, nor does he really encourage others to do so.

By walking, Thoreau is not rejecting civilization but rather seeking what he calls in *Walden* "the tonic of wildness," for "our village life would stagnate if it were not for the unexplored forests and meadows which surround it." [13] The purpose of wildness is to refresh civilization, not to reject it. Walking works according to Guyot's "mutual exchange of relations" in which "a simple difference . . . of position excites a manifestation of vital forces." Thoreau's emphasis, as Laura Dassow Walls has suggested, "is not on a place or a 'center' but on a process, 'walking,' which conducts him to a state of being: 'the wild.'"[14] In "Walking," Thoreau marvels at how shopkeepers and housewives can remain nearly motion-less cooped up in their shops and houses all day (208–9), for he finds physical change to be the necessary catalyst without which "I cannot pre-serve my health and spirits" (207). The wildness of nature gives him the psychological and spiritual wildness to function creatively when he re-turns to civilization; he brings back wildness civilized. Nor does he need wilderness to achieve inner wildness, for "a single farmhouse which I had not seen before is sometimes as good as the dominions of the King of Dahomey" (211). Wildness cannot be a tonic for civilization unless the walker returns to import it psychologically into the village.

If, on the one hand, the individual saunterer should be equally at home anywhere and any change in position should be able to excite his vital forces, on the other hand, place is vitally important for symbolic reasons. "It is not indifferent to us which way we walk," Thoreau says; "there is a right way" (216). That way is west, the way of Guyot's historical civilization. The individual walker reenacts symbolically the movement of civilization. Thoreau prefers walking west because "the future lies that way to me, and the earth seems more unexhausted and richer on that side" (217). To migrate west "is the prevailing tendency of my country-men. I must walk toward Oregon, and not toward Europe. And that way the nation is moving, and I may say that mankind progress from east to west" (218). "We go westward as into the future," he says, "with a spirit of enterprise and adventure" (218).

Thoreau at this point in the essay has not yet mentioned Guyot spe-cifically; he will quote him a page or two later. But the idea of Manifest Destiny and the westward movement of civilization that he describes is drawn straight from Guyot. Thoreau, like Guyot, finds little potential in directions other than west. Guyot argues that movements south from Europe and the Caucasus lead to a lack of moral development because of the enervating heat. Thoreau acknowledges the recent migrations south-east to Australia but is skeptical of their success: "this affects us as a ret-rograde movement, and, judging from the moral and physical character of the first generation of Australians, has not yet proved a successful ex-periment" (218). Guyot argues that movements east into Asia at first lead to impressive cultural development, but that development is eventually stifled by the vastness and isolation of that continent's huge mountain ranges and vast wastelands. Thoreau echoes this view when he comments on the limitations of the Asian world view: "the eastern Tartars think that there is nothing west beyond Thibet. 'The world ends there,' say they;

'beyond there is nothing but a shoreless sea.' It is unmitigated East where they live" (218).

By contrast Thoreau, the American, can "believe that the forest which I see in the western horizon stretches uninterruptedly toward the setting sun, and there are no towns nor cities in it of enough consequence to disturb me" (217–18). This limitless vista is part of the idea of "American exceptionalism," the idea that North America was an extraordinarily fertile and healthy place, exceptionally well suited to be the next stop on the march of civilization. "Where on the globe," he asks, "can there be found an area of equal extent with that occupied by the bulk of our States, so fertile and so rich and varied in its productions, and at the same time so habitable by the European, as this is?" (220). He then cites authorities to verify these exceptional qualities: first Michaux, who observes that there are more large trees in North America than in Europe; next Humboldt (Guyot's mentor), whose books describe the vast tropical wilderness of the Amazon; and then Guyot, whom he quotes at length, emphasizing Guyot's affirmation of America's special place in history.

He introduces the quote from Guyot with a brief reservation: "The geographer Guyot, himself a European, goes farther, — farther than I am ready to follow him" (220). This reservation most likely refers to Guyot's Christian agenda, which Thoreau surely did not share. (The "Holy Land" of Thoreau's "saunterer" is not Guyot's Christian Heaven.) But he retracts his reservation — "farther than I am ready to follow him" — when he comes to Guyot's expression of America's destiny:

> yet not when he says: "As the plant is made for the animal, as the vegetable world is made for the animal world, America is made for the man of the Old World. . . . The man of the Old World sets out upon his way. Leaving the highlands of Asia, he descends from station to station towards Europe. Each of his steps is marked by a new civilization superior to the preceding, by a greater power of development. Arrived at the Atlantic, he pauses on the shore of this unknown ocean, the bounds of which he knows not, and turns upon his footprints for an instant." When he has exhausted the rich soil of Europe, and reinvigorated himself, "then recommences his adventurous career westward as in the earliest ages." So far Guyot. (220–21; Guyot 233)

Positioned as it is in the center of Thoreau's parade of authorities who support American exceptionalism, this quote is clearly one which Thoreau strongly endorses. Thoreau genuinely believes with Guyot that America is destined to be the next home for the civilization of the Old

World. Rather than arguing for the preservation of the wilderness, he is actively endorsing its invasion and eventual destruction to serve the needs of civilization.

Thoreau's next paragraph begins with another reference to an idea from Guyot, the idea that human access to seacoasts is a requirement for the "mutual exchange of relations" that allows civilization to progress. Thoreau says that "from this western impulse coming in contact with the barrier of the Atlantic sprang the commerce and enterprise of modern times" (221). He likely has in mind Guyot's argument that European and American access to the Atlantic Ocean is crucial to the progress of civilization. Guyot asks in *The Earth and Man*, "is it not on the shores of the Atlantic that life is developed in its most active, most intense, and most exalted form?" (184). A couple of sentences later Guyot continues by saying that "the life of nations is in the commerce of the world, not only in a material, but even more in a moral point of view" (184), a view with which Thoreau the transcendentalist would surely have agreed. Thus America, with its long Atlantic coastline facing Europe and its destined access to the Pacific, is, according to Guyot, "enthroned queen-like upon the two great oceans" and will "be called to play a part as mediator between the two extremities of the world" (184). Given this historical role, it would be difficult for America not to make commercial use of its vast wilderness of resources. Neither Guyot nor Thoreau seems aware of the inevitable conflict between the material and the moral impulses.

After another quote from Michaux illustrating America's position as a global meeting place, Thoreau sums up Guyot's geographical version of history by coining a Latin phrase: "*Ex Oriente lux; ex Occidente* FRUX. From the East light; from the West fruit" (221). This phrase extends one of the metaphors crucial to Guyot's argument, that history is a matter of the dispersion of cultural seeds or "germs." For Guyot, Asia is "the continent of *the germs*" of civilization (30), but it does not have a suitable geography to allow those seeds to develop fully. Europe provides a better bed to nurture the seeds of civilization. In a passage that Thoreau omits from the long quotation from Guyot above, Guyot says that it is in Europe that humanity "works out slowly the numerous germs wherewith he is endowed" (233). Eventually, however, the resources of Europe are exhausted and humanity must look elsewhere: "He has tilled the impoverished soil, and yet the number of his offspring increases" and so he "sets out in search of new countries" (233) and casts his glance westward toward America. Thus, Guyot says, "the Old World is the world of germs; the New, the fruitful bosom giving them increase. Europe thinks; America acts" (238). Thoreau's Latin phrase, it turns out, is simply a paraphrase of Guyot, with the metaphors mixed to achieve the Latin rhyme.

This metaphor of America as the fruit of civilization is one which Thoreau kept in his literary tool bag and would likely have used again in his projected works on fruits and on the dispersion of seeds. In his Journal for September 18, 1859, amid a number of observations about fruits and seeds, Thoreau writes,

> One might at first expect that the earth would bear its best men within the tropics, where vegetation is most luxuriant and there is the most heat. But the temperate zone is found to be most favorable to the growth and ripening of men. This fruit attains to the finest flavor there. So, methinks, it is neither the stem nor blossom end of a fruit that is sweetest and maturest, but its blossom cheek or temperate zone, the portion that lies under its temperate zone. I suspect that the south pole is the stem end of the globe and that Europe and America are on its rosy cheek, and fortunate are we who live in America, where the bloom is not yet rubbed off.[15]

The first part of this passage refers to Guyot's theory that a tropical climate is best for the development of vegetable and animal species, but that a temperate climate is best for the development of humans, the only species to which God has given the gift of moral sensibility. Guyot cites data that "in America, the temperate zones of the two hemispheres furnish scarcely more than four thousand species of plants, the tropical region of this same continent has already made known more than thirteen thousand" and that "the animal kingdom is no less developed . . . in this privileged zone" (252). From such data Guyot extrapolates a law about physical nature: "the degree of perfection of the types is proportional to the intensity of heat, and of the other agents stimulating the display of material life" (264). The largest and most beautiful physical specimens will thus be found in the tropics. Guyot argues that there is a different law for humans, however, one based on moral rather than physical development: "In man, the degree of perfection of the types is in proportion to the degree of intellectual and moral improvement" (264). Thus "while all the types of animals and of plants go on decreasing in perfection, from the equatorial to the polar regions, in proportion to the temperatures, man presents to our view his purest, his most perfect type, at the very centre of the temperate continents" (254). The racial implications of this theory and Thoreau's acceptance of it are, of course, quite troubling, but that is another essay.

The second half of Thoreau's Journal passage suggests how he might eventually have connected his interest in fruits and seeds to his interest in the development of civilization by making symbolic connections between physical and moral law. That potential connection is illustrated by an interesting passage in "The Dispersion of Seeds" in which Thoreau discusses accidental human agency in distributing seeds. To demonstrate that "the civilized man transports more . . . seeds than the savage does,"[16] Thoreau quotes Charles Pickering, a medical doctor and explorer whose *The Races of Man* argued for less of a connection between climate and race than Guyot posits: "Pickering, in his work on races, says that 'the natives of Australia, being for the most part devoid of clothing, and possessing very few manufactures, have contributed perhaps less than any other branch of the human family to the dispersion of seeds and plants.'"[17] Thoreau thus intertwines the dispersion of seeds and the dispersion of civilization's "germs." Such passages suggest that the split between Thoreau's interests in science and in social reform that has long been a commonplace of Thoreau criticism is in fact a myth. If as Robert D. Richardson suggests, "The Dispersion of Seeds" is "about the growth of communities and the rise of new generations,"[18] it is so not only regarding the plant world, but implicitly regarding human communities and the rise of civilization as well. Both "Walking" and "The Dispersion of Seeds" are thus part of what Joel Porte has called Thoreau's lifelong "fable of dissemination."[19]

Thoreau clearly believes with Guyot that the seeds of civilization transported from Europe to America will blossom into the most fully mature moral fruit that civilization has ever seen. Thoreau continues in "Walking" with more authorities praising America's exceptional glories: Sir Francis Head claiming that everything is bigger and better in America, and Linnaeus commenting on the scarcity of dangerous wild beasts. "These," Thoreau says, "are encouraging testimonies" containing facts which, he continues, "are symbolical of the height to which the philosophy and poetry and religion of her inhabitants may one day soar. At length, perchance, the immaterial heaven will appear as much higher to the American mind, and the intimations that star it as much brighter" (222). He then emphatically reaffirms Guyot's most basic assumption: "I believe that climate does thus react on man, — as there is something in the mountain air that feeds the spirit and inspires. Will not man grow to greater perfection intellectually as well as physically under these influences?" (222). This creed is crucial both to his and to Guyot's view of

America: "Else to what end does the world go on, and why was America discovered?" Thoreau asks (223).

In the context of this view of history, Thoreau's comments on the wild acquire a meaning which might seem troublesome to Thoreau's reputation as the father of American environmentalism. He begins the next section of "Walking" with the stirring pronouncement that "The West of which I speak is but another name for the Wild; and what I have been preparing to say is, that in Wildness is the preservation of the World" (224). This statement has most often been misunderstood as a defense of a certain kind of place, the wilderness (see Barbara Nelson's essay in this volume), but it is in fact a defense of a state of mind, what Thoreau calls later in the essay "Useful Ignorance" (239), the potential for growth and learning.

In the individual, "the tonic of wildness" is a healthy restlessness, a desire for more knowledge and new experiences. Thoreau argues that particular untamed places — "the impervious and quaking swamps" (226–27) or "the ocean, the desert, or the wilderness!" (228) — can foster this wildness, but he also says that it can be found in the forests and meadows nearer home (225). It can be in the sound of music — "the sound of a bugle in a summer night," for instance — or in a show of spirit in a domestic animal: "I love to see the domestic animals reassert their native rights, — any evidence that they have not wholly lost their original wild habits and vigor; as when my neighbor's cow breaks out of her pasture early in the spring and boldly swims the river" (234). Each person has a potential, though perhaps repressed, strain of wildness within: "We have a wild savage in us, and a savage name is perchance somewhere recorded as ours" (237). "In short," he says, "all good things are wild and free" (234).

Wildness is clearly not restricted to wilderness. Wildness is but one, though a necessary, dimension of life. One should strive for a balance between civilization and wildness: "the natural remedy is to be found in the proportion which the night bears to the day, the winter to the summer, thought to experience" (210). The problem is that most people acquiesce to civilization early in life — "when we should still be growing children, we are already little men" (237) — and they lose touch with their "wild" side completely. Hence the value of walking in stimulating that suppressed wildness. Thoreau himself admits that "for my part, I feel that with regard to Nature I live a sort of border life on the confines of a world into which I make occasional and transient forays only, and my patriotism and allegiance to the state into whose territories I seem to retreat are those of a moss-trooper" (242). Walking, in short, provides for Thoreau that "mutual exchange of relations," that duality between tameness and wildness that both Thoreau and Guyot believe to be necessary for the mental and physical health of a civilization.

In civilization at large, Thoreau's wildness is the desire for more space and more resources with which to improve the quality of life physically, morally, and spiritually. It is the restlessness of the individual extended to society at large: "something like the *furor* which affects the domestic cattle in the spring, and which is referred to a worm in their tails, affects both nations and individuals, either perennially or from time to time" (219). That furor in Thoreau's day was the westward movement, which Guyot describes as "a perpetual movement, a fever of locomotion" which "rages from one end of the continent to the other" (323–24). The causes of such a migration, Thoreau suggests, are physical and social stagnation. Physically a culture needs a fertile soil to sustain it, and it must move when it exhausts its own agricultural resources: "The civilized nations — Greece, Rome, England — have been sustained by the primitive forests which anciently rotted where they stand. They survive as long as the soil is not exhausted. Alas for human culture! little is to be expected of a nation, when the vegetable mould is exhausted, and it is compelled to make manure of the bones of its fathers" (229). The social problem, as Thoreau sees it, is that urbanization is a sort of social incest caused by too much human interaction without any "tonic of wildness": "we are so early weaned from [Nature's] breast to society, to that culture which is exclusively an interaction of man on man, — a sort of breeding in and in, which produces at most a merely English nobility, a civilization destined to have a speedy limit" (237).

The cure for this stagnation for both Thoreau and Guyot is the westward movement, with the farmer in the vanguard plowing up new soil to make a new life amid the wilds of the forests and prairies. On this subject Thoreau again quotes Guyot silently but approvingly: "It is said to be the task of the American 'to work the virgin soil,' and that 'agriculture here already assumes proportions unknown everywhere else'" (229–30; Guyot 236). The farmer is thus the hero of the westward movement: "I think that the farmer displaces the Indian even because he redeems the meadow, and so makes himself stronger and in some respects more natural" (230). The victories that the farmer wins are the results of technology, which here receives high praise from Thoreau: "The weapons with which we have gained our most important victories, which should be

Frances F. Palmer, Across the Continent: Westward the Course of Empire Takes Its Way, *1868. Currier and Ives lithograph. 20 × 27. Library of Congress.*

handed down as heirlooms from father to son, are not the sword and the lance, but the bushwhack, the turf-cutter, the spade, and the bog hoe, rusted with the blood of many a meadow, and begrimed with the dust of many a hard-fought field" (230).[20] As evidence of the enterprising spirit and persistence of pioneering agriculture, Thoreau describes a farmer for whom he had done some surveying who refused to despair of making productive three seemingly impenetrable swamps that he owned. "That man," Thoreau says with admiration, "intends to put a girdling ditch round the whole in the course of forty months, and so redeem it by the magic of his spade. I refer to him only as the type of a class" (230).

In the face of such technological ingenuity and persistence, the Indian, Thoreau and Guyot agree, must be doomed to extinction. Placed in a temperate climate the most conducive in the world to moral and intellectual development, the Indian has proven unworthy of such blessings by an inability to make full use of them. "The very winds," Thoreau says, "blew the Indian's cornfield into the meadow, and pointed out the way which he had not the skill to follow. He had no better implement with which to intrench himself in the land than a clamshell. But the farmer is armed with plow and spade" (230–31). Thoreau here expresses no more regret than does Guyot for the fate of the Indian, who has proven himself unable to make use of the natural "dispersion of seeds" or to participate in the historical dispersion of cultural seeds. Thoreau instead settles for using the "savagist" technique (see Sayre[21]) of reducing the Indian to a romantic symbol of the wild: "The wildness of the savage is but a faint symbol of the awful ferity with which good men and lovers meet" (234).

Thoreau concludes "Walking" with a vision of hope both for the individual walker and for civilization, a metaphor reminiscent of the ending of *Walden*: "So we saunter toward the Holy Land, till one day the sun shall shine more brightly than ever he has done, shall perchance shine into our minds and hearts, and light up our whole lives with a great awakening light, as warm and serene and golden as on a bankside in autumn" (247– 48). But by now the unintentional irony of that optimism should be clear. While the concept of "the Wild" as a symbol for a healthy state of mind seems useful as a tool for psychological and spiritual healing, its physical and historical implications seem disastrous. If all readers of "Walking" took Thoreau's advice about sauntering, there would by now be no place left to saunter. The woods everywhere would be filled with people. And we know the results of the antidote of the wild that Thoreau proposes for civilization: the westward movement destroyed a continent full of wilderness, as well as its indigenous people.

Thoreau is not entirely unaware of this potential irony; in "Walking" he does express some concern about the destruction of nature. He sees signs of such destruction already in Concord: "A hundred years ago they sold bark in our streets peeled from our own woods. . . . already I shudder for these comparatively degenerate days of my native village, when you cannot collect a load of bark of good thickness, and we no longer produce tar and turpentine" (229). He also predicts that "possibly the day will come when [the landscape] will be partitioned off into so-called pleasure-grounds, in which a few will take a narrow and exclusive pleasure only, — when fences shall be multiplied, and man traps and other engines invented to confine men to the *public* road, and walking over the surface of God's earth shall be construed to mean trespassing on some gentleman's grounds. . . . Let us improve our opportunities, then, before the evil days come" (216). His suggested solution to such environmental problems is stated rather unemphatically late in the essay: "I would not have every man nor every part of a man cultivated, any more than I would have every acre of earth cultivated: part will be tillage, but the greater part will be meadow and forest, not only serving an immediate use, but preparing a mould against a distant future, by the annual decay of the vegetation which it supports" (238). This statement amounts to a call for spacious public greenbelts of forests and meadows around each town to provide "vegetable mould" to fertilize the soil and walking room for all inhabitants who wish to "improve their opportunities" for communion with nature. But it is hardly the resounding battle cry for preserving the wilderness that "Walking" is thought to contain, and it is mostly overwhelmed by the opposite and dominant idea of "Walking" that both individuals and civilizations should explore nature more fully, the likely result being the destruction of the wilderness for human use.

"Walking" is thus not the best — or even a very good — American document to support environmental causes of conservation or preservation, causes more directly championed in Thoreau's own day by George Catlin's call for "a nation's park" to preserve the buffalo and Indian culture[22] or by George Perkins Marsh's *Man and Nature* and its warning about humanity's destruction of natural resources. In arguing that "Walking" contains "the most powerful and uncompromising statements regarding nature Thoreau publicly espoused in his lifetime," Robert Kuhn McGregor (along with many other readers) mistakes Thoreau's rhetorically defiant introduction, intended initially to get the attention of a live lyceum audience, with the essay's much less extreme main argument.[23] Within Thoreau's own works, one will find better support for conservation in his study of forest succession, more concern about the wilderness in *The Maine Woods*, firmer roots for ecological approaches to nature in the bioregional ecological data in his Journal and in his studies of seed dispersion, and a more extreme statement in his moving to Walden Pond. Sauntering out of town and into the woods for a few hours each day is, after all, hardly as extreme as moving there entirely for two years.

Nonetheless, "Walking" remains an important document in American environmental history. In its merging of Thoreau's own romantic transcendental philosophy and of Guyot's romantic Humboldtian science, "Walking" is typical of the symbolic approach to nature which placed nature in the forefront of American consciousness, a consciousness necessary before conservation could become important. Thoreau valued "Wildness" and "the West" primarily for their psychological and symbolic meaning. As he wrote to his friend Thomas Cholmondeley in 1856, "The *great west* and *northwest* stretching on infinitely far and grand and wild, qualifying all our thoughts. That is the only America I know. I prize this western reserve chiefly for its intellectual value. That is the road to new life and freedom. . . . That great northwest where several of our shrubs, fruitless here, retain and mature their fruits properly."[24] In its symbolic and anthropocentric appropriation of nature as a symbol for progress, "Walking" also provides important insights into the American ambivalence toward nature which pervades American history. But in doing so, it does not so much look forward to the preservationist programs of the Sierra Club as it reflects the nineteenth-century westering myth of Arnold Guyot and Frederick Jackson Turner.

NOTES

1. Thoreau, "Walking," in *Writings of Henry David Thoreau*, ed. Torrey, vol. V, 205. Subsequent page references are cited parenthetically in the text.

2. Nash, *Wilderness and the American Mind*, 84.

3. McIntosh, *Thoreau as Romantic Naturalist*, 287.

4. Peck, *Thoreau's Morning Work*, 162.

5. Buell, *Environmental Imagination*, 115.

6. Harding, *Thoreau Handbook*, 70.

7. Garber, *Thoreau's Redemptive Imagination*, 43.

8. Ibid., 45.

9. Robinson, "Thoreau's 'Walking' and the Ecological Imperative," 171.

10. Richardson, *Henry David Thoreau*, 288.

11. Guyot, *Earth and Man*. Subsequent page references are cited parenthetically in the text.

12. Turner, *Frontier in American History*, 1.

13. Thoreau, *Walden*, 317.

14. Walls, *Seeing New Worlds*, 232.

15. *Journal of Henry David Thoreau*, ed. Torrey and Allen, vol. XII.

16. Thoreau, *Faith in a Seed*, 99.

17. Ibid., 99.

18. Richardson, "Introduction," 4.

19. Ibid., 15.

20. See David R. Foster's comments on Thoreau's view of the farmer as hero in *Thoreau's Country: Journey through a Transformed Landscape*, 33–47.

21. Sayre, *Thoreau and the American Indians*.

22. Catlin, "Buffalo Country," 70.

23. McGregor, *A Wider View of the Universe*, 94.

24. Qtd. in Paul, *Shores of America*, 415.

"In Search of a More Human Nature"

Wendell Berry's Revision of Thoreau's Experiment

TED OLSON

The first published work to investigate the literary kinship of Henry David Thoreau and Wendell Berry was scholar Herman Nibbelink's 1985 essay "Thoreau and Wendell Berry: Bachelor and Husband of Nature." Asserting that Berry was an intellectual and spiritual disciple of Thoreau, Nibbelink's essay identified several similarities between the two authors — belief in the restorative powers of nature, commitment to living deliberately, valuing of simplicity, and disdain for materialism — mentioning only one major difference: "the place of agriculture in the relationship of nature and culture."[1] This difference, Nibbelink conjectured, resulted from Thoreau's belief that farming and husbandry robbed a person of individual freedom, while Berry held that "in agriculture . . . nature and culture are married" (151).

As illuminating as it might have seemed when first published, Nibbelink's essay is outmoded today, since the scholar focused his exploration of this particular literary kinship on just two texts: Thoreau's bean field chapter from *Walden* and Berry's poetry collection *Clearing*. However, Berry's worldview, as well as his attitude toward Thoreau, changed markedly after the publication of that 1977 volume. Berry's writings of the 1960s and early 1970s — particularly in the genres of nonfiction and poetry — tended to be ecocentric in outlook. That is, Berry — whether evoking the natural world, celebrating spiritual values in nature, or safeguarding natural places through political action — tended to privilege nature over culture. His writing since the mid-1970s has grown steadily anthropocentric, however, displaying increasing confidence in the power of human culture, if based on an ecologically sound way of life, to bind people and nature together in a constructive — not destructive — interrelationship. Nibbelink did not address the fact that *Clearing* was a transitional work in Berry's oeuvre; some of the poems in that volume were ecocentric in outlook, and others were anthropocentric. The former perspective was the central motivation of the poem "History," in which Berry decried European settlers' treatment of the land on which he was now living, while the latter perspective infused "The Clearing," in which Berry imagined himself a new kind of pioneer, one who, chastened by the mistakes of previous settlers, has discovered a way to live on the earth without hurting the natural world or himself. *Clearing* marked Berry's realization that, though unscrupulous humans have despoiled the earth, a more enlightened culture, through reclaiming a sense of place, would instill in people a deeper respect toward the land and thus repair at least some of the accrued environmental damage. That poetry volume, though, does not — and, given the date of its composition, cannot — reveal the extent to which Berry in his later writings would commit to finding cultural solutions to environmental problems.

Just as *Clearing* cannot represent Berry's current thinking regarding the interrelationship between people and nature, Nibbelink's essay cannot account for Berry's present-day attitude toward Thoreau. In this essay I intend to explore Berry's changing attitude toward his literary predecessor, as I sense that such a study will elucidate some of the reasons for Berry's shift from an ecocentric to an anthropocentric perspective.

The anthropocentric bent of Berry's later work, it should be noted, was not a result of diminishing interest in environmental issues on his part; Berry has remained a tireless proponent of people being in "a continuous harmony" (to borrow one of his more memorable phrases) with other living things. Nevertheless, by the mid-1970s, Berry had become convinced that most environmentalists, exhibiting a penchant for fervent ecocentrism, overrelied on politics when addressing environmental problems. Although he continued to demonstrate against environmental threats (participating, for instance, in protests against a proposed nuclear power plant near his north-central Kentucky home), Berry by the mid-1970s was rejecting politics as the most effective means by which to confront our environmental crisis, insisting instead upon cultural reform. "Our environmental problems . . . are not, at root, political; they are cultural," he observed in 1985. "Our country is not being destroyed by bad politics; it is being destroyed by a bad way of life. Bad politics is merely another result. To see that the problem is far more than political is to return to reality."[2]

From the mid-1970s onward, recognizing that culturally created problems required cultural solutions, Berry progressively broke from the ecocentric perspective of mainline American environmentalism, a move which brought criticism from some environmentalists. In a 1985 essay defending friend and fellow writer Edward Abbey from the charge that he was a traitor to environmentalism, Berry revealed the degree to which he was now committed to finding anthropocentric, cultural solutions, rather than ecocentric, political solutions: "Edward Abbey is fighting on a much broader front than that of any 'movement.' He is fighting for the survival not only of nature, but of *human* nature, of culture, as only our heritage of works and hopes can define it. He is, in short, a traditionalist — as he has said himself, expecting, perhaps, not to be believed."[3]

In that same essay, when attempting to identify an appropriate literary context for Abbey's work (and, by implication, his own), Berry challenged a belief widely held among environmentalists from the 1960s through the 1980s (the years of his own and Abbey's emergence as writers): the notion that Thoreau was the progenitor of all American nature writing. "One of the strongest of contemporary conventions," wrote Berry, is that of comparing to Thoreau every writer who has been

as far out of the house as the mailbox. But I do not intend to say that Mr. Abbey writes like Thoreau, for I do not think he does, but only that their *cases* are similar. Thoreau has been adopted by the American environment movement as a figurehead; he is customarily quoted and invoked as if he were in some simple way a forerunner of environmentalism. This is possible, obviously, only because Thoreau has been dead since 1862. Thoreau was an environmentalist in exactly the sense that Edward Abbey is: he was for some things that environmentalists are for. And in his own time he was just as much of an embarrassment to movements, just as uncongenial to the group spirit, as Edward Abbey is, and for the same reasons: he was working as an autobiographer, and his great effort was to conserve himself as a human being in the best and fullest sense. (40, Berry's emphasis)

This 1985 passage denying Thoreau a central position in the canon of American nature writing was not Berry's first reevaluation of his former literary hero — that, as shall be discussed later, took place in the mid-1970s. Nonetheless, while Nibbelink's essay cited passages from Berry's early work which professed a debt to Thoreau, the scholar ignored passages which projected a fundamentally different worldview from Thoreau's; thus, Nibbelink missed clues which would have intimated Berry's inevitable break from his literary predecessor.

This "anxiety of influence" regarding Thoreau is evident in some of Berry's earliest published writings, wherein he exhibited a tendency to revise Thoreau even as he praised him. For instance, in "A Native Hill," a 1969 essay addressing the need of people to escape periodically the pain wrought by human history, Berry imitated Thoreau stylistically and thematically, revealing the depth of his psychic identification with the author of *Walden*. Yet, even as he, in a passage from "A Native Hill," mimicked the mission statement from *Walden*, Berry proffered corrections. Thoreau's mission statement, in which that author justified his Walden Pond experiment, is well known:

I went to the woods because I wished to live deliberately, to front only the essential facts of life, and see if I could not learn what it had to teach, and not, when I came to die, discover that I had not lived. I did not wish to live what was not life, living is so dear; nor did I wish to practise resignation, unless it was quite necessary. I wanted to live deep and suck out all the marrow of life, to live so sturdily and Spartan-like as to put to rout all that was not life, to cut a broad swath and shave close, to drive life into a corner, and reduce it to its lowest terms, and, if it proved to be mean, why then to get the whole and genuine meanness of it, and publish its meanness to the world; or if it were sublime, to know it by experience, and be able to give a true account of it in my next excursion. For most men, it appears to me, are in a strange uncertainty about it, whether it is of the devil or of God, and have *somewhat hastily* concluded that it is the chief end of man here to "glorify God and enjoy him forever."[4]

The aforementioned passage from Berry's "A Native Hill" reads as follows:

Sometimes I can no longer think in the house or in the garden or in the cleared fields. They bear too much resemblance to our failed human history — failed, because it has led to this human present that is such a bitterness and a trial. And so I go to the woods. As I go in under the trees, dependably, almost at once, and by nothing I do, things fall into place. I enter an order that does not exist outside, in the human spaces. I feel my life takes its place among the lives — the trees, the annual plants, the animals and birds, the living of all these and the dead — that go and have gone to make the life of the earth. I am less important than I thought, the human race is less important than I thought. I rejoice in that. My mind loses its urgings, senses its nature, and is free. The forest grew here in its own time, and so I will live, suffer and rejoice, and die in my own time. There is nothing that I may decently hope for that I cannot reach by patience as well as by anxiety. The hill, which is a part of America, has killed no one in the service of the American government. Then why should I, who am a fragment of the hill? I wish to be as peaceable as my land, which does no violence, though it has been the scene of violence and has had violence done to it.[5]

However much it echoes the phrasing and premise of Thoreau's original, Berry's passage is less a paraphrase than a revision — Berry displays a radically different literary persona. While both authors advocate dwelling in a natural place to avoid the compromises of living in human society, Berry's passage is alarmingly confident, metaphysically assured, while Thoreau's is uncertain, naively speculative. The author of *Walden* views his time in the woods as being in essence an experiment (he was not sure what he would learn), but Berry knew exactly what he would gain from nature (peace, freedom from human compromise) before he ever entered the woods. Furthermore, Thoreau remained obligated to a human community while he was in the woods; his self-appointed mission there was to experience life and to communicate its "meanness" to the world. Berry's reason for being in the woods, however, was to become one with the transhuman order and so escape his isolated self and the constraints of human society. By juxtaposing the natural order he had entered and the human world he had left behind, Berry is avouching a belief that the natural world is separate from and superior to the human world. All told, Berry's passage is more ecocentric than Thoreau's — a revelation, indeed, given Berry's later shift to a more anthropocentric stance.

What compelled Berry to make that shift is doubtless also what led him to reject Thoreau as his philosophical and literary mentor: concern for agriculture, a deepening commitment to marriage, family, and community, and growing faith in Christianity. Increasingly disrespecting Thoreau's positions on these issues, Berry began to question the wisdom — even, given his utilitarian aesthetics, the literary merit — of Thoreau's work. Nowhere did Berry criticize his predecessor more consistently or convincingly than in his writings about two of his Kentucky neighbors, Harlan and Anna Hubbard. From the early 1950s to their deaths in the 1980s, the Hubbards lived beside the Ohio River on a small farm known as Payne Hollow. Happening upon that farm during a canoe trip in 1964, Berry, who only weeks before had bought his own small farm not far away, was awed by what he witnessed:

> What the Hubbards had done there was done in full respect for the place's essential dignity and integrity. Because of this, their life and work there could be called "original." I certainly have never seen another place like Payne Hollow, and have known no other lives like the Hubbards' and no other paintings and writings like Harlan's; I am confident that I never will. But far higher principles and far dearer results are involved than what we call originality. The Hubbards' life at Payne Hollow — and I think I felt this on that first visit — was not a life merely personal in its significance; it was an exemplary way of living in America.[6]

Then teaching at the University of Kentucky and embarking on his writing career, Berry did not return to Payne Hollow for five years. In the early 1970s, though, he frequently visited the Hubbards, and a friendship developed. Harlan and Anna Hubbard inspired Berry and his wife, Tanya, who were then establishing their own small farm nearby; the Berrys reciprocated by helping Harlan Hubbard, who was an author and a painter, prepare his manuscripts for publication. (Berry wrote the foreword to an edition of Hubbard's *Shantyboat: A River Way of Life*, while his wife typed the manuscript of another Hubbard book, *Payne Hollow*.)

After Harlan Hubbard's death in 1988 (Anna Hubbard had died in 1986), Berry committed himself to keeping the Hubbards' memory alive. One result of this endeavor, the biographical study *Harlan Hubbard: Life and Work*, celebrated the Hubbards as examples of contemporary lives well lived. In that book, Berry wrote:

> [The Hubbards] lived and thrived in a place in which, by the conventional assumptions of our time, all human possibilities were exhausted. When they settled at Payne Hollow, the place was abandoned, but a stone chimney, a root cellar, and other relics testified to a life that had been lived there once and given up. The place was available to the Hubbards because no one else saw any good in it. Harlan himself had seen the old rural life come to an end in such places: the hill country south of the Ohio is full of abandoned homesites in hollows and small creek valleys. If, as I said, the traditional farming of the country was good at its best, at its worst it was extremely destructive, and it tended to grow worse in proportion to the steepness, shallowness, or rockiness of the land. We never developed a good way of using

such places; the families who farmed them wore them out. The example of the Hubbards' life at Payne Hollow puts that failed history into proper perspective, and suggests a proper corrective. (96–97)

In his foreword to *Shantyboat: A River Way of Life*, published in 1977, Berry cited two writers who had influenced Harlan Hubbard's work: Thoreau and Mark Twain. "It has not been fully appreciated," claimed Berry, "how their work is brought to maturity and [is] fulfilled in his [Hubbard's] work. My point and my difficulty are equally embedded in the realization that this is not purely a literary judgment. I do not mean to argue that Harlan Hubbard surpasses these two predecessors as a writer. But he does surpass them, I think, in the practical force of his wisdom that, among other things, makes it impossible to judge him in purely literary terms."[7]

Also in that foreword, Berry identified the lessons Thoreau and Hubbard learned while living deliberately in their respective natural places. In Berry's estimation, Thoreau at Walden Pond discovered a new moral perspective, whereas Harlan Hubbard, with the help of Anna Hubbard, developed at Payne Hollow a new way of life (viii). Berry — displaying a preference for the Hubbards' practicality over Thoreau's transcendentalism — lauded Harlan Hubbard for

the *justness* of his speech, his care to write of each thing as no more or less than it is. He will let nothing stand either for its price or for some alien "meaning." He would not say, like Thoreau, that "The sun is but a morning star." Harlan is neither lecturing nor prophesying; he makes no such presumption upon our attention or our understanding. He is speaking to us simply because we happen to be listening, which is both discriminating and polite. And the sun is the sun to him; aside from seeing well by it, he shows no wish to improve it. (ix, Berry's emphasis)

This 1977 passage, his first significant published criticism of Thoreau, signaled Berry's growing conviction that the Hubbards' quiet life at Payne Hollow was more successful than Thoreau's internationally recognized experiment in simple living at Walden Pond. In *Harlan Hubbard: Life and Work* (published in 1990), Berry related that, while "Harlan's and Anna's economy at Payne Hollow descended in principle from Thoreau's economy at Walden Pond, it differed from Thoreau's economy radically in some respects, and also advanced and improved upon it" (24). From Berry's perspective, several shortcomings in Thoreau had compromised the effectiveness of the Walden Pond experiment, including Thoreau's refusal to work with others in performing the tasks of everyday survival (26), his belittling of farming and husbandry (27), and his living in excessive austerity and asceticism (28). For proof of the superiority of the Hubbards' way of life, Berry cited the fact that Thoreau stayed at Walden Pond for just over two years, whereas the Hubbards remained at Payne Hollow for over three decades (25). Also observing that "Thoreau's was a bachelor's economy, [while] the Hubbards' was that of a married couple" (24–25), Berry stated that the Hubbards' "more elaborate household, enlarged necessity, and twenty-times-longer tenure provide far better elucidation and proof of their common principles than Thoreau was able to provide" (25).

In a more daring conjecture, Berry asserted that Harlan Hubbard's philosophical viewpoint and literary style were superior to Thoreau's because they emanated from a fundamentally better way of life. According to Berry, "*Walden* is a young man's book" in which Thoreau exhibited "bumptious self-assurance"; by comparison, Harlan Hubbard's writings are more modest yet wiser (26). "By enlarging Thoreau's experiment into a life," argued Berry, "Harlan showed that one may indeed follow the bent of one's genius, but only by subordinating one's genius to many necessities. He [Harlan Hubbard] was 'anchored,' not only to a wife, but to the land and herd of animals of which Thoreau spoke with condescension. . . . Thoreau's conflict of economy and genius was resolved in Harlan's life by his enjoyment of the details that he was required to have in mind and the work that he was required to do" (27).

It should be noted that Harlan Hubbard, a lifelong reader of Thoreau, did not concur with Berry's negativity toward the author of *Walden*. Much of the Hubbards' original inspiration for living "a life of simplicity, independence, magnanimity, and trust" in isolation from society had come from Thoreau's example (18). Thus, when Berry sent him for perusal a draft of the *Shantyboat* foreword in 1976, Harlan Hubbard quietly yet firmly insisted that Berry remove a "disrespectful" comment concerning Thoreau (91).

Although his early work frequently reflected, stylistically as well as thematically, the influence of Thoreau, Berry has revealed considerable ambivalence toward his literary predecessor since the mid-1970s, the consequence of increasing disagreement with Thoreau's positions on agriculture, marriage, family, community, and Christianity. At times, Berry has referred to Thoreau's experience at Walden Pond as a failed experiment; at other times, he has been more subtly dismissive, as in the fol-

lowing 1982 statement from a published letter: "It's the connection between nature and culture, the wild and the domestic, that concerns me
(agriculture *is* such a connection . . .) and I don't think Thoreau can help
much with that."[8]

Despite such criticism, Berry in recent years has confessed occasional,
grudging respect for Thoreau. In 1982, for instance, Berry wrote, "[Tho-
reau] went far beyond the Romantic poets as an observer and under-
stander and advocate of nature, and he is indispensable to us for that,"[9]
while in an early 1990s interview, Berry recalled how, upon first recognizing that his own writing would be "necessarily centered about one
place," he turned for inspiration to Thoreau and seven other authors
similarly concerned with exploring the meaning of "place." In this list of
his main literary influences, Berry revealingly mentioned Thoreau first.[10]

NOTES

1. Nibbelink, "Thoreau and Wendell Berry," 136. Subsequent page references
are cited parenthetically in the text.

2. Berry, *What Are People For?* 37–38.

3. Ibid., 40, Berry's emphasis. Subsequent page references are cited parenthetically in the text.

4. Thoreau, *Walden*, 90–91, Thoreau's emphasis.

5. Berry, "A Native Hill," in *Recollected Essays*, 104.

6. Berry, *Harlan Hubbard*, 88–89. Subsequent page references are cited parenthetically in the text.

7. Berry, foreword to Hubbard, *Shantyboat*, vii. Subsequent page references are
cited parenthetically in the text.

8. Nibbelink, "Thoreau and Wendell Berry," 151, Berry's emphasis.

9. Ibid., 151.

10. Weinreb, "A Question a Day," 41.

Water-Signs

Place and Metaphor in Dillard and Thoreau

JAMES A. PAPA, JR.

Thoreau's position at the center of American nature writing has been long established, and few writers in the genre escape his influence. Some, such as Joseph Wood Krutch, are quick to acknowledge the debt. Others, such as Edward Abbey, who referred to Thoreau as a "spinster-poet" who "led an unnecessarily constrained existence,"[1] attempt for various reasons to distance themselves from Thoreau. Even Henry Beston, whose *The Outermost House* borrows much from Thoreau's sojourn at Walden, felt Thoreau "had very little heart" and would not acknowledge much if any connection to him.[2] But traces of Thoreau's works appear not only in the written works but sometimes even in the lives of those writers who follow in his tradition. The line of descent is often so clear that Edward Abbey has called such writers "sons and daughters of Thoreau."[3]

Annie Dillard is one such daughter, and *Pilgrim at Tinker Creek*,[4] the work for which Dillard is best known and for which she won a Pulitzer Prize, is an especially appropriate choice to compare with Thoreau's *Walden* in terms of how place and nature are observed and perceived.[5] Both Dillard, in *Pilgrim at Tinker Creek*, and Thoreau, in *Walden*, inhabit transitional landscapes, in the sense that neither the woods around Walden Pond nor the environment surrounding Tinker Creek is either wilderness or town. Dillard's choice of place is a semirural area in "a valley in Virginia's Blue Ridge" (*PTC* 2) at the beginning of the last quarter of the twentieth century; Thoreau's narrative locus is a wooded area on the outskirts of the New England village of Concord in the first half of the nineteenth century. Despite the different historical periods, both landscapes contain or are not far removed from permanent dwellings; both support residential (even if, in the case of *Walden*, the sole residence is Thoreau's) or commercial activity, however limited; and both are crossed or bordered by public thoroughfares, such as roads or railroad tracks. Still, each landscape also provides, by way of daily rambles on foot, extensive contact with more or less unspoiled natural settings. In short, both landscapes allow for similar types of pastoral experience. Even more important, given the discussion to follow, is that each text takes as its metaphorical center a natural body of water to which each narrator makes nearly daily solitary excursions. These excursions then serve as both inspiration and stage for observation and revelation regarding the natural world.

Given that Dillard and Thoreau live relatively solitary lives in close proximity to nature, they come into repeated contact with relatively ordinary and common natural phenomena such as sandbanks, ice, cedar trees, muskrats, and dead frogs. These things are then called upon to illustrate, and in the case of Thoreau to articulate through metaphor, deeper universal truths. In *Pilgrim*, such things are not, however, called up simply to suggest or represent higher transcendental truths, as they are in *Walden*. Dillard means us to see these things for truth itself, absolving us of the need to translate them into a new literary language. She comes finally to understand in *Pilgrim* that "what I have been after all along is not an explanation but a picture" (182). Things in the natural world do not need to be made to mean anything beyond what they are. The lesson in *Pilgrim* is that the primacy of experience, the moment of felt realization, *is* truth itself, and not merely a metaphor. Language is meant to reveal, not create, truth. Dillard means to teach herself only how to finally see what is actually in front of her, so that she might find the words to put it in front of the reader as well.

Such a position is radically different from that taken by Thoreau in *Walden*, where the use of nature (or the material world) as metaphor is clearly illustrated in Thoreau's comments about working in the "fields if only for the sake of tropes and expression, to serve a parable maker one day" (*W* 162). The use of the word "serve" is critical, since it suggests a hierarchical relationship and reinforces the notion that nature is simply raw material to be used for literary ends. Thoreau does not mean to see what is there in nature and tell us. He means instead to teach us that what we see is simply evidence of what we are already capable of knowing through our own understanding if we will only still ourselves enough to listen to it. He proposes to tell us what to see before we even look.

The truly interesting thing is that not only do Dillard and Thoreau approach what they see in nature in fundamentally different ways, but what they see, as well as how they see, is remarkably dependent upon the different landscapes in which each narrative is set. Again, the primary difference is that whereas Thoreau attempts to uncover some kind of preexisting divine form and render it visible, Dillard surrenders instead to the possibility of formlessness or chaos in the universe, though she does eventually come to believe in a deific force that creates in "solemn incomprehensible earnest" (*PTC* 278). That much being said, the focus here is on the ways in which the narratives differ in their treatment of *how* and *what* each narrator sees, and in how the different landscapes shape these narratives. James Aton refers to this process as an "episte-mology" of seeing,[6] but Aton's reading of Dillard differs from the one at hand. Aton sees Dillard in *Pilgrim* as a "conscious metaphysical poet, transforming natural facts into metaphors of the mind" (78). The argument here is that Dillard resists the urge to transform observation into metaphor, and instead struggles simply to come to grips with what it is that she actually sees. In doing so, Dillard leaves the subsequent movement from observation to metaphor to the reader.

The way in which landscape shapes and is shaped by the ways Dillard and Thoreau see and interpret the natural world around them is best explored by focusing on the use of water imagery in each text. More than anything else, the use of water imagery serves to create and validate the ways in which Dillard and Thoreau see nature and the cosmos. Water, because of its inherent properties — it is mirrorlike, windowlike, possesses a penetrable surface, has no definite shape, and so on — is a fertile breeding ground for metaphor, and both narratives rely heavily on water imagery for their most poetic and powerful passages. Water, with its various colors, moods, and properties, serves as a controlling metaphor in each text, one from which each narrative might be said to spring.

For Dillard, *how* we see all but determines *what* we see. Though she tries "for weeks" to see the world around her as "color patches," like newly sighted cataract patients do, she cannot "sustain the illusion of flatness." She had, she tells us, "been around for too long" to *really* see differently than she always had. She simply "couldn't unpeach the peaches" (*PTC* 31). Instead, she comes to the realization that "form is condemned to an eternal dance macabre with meaning." She cannot "re-member ever having seen without understanding" (31). Perception then is inextricably tied to the context in which it is learned and practiced. But there is no denying that when it comes to Tinker Creek itself, *what* the narrator sees also determines *how* she sees.

Tinker Creek, unlike Walden Pond, is a fluid, dynamic entity without fixed boundaries. In time of flood "everything looks different" (*PTC* 153), and Dillard can "expect to see anything at all" (155). The creek is continually rushing by her; even the stiller sections are always moving, however slowly. Stillness is an illusion when looking at the creek, just as stillness in the mind is an illusion: "Scenes drift across the screen [of the mind] from nowhere. I can never discover the connection between any one scene and what I am more consciously thinking, nor can I ever conjure the scene back in full vividness. . . . the scene is always just slipping out of sight" (95). Consciousness operates in the same manner as the creek, and it can no more anchor itself in the present than the creek can cease flowing. Dillard comes to realize that "the present of [her] consciousness is itself a mystery which is always rounding a bend like a floating branch borne by a flood" (95).

The implications of such a realization, or conceptualization, of consciousness are staggering: chaos, understood in the sense of a constant flow of disordered and nonteleological phenomena, exists not only in the cosmos, and in nature, but in the mind as well. Consciousness cannot *fix* itself, even for a moment, among the swirling chaos of the cosmos. "Where am I? But I'm not," says Dillard, suggesting that the conscious self can never, even for an instant, locate itself with any certainty. Consciousness itself, then, does not allow for stasis in nature and the cosmos even were it to exist there, since consciousness itself constantly fragments and disorders the world around it. Just as a "fish flashes, then dissolves in the water before [Dillard's] eyes like so much salt," so does all of creation manifest itself in a "now-you-don't-see-it, now-you-do" fashion. The same holds true for human consciousness. It will not allow the self to grasp hold of the present for more than several seconds (94), and even that relatively short span of imagined stasis may be nothing more than an illusion. "Time is a live creek bearing changing lights. As I move, or as the world moves around me," Dillard tells us, "the fullness of what I see shatters"; the present "is constantly being ripped apart and washed downstream" (84).

This inability to center on the wholeness of any one thing or moment leads in *Pilgrim* to a preoccupation with the "fringe," or the edges, of things, whether they be material (the natural world) or immaterial (time). Throughout the narrative, Dillard finds herself continually drawn to "the sheer fringe and network of details" of things; they "[assume] primary importance. That there are so many details seems to be the most important and visible fact about the creation" (131). Perception is splintered into finer and finer foci until meaning is lost and science fails under the weight of its own incredible ability to catalog and decipher: "All the theories botanists have devised to explain the functions of various leaf-shapes tumble under an avalanche of inconsistencies. They simply don't know, can't imagine" (135). Here the failure of the imagination to even posit potential explanations suggests that humanity's poetic capabilities are not up to the task. The use of the word "tumble" reinforces as well the way Tinker Creek itself spills over and around the things that lie both in it and in its way. Reality is as fluid as moving water.

Poetry may, as Robert Frost claims, offer us "a momentary stay against confusion,"[7] but no lasting foundation beyond that on which to rest or proceed. The sheer "fecundity" of nature "that so appalls" Dillard, the ever expanding universe and the infinite reaches of space, all of these serve to ensure that we will never know anything but the intricate details of the fringes we are forever trying to grab hold of and examine. Like Tinker Creek itself, the universe will not still itself, will not allow human consciousness to find a true anchor hold. And though Dillard may at times suppose her house by the creek an "anchor" that keeps her "stead-ied in the current," it is only a "sea anchor" (*PTC* 2–3), which, as any mariner knows, does nothing more than keep one head on to the seas while the vessel continues to drift downwind.

Walden, on the other hand, takes as its central metaphor the pond near which Thoreau builds his cabin and conducts his "experiment" in living. The pond is a far tamer body of water than Tinker Creek, and Thoreau refers to the pond at various points as a "well" dug by an "an-cient settler" (i.e., the Creator), as "*Walled-in* Pond" (*W* 183), and as "the quiet parlor of the fishes" (283), suggesting both domesticity and re-straint. The pond may rise and fall, creating new, or rather revisiting old, shorelines (180), but it is important to remember that Walden Pond doesn't ever abandon its shape or its banks, as the creek does when it floods. The fact that the pond serves as a site for commerce also rein-forces its domestic nature: the railroad causeway runs close by the pond's shore, and in winter men harvest the pond's ice (293–97). And so while it is also a place for communion with the natural world, having the ability to "link you to Nature" (175), the pond lacks the wild "fecundity" of Tinker Creek, being "not very fertile in fish" (184), and tolerating "at most . . . one annual loon" (185). It is a symbol of constancy and order, "nations come and go without defiling it" (188), and it remains perpetu-ally "unchanged . . . perennially young" (193). More important, while Tinker Creek often bears things quickly away from Dillard, Walden Pond "is a mirror which no stone can crack" (188), reflecting back to Thoreau those things he brings to it. At times he cannot even distinguish himself from it. "I am its stony shore," Thoreau tells us, "And its deepest resort / Lies high in my thought" (193). "It is earth's eye," and "looking into" it, "the beholder measures the depth of his own nature" (186), not that of nature or the Creator.

The point is clear. Thoreau sees himself, not the cosmos, in the waters of the pond. And the self that he sees is the artist, concerned with form, structure, harmony, and balance, brother finally to the scientist, who like the artist is engaged in a search for a framework with which to make sense of and understand the world. The pond suits Thoreau's conception of an ordered universe that can be known and understood: "not a fish can leap or an insect fall on the pond but it is thus reported in circling dimples" (188). The fact that the pond, less than two miles in circumference (175), can be circumambulated with ease in a relatively short time only adds to Thoreau's sense of its measurability. The pond exists to serve his imagination, and it "grind[s] such grist" as he will "carry to" it (197).

In the end, Walden Pond is both predictable and knowable; it has been pressed into service by the merchant and the poet. The pond's bottom has been sounded, and the surrounding topography recorded. The environs of the pond have been "profaned" by "the woodcutters," the railroad, and even Thoreau, insofar as he has made literary use of it. Despite all of this, if Thoreau at times grants the lake a mysticalness beyond what others recognize or grant, it is a mysticalness tempered by the limits of Wordsworthian romanticism. The pond and its environs, Thoreau tells us, represent his own "lake country" (197).

Such is not the case with Dillard, who, confronted with the indifference and chaos of nature and the cosmos, finds herself on the verge of madness: "wild-eyed, flying over fields and plundering the woods, no longer fit for company" (PTC 274). Like any true mystic, revelation has made her unfit for a life "making itsy-bitsy friends and meals and journeys for itsy-bitsy years on end" (276). Where Thoreau has, paradoxically, demythologized the pond and the woods (and at the same time unknowingly and paradoxically made possible its future status as a legendary if not mythic cultural symbol), carefully sounding the pond's bottom, as well as society's, Dillard has instead "'gone up into the gaps'" in search of "the spirit's one home" (276).

She has "been bloodied and mauled, wrung, dazzled, drawn." Her eyes are "ashes, or fiery sprouts" (278), and "everywhere I look I see fire . . . the whole world sparks and flames" (10). She knows that she is "dealing with a maniac" (277), and that the "divinity is not playful," but

a "power that is unfathomably secret, and holy, and fleet. There is nothing to be done about it, but ignore it, or see." And seeing, there is nothing
she can do but "gape appalled" (278).

Certainly, no other disciple of Thoreau confronts the brute horror and
violence of nature as fearlessly or as wholly as Dillard, or is more willing to question one of the most basic of human assumptions — that the
Creator is a moral and rational being, and the world a sensible and ordered place. If Dillard has in her the poet's love of beauty and wonder,
and she does, she is also not afraid to seek out and seize from what Joseph
Conrad called "the remorseless rush of time" a glimpse of the bizarre or
the frightening, the horrific and the grotesque, and demand it "reveal the
substance of its truth — disclose its inspiring secret."[8] She is a clear exception to Thomas J. Lyon's claim that "nature literature since Darwin
does not reflect any sense of terror at being adrift in a blankly material-
istic universe."[9]

For Dillard, Conrad's "secret" is the elusive answer to the enigma of
human existence: does that existence have meaning and does the natural
world in which we live exist for a purpose, or is it simply a lucky accident
in a dark and inhospitable universe? Dillard raises this question early in
the text, informing us that "in the Koran, Allah asks, 'The heaven and the
earth and all in between, thinkest thou I made them *in jest?*'" Dillard
attempts to answer this very question and to explore the spiritual rami-
fications that arise simply from daring to ask it, since to do so is to run
up against the frightening possibility that all of existence is, in the end,
without any inherent meaning or value beyond what humans might attribute to it. For Dillard, however, who "propose[s] to keep . . . what
Thoreau called a 'meteorological journal of the mind,'" narrative serves
as a redemptive act that negates the spiritually horrific reality of a meaningless world, and allows her, as well as the reader, to realize and explore
the "unmapped dim reaches and holy fastnesses" (*PTC* 12) where "the
spirit can discover itself for the first time like a once-blind man un-
bound" (276). Narrative, the construction and imposition of order and
meaning through language, provides Dillard the means to make sense
not only of the world, but of her responses and reactions to it. The literary act reaffirms the self's value and place in the world. The quest for
meaning, through art, *becomes* meaning. As Dillard says in *Living by
Fiction*, "We find in art objects qualities in which the great world and its
parts seem often wanting: human significance, human order, reason,
mind, causality, boundary, harmony, perfection, coherence, purity, purpose, and permanence."[10]

In *Walden,* Thoreau takes a fundamentally different position than Dillard does regarding both the natural world and the relationship between language and meaning. Unlike Dillard, Thoreau never truly entertains the notion that human life may ultimately be meaningless, or that the universe may be amoral and chaotic. The transcendental assumption in *Walden* is that the natural world is the physical manifestation of divine order. No real existential doubt can exist in the mind of a narrator like Thoreau, who, declaring that "men labor under a mistake" (*W* 5), determines to show by clear example how men might live otherwise. While *Walden* may pose itself as a quest for meaning in the form of truth, for "that which we can call '*reality*'" (98), the fact is that it is not. On the contrary, Thoreau sets out for Walden Pond with full confidence that the world and life *do* have meaning, but that the true meaning of our existence, and of the world's, is only recognizable by those who live according to the correct set of values and habits. As he puts it, "The morning wind forever blows, the poem of creation is uninterrupted; but few are the ears that hear it" (85). That he refers to the "*poem* of creation" (emphasis added) suggests that the universe, with everything in it, does have form, structure, meaning, and purpose, since poetry can also be said to have all of these things. If the creation is a "poem," it cannot be meaningless or without form, though to understand its meaning or to recognize its structure may require careful study.

For Dillard, it is impossible to create or even to discover meaning, or even to be sure of what it is one sees, except through "verbalization." As she puts it, "Seeing is of course very much a matter of verbalization. Unless I call attention to what passes before my eyes, I simply won't see it" (*PTC* 32). Without language, the natural world remains inaccessible. Dillard can perceive only those things, or states, that she can articulate through writing or speech. The problem is that the perceived *experiences* put forth in both narratives under discussion are as much products of the act of literary composition as they are written records of various actual happenings or perceptions. As Peter Fritzell points out, to write about observing nature is not the same thing as to observe nature.[11] I would even argue that the experiences and revelations put forth by Dillard in her narrative are more products of the act of composition than they are of the moments that may have inspired her to want to write them down. In Dillard's case, this debt is at least acknowledged, given the passage quoted above. And though she is quick to point out that "there is another kind of seeing that involves a letting go" of "this running description of the present," the fact that the text itself exists at all serves to dispute this claim (*PTC* 33, 32). Dillard is dependent upon written language not only to communicate but to perceive.

Thoreau does not claim this kind of limitation. The scope of his vision is no more than a starting point, and he does not let it constrain him. Looking out one spring morning from the doorway of his cabin, he remarks that "though the view from my door was . . . contracted, I did not feel crowded or confined in the least. There was pasture enough for my imagination" (*W* 87).

In *Pilgrim*, imagination does not take as active a role as it does in *Walden*. It is not the imagination per se that is awakened when Dillard sees. Indeed, nature as she encounters it in the somewhat tame environment of Tinker Creek is more incredible than anything her own imagination could ever imagine, and what she does see often turns out, upon closer inspection, to be something quite different from what she originally thought it to be. Because Dillard reads so much science, the more she observes and studies the world, the less comprehensible it becomes to her.[12] While Thoreau takes what he sees as a solid base from which to proceed outward along the lines of his own imagination, Dillard finds over and over again that even sight itself cannot be trusted. Over and over again, Dillard tells us that she "can't believe [her] eyes" (*PTC* 68, 156). This being the case, in her observations of the natural world, she never proceeds outward from the thing itself in the direction of the imagination, but instead attempts to see further *into* whatever scene, object, or phenomenon lies in front of her. For Dillard nature is an oracle: she wants it to speak *to* her. The same is not true for Thoreau, whose primary concern seems to be to speak *for* nature, though he attempts to convince us that his message is in fact nature's own.

The difference here is subtle but significant. Living as she does near the banks of Tinker Creek, Dillard cannot escape the pronouncement of Heraclitus that one can never step into the same river twice. The world and the self are nothing but flux, and any kind of faith must fashion itself upon this realization. Thoreau, on the other hand, living on the shore of Walden Pond, hoeing his bean field, and carefully recording his experiment's expenses, naturally puts his faith in an orderly and predictable world. The landscapes, or in this case the waterscapes, near which Thoreau and Dillard live do much not only to reinforce the consciousness each writer brings to his or her observations of nature, but to shape such consciousness as well. And yet, as this reading shows, Dillard's metaphors seem much more derivative of or dependent upon what she sees in nature than are Thoreau's, which might be said to impose upon or define nature more. At the very least, Thoreau's choice of a pond as a primary symbol reveals his affinity for landscape features that reinforce rather than undermine his romantic predispositions. Dillard, adrift in the late twentieth century, a time of fragmented narratives and indeterminate science, could never be confined by such certain limits. And so she is drawn instead to the paradox of Tinker Creek, which, though fixed in the landscape like the pond, is itself in perpetual motion, never to be pinned down.

NOTES

1. Abbey, *Down the River*, 22.

2. Coatsworth, *Especially Maine*, 2.

3. Abbey, *Abbey's Road*, xx.

4. Dillard, *Pilgrim at Tinker Creek*. All citations refer to the Bantam edition, hereafter referred to as *PTC* in parenthetical citations.

5. Thoreau, *Walden*. Hereafter referred to as *W* in parenthetical citations.

6. Aton, "'Sons and Daughters of Thoreau,'" 80.

7. Frost, *Selected Poems*, 2.

8. Conrad, *Portable Conrad*, 62.

9. Lyon, *This Incomperable Lande*, 62.

10. Dillard, *Living by Fiction*, 176.

11. Fritzell, *Nature Writing and America*, 247.

12. Becker, "Science and the Sacred."

II. IMAGING PLACE

Finding a Discourse to

Match Discovery

The Written World

Place and History in Thoreau's "A Walk to Wachusett"

DAVID M. ROBINSON

Thoreau's development of a sense of place depended upon his developing a form of description for his excursions into nature which would also allow him to elaborate their larger spiritual and ethical significance. Many of his Journal entries have their origins in the observations and meditations that he made during and after walks in the countryside or into the woods, a pattern that would become almost sacramental for him in his later Journals.[1] Such a walk, a "sauntering" into nature as he would later define it in "Walking," was a self-conscious expedition of exploration in which Thoreau tried to examine and understand natural phenomena and their patterns of interaction, and to test and refine his own capabilities as observer. Thoreau's published work also evolved through his use of the excursion as the basis of an essay, the genre of *A Week on the Concord and Merrimack Rivers, Cape Cod, The Maine Woods,* and in some respects, *Walden.* This pattern began with "A Walk to Wachusett," an account of a July 1842 hike to Mount Wachusett with Richard Fuller in which Thoreau uses the narrative of his journey into a natural setting as the framework for descriptive observations and, in Linck Johnson's phrase, "a vehicle for an inward journey of mind and spirit."[2] The excursion was devoted in large part to description of the countryside and its natural environment through which Thoreau demonstrates that he comprehends nature in all its forms. But the excursions also become meditations on Thoreau's spiritual strivings, giving them an important philosophical and ethical dimension.

A sense of Thoreau's shaping of the essay is indicated by his initial reference to their destination, "the dim outline of the mountains in our horizon," a hovering presence whose "distance and indistinctness" becomes a reference point for imaginative projections of purpose that lend the authority of myth, antiquity, and scientific discovery to Thoreau's excursion: "with Homer, on a spring morning, we sat down on the many-peaked Olympus, . . . with Virgil and his compeers [we] roamed the Etrurian and Thessalian hills, . . . with Humboldt [we] measured the more modern Andes and Teneriffe."[3] Thoreau makes his expedition a heroic undertaking, equal in gravity to anything recounted in classical literature, or anything accomplished by modern scientists. As Sherman Paul has written, "To go to the mountain, then, was to go westward and heavenward, to experience transcendentally" (159).

Thoreau's reference also contains, more subtly, another claim, which he will weigh throughout the course of the essay. Thoreau implies that modern experience, as represented in Humboldt's exploration, is the equivalent of the ancient experience recorded in Homer and Virgil. In many ways the excursion is a test of this thesis, and Thoreau is battling against the suspicion that modernity is a diminished state. While the mythical past is in some sense an escapist concept for him, it is also a utopian projection, a realm of promise and potential, or the place of origin from which human culture has unfortunately strayed.

While this framework of mythical expectation colors the essay, the motif of the heroic quest is reinforced by the exhilarating physical impact of the landscape. The heroic past and the Edenic landscape merge in their promise of a heightened or intensified awareness. Leaving before daybreak, Thoreau and Fuller enter a natural world absent of all human activity. "As we traversed the cool woods of Acton, with stout staves in our hands, we were cheered by the song of the red-eye, the thrushes, the phoebe, and the cuckoo; and as we passed through the open country, we inhaled the fresh scent of every field, and all nature lay passive, to be viewed and traveled" (136). Thoreau communicates here a sense of entering newly into the world, of first-seeing, in which the vitality of physical exertion and sensory experience coheres with a feeling of consonance with the landscape, which is Edenic in its freshness and its benignity. The sense of renewal is heightened by the predawn quiet, in which human activity has almost completely subsided, and the world is restored to a pristine serenity. "Every rail, every farmhouse, seen dimly in the twilight, every tinkling sound told of peace and purity, and we moved happily along the dank roads, enjoying not such privacy as the day leaves when it withdraws, but such as it has not profaned" (136).

The terms "purity" and "profaned" indicate clearly that a further polarity underlies the intellectual structure of the essay, that between the natural world and human society. Thoreau's contrast between the ancient and modern worlds is in a sense reiterated in his opposition of nature and the village, with the ancient world and the natural world each serving as symbolic alternatives to the limitations of ordinary perception and experience. The sensuous appeal of the early morning scene has emphasized this contrast, for Thoreau feels not only as if he is exploring new territory in nature, but that he is escaping the confinements and exhaustion of his accustomed social world. Thoreau enters a new landscape, and finds exhilaration in its freshness, but he is also conscious of entering it as a refuge from the ordinary patterns of human social and economic interaction, which have been profaned by greed, competition, and the loss of real insight into the simplicity and harmony of nature. He thus links this landscape with the refuge of classical poetry. "Before noon we had reached the highlands overlooking the valley of Lancaster (affording the first fair and open prospect into the west), and there, on top of a hill, in the shade of some oaks, near to where a spring bubbled from a leaden pipe, we rested during the heat of the day, reading Virgil and enjoying the scenery" (137–38). Thoreau paints the scene in pastoral terms, making particular note of the fact that they had reached an elevation that provided a broader perspective on their journey. "It was such a place as one feels to be on the outside of the earth," he explains, allowing them to "see the form and structure of the globe" (138).

It seems, however, that Thoreau is conscious of a forced quality in his attempt to remake himself as a modern Virgil. He worries about his temporal and geographical separation from the ancient world, and fears the separation may be too great to be overcome. "Virgil, away in Rome, two thousand years off, should have to unfold his meaning, the inspiration of Italian vales, to the pilgrim on New England hills." To speak over such a distance seems at first an impossible task — "this life so raw and modern, that so civil and ancient" (138). Even though Thoreau eventually dismisses this fear, claims his brotherhood with Virgil, and stresses Virgil's affirmation of "the identity of human nature in all ages," his eventual declaration of Virgil's relevance is less important than his initial ambivalence. This is suggested most persuasively by his choice of the words "raw and modern" to contrast "civil and ancient." Like the mountains in the west, classical poetry is appealing because it represents an escape from the modern world, or an alternative to it. The clearly self-dramatizing way that Thoreau reads Virgil as an integral part of the excursion is part of a posture of alienation that will come to more complete fruition in *A Week* and the "Reading" chapter of *Walden*, where Thoreau's critique of contemporary society becomes more pointed, and his search for an imaginative alternative more intense.

Thoreau's difficulties with modernity are in part a reflection of his growing discomfort with the commercial, competitive, and exploitative society that America had become, and they represent a growing critical consciousness of political and socioeconomic questions. The urgent discourse of the reform movements of the day, reflected in works by transcendentalists such as Emerson, Orestes Brownson, Margaret Fuller, Theodore Parker, and George Ripley, were clearly contributing to this dissident sensibility. The founding of the Brook Farm community in 1841, the year before Thoreau's Wachusett excursion, was the direct result of the ferment of social opinion and political dissent that had begun to mark transcendentalism, and which certainly was having its impact on Thoreau. But it is important to remember that in addition to this widespread political dissent which Thoreau shared, struggles of a more personal sort, those connected directly with his vocational instability and ambivalence, were also at work. "The Transcendentalist," as described by Emerson in an 1841 lecture by that title, was an individual struggling not only with religious and philosophical questions, but with the problem of finding a fulfilling vocation. Emerson could have had any of several of his younger friends in mind in constructing this portrait, and it is meant to be a composite, representing a more general generational problem. But the description is strikingly apt for Thoreau in the early 1840s. Living a heroic life had become in some ways synonymous with living the life of a poet or essayist, and as Steven Fink has shown in convincing detail, that life was a difficult one for Thoreau to negotiate, given the literary marketplace of nineteenth-century America.[4] The sense of alienation and the yearning for an experience that is closer to myth or poetry that we find in "A Walk to Wachusett" are quite revealing of Thoreau's struggles as a young intellectual, hoping to find a place in pragmatic American culture.

Although it seems on the surface to be an unproblematic description of Massachusetts scenery and local customs, "A Walk to Wachusett" suggests how Thoreau's growing social dissidence was inseparable from his devotion to the landscape. He is able to express his uneasiness and social alienation through humor, comically mocking his efforts to be free from his accustomed world, and his discovery that it seems to follow him, wherever he meets other humans. Stopping overnight after the first day's hike in a remote village near the base of Mount Wachusett, he was chagrined to have "our own village newspaper handed us by our host, as if the greatest charm the country offered to the traveler was the facility of communication with the town" (141). For Thoreau, the newspaper is a somewhat unpleasant reminder of the world from which he is seeking at least a temporary respite, and a confirmation that habits and social patterns have changed little even in this recently established settlement.

But Thoreau does begin to find fulfillment as he begins his ascent of Wachusett early the next morning. "It was only four miles to the base of the mountain, and the scenery was already more picturesque," he observes, communicating a level of rising expectation associated with ascending the mountain. Picking raspberries by the roadside, he declares in a half-elevated, half-fanciful tone that "the traveler who ascends into a mountainous region should fortify himself by eating of such light ambrosial fruits as grow there" in preparation for inhaling "the subtler and purer atmosphere of those elevated places." Such eating of the berries will propitiate "the mountain gods by a sacrifice of their own fruits" (142). This is of course an elaboration on the essay's general motif of ascent toward the heavens, and it reflects the sense of a building toward enlarged spiritual insight that the mountain ascent has come to represent metaphorically. But its tone borders on the mock-heroic, and thus while it links ascent of the mountain with spiritual progress, it also seems self-conscious about that linkage, undercutting to some extent the motif of mythic quest in the narrative.

Gauging Thoreau's tone and mood is always a difficult task, although it is the complexity of his tone, our sense of the unsettled and shifting quality of the authorial persona, that gives works such as Walden and "Walking" their textual richness and appeal. "A Walk to Wachusett" is in this sense an experimental piece, in which Thoreau is trying out his attitude toward his excursion even as he reconstructs it in his narrative. Both a sense of elevated and refined purpose, and a lighter feeling of gaiety and refreshment, mixed with a tendency to self-deflation, mark the early stages of the essay, alternating and in some instances colliding. But as Thoreau begins to describe the actual ascent of the mountain, a tone of serious intellectual elevation prevails, and the lighter touches of gaiety give way to a more rapt engagement with the expansion of perspective that the mountain offers.

Thoreau speaks literally of his sense of an enlarged vision, since his gradually increasing altitude gives him a larger and larger perspective of the landscape that he has just traversed. Even though Mount Wachusett is a small summit, by its "slight elevation it is infinitely removed from the plain," and Thoreau reports that "when we reached it we felt a sense of remoteness, as if we had traveled into distant regions, to Arabia Pe-træa, or the farthest East" (142–43). Haunted by the familiarity of people and their ways all along his trek, Thoreau has finally achieved a sense of the strangeness of the world and those who inhabit it. Here finally is the sense of difference for which Thoreau has been searching, the impression that he has indeed left his normal state of affairs behind and can therefore view things differently. He immediately immerses himself in a detailed description of the plant and animal life he finds at the summit, and of its geographical contours. These things help to constitute the difference he feels, given his already well-developed sensitivity to changes in natural environments. But it is the view that is made possible by the summit's elevation that confirms his sense of being in a completely new place.

The view is somewhat obscured by hazy conditions on their arrival at the summit, but this phenomenon itself adds to the feeling of novelty, almost of dislocation, that Thoreau describes. "The first day the weather was so hazy that it was in vain we endeavored to unravel the obscurity. It was like looking into the sky again, and the patches of forest here and there seemed to flit like clouds over a lower heaven" (143). The visual reversal here, in which heaven comes to look like earth, and earth like heaven, is indicative of a shift in seeing that has important metaphorical reverberations in the essay. Thoreau begins to look back on his home differently, finding the once familiar now interestingly disordered. "As to voyagers of an aerial Polynesia," he now says, referring to himself and his companion, "the earth seemed like a larger island in the ether; on every side, even as low as we, the sky shutting down, like an unfathomable deep, around it, a blue Pacific island, where who knows what islanders inhabit" (143). In this moment when the visual illusion caused by the mist leads him to see the earth as a strange and exotic place to be discovered and explored, Thoreau confirms the theme that he had hinted at from the beginning: we must see the world as new.

That new world begins to open to Thoreau during the night he spends on the summit. As the atmosphere begins to clear by sunset, he has both a sunset vista of the surrounding valleys, and in the evening a nearly full moon to illuminate the summit. "Before sunset, we rambled along the ridge to the north, while a hawk soared still above us. It was a place where gods might wander, so solemn and solitary, and removed from all contagion with the plain" (144). He is able to celebrate even the chilly wind that drove him into his tent: "It was thrilling to hear the wind roar over the rocks, at intervals when we waked, for it had grown quite cold and windy. The night was, in its elements, simple even to majesty in that bleak place, — a bright moonlight and a piercing wind" (145). It is as if the elements of nature have been restored to their fundamental power, and the exposure that Thoreau and Fuller feel in camping at the summit becomes a form of humble acceptance of their place in the natural world.

The transformation worked by the achievement of this elevation is represented in the range and clarity of vision that the clearing of the skies provides them the next morning. "At length we saw the sun rise up out of the sea, and shine on Massachusetts," Thoreau says, adding that "the atmosphere grew more and more transparent till the time of our departure." Looking down "over successive circles of towns, rising one above another, like the terraces of a vineyard" (146–47), Thoreau finds himself in a position in which nature seems overwhelmingly powerful, framing and controlling all human activity, which seems, by comparison, less commanding and less confining. He has achieved the freedom that he has been seeking in the entire excursion, and he can look back to his starting point with a fuller comprehension of it and a renewed understanding.

Thoreau's feeling of deeper understanding is revealed metaphorically in his description of the patterns of the landscape that he is able to comprehend from the summit of Wachusett. "There lay Massachusetts, spread out before us in its length and breadth, like a map" (147). He is able to see the ranges of hills in New Hampshire and the Hoosac and Green Mountains, and, to the east and south, the sea. In describing the landscape as a map, Thoreau is asserting a more comprehensive understanding of it, one that is also linked to a new recognition of the controlling influence of the landscape and the environment on the development of human society. "A mountain chain determines many things for the statesman and philosopher," he comments, observing that "the improvements of civilization rather creep along its sides than cross its summit." This controlling power of the landscape can have an important impact on human development by restraining the worst effects of human social interaction. "How often is it a barrier to prejudice and fanaticism!" he exclaims, returning to nature's capacity to purify the human spirit. "In passing over these heights of land, through their thin atmosphere, the follies of the plain are refined and purified" (148).

Thoreau has felt a personal sense of release from "the follies of the plain" in his excursion, an unburdening that, while postponed, finally comes to predominate his mood. His comments on the restraint that the environment can place on human error is an enlargement of this mood, in which he applies his own experience in the excursion to human history, and the human future. At this point, Thoreau begins to transform the excursion from a pursuit of refuge, with implications of escapist fantasy, into a vehicle of renewal in which he is able to observe society with both deeper understanding and a more profound courage and hope.

One important confirmation of this renewed hope is Thoreau's account of passing the site of Mary Rowlandson's capture by Indians near Lancaster, the incident that is recounted in the most famous of the New England captivity narratives. Thoreau notes the "unexpected refinement" of the scenery as he passes through; its "level prairies of great extent, interspersed with elms and hop-fields and groves of trees, give it almost a classic appearance." That appearance of refinement of course contradicts the weight of the dark history of the place. "From this July afternoon, and under that mild exterior," he says, "those times seem as remote as the irruption of the Goths." Thoreau comments at some length about his inability to connect the landscape with the violence of the past, and with a consequent inability to connect his own experience with that "dark age of New England" (149). "On beholding a picture of a New England village as it then appeared," he writes, "with a fair open prospect, and a light on trees and river, as if it were broad noon, we find we had not thought the sun shone in those days, or that men lived in broad daylight then." The nature into which Thoreau has recently immersed himself seems far removed from that tragic history. "We do not imagine the sun shining on hill and valley during Philip's war. . . . They must have fought in the shade of their own dusky deeds" (150).

This is a revealing claim, but perhaps ironically revealing. At the same time that Thoreau is asserting nature's authority over history, its capacity to cancel or override the past, he is in fact contemplating that very past, recalling its violence and tragedy. To say that the entire New England past is shaded in a kind of dim twilight is to depict in pictorial terms the burden of its history, and to suggest that Thoreau is aware of that burden. While he asserts the landscape's Edenic innocence, he is simultaneously remembering the tragic history of this particular place.

This meditation on the Indian wars, brief though it is, is a significant element of "A Walk to Wachusett," constituting a contrasting pole to the mythical dimension of the narrative, with its allusions to Virgil and its sense of a quest to move into a timeless realm. When nature, especially a particular natural place, becomes the vehicle for historical memory rather than its obviation, the somewhat simplified dichotomy between town and country, of social contamination and natural purity, on which Thoreau has built the essay, is complicated. This is important not only to

"A Walk to Wachusett," but a recurring development in later Thoreau excursion narratives. In *A Week,* Thoreau would offer another meditation on the captivity and escape of Hannah Dustan as he traveled down her escape route on his return to Concord, making even more vivid the unbreakable connection between place and history. "Ktaadn," Thoreau's account of his excursion into what he considered a truly wild landscape, is punctuated by encounters with the social world, especially the signs of the lumber industry which was transforming the landscape that Thoreau was hoping to observe. Even in *Walden,* Thoreau's descriptions of the purity and beauty of the pond and the vitality of the nature around it are interwoven with descriptions of the railroad, of the poverty-stricken immigrant John Field and his family, and of the former inhabitants of the woods around Walden Pond, in whose historical shadow Thoreau conducts his new experiment.[5]

While Thoreau's attempt to distance himself from history is not completely successful, it does provide him the opportunity to use the return from Mount Wachusett to affirm a sense of a new beginning, and reenter with renewed strength and purpose the social world that he has left in making the excursion. "And now that we have returned to the desultory life of the plain, let us endeavor to import a little of that mountain grandeur into it" (151). We can find in this declaration something of the resolution to renewed engagement with the world that is the concluding note of *A Week,* "Ktaadn," and *Walden.* While in one sense such a stance undercuts the whole gesture of escape at the core of each excursion, it is better to understand the desire for escape itself as part of a larger pattern of a removal that generates a renewed sense of presence and belonging, not only in nature but in society. "There is elevation in every hour," he declares; "we have only to stand on the summit of our hour to command an uninterrupted horizon" (151). The gesture here certainly points ahead to the more elaborate excursions and meditations of the next decade, and shows us Thoreau devising a form of expression that would yoke his social alienation and desire for escape into a sustainable ethical stance.

NOTES

1. See Don Scheese, "Thoreau's *Journal*. The Creation of a Sacred Space."

2. Johnson, *Thoreau's Complex Weave,* 12. See also Sherman Paul's discussion of "A Walk to Wachusett" and its relation to the development of Thoreau's later works in *The Shores of America: Thoreau's Inward Exploration,* 157–65; Lawrence Buell's discussion of Thoreau's use of the literary excursion in *Literary Transcendentalism: Style and Vision in the American Renaissance*; and Robert Sattelmeyer's

discussion of "A Walk to Wachusett" in the context of Thoreau's development of the excursion narrative as an effective literary genre for his vision in "A Walk to More Than Wachusett."

3. Thoreau, "A Walk to Wachusett," in *Writings of Henry David Thoreau*, ed. Torrey, vol. V, 133. Subsequent page references are cited parenthetically in the text.

4. Fink, *Prophet in the Marketplace*.

5. See H. Daniel Peck, *Thoreau's Morning Work: Memory and Perception in "A Week on the Concord and Merrimack Rivers," the Journal, and "Walden."*

Thoreau, Thomas Cole, and Asher Durand

Composing the American Landscape

ISAIAH SMITHSON

Thomas Cole (1801–1848) and Asher Durand (1796–1886) constituted the first generation of the Hudson River school of landscape painters. Cole, the "father" of the school, was the artist most responsible for making landscape painting respectable and popular in America; heretofore, only historical paintings had been accepted as "serious art." Durand, an established engraver before turning to painting, introduced to American landscape painting both precision and an emphasis on scenes lacking human presence. When Henry David Thoreau graduated from Harvard in 1837, Cole had been famous for a decade and Durand was just emerging as a painter. Thoreau, Cole, and Durand were not only contemporaries. They were also fellow landscape painters.

Whereas Cole and Durand walked and made sketches primarily in the forests of New York's Catskills and Adirondacks, Vermont's Green Mountains, and New Hampshire's White Mountains, Thoreau walked and made notes primarily in the forests of Maine and New Hampshire, on the seashore of Cape Cod, and among the woodlands, ponds, and farms surrounding Concord. Thoreau visited museums and galleries in New York and Boston in which paintings of Cole and Durand were exhibited; had access to publications that reproduced landscape paintings;[1] and read works by some of the landscape theorists who directly or indirectly influenced Cole and/or Durand: Edmund Burke, Archibald Alison, William Gilpin, Uvedale Price, and John Ruskin.[2] Although Thoreau was probably not directly influenced by Cole or Durand, he was influenced by the same landscape aesthetics that affected them, and he conceived of himself as a landscape painter. Indeed, Robert Sattelmeyer says Thoreau sought to develop in himself the "eye of the painter and the art critic," and Lawrence Buell describes Thoreau as "obsessed with how land is seen aesthetically: as landscape, as scenery."[3] Thoreau often referred to his prose depictions of nature in terms of a "painting," "picture," or "gallery."[4] Given all this evidence of Thoreau's affinity with landscape painting, I believe that a "gallery" in which the prose paintings of Thoreau are hung amid works by Cole and Durand will effectively highlight some of the characteristics and singularity of Thoreau's work. My own canvas is small and my strokes necessarily broad, but I will juxtapose works by Cole, Durand, and Thoreau to delineate, first, their methods of composition and, second, their philosophies of place.

Composing Landscapes

Cole usually walked and sketched when the weather was pleasant; he would paint in his Catskill and New York City studios during the winter months, basing his paintings on his sketches. Durand was more likely to paint as well as sketch outside. Regardless of where they worked, Cole and Durand were unabashed composers rather than recorders. Cole asserts in an 1826 letter that "the finest pictures which have been produced . . . have been compositions" rather than "actual views."[5] Durand agreed. In his 1855 "Letters on Landscape Painting," published for the benefit of novice painters, Durand distinguishes between "imitation" and "representation," arguing that, "Although painting is an imitative Art, its highest attainment is representative, that is, by the production of such resemblance as shall satisfy the mind that the entire meaning of the scene represented is given."[6] Durand also agreed with Cole's claim that "a departure from Nature is not a necessary consequence in the painting of compositions: on the contrary, the most lovely and perfect parts of Nature may be brought together, and combined in a whole that shall surpass in beauty and effect any picture painted from a single view."[7]

In accordance with these tenets, Cole usually followed the tradition of inserting a withered tree as a framing device; usually elevated the viewer's vantage point; sometimes reduced the size of human figures to emphasize the grandeur and indifference of the surrounding landscape; experimented with different sizes, textures, spatial relationships, and tones; created specific weather and light conditions; and ignored some actual features and invented others (e.g., a browsing deer). These compositional strategies were designed to treat the viewer to well-defined *foregrounds*, more relaxed side frames that create a coulisse effect, and infinite *background* horizons — simultaneously guiding the viewer's primary attention to well-lighted, arresting *middle grounds*. Thus, Cole's landscapes are composed not only in the sense that they freely arrange nature's furniture, but also in the sense that the arrangement occurs according to a pattern not derived from nature. Cole usually composed his canvases according to the tripartite model he had learned from examining dozens of landscapes by Claude Lorrain (1600–1682); indeed, Cole was known as the "American Claude" by his contemporaries.

I believe the most dramatic (and humorous) examples of Cole's composing license are found in the Kaaterskill Falls paintings. In these paintings of the seemingly remote, unspoiled upper and/or lower falls, Cole omits the tourists who would have gathered at the popular Catskills site, ignores the observation platform and refreshment stands, does not suggest the near proximity of the luxurious Catskill Mountain House hotel, and does not hint that the cascading water could be abruptly stopped by an upstream dam when increased power was needed for the nearby sawmill.[8] Instead, in one of the paintings — *The Falls of Kaaterskill* (1826) — Cole inserts a lone, tiny, partially clad Indian, complete with hunting bow and feathered headdress. Cole's composition decisions resulted in landscapes decidedly more pristine than the falls actually visited by tourists in the 1820s.

Thoreau, too, was a composer. He *did* profess disdain for landscape painting because it presents "Nature as somebody has portrayed her," rather than "Nature as she is."[9] Nevertheless, as Richard Schneider points out, Thoreau's "vision is essentially pictorial" and his "writing encompasses virtually all of the approaches to understanding nature taken by American landscape painters of the nineteenth century."[10] Like a painter, Thoreau constantly noted the quality of and changes in light — innumerable passages in his Journal testify to this awareness. Working within the varying light conditions, Thoreau organized his prose descriptions from a set point of view, or along a sight line created by the walking observer, or in accordance with a controlling metaphor (e.g., a painting, journey, or seasonal cycle), or according to color and space relations seen typically on a canvas.[11]

Thoreau's compositional repertoire included elements and strategies unavailable to painters. Some elements are obvious: odors of plants, sounds of wildlife, and moonless night scenes. Some strategies are more subtle. First, Thoreau employed the equivalent of a highly mobile lens — making full use of the "wide angle," "zoom," and "macro" variations allowed by the human eye. Second, he usually insisted on the presence of the observer, sometimes to the extent that the observer became the object

Thomas Cole, The Falls of Kaaterskill, *1826. Oil on canvas. 43 × 36. The Warner Collection of Gulf States Paper Corporation, Tuscaloosa, Alabama.*

observed. And, third, he sometimes juxtaposed images of the same object painted at different times. Often these techniques were employed simultaneously. I will draw briefly on "Autumnal Tints" to illustrate these three techniques.

Cole, Durand, and other landscape painters were restricted to one middle ground per painting. To multiply foci, a painter would have to create more than one painting of a scene, each offering a different perspective, as Cole did with the Kaaterskill Falls paintings and as Durand did with his Lake George paintings. Or a painter could create structurally and thematically connected panels — allegorical landscapes such as Cole's four-part *The Voyage of Life* (1840) and Durand's two-part *The*

Morning and Evening of Life (1840).[12] Thoreau solved the problem with merely a phrase. In the "Red Maple" section of "Autumnal Tints," for example, Thoreau directs the viewer to "Look at yonder swamp of maples mixed with pines . . . a quarter of a mile off, so that you get the full effect of the bright colors, without detecting the imperfections of the leaves."[13] Having described some of the leaf colors and branch formations available from this perspective, Thoreau simultaneously asserts the artist's presence and changes the point of view, creating a second middle ground for his prose painting: other trees "of more irregular form, when I turn my head slightly . . . seem to rest heavily flake on flake, like yellow and scarlet clouds" (150). Having thus described the varied hues and shapes from two perspectives, Thoreau offers an aside with reference to that other kind of landscape artist: "Yet a painter would hardly venture to make them thus distinct a quarter of a mile off" (150). As if to correct the landscape artist's inadequacy, Thoreau follows this remark by directing the viewer's attention to another maple grove at a distance, and then walks toward it: "As I advance, lowering the edge of the hill which makes the firm foreground or lower frame of the picture, the depth of the brilliant grove revealed steadily increases" (150). Again Thoreau has asserted the artist's presence, but this time he has employed a human "zoom lens" by walking forward, instead of merely shifting the direction in which the head is aimed. Durand would have recognized the pedagogical value of this compositional technique: he instructs the novice painter to isolate trees or other objects and then walk: "at times shortening, at others lengthening, the space before you" to learn about changes in light, texture, density, and distinctness.[14]

Thoreau, like all humans, had access to a macro lens, too. He displays it in the "Scarlet Oak" section when he invites the viewer to see "how finely" the oak "leaves are cut against the sky."[15] Having set the sky as a background, Thoreau gives a close physical and philosophical description of the oak leaves constituting the middle ground — and then shifts from this panegyric to an extended description of the leaves "when, a month later, they thickly strew the ground in the woods, piled one upon another under my feet" (167). Interjecting once more the picture metaphor that weaves through his prose, he says, "If I were a drawing master, I would set my pupils to copying these leaves, that they might learn to draw firmly and gracefully" (167). Durand *was* a "drawing master," and he instructed students to do just what Thoreau suggests; Durand gives explicit instructions on creating drawings that distinguish one "species" from another and capture "traits of individuality" within natural objects.[16] Both Durand and Thoreau insist on the importance of the macro lens; however, Thoreau illustrates the greater versatility allowed the prose lens. Thoreau shows in the "Red Maple" and "Scarlet Oak" sections that, while a single landscape painting cannot simulate the visual changes that occur as one turns one's head, or walks in different directions, or returns to a scene in different seasons, a prose description can readily accommodate these spatial and temporal shifts.

Hudson River school landscape painters seldom insisted on the painter's presence. Cole inserted an unobtrusive artist into only a few of his landscapes (*View from Mount Holyoke*, 1836, and *Portage Falls on the Genesee River*, 1839). Similarly, Durand was noted for several "precise outdoor studies" that "were among the most selfless in a generation of landscapists for whom selflessness was an ideal."[17] Thoreau, though, conceived of the author's "self" — or persona — as an attractive element of his compositions. He not only spoke in first person throughout his descriptions but also took opportunities to make his persona the focus of some passages. One of the most extraordinary insertions of the artist into the scene occurs when Thoreau's persona *becomes* the natural event described. In the "Elm" section, Thoreau describes the ripeness of the autumn elm leaves, wonders whether "there is any answering ripeness in the lives of the men who live beneath them," and humorously finds the answering spiritual ripeness in himself: "When I stand where half a dozen large elms droop over a house, it is as if I stood within a ripe pumpkin-rind, and I feel as mellow as if I were the pulp, though I may be somewhat stringy and seedy withal."[18] The artist's persona has simultaneously become the organic state and the focus of the scene.

Are Thoreau's landscape representations as calculated as Cole's and Durand's? Yes, in spite of Thoreau's distinction between nature as portrayed and "Nature as she is." Thoreau does not insert tiny, ornamental Indians in his descriptions; however, he necessarily allows readers to see only from particular perspectives, necessarily emphasizes or ignores particular natural features, and must choose landscapes bathed with certain hues of light, sound, and fragrance rather than others. Thoreau knew that all landscape artists — whether using the medium of prose or paint — necessarily compose. Thoreau asserted the notion of "Nature as she is" — intimating that nature could be known apart from representation — yet he constantly and overtly called his audience's attention to his own representational devices. In fact, Thoreau made representation one of the themes of "Autumnal Tints." Thoreau states that his depictions of autumn's "bright tints" are "extracts from my notes,"[19] emphasizing that he, too, relied on "sketches" as a step toward the polished canvas and away from raw nature.[20] Thoreau also states that he has chosen this prose project over a type of book in which he would "get a specimen leaf from each changing tree, shrub, and herbaceous plant . . . outline it, and copy its color exactly with paint," and over another type of book that would "preserve the leaves themselves."[21] In "Autumnal Tints," then, Thoreau conspicuously chooses prose over painting and actual leaves. According to Sharon Cameron, "Thoreau is not interested in nature as a composition . . . but is rather interested in the composition of nature, and, in fact, hopes to replicate it."[22] But as Cameron acknowledges, this distinction is not tenable, and "purified" landscapes are impossible (115). The result, she says, is that "Thoreau's pictures" are often characterized by a "tension" between Thoreau's sought-after replication and his indications that nature cannot, finally, be "seen purely" (115). Thoreau's many references to natural surroundings as "pictures" and his constant highlighting of his own presence within outdoor scenes emphasize this "tension" between the pure landscape he would like to experience and the composed landscape he sees, walks through, and writes about.

Humans — whether or not they are landscape artists — cannot conceive of nature apart from their personal and cultural conceptions of nature. Thoreau evidently knew he could not escape this self referential situation. His deifying and gendering of nature in the phrase "Nature as she is" are two compressed, ironic examples of an artist having incorporated common nineteenth-century cultural conceptions of nature into his own experience of nature. Landscape artists differ from most humans, though, in that they create works in which the means through which places are composed become as much the subject as the places being composed. Thus, the issue, for me, is not *whether* Thoreau, Cole, and Durand composed their paintings, but *how* and *why*. Having pointed out some of the *how's* expressed in Cole's paintings, Durand's letters, and Thoreau's essay, I will now explore some of the *why's* motivating their work. I wish to show that, in the case of each artist, *how* they composed their landscapes was founded on particular *why's* — on their respective philosophies of place.

Philosophies of Place

One useful way to approach the compositional *why's* of Cole, Durand, and Thoreau is through their reactions to two European aesthetic concepts — primarily to the picturesque, but also to the sublime. In the first half of the nineteenth century, the sources of American intellectual life were still overwhelmingly European (especially British). European aesthetic theories and terms formed the accepted parlance in American intellectual and popular culture. Like all literate Americans, Cole, Durand, and Thoreau saw the American landscape through European theories and discussed local landscape aesthetics with European terminology. Cole and Durand toured Europe to see picturesque paintings of Claude Lorrain and Thomas Gainsborough (1727–1788), sublime works by Salvator Rosa (1615–1673) and Joseph M. W. Turner (1775–1851), and many other paintings and sites constituting the European landscape tradition that had begun in the seventeenth century. Thoreau read eight books by Gilpin (1724–1804) — the chief arbiter of the picturesque for Americans — assiduously commenting on them in his Journal. European aesthetics encountered through travel and reading became valuable models as well as posed significant obstacles for Cole, Durand, and Thoreau. Their philosophies of place derived, at least in part, from their responses to these theories.

The picturesque was a way of seeing, conceiving, and valuing a particular category of places. Seventeenth-, eighteenth-, and nineteenth-century European poets and painters who provided models of the picturesque, European aestheticians of the eighteenth and nineteenth centuries who defined the picturesque mode and differentiated it from the beautiful and sublime, wealthy English landowners who transformed their classical gardens into picturesque gardens in the late eighteenth century, and nineteenth-century American tourists who sought picturesque sites that had been described for them in guidebooks and who used a "Claude glass" to exclude the mass of surrounding natural features that did not "fit" into the picturesque frame — all of them were engaged in imposing an aesthetic ideal onto particular places.[23] Humans were required to do so, according to Gilpin, because "Nature is always great in design; but unequal in composition."[24]

"Beautiful," "sublime," and "picturesque" are slippery concepts that historically have been defined in relation to one another. Joshua Reynolds, Burke, Gilpin, Alison, Payne Knight, Price, and others were not in total agreement, and not all of them discussed all three concepts. In general, though, a beautiful landscape (either a physical place or a painting) is characterized by a balanced (classical) structure, smooth surfaces, gradual variations in light and color, idealized natural forms in a pastoral setting, and a placid mood. The picturesque (sometimes called "picturesque beauty") developed in the second half of the eighteenth century as a supplement to the tradition of classical beauty. Picturesque landscapes feature rough or craggy surfaces, sharp juxtapositions among dark and light masses, varied and irregular shapes, individualized natural forms, and ruins or some other vestiges suggesting past human habitation. The mood includes nostalgia for a rural past. The sublime scene — also receiving pronounced attention in the second half of the eighteenth century — is characterized by a vast scale and landscape features such as an ominous mountain, mysterious valley, crashing sea, or threatening thunderclouds. Terror, wonder, and awe are elicited by a "sublime" landscape; for sensitive viewers, the result is spiritual insight, such as realization of the diminished role of humans within the natural world's geologic past and present grandeur. Although human figures are often absent from sublime settings, when they do appear they are diminished in size and are at risk; in beautiful and picturesque landscapes, human figures are more likely to appear at peace with their physical surroundings.

Cole's 1835 "Lecture on American Scenery" refers to these three landscape categories as it announces the philosophy of place that guided Cole during the latter part of his career.[25] Cole praises American scenery for aesthetic reasons, saying, "in the Adirondacks of this state and the White Mountains of New-Hampshire, there is a union of the picturesque, the sublime, and the magnificent . . . the sublime melting into the beautiful, the savage tempered by the magnificent."[26] But Cole reserves special praise for "the most distinctive, and perhaps, the most impressive, characteristic of American scenery, its wildness" (201). Cole then uses these *aesthetic* claims as a basis for developing *political, moral,* and *religious* tenets.

With respect to connections between the aesthetic and the political, Cole insists that the "stern sublimity of the wild" helps to define America (199). He transforms what European observers viewed as an aesthetic weakness — that America lacked picturesque scenery because it lacked objects that had been imbued with meaning by association with a distant past — into a political strength: "American associations are not so much of the past as of the present and the future. . . . You see no ruined tower to tell of outrage, no gorgeous temple to tell of ostentation; but freedom's offspring — peace and security dwell there, the spirits of the scene" (210).[27] Cole sought to establish America's free, wild landscape as part of the national identity that was emerging after the definitive break with England that occurred with the War of 1812.

With respect to connections among aesthetics, morals, and religion,

Cole asserts the Platonic precept that "there is in the human mind an almost inseparable connexion between the beautiful and the good, so that if we contemplate the one, the other seems present" (198). Further, according to Cole, America's "rural nature" and the "Poetry and painting" that represent it elicit from the viewer "a more profound reverence for the Creator of all things" (197–98). When "gazing on the pure creations of the Almighty, he feels a calm religious tone steal through his mind" (199). The work of Alison and others had taught Cole to value associations that can arise when viewers contemplate nature, whether in actuality or as represented through painting. In "American Scenery" and throughout Cole's artistic maturity, Cole championed associations readily available through America's rural and wild scenes: associations that he hoped would lead Americans to identify their emerging nation with their landscape, and to contemplate freedom, goodness, and God.[28]

To highlight the "wild" scenery peculiar to America, to help Americans conceive of their native places as integral to their national identity, and to make viewers aware of the moral and religious implications of American places, Cole emphasized the sublime and stretched the boundaries of the picturesque, as the following three examples illustrate. First, the five-part Course of Empire series (1834–1836) — marking the midpoint of Cole's career — combines one sublime and two picturesque panels with two panels in which governmental and religious edifices, along with war scenes, almost completely conceal the landscape. Sublime and picturesque conventions are made the vehicle for an unusually complex political message in this depiction of an empire that rises when it is in harmony with the landscape and falls as it loses contact with the surrounding terrain. Second, the famous *View from Mount Holyoke* (1836) mixes a touch of the sublime with predominantly picturesque characteristics — in a single canvas in this case — not to portray the conventional European arcadia of the distant past, but to dramatize the pressing loss of America's wild landscapes to industry and cultivation in the immediate present. Finally, in the last years of Cole's career, picturesque and sublime characteristics are overlaid by religious allegory. Cole was a sincere Christian who was baptized into the Anglican Church in 1842, at age forty-one. In the Voyage of Life series (1842), sublime features dominate over the picturesque. In all four paintings, landscape conventions continue to express traditional painterly conventions, but they are also forced to express Cole's insistence on faith in what he labels a "Guardian Spirit" and an "angelic Being."[29] As Elliot Vesell observes with respect to Cole's final years, "From the start of his career Cole had employed religious themes, but they had served largely as vehicles for depicting . . . nature. Now religious themes took precedence over nature and became ends in themselves."[30] This shift is obvious even in the title of the Cross and the World series that remained unfinished at Cole's death. In effect, Cole, along with other American painters and poets, participated in what Barbara Novak labels the "Christianized sublime," a "sublime . . . absorbed into a religious, moral, and frequently nationalist concept of nature."[31] The European sublime and picturesque allowed for the use of landscape to instruct as well as to please, but in Cole's philosophy of place, instruction became the predominant objective. By the end of Cole's career, an Americanized picturesque and a Christianized sublime prevailed: political and moral concerns had been subsumed by religious themes, and aesthetics existed almost wholly to serve Cole's religious vision.

Like Cole's "Lecture on American Scenery," Durand's "Letters on Landscape Painting" provide a valuable, mature statement of the artist's philosophy of place. The nine "Letters" make clear that Durand found the picturesque to be even more inadequate than Cole did. According to Gilpin, nature should be valued and labeled "picturesque" if it "would look well in a picture";[32] Durand would reverse the terms so that a picture would be valued if it looked like nature. Though Durand grants that picturesque paintings are "not without their moral," he wonders whether they do "not belong more to the service of the tourist and historian than to that of the *true* landscape artist."[33] Also like Cole's "Lecture," in Durand's "Letters," thoughts on *aesthetics* lead inevitably to meditations on *religion*. Durand encourages the inexperienced painter to study "Nature early" for aesthetic reasons — in order to receive the "first impressions of beauty and sublimity" from Nature, "unmingled with the superstitions of Art" (34). However, there is "another motive for referring" the artist to the "study of Nature early — its influence on the mind and heart," for the "external appearance of this our dwelling-place . . . is fraught with lessons of high and holy meaning, only surpassed by the light of Revelation" (34). Art's "true purpose," according to Durand, is "impressing the mind through the visible forms of material beauty, with a deep sense of the invisible and immaterial" (97); "the true province of Landscape Art is the representation of the work of God in the visible creation, independent of man" (354). In Durand's view, "*picturesqueness*" fails to fulfill this purpose because it gives "preference to scenes in which man supplants his Creator, whether in the gorgeous city of domes and palaces, or in the mouldering ruins that testify of his 'ever fading glory' "

(66). Because of the inability of the picturesque to convey the moral and religious values important to Durand, he categorizes it as merely one of the "externals of painting" (66).

Durand's philosophy of place emphasized the spiritual reality beyond the visible place. As was true for Cole, Durand's composition choices were intimately connected with his philosophy of place. Not surprisingly, then, although Durand insisted on the painter's right to compositional "license," his philosophy of place included definite limits (16). The artist may "displace a tree," for example, but elements such as "the elevations and depressions of the earth's surface composing the middle ground and distance . . . may not be changed," for "on these God has set his signet" (16).

Durand's philosophy of place also paid special attention to places from which humans are absent. Accordingly, beginning in the 1850s, Durand distinguished himself with dozens of small-scale studies of natural objects, and the play of light on these objects. Certainly Durand also created many picturesque landscapes similar to Cole's. However, "Durand was one of the first Hudson River men who was able . . . to surrender the Claudian-derived cliché in his landscape compositions, and to assume a plein-air objectivity in which the inherent components of *landscape* determined design, while *weather* determined properties of atmosphere and light." [34] Durand's studies allowed "new laws of composition to grow from within the province of nature itself." [35] Many of Durand's landscapes place his viewers *inside* the forest and confine their viewing area to a few square feet of ground-level or eye-level boulders, shrubs, water, and soil; human subjects are not included (e.g., *Interior of a Wood*, n.d.; *Study of Rocks*, 1869; *Landscape*, n.d.; and *Catskill Study*, n.d.). Even in cases where a somewhat more open viewing space allows the viewer to look up and toward several trees within the enclosed space, human figures are absent. Within this second category, arching trees often form a churchlike "nave" familiar to Christians (e.g., *Woodland Interior*, 1854; *In the Woods*, 1855; *Through the Woods*, 1856; and *Forest Study*, n.d.).

Durand's dismissal of the picturesque and his precise landscape studies illustrate that he — unlike Claude and Cole — valued close, precise renditions of natural objects, moved out of the picturesque into realism in some of his work, and truly was committed to landscape "independent of man." [36] In Durand's philosophy of place, neither picturesque conventions nor human presence was required for the "work of God" to become manifest. In spite of these differences, in some of the "nave" studies and in other landscapes, Durand recapitulated the movement seen in Cole's last years: aesthetic considerations served primarily to express a religious vision.

Although Cole and Durand were critical of the traditional picturesque mode of rendering landscapes, Thoreau would necessarily have been critical of their stances, in turn. Thoreau's responses to both the picturesque and the sublime were different from those exhibited by Cole and Durand. Thoreau's writing, like the writing of most nineteenth-century travel and nature writers, includes picturesque images and strategies. The 1843 "A Winter Walk," for example, has been called a "catalogue of conventional images of picturesque New England."[37] The "deserted woodman's hut" that Thoreau likens to the "ruins of Palmyra or Hecatompolis" in this essay is just one of the obvious instances of the picturesque. According to one scholar, "time after time, year after year, Thoreau gave evidence of a picturesque point of view."[38] However, Thoreau evidently did not read and think seriously about the picturesque until he read Gilpin's works during an approximately two-year period beginning in spring 1852 and ending in winter 1854. Once Thoreau began to think about the picturesque, he became fascinated. His Journal contains more comments on Gilpin than on any other person, except for a few close friends (885); *Walden*, *Cape Cod*, *The Maine Woods*, and Thoreau's letters also contain quotations from or allusions to Gilpin (865–66). In spite of his sometimes high regard for Gilpin and his obvious interest in the picturesque, Thoreau was, finally, critical of both.[39] His comments on Gilpin, as well as other passages written mostly during Thoreau's final years, constitute a criticism of the picturesque, a theory of the sublime, and a philosophy of place that deviate sharply from the views developed by Cole and Durand.

Thoreau *did* share some aesthetic complaints with Cole and Durand. For example, his dismissal of Gilpin because it is "all side screens and fore screens — and near distances — & broken grounds with him" and because "scenery" seems "not worth beholding" to Gilpin if it is not "*picturesque*"[40] is similar to Durand's dismissal of the picturesque as being concerned with only the "externals" of landscape painting and to Durand's objection that the picturesque values nature that is pictorial instead of valuing paintings that are faithful to nature. However, as has been shown, Cole's and Durand's aesthetic responses to the European picturesque and sublime blended inextricably into nationalistic, moral, and religious concerns. It is here that significant differences emerge:

Thoreau's aesthetics were not devoted to nationalistic causes; his *aesthetics* served *moral* and *spiritual* motives, rather than *moral* and *religious* motives.

Cole used picturesque and sublime compositions to emphasize America's wild landscapes and American political freedom associated with this wildness. Thoreau used mostly picturesque and a few sublime compositions to emphasize a different concept of wildness — a type of landscape, culture, and individual attitude not restricted to any one country or nation. In "Walking," Thoreau admits to being a "true patriot"[41] and distinguishes America from the Old World by quoting Sir Francis Head to the effect that in America "the mountains are higher, the rivers longer, the forests bigger, the plains broader" (109–10). However, Thoreau also maintains that the "secret of successful sauntering" is "having no particular home, but [being] equally at home everywhere" (93). He insists that, although he may walk on the readily identifiable Marlborough Road, he walks "out into a nature such as the old prophets and poets, Menu, Moses, Homer, Chaucer, walked in. You may name it America, but it is not America" (102). Indeed, says Thoreau, "You may go round the world / By the Old Marlborough Road" (104). Although Thoreau's depictions of wild landscapes are firmly grounded in American places such as Concord or Mount Katahdin, the emphasis is not on the "Americanness" of these places, but on their wildness. For Thoreau, wildness is exhibited in selected landscapes, personalities, and works of art from all places and eras; exists in opposition to mere civility; can connect humans with their nonhuman neighbors; and entails freedom that goes beyond nationalism.

The differences between the moral and *religious* emphases found in Cole and Durand and the moral and *spiritual* emphases found in Thoreau's philosophy of place are apparent in both picturesque and sublime contexts. Alongside the nineteenth-century "Christianized sublime" expressed in Cole's later work, there existed also what I will label the "Christianized picturesque." Durand's *Early Morning at Cold Spring* (1850) is a clear example. It reproduces the Claudian compositional stage, with the foreground, surrounding birches, and midlevel body of water highlighting a man looking at not one, but two, distant church spires. The barely disguised Christianity that is expressed in this painting and that Cole and Durand integrated into many of their landscapes and into their philosophies surely would not have been affirmed by Thoreau. Thoreau did not object to using aesthetics to serve what he terms a "higher law."[42] As has already been seen in "Autumnal Tints," Thoreau's persona admires dying

Asher B. Durand, Early Morning at Cold Spring, *1850. Oil on canvas. 60 × 48. Museum purchase, Lang Acquisition Fund, 1945.8.*

leaves not merely for their hues but also for their suggestion of an analogous spiritual ripeness in humans and of a oneness shared by the persona and the pumpkin pulp. Accordingly, Thoreau vehemently criticized Gilpin for seeming to suggest that nature could be separated from morality and appreciated merely for its aesthetic qualities: "Gilpin talked as if there was some food for the soul in mere physical light and shadow, as if, without the suggestion of a moral, they could give a man pleasure or pain!" (*J* VI:103). Thoreau was equally critical of Gilpin for suggesting that "'we have scarce ground to hope every admirer of *picturesque beauty* is an admirer also of the *beauty of virtue*'" (*J* VI:59, Thoreau's emphasis).[43] "And he a clergyman, 'vicar of Boldre!'" is Thoreau's indignant response (59). Like his transcendentalist colleagues, Thoreau perceived nature as a nonhuman repository for symbols bearing on how human life should be understood and conducted. But Thoreau had his own precise ideas of what messages are to be found in nature and of what constitutes the "higher law." Christian doctrine would not have qualified.

As has been illustrated above, in his 1855 "Letters," Durand envisioned nature as a source of religious teachings "only surpassed by the light of Revelation." Thoreau reversed this evaluation in 1857: the "love of Nature" and the "revelations" available through nature are superior to and are "not compatible with the belief in the peculiar revelation of the Bible" (J X:147). As early as his 1839 Sunday excursion on the Merrimack, Thoreau contrasted the "people coming out of church" with himself and his brother in their canoe and concluded, "we were the truest observers of this sunny day."[44] Thoreau mistrusted Christianity because, in his view, its emphasis on "another world" slights current "tough problems" (73–74) and because its focus on "man and man's so-called spiritual affairs" ignores nonhuman life (73). Thoreau's philosophy of place includes a stark opposition between the "husk of Christianity" and the "higher law" — only the latter is revealed through nature.[45]

Thoreau's "higher law" is sometimes associated with the wild ("Autumn Tints" and "Huckleberries") and sometimes opposed to it ("Higher Laws" section of Walden). But the quest for this "higher law" — or what Thoreau also terms a "higher nature" or "spiritual life" — always involved viewing nature symbolically.[46] And Thoreau's viewing of nature seems to have revealed two contradictory faces: one asserting a kinship shared by human and nonhuman life, and the other insisting on an irreconcilable divide between human and nonhuman life. The first face is portrayed by Thoreau through picturesque rather than sublime landscapes. Thoreau's persona undertakes several "pilgrimages" featuring many picturesque settings in "Walking," "Autumnal Tints," and the other lectures and essays written in Thoreau's last years. However, these pilgrimages lead not to traditional Christian symbols, but to older, vegetation rites asserting their presence in defiance of Christian overlays. For example, "Wild Apples" includes descriptions of pre-Christian, ritualistic gestures, songs, and dances undertaken to ensure productivity — some of the activities occurring on Christmas Eve;[47] "Huckleberries" includes reference to eating fruits "in remembrance" of Nature, as a "sort of sacrament — a communion — the *not* forbidden fruits, which no serpent tempts us to eat."[48] These picturesque descriptions feature rites suggesting spiritual communication and identity between human and nonhuman life that continues to exist in spite of, or in opposition to, Christian symbols. Thoreau's saunterers encounter forest "temples not made with hands," but they are only superficially similar to the "naves" painted by Durand (253). Having climbed to the top of New Hampshire's Mount Washington, Thoreau's pilgrim encounters one of these places long ago made "sacred" by Amerindians; he "rises above himself, as well as his native valley" in that picturesque setting, but he does not encounter symbols of the Christian God (255–56).[49]

Thoreau created many more picturesque than sublime landscapes. The ascent of Mount Katahdin is not only the best known of Thoreau's few sublime landscapes, it is also the best illustration of the alternate face insisting on the gap between human and nonhuman life. In an 1852 Journal entry, Thoreau writes, "There is something worth living for when we are resisted — threatened. . . . What would the days — what would our life be worth if some nights were not dark as pitch . . . How else could the light in the mind shine!" (*PJ* 4: 407). Thoreau's experience on Mount Katahdin six years earlier constituted one of those dark nights. Ascending Mount Katahdin alone, Thoreau (or his persona) relies on the European vocabulary of the sublime to depict a "primeval" Nature that is "vast, and drear, and inhuman . . . savage and awful, though beautiful."[50] Mount Katahdin is definitely not picturesque: it is neither "man's garden," nor his "lawn, nor pasture, nor mead, nor woodland" (70). Therefore, Thoreau's Mount Katahdin painting insists on alienation rather than the sense of kinship that pervades his picturesque landscapes; the persona emphasizes that nature "does not smile on him as in the plains" (64), that "Man was not to be associated with it. It was Matter, vast, terrific, — not his Mother Earth" (70). Ritual is encountered here, as in Thoreau's picturesque landscapes, but it is so ancient as to be alien; modern humans are cut off from Mount Katahdin's "heathenism and superstitious rites, — to be inhabited by men nearer of kin to the rocks and to wild animals than we" (71). Thoreau's sublime landscape does not feature traditional religious images like those found in Cole's sublime works: John the Baptist, Adam and Eve, or the Guardian Spirit. Instead, Thoreau's encounter with sublime spiritualism evokes a more fundamental response in the famous "contact" passage: "Talk of mysteries! — Think of our life in nature, — daily to be shown matter, to come in contact with it. . . . Who are we? *where* are we?" (71, emphasis added).

Thoreau's sublime landscape, unlike his own picturesque paintings and unlike the religious paintings of Cole and Durand, leads to a fundamental, unanswered question of place — of relations between humans and "the *solid* earth."

Conclusion

Because I have based my comparison of composition techniques on only a few compositions by Cole, Durand, and Thoreau, and because I have narrowed the discussion of philosophies of place to the artists' responses to the picturesque and sublime, I am leaving much unsaid. However, the preceding discussion of composition techniques and philosophies of composition does allow me to make three assertions with respect to the *how's* and *why's* of the landscapes of Cole, Durand, and Thoreau. First, Cole and Durand offered their audiences messages that were valuable but less original than those Thoreau offered his audience. It is true that, in composition, Cole strained against the Claudian model and that Durand's "studies" were rare in their close focus on natural objects and their exclusion of human subjects. It is also true that Cole and Durand created many fine landscapes. Thematically, though, the depiction of nature as a source of national, moral, and religious beliefs had become culturally sanctioned long before Cole and Durand began to present it. Rather than being original, Cole and Durand followed a path well worn by American romantic writers such as James Fenimore Cooper, Washington Irving, and William Cullen Bryant, as well as by many eighteenth- and nineteenth-century English painters and writers. Second, the original themes offered by Thoreau constitute paradoxes rather than overt statements. In Thoreau's compositions, claims with respect to representing "Nature as she is" are countered by reminders that pure nature cannot be represented. In his philosophy of place, Thoreau indicates that the "higher law" found in nature should be the goal of landscape compositions, but he shows that the quest for the "higher law" sometimes reveals a nature with whom humans have close kinship and sometimes reveals a nature that is irrecoverably distant from modern humans. Neither paradox is resolved — this irresolution *is* the original vision Thoreau offers his audience. Finally, placing Thoreau's picturesque and sublime prose landscapes and philosophical meditations against the backdrop of work done by Cole and Durand makes clear that Thoreau's work was not only original, but also less comforting, more complex, and more challenging.[51] Accordingly, while a small number of academics continues to study the work of Cole and Durand for its historical value, a large number of people — academics and general readers — continue to grapple with Thoreau's work. Today, the questions raised by Thoreau's paradoxes are more compelling than the answers offered by Cole and Durand.

NOTES

1. Schneider, "Thoreau and Nineteenth-Century Landscape Painting," 69.

2. Thoreau wrote an undergraduate essay on Burke's concept of the "sublime." With respect to Alison, Thoreau read his four-volume *History of Europe*, rather than his *Essays on the Nature and Principles of Taste* (1790), the Alison publication of most interest to landscape artists, art theorists, and critics interested in associationism. See Robert Sattelmeyer, *Thoreau's Reading: A Study in Intellectual History with Bibliographical Catalogue*, 70, 119.

3. Ibid., 70; Buell, *Environmental Imagination*, 409.

4. For examples and discussion of Thoreau's use of "painting" and "picture" in reference to nature, see Schneider, "Thoreau," 73 and note 30, and Sharon Cameron, *Writing Nature. Henry Thoreau's Journal*, 108–18. For an account that minimizes Thoreau's interest in and desire to see paintings, see Edward Wagenknecht, *Henry David Thoreau: What Manner of Man?* 32–33.

5. Merritt, "Appendix I," 47.

6. Durand, "Letters on Landscape Painting," 146.

7. Merritt, "Appendix I," 47.

8. Baigell, *Thomas Cole*, 30.

9. Thoreau, *Journal of Henry David Thoreau*, ed. Torrey and Allen, vol. X, 69. Subsequent volume and page references to this work are cited parenthetically in the text with *J*.

10. Schneider, "Thoreau," 71, 67. Schneider also states that, "although verbal landscapes containing the compositional elements and aesthetic categories of landscape painting occur throughout Thoreau's career, they are much more frequent in his writings prior to 1851" (74).

11. Ibid., 73.

12. Cole also created "panoramic" canvases, forerunners of the "wide angle" paintings for which Hudson River school painters Frederick Church and Albert Bierstadt became famous. Although panoramic depictions do not necessarily create multiple middle grounds, they do create a dramatic viewing angle that *seems*, in some cases, to approach 180 degrees. For a discussion of Cole's *View from Mount Holyoke* as a "panoramic," or "panoptic," painting, see Alan Wallach, "Making a Picture of the View from Mount Holyoke."

13. Thoreau, "Autumnal Tints," in *Natural History Essays*, 149.

14. Durand, "Letters," 146.

15. Thoreau, "Autumnal Tints," 166.

16. Durand, "Letters," 34.

17. Baigell, *Concise History of American Painting and Sculpture*, 79.

18. Thoreau, "Autumnal Tints," 151. Sattelmeyer notes that "Autumnal Tints" was "prepared by Thoreau on his deathbed" and that Thoreau's depiction of some subjects "closely reflects his own condition." Accordingly, this passage takes on somber as well as humorous tones. See the introduction to *Natural History Essays*, xxviii.

19. Thoreau, "Autumnal Tints," 139.

20. Thoreau's Journal entries often constituted the notes or sketches for his lectures and essays (and the Journal entries themselves were often based on notes taken by Thoreau during his walks). The Journal entries, though, cannot always be considered sketches for polished works, because in his later years Thoreau came to think of the Journal as a final, publishable product.

21. Thoreau, "Autumnal Tints," 139.

22. Cameron, *Writing Nature*, 114.

23. Christopher Hussey states that, before the emergence of the picturesque, "landscapes as such gave . . . no aesthetic satisfaction whatsoever. It was not until Englishmen became familiar with the landscapes of Claude Lorrain and Salvator Rosa, Ruysdael and Hobbema, that they were able to receive any visual pleasure from their surroundings." See *The Picturesque: Studies in a Point of View*, 2.

24. Gilpin, *Observations on the River Wye*, 18.

25. Cole first delivered his "Lecture on American Scenery" before the American Lyceum Society on May 8, 1835, in New York; this lecture was revised and published in the *American Monthly Magazine* in 1836 as the "Essay on American Scenery." On April 1, 1841, Cole delivered a modified version of the "Essay" as a lecture to the Catskill Lyceum Society; this lecture was published in the May 1841 issue of the *Northern Light*. Barbara Novak describes the "Essay on American Scenery" as "an essay that articulates the spirit that was to dominate much American landscape painting for thirty years." See *Nature and Culture: American Landscape Painting, 1825–1875*, 4.

26. Cole, "Lecture on American Scenery," 203.

27. The absence of ruins suggested not only a historical deficiency, but also philosophical and aesthetic problems. In the European picturesque, ruins were considered no longer to be controlled by humans, but to have returned to nature. In this condition, ruins provided supposedly natural art, since they would be characterized by the irregular lines typical of nature. See Malcolm Andrews, *The Search for the Picturesque: Landscape Aesthetics and Tourism in Britain, 1760–1800*, 49–50.

28. Cole admitted that his work did not always fulfill these lofty objectives. He noted that sometimes he was forced to settle for "painting for money & to please the many." See Ellwood Parry III, *The Art of Thomas Cole: Ambition and Imagination*, 310.

29. Louis Noble, *Life and Works of Thomas Cole*, 216.

30. Vesell, introduction to *The Life and Works of Thomas Cole*, xxiii.

31. Novak, *Nature and Culture*, 38.

32. Gilpin, *Observations on the Western Parts of England*, 328.

33. Durand, "Letters," 66.

34. Novak, *American Painting of the Nineteenth Century*, 84.

35. Durand, "Letters," 87.

36. Novak defines the "Claudian-derived mode" typical of Cole's paintings as only one of several "threads" that constituted the "American landscape tradition." She maintains that Durand's more realistic paintings illustrate a thread that "involved the deliberate abandonment of all the overtones of the picturesque." See Novak, "Influences and Affinities: The Interplay between America and Europe in Landscape Painting before 1860," 30.

37. Fink, *Prophet in the Marketplace*, 120.

38. Templeman, "Thoreau, Moralist of the Picturesque," 864.

39. For discussions of Thoreau's reading of Gilpin, see Templeman; James Southworth's response to Templeman, "Thoreau, Moralist of the Picturesque"; Gordon Boudreau, "H. D. Thoreau, William Gilpin, and the Metaphysical Ground of the Picturesque"; and Schneider, "Thoreau," 74. Whereas Templeman describes Thoreau's attitude toward Gilpin as being almost wholly laudatory, Boudreau argues that Thoreau's initial respect for Gilpin's work and for the picturesque had disappeared by the winter of 1854.

40. Thoreau, *Journal, Vol. 5: 1852–1853*, 284. Subsequent volume and page references to the Princeton edition of the Journal are cited parenthetically in the text with *PJ*.

41. Thoreau, "Walking," in *Natural History Essays*, 111.

42. Thoreau, "Huckleberries," in ibid., 212.

43. Thoreau wrote in 1859 that "There is no beauty in the sky, but in the eye that sees it. Health, high spirits, serenity, these are the great landscape-painters. Turners, Claudes, Rembrandts are nothing to them. We never see any beauty but as the garment of some virtue" (see *J* XII:368).

44. Thoreau, *A Week*, 63.

45. Thoreau, "Huckleberries," 212.

46. Thoreau, *Walden*, 219, 210.

47. Thoreau, "Wild Apples," in *Natural History Essays*, 185–86.

48. Thoreau, "Huckleberries," 241.

49. Perhaps the most dramatic example of "higher laws" is the statement that autumn leaves "contentedly . . . return to dust again . . . resigned to lie in decay at the foot of the tree, and afford nourishment to new generations of their kind, as well as to flutter on high! They teach us how to die." Here, too, the contrast between "higher laws" and Christianity is evidently maintained as Thoreau follows this statement with, "One wonders if the time will ever come when men, with their boasted faith in immortality, will lie down as gracefully and as ripe" ("Autumnal Tints," 158).

50. *Maine Woods,* 69–70.

51. I am grateful to the Graduate School and College of Arts and Sciences at Southern Illinois University at Edwardsville for supporting travel to New York, New Hampshire, and Massachusetts to study sites depicted by Cole, Durand, and Thoreau, and for supporting travel to museums in Albany, New York City, Boston, and Washington, D.C., to study Hudson River school paintings. I am also thankful to Richard Schneider for suggesting significant bibliographical resources.

Reading Home

Thoreau, Literature, and the Phenomenon of Inhabitation

PETER BLAKEMORE

In the summer of 1851, Henry Thoreau was wrestling with questions about the naturalist's role in the world. His Journal shows how fascinated he had become with the scientific exploration and expeditionary travel writing of such notable scientists as Darwin, Michaux, Gray, and Humboldt. Steeping himself in these works, Thoreau realized something important about the nature of perception and how traveling in foreign lands limited the observer. The scientist's keenly trained eye and taxonomic method of division was valuable, but it was not all, and could, in fact, cause one to miss the wheat among the chaff. As he noticed that the "character" of his own "knowledge" was gradually becoming "more distinct & scientific," Thoreau realized that the traveling scientist risked losing his "views as wide as heaven's cope" by focusing "down to the field of the microscope."[1]

As usual, he solved the problem by walking. Thoreau finally realized that his practice of recording impressions from walks in his Journal led toward a different way of seeing. By the early 1850s, Thoreau understood the distinction geographer David Seamon wrote of more than a century later: a strictly scientific view of the land "can investigate only the empirically discernible, objective parts of human behavior and experience. The less visible, more subtle portions of human existence — at-homeness, habit, modes of encounter, dwelling — are ignored or reduced to recordable manifestations."[2] Thoreau decided he would practice a different kind of observation; he would develop a method of local travel, and bring to his work something objective scientific travelers could not — a reverence for home.

As anyone who has followed him into the Journal or the late natural history essays such as "The Dispersion of Seeds" will realize, Thoreau's project led him deeper into an ecologically connected self than we can find in practically any work by an American before or after. Thoreau devoted most of his last decade on earth to living, thinking, and writing a life and a place into imaginative existence together. And beyond the importance of Thoreau's evolving method for our study of his work, the kind of phenomenal interpretations of time and place he practiced in the 1850s can help us to develop terms and perceptual viewpoints with which we can better interpret a large body of American literature. The practice of intentional perception employed by literary naturalists like Thoreau, John Muir, and Mary Austin can guide us toward new ways of understanding inhabitation in our literature as well as our world.

One of the most illuminating studies of Thoreau's practice in the Journals is H. Daniel Peck's *Thoreau's Morning Work*. Here Peck explains that with the Journal's "repeated description of phenomena," Thoreau was able to develop a "middle level of response" between the Emersonian all-encompassing eye and an "evolving scientific naturalism." According to Peck, Thoreau's method gave his observations "an almost empirical status lying halfway between subjective and objective reality." Through this continuous record, Thoreau was able to find "the meeting place of the perceiver and the perceived." [3]

Peck and other analysts of the Journal have demonstrated the important reorientation in thinking Thoreau made during his last ten years of life. The work he had embarked upon in the early 1850s would become clearer with time, so that by 1857 he would conclude that "the man of science makes this mistake, and the mass of mankind along with him: that you should coolly give your chief attention to the phenomenon which excites you as something independent on you, and not as it is related to you" (*J* X:164–65). By this Thoreau does not mean one should dispense with the separation of object from self. His claim here speaks neither to a transcendent incorporation, nor a romantic anthropomorphosis or pathetic fallacy. Thoreau is after something much more specific. "The important fact is [the phenomenon's] effect on me." Thoreau continues: "He [the man of science] thinks that I have no business to see anything else but just what he defines the rainbow to be, but I care not whether my vision of truth is a waking thought or a dream remembered, whether it is seen in the light or in the dark. It is the subject of my vision, the truth alone, that concerns me. The philosopher for whom rainbows, etc., can be explained away never saw them. With regard to such objects, I find that it is not they themselves (with which the men of science deal) that concern me; the point of interest is somewhere *between* me and them (*i.e.* the objects)" (*J* X:165, Thoreau's emphasis). Thoreau knew that a rainbow was not a "bow or arch exhibiting, in concentric bands, the several colors of the spectrum, and formed in the part of the hemisphere opposite to the sun by the refraction and reflection of the sun's rays in the drops of falling rain," as the dictionary would have it. A rainbow cannot be contained by such an abstract and general description, nor can it exist absent of the precise time, place, and weather in which it occurs. As a specific event, the rainbow requires all the other aspects of its context — the background of hills, the air temperature, the exact angle of sunlight, the observer's sense of time, all of what David Abram terms the "dynamic affordances" that make it perceivable, that make it an actualized part of the physical universe.[4] Most of all, an actual rainbow requires an actual perceiver for it to be seen and, more importantly, significant.

To conclude from this that Thoreau shunned natural science or distrusted empiricism would be wrong; he simply knew their limitations. He understood from experience that, by themselves, taxonomy and empirical analysis could never provide a groundwork for the practice of inhabitation. For Thoreau, who wrote in his journal in May of 1854 that "there is no such thing as pure *objective* observation. Your observation, to be interesting, *i.e.* to be significant, must be *subjective*" (*J* VI:236, Thoreau's emphasis), the essential value of observation goes beyond the need for abstract laws and description of phenomena to the cultivation of a local, specific way of knowing.

Philosopher Alfred North Whitehead touches upon the reality Thoreau recognized when he writes that the "disadvantage of exclusive attention to a group of abstractions, however well-founded, is that, by the nature of the case, you have abstracted from the remainder of things."[5] In *Science and the Modern World*, Whitehead questions the idea of "simple location" — the notion that reality can be described accurately as points on a graph — and in doing so he moves us toward Thoreau's recognition of a century before. Whitehead's "remainder of things" represents the things themselves, the phenomenological "sense objects," the "given" and "evident" materials that excite our perceptions and create for the sensing subject a world to perceive. As Whitehead describes the cognitive process, he shows that if the physical presences that have been "excluded" due to relying on abstraction "are important in your experience, your modes of thought are not fitted to deal with them." But since we "cannot think without abstractions," Whitehead believes it is "of the utmost importance to be vigilant in critically revising [our] *modes* of abstraction. It is here that philosophy finds its niche as essential to the healthy progress of society. It is the critic of abstractions."[6] Thoreau's continual return to questions of perception and cognition — the how, why, and what — is an example of precisely this philosophical niche. Karl Kroeber's complaint that Thoreau's Journal too often turns inward toward an unecological "self-centeredness" fails to understand this philosophical necessity and how crucial it is to the project of inhabitation.[7] Seeing home and writing accurately about it is no mean task. As Thoreau realized, it requires a cold, distant eye, a loving heart, and continuous vigilance over the mode of perception one chooses to employ. Gushing sentimentalism will never do when the subject is home, but neither will the cool abstraction of the perfect taxonomist.

Thoreau found local observation the best way to sharpen his instruments of perception and arrive at insight that would be significant to himself, his neighbors, and his home ground. In the week to week calibration and improvement of his method, Thoreau practices what philosopher Edmund Husserl calls the "return to the intuition of the essence in its givenness."[8] By recording impressions from year to year and keeping track of their effect upon the perceiving self, coming back as a home traveler might, over and over to the same places, the same ponds, the same trees, Thoreau created one of the most fully imagined landscapes in our literature and one of the most carefully and continuously constructed records of identity in relation to the land.

I offer an example of his situating perceptions in a single place over time. One might open the Journal to any of hundreds of pages after 1851 and find Thoreau deep in the practice and perfection of this method, but I choose a single passage from an entry of May 7, 1854, because Thoreau draws a connection between the transformation of spring and its outward expression as his world begins to bloom:

> The earliest flowers might be called May-day flowers, — if indeed the sedge is not too far gone for one then. A white-throated sparrow still (in woods). *Viburnum Lentago* and *nudum* are both leafing, and I believe I can only put the former first because it flowers first. Cress at the Boiling Spring, one flower. As I ascend Cliff Hill, the two leaves of the Solomon's-seal now spot the forest floor, pushed up amid the dry leaves. *Vaccinium Pennsylvanicum* leafing. Flowers, *e.g.* willow and hazel catkins, are self-registering indicators of *fair* weather. I remember how I waited for the hazel catkins to become relaxed and

shed their pollen, but they delayed, till at last there came a pleasanter and warmer day and I took off my greatcoat while surveying in the woods, and then, when I went to dinner at noon, hazel catkins in full flower were dangling from the banks by the roadside and yellowed my clothes with their pollen. If man is thankful for the serene and warm day, much more are the flowers. (*J* VI: 241)

Spiraling in and out through time, Thoreau puts himself in *that* morning at the moment of writing, in yesterday's walk, in the distant past when he experienced the phenomenon of the catkins blooming, and in the future, when these flowers will bloom and once again lay their pollen open to the air. His play on thankfulness, fulfillment, and blooming represents the kind of significant discovery Thoreau believed one could make by keeping track of home. This relocation through time and space becomes grounded and meaningful because it does not simply happen in the abstract, in any time or any space, but in *place* — and in the *home* place, to be specific. Thoreau knows that the human imagination must lie at the center of knowledge. The phenomenal life-worlds Thoreau sees and his archaeological sense of experience and human, floral, and faunal emplacement reveal for us, as it did for him in his time, the value of place itself. We recover incidents and events by returning, either in our imagination or in bodily form, as Thoreau did on his daily walks, to places where memory has kept the patterns of the past.

By starting with the intention to perceive, there can be no indifference where the variations and physical subtleties of one's home place are tracked, accounted for, and recorded week to week, season to season, year to year. By registering the way changes in the land affected him, and in turn, keeping track of how his own intentionality prepared him to see or experience home, Thoreau intertwines the two inextricably and creates an embodied identity that cannot be abstracted from place. Contrary to Sharon Cameron's claim that the "fiction of the *Journal* is that consciousness is displaced by [natural phenomena],"[9] Thoreau had found the same truth that Edmund Husserl realized more than half a century later: consciousness does not exist separated from physical reality. There is no thing called consciousness — there is only "consciousness-of."[10] Natural phenomena cannot displace consciousness, nor would Thoreau "fictionalize" them into doing so. Natural phenomena *are* consciousness — or to put it more precisely, neither consciousness nor phenomena exist alone. They create one another in reciprocating interanimation.

Like geographer Yi-Fu Tuan, Thoreau recognized that living fully at home meant more than a romantic view of place. Explaining the difference between two views of a landscape, Tuan writes that the visitor uses vision to "compose pictures. The native, by contrast, has a complex attitude derived from his immersion in the totality of his environment. The visitor's viewpoint, being simple, is easily stated. . . . The complex attitude of the native, on the other hand can be expressed by him only with difficulty and indirectly through behavior, local tradition, lore, and myth." [11] We could extend the analogy, as Thoreau did, to say that the world traveler can draw only from wide-ranging factual knowledge, while the local traveler learns something about himself from locality. Writing in his Journal on this perceptual distinction, Thoreau discovered that if the observer "should begin with all the knowledge of a native — & add thereto the knowledge of a traveler — Both natives & foreigners would be obliged to read his book. & the world would be absolutely benefited" (PJ 3:357). Such a paradoxical native foreigner, or local traveler, represents an attempt by Thoreau to answer this age-old epistemological conundrum: If we see the world as part of ourselves, and ourselves as part of the world, how do we express it? How does a person in the position of being "nature looking into nature," as Thoreau put it, describe the event? [12] It is the same apparent constriction David Seamon points to when he writes, "For most moments of daily living, we do not experience the world as an object — as a thing and stuff separate from us. Rather, we *interpenetrate* that world, are *fused with it* through an invisible, weblike presence woven of the threads of body and feelings." [13] How does a person *describe* such an awareness?

To focus on what happens when the givenness of objects and the world and the being and significance of the perceiving self meet, one must strive for a new means of perception. Thoreau knew what Maurice Merleau-Ponty emphasized in his study of the body, perception, and phenomena. Pointing to the sort of paradox Thoreau often employed to move over an impasse, Merleau-Ponty writes that "empiricism cannot see that we need to know what we are looking for, otherwise we would not be looking for it, and intellectualism fails to see that we need to be ignorant of what we are looking for, or equally again we should not be searching." [14] Striving for such a balance between preconception and naïveté, phenomenologists like Merleau-Ponty and Husserl developed ideas that might well have been the bylaws for the Society for the Diffusion of Useful Ignorance Thoreau half-jokingly proposed in "Walking." [15] Thoreau was jabbing at the hubris of taxonomy for taxonomy's sake, but as is almost always the case with his quips, a kernel of truth lies at the center. The practice of walking, of returning slowly, carefully, lovingly, again and again, with an open, receptive, uncertain point of view to the things themselves puts the perceiving subject in a continuously evolving relationship. Such a home scientist knows that change will occur, but not precisely when or how. Developing this type of Useful Ignorance can have momentous consequences. "How much, what infinite, leisure it requires, as of a lifetime, to appreciate a single phenomenon! You must camp down beside it as for life, having reached your land of promise, and give yourself wholly to it," Thoreau decided in the winter of 1852. "It must stand for the whole world to you, symbolical of all things" (*PJ* 5: 412–13).

If we conclude from such remarks that Thoreau was allowing flights of fancy to take wing, or that he believed he might find a religious realization in the bark of a tree or the blooming of a flower — in the way that William Blake might use nature as a doorway providing access to his religion of the imagination — we misread Thoreau's project. In fact, Thoreau is far from this sort of romanticism. Instead, as we read in the Journal, we begin to realize the care he took to balance his empirical mind with his imagination. Of course, abstracting from things themselves by performing such scientific practices as taxonomic noting of species on, say, location grids or in population graphs is vital to understanding the world. Taxonomy "is the way in which we think of things, and without these ways of thinking, we could not get our ideas straight for daily use," Whitehead reasoned.[16] But Whitehead understood that we must also on occasion question this mode of perception, and I believe Thoreau understood it as well. The more carefully we look at the last decade of Thoreau's life, the more clear it becomes that he would have known precisely what Edith Cobb meant when she wrote of the "adolescent fixation on selfhood" that plagues the reductive mind.[17] Believing that a taxonomic description of range and philogeny is enough to make meaning is a delusion; of course, taxonomy has its purpose and its own essential value as a tool toward greater understanding. But still greater meaning arises from the continuous recording of a life, and going back to places over and over turns the "symbolical" significance of a phenomenon into realized experience — as the rainbow, or the interpretation of mouse tracks in ice, or the reassessment of thermometer readings, or any other phenomenon connected to specific places keeps track of the things themselves — not their representation through abstractions. "Consciousness must be faced with its own unreflective life in things and awakened to its own history which it was forgetting," Merleau-Ponty exhorts.[18] For this reason, Thoreau realized that the self could not be separated from place. By hybridizing the intentionality, expectation, and recovery that come out of local familiarity with the heightened receptivity of the traveler, whose wits must be at the ready, who must be prepared for surprises not mentioned in the guidebooks, we might explore our homes with both sentiment and empiricism — we might *feel* home as much as we analyze and keep track of it.

Gary Snyder has called this way of knowing the "spirit of place." According to Snyder, to "know" a place in this way is to participate in its "gossip," to be a neighbor, literally a "near-dweller," in the land.[19] Edith Cobb labeled it "compassionate intelligence" and believed that it led to "the kind of understanding and sharing of 'otherness' that we call 'identification.'"[20]

Thoreau's recognition that observation, experience, reason, history, and sentiment led into a deeper knowledge, and that he himself could know his identity only through his home, made him feel the value of place all the more intensely. He saw that place itself could be lost. And worst of all, it could be lost for mere lack of attention. For the man who practically shouted at his neighbors, "Employ your senses!" such a loss would seem the most ironic and bitter event imaginable.

As an antidote to the leveling of place, Thoreau promoted wildness. For him, the more naturally diverse and complex a landscape, the more that place presented itself as a desirable subject for attention. He knew the danger of *in*attention that Neil Evernden points to when he writes: "So long as we neglect the development of perceptual skills the world is diminished in equal measure. As our awareness expands so too does the reality we inhabit."[21] John Muir, Mary Austin, and other literary naturalists recognized this as well. They too found ways to create their identity in response to the land. Muir's realization came during his first summer in California's Sierra Nevada, where he discovered that one might feel a sense of calm and sustained rightness of inhabitation — a perception of being in the place that felt like home — even in the wild mountains. "Another inspiring morning," he writes, "nothing better in any world can be conceived. No description of Heaven that I have ever heard or read seems half so fine. At noon the clouds occupied about .05 of the sky, white filmy touches drawn delicately on the azure."[22] Like Thoreau, Muir sees the value of precision, right down to the percentage point of cloud cover. To identify a place as home, one's world must be specific. Accurate descriptions of the sky matter. To think with both the mind of a scientist, using intelligence, and the mind of a like being, or neighbor, using sympathy, moves one into another order of existence in place. It is to meet one's home as one would a friend, to accept its being as given, to dwell with the land rather than upon it.

Characterizing Muir as primarily an anthropomorphizer of nature, Lawrence Buell focuses his attention on tropes and Muir's artistic movement toward the pathetic fallacy and "the quaint usage favored by the neoclassical poets." [23] But if we encounter Muir during his first inklings that the rugged, wild mountains of California might be home, and adopt a more charitable stance, seeking instead an answer to how Muir arrived at his choice to personify, we will soon see that phenomena led him toward recognition of sympathy. Buell is right, of course. Perhaps no one else has shown more of an affinity for anthropomorphism than John o' the Mountains, with his Douglas squirrel as the "peppery, pungent autocrat of the woods" and "the small forest birds" who turn into "little feathered people of the trees." [24] Such metaphors may on occasion cloy us with their sentimentality, but we should not allow this aspect of Muir's writing to distract us from the deeper significance of his work.

By going to the mountains and encountering the phenomena of the region, Muir builds up a store of experience that grants him a more deeply imagined and deliberate sense of place. At such times he becomes a conduit for description of phenomena, and as the perceiving subject, in spite of his predisposition toward abstracted anthropomorphosis and sentimentality, Muir can outdo himself, locating a transcendent "fact" within the smaller sight, as when he relates this experience of arising to a morning's condensation: "Fine calm morning; air tense and clear; not the slightest breeze astir; everything shining, the rocks with wet crystals, the plants with dew, each receiving its portion of irised dewdrops and sunshine like living creatures getting their breakfast, their dew manna coming down from the starry sky like swarms of smaller stars." At this point, we might recoil somewhat to hear Muir's fabrication — his whole-cloth rendering of dew as correspondent with stars seems hard to stomach at first — but continuing on, we can see that a sort of familiarity and more purposeful and evident connection can be drawn out of Muir's conceit: "How wondrous fine are the particles in showers of dew, thousands required for a single drop, growing in the dark as silently as the grass! What pains are taken to keep this wilderness in health, — showers of snow, showers of rain, showers of dew, floods of light, floods of invisible vapor, clouds, winds, all sorts of weather, interaction of plant on plant, animal on animal, etc., beyond thought! How fine Nature's methods! How deeply with beauty is beauty overlaid! the ground covered with crystals, the crystals with mosses and lichens and low-spreading grasses and flowers, these with larger plants leaf over leaf with ever-changing color and form, the broad palms of the firs outspread over these, the azure dome over all like a bell-flower, and star above star."[25] Here Muir recognizes the beauty in order, twin concepts that Thoreau reminds us the Greeks conflated into the single term "Kosmos."[26] Out of a familiarity and continuous presence in relation to the given phenomena, Muir is able to see the underlying interconnections, and while we in our more prosaic times may quibble with the notion that dewdrops are like manna, Muir is accurate to point out that the drops condense out of apparent nothingness and sustain plant life, just as any other living thing relies on sources of food. Connecting the light and the water with the flora — in a sort of photosynthetic enactment of digestion — Muir develops a metaphorical reality. A continuous sense of the life-world, including the overlaid processes of condensation and phototropism and their effect on photosynthesis, becomes visible in observation over time in place.

D. H. Lawrence complained that "America hurts because it has a powerful disintegrative influence upon the white psyche."[27] I think he meant that the North American sense of wildness, and of the wilderness as possible home, presents a threat to the European ideal of order and boundaries. Muir's impression that "more and more, in a place like [the Sierra], we feel ourselves part of wild Nature, kin to everything" is a way of thinking that threatens the European sense of control and rationality that, try as he might, Lawrence himself could never escape.[28]

This same wildness and disinterest in human motivations broods like the desert sun over Mary Austin's remarkable book, *The Land of Little Rain*. Austin finds her own home subject in the country of indeterminate border between the Mojave and Great Basin Deserts, a place where "whether the land can be bitted or broken" for the sake of humankind "is not proven."[29] And just as Muir and Thoreau recognize the need to sojourn in order to "know" a place, she warns those who might visit on a lark that "the real heart and core of the country are not to be come at in a month's vacation. One must summer and winter with the land and wait its occasions."[30] To know a wild country, to perceive it without fear, to walk out into it on its terms is to reimagine one's self in relation to that land.

For Austin, the desert's attraction was more than pastoral quietude or the thrill of living a charmed life in a dangerous world. Her whole project of developing a North American sense of consciousness was tied into landscape and how it made its presence known to the mind. Mary Austin's sense of connection to California's Owens Valley is a prime example of the sense of insideness that geographer Edward Relph describes. "From the outside," Relph writes, "you look upon a place as a traveller might look upon a town from a distance; from the inside you experience a place, are surrounded by it and part of it."[31]

Being inside such a place and drawing one's identity can have interesting side effects. Vera Norwood rightly claims that Austin's unforgiving, hard-edged landscape "liberates Anglo women in particular from the silencing strictures of femininity."[32] Turning the common idea of the secure on its head, the wild and untamed becomes a sanctuary, but not as a new territory to light out for, not as a desperado's Hole in the Wall, or a country beyond the pale; the desert offers a haven because it reflects back to us our own imaginative and creative capacities. In "The Pocket Miner" chapter of *The Land of Little Rain*, the narrator tells us of a hapless, small-scale prospector who wakes up one morning in "a lonely, inhospitable land, beautiful, terrible. But he came to no harm in it," she follows up quickly; "the land tolerated him as it might a gopher or a badger. Of all its inhabitants it has the least concern for man."[33] Far from the gendered-feminine landscape metaphorically prepared for rape and violation that Annette Kolodny has found in earlier European tropes of the New World, Mary Austin's southwestern motherland represents a power to be reckoned with. It brings to mind Thoreau's more ambiguous feminine presence, Nature "this vast, savage, howling mother of ours . . . lying all around with such beauty and such affection for her children as the leopard."[34]

Indeed, in much the same way that Thoreau's study of wildness in the countryside around Concord led him away from social or scientific conventions, Austin's narrator in *The Land of Little Rain* breaks out of the social bindings most women lived under at that time to make her home space in a place where one's wits and powers of observation become essential equipment for survival. Dwelling becomes possible in the desert wilds only when a person's consciousness seeks to perceive the given world. The Owens Valley which gives rise to Mary Austin's perceptual skill provides a constant reminder of Merleau-Ponty's claim that "to return to things themselves is to return to that world which precedes knowledge, of which knowledge always *speaks*, and in relation to which every scientific schematization is an abstract and derivative sign-language, as is geography in relation to the countryside in which we have learnt beforehand what a forest, a prairie or a river is."[35] Just as Muir and Thoreau found their sensitivity increasing as they became inhabitants, so

Austin recognizes this place as the proper means to understanding the self. "Let me loose in the desert with the necessity of discovering truth about any creative process of the human mind," she writes to a friend, "and I can pick up the thread from the movement of a quail . . . from anything of beauty that comes my way."[36] Though her faith in the landscape's instructive qualities went further than most would allow for today — for instance, she believed that poetic meter and rhyme schemes directly correspond to specific topography — Austin has also recognized the truth that in the median point between observer and observed, place and person together become significant. The "ordinary traveler," according to Austin, will bring "nothing away from [the mountain arroyos] but thirst."[37] Establishing identity is an aspect of time and space, which together equal place.

Just as Austin, Muir, and Thoreau recognize the need to sojourn in order to know a place, the narrator of Sarah Orne Jewett's *The Country of the Pointed Firs* comes to understand her sanctuary on the Maine coast as a place that might improve her ability to perceive. Here, too, meaning arises in direct response to phenomena, and the reader's mind is made to confront the physical as embodied experience. The novel also presents a little problem, but a useful problem, one that I think can help us to see a way into reading works of fiction from the perspective of inhabitation and the storying of place.

In *The Environmental Imagination,* Lawrence Buell expresses concern about whether narrative forms, characterization, and the plotting that authors have relied upon throughout history can withstand an ecologically based literature. "What sort of literature remains possible if we relinquish the myth of human apartness?" he laments, then goes on to claim that such a literature would have to abandon "or at least question what would seem to be literature's most basic foci: character, persona, narrative consciousness."[38] Though Buell may have been thinking in terms of narration pretending to arise from a nonhuman perspective, such as Gaia or a forest speaking, Jewett's *The Country of the Pointed Firs* offers an example of at least one aspect of a more ecologically conscious work that might trouble him; as a novel with practically no sense of rising or falling action and few if any remarkable tragic or comic events, it is one of the quietest, least dramatic books imaginable. Even the narrative voice and tone created by Jewett seem to soften a description of place that is already calm, collected, and holding itself firm along the coast.

Yet in spite of the apparent inertia among her characters, we readers may be moved in the most psychically imaginative and physical ways.

Coming to such a book after reflecting upon the processes of inhabitation enacted by Thoreau, Muir, Mary Austin, and other literary naturalists, we gain a much more fruitful appreciation. Jewett's *The Country of the Pointed Firs* calls us to mindfulness, both for the way its narrator discovers significance out of intention, and for the way the book draws us sympathetically and imaginatively into what might seem like the most uneventful place on earth. The lesson of a novel that shuns the classic requirements for dramatic action is its very uneventfulness. Paradoxically, this lack of individual plotting among characters forces us to see that the mundane, ordinary occurrences are what really matter. In Jewett's novel, almost nothing comic or absurd or grotesque happens: a visitor arrives on the Maine coast to spend a summer writing in solitude. Instead, she learns how — precisely how — people in this part of the world get a living, and soon begins to feel herself becoming fastened to the place. That is the story.

Some like Buell might criticize the fact that there is little or no development beyond that of the few characters who turn up in more than one scene, such as the narrator's landlady, Almira Todd. But as I see it, this is the book's genius. Here human and geographic meaning flow together — create one another. We are reminded that a hundred or a thousand small but powerful stories exist at the center of every real land community. *The Country of the Pointed Firs* tells us what happens to a place when people live in it, how the place itself changes and offers its inhabitants ways of living, seeing, and telling stories. Turning back to the perceptual experimentation Thoreau developed in order to read his own sense of place, we see how the imaginative insights stimulated by Jewett's novel open the doors of experience in a manner that is so productive and generative as to offer the reader new ways of looking at a coastal town and its people. Thus the book fronts us with a landscape full of meaning, a landscape so actively present and attractive of our attention as to call us to our senses. It is in itself, through the very experience of reading and visualizing, a turn toward phenomena and the life-world — and also a *re*turning to ourselves in place.

Like Thoreau the native traveler, Jewett's narrator imagines herself as someone between knowledge and naïveté. From the opening pages she describes herself as "a lover of Dunnet Landing returned to find the unchanged shores of the pointed firs, the same quaintness of the village with its elaborate conventionalities; all that mixture of remoteness, and childish certainty of being the centre of civilization of which her affectionate dreams had told." [39] Thus she is both prepared to see what she has already known and hopeful of learning more. And like Thoreau, her observations tend toward the transcendental, allowing her to see the deeper significance underlying facts. The first thing she finds is that the houses have a cheerfulness and determination in the way they face the shoreline. Their "small-paned windows in the peaks of their steep gables" seem like "knowing eyes that watched the harbor and the far sea-line beyond" (1). Of course, the windows *are* knowing eyes, or at least by extension they are the places where knowing eyes would watch for returning ships.

The narrator continues along this metaphorical path, pointing out that getting to know such a place is like "becoming acquainted with a single person" (1). If as with Muir's anthropomorphism and strained sentimentality, we feel overindulged and incapable of suspending our disbelief, we might stop and ask ourselves how else an observant person should describe approaching a Maine bay town by boat? The rocky promontories, the scattered crags of island giving themselves inward finally to a purchase of small homes, docks, churches, and the other vestiges of inhabitation — all of this calls to our attention the welcoming quality of a coastal village. And Maine coastal communities sit very much as single entities rising up from out of the dark green land. The town buildings, docks, and streets form not only our perception of the village, but also create there on the water's edge a place of safety, a symbolic human project, a refuge from storms, and a rest from the work of guiding and keeping a craft on course. They welcome us after long passages, offering even in the distance as we approach, a story of human ingenuity, design, and forbearance.

The landing action as we arrive carves out a place in space, and in the building of such towns we are constantly reminded of the twin reality of going and staying — of departing and arriving — of launching outward on yearlong voyages, and returning to home. For many of the villagers, including the central character, the narrator's landlady, hostess, and chief informant, Almira Todd, the "away" of the horizon is not pure mystery, not an alien, other place. Their seafaring lives connect them to the larger world in a physically, chronometrically *real* way. They know by experience precisely what it is to lose sight of land and can count the hours it takes to sail that distance. They also know what it means to make landfall again, a fact which highlights the importance of the town's name, Dunnet Landing. It holds in language the physical act of arrival, of safety, of coming ashore. Our narrator wants us to see that it is not only the place that shapes the people, but that the people and place together give character to a sense of dwelling. Out of this communion, the town acquires, or adapts, a presence that is nearly distinguishable as personality.

The portrait of Dunnet Landing also reminds us how remote such places can be. Where the system of roadways at this time was still quite rudimentary — possibly connecting by one or two narrow lanes to a larger turnpike, which in turn connected larger towns and cities — the people mainly traveled by sea. In such a location, conceiving and balancing a sense of wildness with the habitation of more urban settings, the mind envisions outlying population centers by turns in the jagged coastline, and we are forced to imagine other people's accessibility contingent upon wind direction, wave height, the number of tacks, and the length of time, including the seasonal aspects of daylight, that would make up a voyage to the nearest neighboring town.

Outside the visual attractions of the village, we soon discover how islands draw the eye outward to the horizon and engage people in imaginative fusion with time and space. Our visiting-native narrator arranges a trip out to Green Island to meet Mrs. Todd's mother and brother. Fully prepared by earlier scenes for the concept of distance and topography, we experience this voyage, and another taken to Shell-Heap Island, as little masterpieces of small craft lore and sailing skill. Anyone who has ever heard the main sheet snap as they've come about, or ridden a swell and pulled the dagger board as they've beached their craft will have had this ancient place-centered knowledge and embodied experience revived by Jewett's writing.

Finally, this story of place, and the place itself, this Country of the Pointed Firs, serve the narrator as a territory for recovery. Her solitary afternoons spent writing at the empty schoolhouse, her original intentions to shut herself up and work on ideas she holds within, fail to interest her enough to remark upon them. Rather, the work of inhabitation, that other experience of becoming a native traveler, of dwelling in the present physical world, seems separated from that less immediate labor of getting a living by her writing. Early on, the narrator's practical life fades into the background, so that by the time the summer is over and she must return to the city, we likely have forgotten her original mission in coming to this place. Dunnet Landing, in all of its intricate expressions, has simply proved too attractive to miss.

From the perspective of describing a sense of home, we cannot find a wiser, more insightful and instructive or interesting book. The askance view of the naive but sympathetic native traveler takes in all that the village has to give: coast, islands, weather patterns, and lifeways, all draw themselves together to form a singleness of experience. In much the same way that Leslie Marmon Silko writes of the Laguna Pueblo people not privileging one story above another, Jewett ensures that we recognize all the parts that make the town itself important. Silko relates a similar sense in the following passage concerning her own village of Laguna:

> Accounts of the appearance of the first Europeans in Pueblo country or of the tragic encounters between Pueblo people and Apache raiders were no more and no less important than stories about the biggest mule deer ever taken or adulterous couples surprised in cornfields and chicken coops. Whatever happened, the ancient people instinctively sorted events and details into a loose narrative structure. Everything became story.[40]

When everything that happens in Dunnet Landing, from gathering herbs to the autumn romance and marriage of an island fisherman and a shepherdess, is significant enough to tell about, then the place itself becomes the story. In the same way that Thoreau understood that all the events of spring and all the variations of those events from year to year are of vital interest, Jewett's novel illuminates the ordinary yet indispensable events of home. The telling of the story becomes the act of inhabitation, and as the story dwells inside us, our imagination sets spark to Dunnet Landing in all its perceptible, specific components — haddock, pennyroyal, schoolhouse, island, clam midden, forest, dory. The space residing within our imaginations, open and awaiting the world to fill it, becomes place.

To the last, our narrator keeps us mindful of the physical world and how it shapes our perceptions. Her final description before the actual end of the book's concluding Dunnet Shepherdess section calls us back to the beginning and to the necessary fronting of the eye and mind with the land. Just as in the beginning the bay and village reveal themselves to her from afar, in the end, drawing the circle to a close, as she watches from shipboard "doubl[ing] the long sheltering headland of the cape," when she "looked back, the islands and the headland had run together and Dunnet Landing and all its coasts were lost to sight" (133). On the jagged shores of Maine, a bit of distance, a doubling back across a point of land, will throw the whole of the shoreline into a new perspective. Openings, bays, coves, islands, and capes disappear in one tack — single places recede backward into memory. The nature of the landscape impresses itself upon our minds once again as we watch it fade into the apparently simple, general line between water and land. Somewhere, nestled in the expanse of horizon behind us, lies the deep affiliation of family, human solitude, coastal lifeways, knowledge, and story held there, awaiting our return, awaiting another landing.

For a person or a town to establish identity requires time. Space experienced over time becomes place. To learn the lessons of inhabitation one must view the spiraling return of seasons, the rhythms of weather, the peculiarities of animal behavior, and the local patterns of human life. One must live the comings and goings, the walking to and fro. One must be, as Thoreau once put it in the pages of his Journal, "prepared for strange things" (*J* IX:54). A novel like Jewett's offers us the chance to inhabit such strange places in our imaginations. It brings us that much closer to the native's point of view. From such books we get a sense of what it means to be *of* this continent, this time and place.

In his typically pithy way, Thoreau may have characterized a dawning sense of North American inhabitation best when he wrote, "Generally speaking, a howling wilderness does not howl: it is the imagination of the traveler that does the howling."[11] His passing quip, dropped in the midst of a description of the sounds one expects to hear in a Maine forest at night, speaks volumes about an American sense of identity at home. Living in a howling wilderness of our own creation, we remain travelers *through* this place. But deciding consciously and intentionally to perceive the things that make up a world can increase our awareness and teach us new ways to experience our stories and the places we call home.

NOTES

1. Thoreau, *Journal, Vol. 3: 1848–1851*, 380. Whenever possible, I cite passages from the Thoreau Edition's updated scholarly version of the Journal published by Princeton University Press (abbreviated as *PJ*). Passages from later in Thoreau's work are taken from the Torrey and Allen edition of the Journal (abbreviated as *J*).

2. Seamon, *Geography of the Lifeworld*, 160.

3. Peck, *Thoreau's Morning Work*, 68. Perhaps the earliest critical recognition of Thoreau's direct experimentation with visual phenomenon is Richard J. Schneider's "Reflections in Walden Pond: Thoreau's Optics." Though Schneider's essay focuses more specifically on ideas of optical experimentation and visual reflection, it also examines the philosophical and epistemological significance of Thoreau's reorientation of subject/object relationships.

4. Abram, *The Spell of the Sensuous*, 82.

5. Whitehead, *Science and the Modern World*, 85.

6. Ibid., 85–66, Whitehead's emphasis.

7. Kroeber, "Ecology and American Literature," 314.

8. Husserl, *Phenomenology and the Crisis of Philosophy*, 113.

9. Cameron, *Writing Nature*, 88.

10. Husserl, *Phenomenology and the Crisis of Philosophy*, 96.

11. Tuan, *Topophilia*, 63.

12. Qtd. in Worster, *Nature's Economy*, 78.

13. Seamon, *Geography of the Life World*, 161.

14. Merleau-Ponty, *Phenomenology of Perception*, 28.

15. Thoreau, *Natural History Essays*, 127.

16. Whitehead, *Science and the Modern World*, 76.

17. Cobb, *Ecology of Imagination in Childhood*, 110.

18. Merleau-Ponty, *Phenomenology of Perception*, 31.

19. Snyder, *Practice of the Wild*, 38.

20. Cobb, *Ecology of Imagination in Childhood*, 107.

21. Evernden, *Natural Alien*, 105.

22. Muir, *My First Summer in the Sierra*, 57–58.

23. Buell, *Environmental Imagination*, 193.

24. Muir, *My First Summer in the Sierra*, 96.

25. Ibid., 128.

26. Thoreau, *Natural History Essays*, 130.

27. Lawrence, *Studies in Classic American Literature*, 73.

28. Muir, *My First Summer in the Sierra*, 243.

29. Austin, *Land of Little Rain*, 3.

30. Ibid., x.

31. Relph, *Place and Placelessness*, 49.

32. Norwood, "Mary Austin's Acequia Madre," 229.

33. Austin, *Land of Little Rain*, 68.

34. Thoreau, *Natural History Essays*, 128.

35. Merleau-Ponty, *Phenomenology of Perception*, ix, Merleau-Ponty's emphasis.

36. Qtd. in Rudnick, "Re-naming the Land," 17.

37. Austin, *Land of Little Rain*, 184.

38. Buell, *Environmental Imagination*, 145.

39. Jewett, *Country of the Pointed Firs*, 2. Further page references are cited parenthetically in the text.

40. Silko, "Landscape, History, and the Pueblo Imagination," 87.

41. Thoreau, *Maine Woods*, 300.

Seeing the West Side of Any Mountain

Thoreau and Contemporary Ecological Poetry

J. SCOTT BRYSON

The needles of the pine,
All to the west incline.
— Thoreau, "The Needles of the Pine"

We know from his Journal that during the latter part of 1841, a year that proved to be his most prolific period as a poet, Thoreau was simultaneously considering abandoning poetry as a form of expression. According to Elizabeth Hall Witherell, Thoreau consistently "harbored fundamental doubts about both the vigor of poetry as opposed to prose and its suitability to his own temperament and particular talent."[1] These doubts sprang from his conviction that, while certain supreme artists like Homer had created poetry worthy of praise, most of what Thoreau called the "effeminate" lyrics of his contemporaries were vapid and impotent in their attempts at conveying the wildness of the natural world. Similar responses have increasingly been offered over the last century and a half, as poets have found traditional nature poetry lacking in its ability to respond to contemporary understandings of the natural world. My purpose here is to use our knowledge of Thoreau's disillusionment with his own poetry, and that of his contemporaries, to help us better understand the response that has taken place within late twentieth-century nature poetry. My central claim is simple and twofold: (1) that the factors that led Thoreau to forsake poetry are quite similar to the factors that have driven contemporary nature poets to produce poems much different from their romantic forebears; and (2) that by understanding these factors, we can better understand what it is that contemporary ecological poets are doing in their work.

It is generally acknowledged that Thoreau's skill as an essayist far out-shone his talent as a poet. It is also widely accepted that most of Thoreau's decision to move away from poetry and toward the natural essay as his primary mode of aesthetic expression was due to his recognition of this same fact. In February 1851, for example, he wrote, "The strains from my muse are as rare nowadays, or of late years, as the notes of birds in the winter, — the faintest occasional tinkling sound, and mostly the wood-pecker kind or the harsh jay or crow. It never melts into song."[2] How-ever, as Witherell makes clear, much of Thoreau's decision to forsake his poetic impulse resulted not only from his doubts concerning his own discordant muse, but also from his disenchantment with what were believed to be the greatest poems of his time and with the ability of po-etry in general to convey the true "Poetry" (in the Emersonian sense) of the natural world. For example, in late 1841, when Thoreau visited the Harvard College Library in order to select poems for an anthology he planned to edit, he experienced a deep disillusionment in respect to the work he discovered there in Cambridge. He writes of "looking over the dry and dusty volumes of the English poets," and of his astonishment "that those fresh and fair creations I had imagined are contained in them. . . . I can hardly be serious with myself when I remember that I have come to Cam. after poetry — and while I am running over the cata-logue, and collating and selecting — I think if it would not be a shorter way to a complete volume — to step at once into the field or wood, with a very low reverence to students and librarians" (November 30; *PJ* 1:337–38).[3]

This type of reaction, preferring the "field or wood" to the "dry and dusty volumes" of civilization, is one we hear throughout Thoreau's work, both prose and poetry. Consider, for example, these lines from his poem "Nature," where he directly addresses the natural world:

> In some withdrawn unpublic mead
> Let me sigh upon a reed,
> Or in the woods with leafy din
> Whisper the still evening in,
> For I had rather be thy child
> And pupil in the forest wild
> Than be the king of men elsewhere
> And most sovereign slave of care
> To have one moment of thy dawn

Than share the city's year forlorn.
Some still work give me to do
Only be it near to you.[4]

We perceive in this passage familiar Thoreauvian themes — his preference for being a lone "pupil in the forest wild" rather than a ruler
in civilization; his redefinition of expected emotional states, where city
dwellers, not the speaker in the "unpublic mead," are the ones who are
isolated and "forlorn."

Yet in spite of penning lines like these, Thoreau apparently found little
in his own verse that was much more effective at rendering the wildness of
the natural world than he discovered in his disappointing journey through
the Cambridge library. The undomesticated quality he searched for was
largely absent from both his own work and that of his most talented contemporaries. As he wrote in a Journal entry from early 1851, "The best
poets, after all, exhibit only a tame and civil side of nature — They have
not seen the west side of any mountain. Day and night — mountain and
wood are visible from the wilderness as well as the village — They have
their primeval aspects — sterner savager — than any poet has sung. It is
only the white man's poetry — we want the Indian's report. Wordsworth
is too tame for the Chippeway" (August 18; PJ 1:321). This frustration
with the inability of "the white man's poetry" to celebrate the "sterner
savager" characteristics of nonhuman nature serves as a major contributor to Thoreau's ultimate abandonment of poetry. As Witherell puts it,
Thoreau was "surprised to find that so little of the poetry he had imagined to be great was actually inspiring to him, and . . . this failure under-
mined his own sense of poetic vocation."[5]

While Thoreau was experiencing these doubts concerning poetry, the
genre itself — especially poetry dealing with the natural world — was
also undergoing a significant revolution. For centuries, what had loosely
been termed "nature poetry" had dominated English literature. From
Beowulf to Blake, much of the literature produced by English-speaking
writers contained heavy doses of natural subject matter and imagery. Yet
as Robert Langbaum has pointed out, by the latter part of the nineteenth
century and the early part of the twentieth, what was considered an
overly romantic nature poetry had lost credibility, largely as a result
of nineteenth-century science and the drastic changes in the way West-
erners envisioned themselves and the world around them. Darwinian
evolutionary theory and modern geology would hardly allow readers to

accept a poem that unselfconsciously anthropomorphized nonhuman nature or celebrated nature's intentional benevolence toward humans. By the early part of the twentieth century, therefore, anything sounding like the old romantic nature poetry was rarely written, and if it was, it was even more rarely taken seriously.[6]

However, in response (and opposition) to this older, romantic vision of nature, a new form of nature poetry began to emerge, produced primarily by such antiromantics as Frost, Jeffers, Stevens, Moore, Williams. And in the latter half of the century, proceeding out of these modern poetic voices, a whole new generation of poets has taken up the theme of nature in a manner quite different from that of Wordsworth and Longfellow. In the work of these contemporary poets — writers like Gary Snyder, Mary Oliver, Wendell Berry, Denise Levertov, W. S. Merwin, Joy Harjo, Pattiann Rogers, A. R. Ammons, Leslie Marmon Silko (the list goes on and on) — we get a perspective on the human/nonhuman relationship that delineates them from their nature poetry ancestors and marks them as what I will call "ecological poets."

Consider, for instance, Snyder's "Front Lines":

> The edge of the cancer
> Swells against the hill — we feel
>   a foul breeze —
> And it sinks back down.
> The deer winter here
> A chainsaw growls in the gorge.
>
> Ten wet days and the log trucks stop,
> The trees breathe.
> Sunday the 4-wheel jeep of the
> Realty Company brings in
> Landseekers, lookers, they say
> To the land,
> Spread your legs.
>
> The jets crack sound overhead, it's OK
>   here;
> Every pulse of the rot at the heart
> In the sick fat veins of Amerika
> Pushes the edge up closer —
>
> A bulldozer grinding and slobbering
> Sideslipping and belching on top of

The skinned-up bodies of still-live bushes
In the pay of a man
From town.

Behind is a forest that goes to the Arctic
And a desert that still belongs to the
　　　Piute
And here we must draw
Our line.[7]

On coming across poems like this one, from Snyder's Pulitzer Prize–
winning *Turtle Island*, we intuitively perceive, whether we have considered the reason or not, that we are reading a new and distinct type of
nature poetry. While it retains many traditional romantic conventions
and perspectives — the reference to the wintering deer, a frustration
with the technology-produced human/nonhuman division, a gaze toward nonhuman nature as refuge from encroaching civilization — the
poem in several ways is markedly different from that produced by earlier
nature poets. For one thing, within the poet's voice a desperation can be
heard, an intense dread of the disaster looming if we neglect to draw
"Our line" and resist the edge of the cancer encroaching into what is
left of the wild. In addition, there is the sympathetic reference to indigenous peoples, the Piute, emblematic (in the poem) of an earlier time
when humans and nonhumans existed in a more interdependent,
symbiotic relationship. Perhaps the most glaring difference is the political
rhetoric employing current inflammatory "ecospeak," as in Snyder's
militaristic title, his analog pointing to the rape of the land, his classifi-
cation of the developers as a "cancer," and his metaphoric equation of
American culture with a heart attack destroying the health of the ecological body.[8] While in many ways "Front Lines" and other ecological
poems clearly fall in line with such canonical nature lyrics as "Contemplations," "Intimations of Immortality," and "Ode to a Nightingale,"
they just as clearly take visible steps beyond that tradition, steps that are
strikingly similar to the ones Thoreau took in his prose writings (as I will
discuss below).

Compare, for instance, the way the clearing of a forest is treated by
two U.S. nature poets from different eras, Walt Whitman and W. S. Merwin. In his "Song of the Redwood Tree," Whitman's speaker, walking
through a "northern coast" forest, hears amid the "crackling blows of
axes sounding musically driven by strong arms," "the mighty tree its
death-chant chanting":

> *Farewell my brethren,*
> *Farewell O earth and sky, farewell ye neighboring waters,*
> *My time has ended, my term has come.*

The speaker explains that even though the "choppers" and the "quick-ear'd teamsters and chain and jack-screw men heard not," "in my soul I plainly heard" the message, which was a "chant not of the past only but the future." The redwood's chant continues:

> *You untold life of me,*
>
> . . . . .
>
> *O the great patient rugged joys, my soul's strong joys*
> *unreck'd by man,*
> *(For know I bear the soul befitting me, I too have*
> *consciousness, identity,*
> *And all the rocks and mountains have, and all the earth,)*
> *Joys of the life befitting me and brothers mine,*
> *Our time, our term has come.*

These lines seem to be setting up their audience for a lesson in ecology, in wise stewardship of the earth, or at least in recognizing the dangers of regarding nonhuman nature as nothing more than inanimate natural resources. In fact, up to this point in the poem, with its espousal of ecological interconnection and its speculation on how sentient nonhuman nature may actually be "unreck'd by man," the poem sounds as if it could easily make the shortlist for quotes likely to appear on a Sierra Club fund-raising letter. In many ways, it sounds like it could have been produced by Harjo or some other American Indian poet.

But the lines that follow the redwood's mystical and ecological pronouncement alter the poem dramatically:

> *Nor yield we mournfully majestic brothers,*
> *We who have grandly fill'd our time;*
> *With Nature's calm content, with tacit huge delight,*
> *We welcome what we have wrought for through the past,*
> *And leave the field for them.*
> *For them predicted long,*
> *For a superber race, they too to grandly fill their time,*
> *For them we abdicate, in them ourselves ye forest kings.*

Thus the poem turns from what sounds like an environmental-movement manifesto to a propagandistic justification for the cutting down of centuries-old redwoods, which are portrayed as willingly yielding to humanity, abdicating their thrones so that a "superber race" can "grandly fill their time."

Now compare Whitman's treatment of the topic with Merwin's in "The Last One," a poem that also narrates the cutting down of a forest but speaks out of a much different vision of the world. The opening lines set the tone for the entire poem as they describe the humans who approach the forest:

Well they'd made up their minds to be everywhere because why not.
Everywhere was theirs because they thought so.
They with two leaves they whom the birds despise.
In the middle of stones they made up their minds. They started to cut.

Well they cut everything because why not.
Everything was theirs because they thought so.

This humanity is much different from that for whom the trees so willingly and lovingly abdicate their thrones in Whitman's "song"; here, rather than a "superber race," humans — "they whom the birds despise" — are portrayed as antagonists, even tormentors, of the natural world.

As the poem continues, we notice that, like in Whitman's poem, human and nonhuman nature interact. But instead of offering a benign natural world that cares for the advancement of the human race, Merwin's parable attempts to render the consequences we can expect from cutting down "the last one," the final tree in the forest (which is emblematic of numerous natural "resources," myopically wasted and destroyed). As the final tree falls and the loggers haul it away, its shadow remains. The men try to remove the shadow by covering it up, by shining lights on it, by building a fire on its roots, by pouring stones into it. But the shadow remains and begins to grow. It eventually begins to take over all with which it comes into contact:

It went on growing it grew onto the land.
They started to scrape the shadow with machines.
When it touched the machines it stayed on them.
They started to beat the shadow with sticks.
Where it touched the sticks it stayed on them.
They started to beat the shadow with hands.
Where it touched the hands it stayed on them.

Eventually, the shadow covers everything within reach, and an ambiguous conclusion tells us that some people were able to escape and that these were "The lucky ones with their shadows."[9]

What becomes clear in the examination of these two poems is that while both "Song of the Redwood Tree" and "The Last One" can technically be labeled "nature poems," their approach to nature is drastically different. One endorses the cutting of trees by giving them a voice that not only absolves but even celebrates humanity for its actions; the other takes as its starting point a condemnation of humanity for the same deeds, then spends the majority of the poem rendering the disastrous consequences. While I find the rhetoric of Merwin's narrative much more persuasive than that of Whitman's, my argument here is not that one poem is a better or worse nature poem, but that the visions offered in the poems are different, and extremely different at that. A poet working from an ecological perspective on the world would not be able to present the poem as Whitman has; an ecological poet, in order to continue to write poems of nature, necessarily must alter his or her poetics.

We can perform the same exercise on any number of different canonical nature poems. Recall, for example, Wordsworth's "Nutting." From a synopsis of the poem, which ends with the "sense of pain" the narrator experiences as a result of his youthful "ravage" of the silent bower, one could easily mistake the lyric for a contemporary environmentalist poem. But the closing line of the poem leaves no uncertainty as to the source of the narrator's guilt: "there is a Spirit in the woods" that has been disturbed. In other words, the speaker has realized that his primary transgression has been committed against some sort of transcendent essence, rather than against the specific and physical natural entities he has ravaged.

Wordsworth's position is similar to Anne Bradstreet's, who in "Contemplations" praises the natural world for its beauty but cannot, according to her worldview, leave it there. Rather, she must assert that "If so much excellence abide below, / How excellent is He that dwells on high." She marvels at the oak, at the thousand winters it has seen, then says that even these centuries "eternity doth scorn." Then addressing the sun after describing its beauty, power, and glory, she remarks, "How full of glory then must thy Creator be, / Who gave this bright light luster unto thee?"

As a contrast, consider Wendell Berry's "Planting Trees," which concludes with these lines:

> Let me desire and wish well the life
> these trees may live when I
> no longer rise in the mornings
> to be pleased by the green of them

shining, and their shadows on the ground,
and the sound of the wind in them.[10]

Here we notice an important distinction between Berry's lyric and the other two poems. Berry — who himself would probably ascribe to the notion that "there is a Spirit in the woods" and allow that it is related to the excellence of "He that dwells on high" — here emphasizes the inherent value of the trees *in and of themselves*, rather than as mere manifestations of a deity that created and permeates them. In other words, whereas Berry values the trees for their own sake, Wordsworth's narrator experiences guilt, less for destroying the brush and trees that make up the bower than for disturbing the spirit in the grove, and Bradstreet praises the beauty of the nonhuman world around her, but only as a manifestation of the glory of God. Again, the claim I want to make here has little to do with the quality of the poems in question, but rather with the explicit differences among their perspectives. For Berry's fervor to "wish well the life / these trees may live" is very different from the somewhat typical romantic desire that, as stated by Shelley, was to "always seek in what I see, the likeness of something beyond the present and tangible object."[11] Berry's outlook is much more akin to Thoreau's, who (as Merwin describes him) views the natural world and sees it as "alive, completely alive, not a detail in a piece of rhetoric. And he leaves open what its significance is. He realizes that the intensity with which he's able to see it *is* its significance."[12]

Differences such as these appear time and again in ecological poetry, as writers attempt to address contemporary issues and concerns that traditional nature poets have either been unaware of or have not been forced to deal with. I tentatively define ecological poetry, therefore, as a subset of nature poetry that, while adhering to many of the traditions of the mode, also takes on distinctly contemporary problems and issues, thus resulting in a version of nature poetry generally marked by three primary characteristics. The first is an emphasis on maintaining an ecocentric perspective that recognizes the interdependent nature of the world;[13] such a perspective leads to a devotion to specific places and to the land itself, along with those creatures that share it with humanity. This interconnection is part of what Black Elk called "the sacred hoop" that pulls all things into relationship, and it can be found throughout ecological poetry. Levertov's "Web," for example, demonstrates this interconnection, ostensibly describing the literal web of a spider, but pointing also to what Levertov calls the "*great web*":

Intricate and untraceable
weaving and interweaving,
dark strand with light:

designed, beyond
all spiderly contrivance,
to link, not to entrap:

elation, grief, joy, contrition, entwined;
shaking, changing,
    forever
     forming,
      transforming:

all praise,
  all praise to the
  great web.[14]

The "great web" here is the one that, "beyond / all spiderly contrivance," moves through and connects all people and things, both human and nonhuman. Levertov's web represents what Mohawk poet Peter Blue Cloud calls "the allness of the creation,"[15] and it points toward the same lesson Harjo offers in "Remember," which concludes with its speaker imploring her audience to

Remember you are all people and all people
are you.
Remember you are this universe and this
universe is you.
Remember all is in motion, is growing, is you.
Remember language comes from this.
Remember the dance language is, that life is.
Remember.[16]

For ecological poets, the world is a community made up of interdependent and interrelated subjects.

This awareness of the world as a community tends to produce the second attribute of ecological poetry, an imperative toward humility in relationships with both human and nonhuman nature. You won't hear ecological poets endorsing Emerson's statement that "Every rational creature has all nature for his dowry and estate. It is his, if he will." Instead, ecological poets are more likely to echo Frost's reminder of how little control we actually have over the wildness of nature: "Something there is that doesn't love a wall." So instead of what Albert Gelpi describes as romanticism's inherent "aggrandizement of the individual ego,"[17] we read a Jeffers poem that depicts extravagant royal tombs, then concludes with the lines, "Imagine what delusions of grandeur, / What suspicion-agonized eyes, what jellies of arrogance and terror / This earth has absorbed" ("Iona: The Graves of Kings").[18] We see Donald Hall, in "An American in an Essex Village," move from a description of a temple's colossal spires, reaching higher than a beech tree, to a recognition that, despite the human pride displayed in the architecture, "the death-watch beetle hollows / six-hundred-year-old / beams."[19] And we hear Blue Cloud define stars as "fire vessels / the universe happening / regardless of man" ("fire/rain").[20]

Related to this humility is the third characteristic of ecological poetry, an intense skepticism concerning hyperrationality, a skepticism that usually leads to a condemnation of an overtechnologized modern world and a warning concerning the very real potential for ecological catastrophe. The opening section of Harjo's *She Had Some Horses*, for example, criticizes time and again the effects of what Abbey dubs modern "syphilization." In "What Music," Harjo grieves with a mother whose sons are living "in another language / in Los Angeles / with their wives";[21] in another poem the poet mourns for those in the cities who are "learning not to hear the ground as it spins around / beneath them" ("For Alva Benson, and For Those Who Have Learned to Speak").[22] Similarly, Jeffers likens modern humanity, with its poor yet immeasurably destructive "wisdom," to "Acteon who saw the goddess naked among leaves and his hounds tore him. / A little knowledge, a pebble from the shingle, / A drop from the oceans." Jeffers concludes the poem with a poignant rhetorical question: "who would have dreamed this infinitely little too much?" ("Science").[23] Snyder is more direct in his reproach, condemning Japan, that "once-great Buddhist nation," for "quibbl[ing] for words on / what kinds of whales they can kill," and "dribbl[ing] methyl mercury / like gonorrhea / in the sea" ("Mother Earth: Her Whales").[24]

Readers familiar with Thoreau will notice the similarities between these characteristics of ecological poetry — ecocentrism, an appreciation of wildness, and a skepticism toward hyperrationality and its resultant overreliance on technology — and the principles that dominate *Walden* and the majority of the Thoreau canon. The essence of my argument is that this similarity is no coincidence. I am not arguing that Thoreau *produced* or *caused* nature poetry's shift from a romantic to a more ecological vision, for of course many complex and interrelated factors have contributed to this transformation.[25] Rather, my point is that just as Thoreau voiced his displeasure with "white man's poetry" and thus offered his prose writings in response, so nature poetry has evolved beyond its romantic ancestry toward a more ecological poetry that attempts to address contemporary environmental issues and concerns and to portray faithfully the wildness of the natural world.

It seems significant that one hundred and fifty years after Thoreau began to give up on poetry, we are only now, within the last couple of decades, producing a significant body of poetic work that takes into account the issues that so concerned him. The cause for this delay is uncertain. Perhaps he was right to doubt "the vigor of poetry as opposed to prose"; or perhaps poetry's evolution, like our society's mindset, is slow to catch up to his vision. But whatever the reason, poets are now attempting to produce work that, among other things, offers what Thoreau called "the tonic of wildness." Whether or not he would say that these poets have "seen the west side of any mountain" is open to question; but the effort is at least being made, as ecological poets attempt to view the mountain "from the wilderness as well as the village."

NOTES

1. Witherell, "Thoreau's Watershed Season as a Poet," 59. My reading of Thoreau's poetry is heavily indebted to Witherell's scholarship.

2. Qtd. in Carl Bode's introduction to *Collected Poems of Henry Thoreau*, xi.

3. This and subsequent references to Thoreau's Journal are from *Journal, Vol. 1: 1837–1844*, which will be cited in this chapter as *PJ* 1.

4. Bode, "Introduction," 216.

5. Witherell, "Thoreau's Watershed Season as a Poet," 60.

6. Langbaum, "New Nature Poetry."

7. Snyder, *Turtle Island*, 32.

8. The phrase "ecospeak" comes from *Ecospeak*, ed. Killingworth and Palmer.

9. Merwin, *The Second Four Books of Poems*, 86–88.

10. Berry, *Collected Poems*, 155.

11. Qtd. in Abrams, introduction to the Romantic Period, in *Norton Anthology of English Literature*, 8.

12. Folsom and Nelson, "'Fact Has Two Faces,'" 34.

13. I use the term "ecocentric" here to describe a worldview that, in contrast to an egocentric or anthropocentric perspective, views the earth as an intersubjective community and values its many diverse (human and nonhuman) members.

14. Levertov, *The Life Around Us*, 17.

15. This line appears in Blue Cloud's "voice play" entitled "For Rattlesnake: a dialogue of creatures," from *The Remembered Earth*, 23.

16. Harjo, *She Had Some Horses*, 40.

17. Gelpi, *Coherent Splendor*, 518.

18. Jeffers, *Selected Poems*, 52.

19. Hall, *Roof of Tiger Lilies*, 24.

20. Blue Cloud, "For Rattlesnake," 20.

21. Harjo, *She Had Some Horses*, 16.

22. Ibid., 8.

23. Jeffers, *Selected Poems*, 39.

24. Snyder, *Turtle Island*, 82. I realize that this distrust of hyperrationality, like the other characteristics, is not completely absent in the work of traditional romantics, whose work also displays an intense mistrust of Enlightenment thinking. Clearly, however, the perspective offered in these poems is different; the original romantic skepticism has risen at the close of the twentieth century to a level never before seen, primarily because we have the "benefit" of a historical perspective that includes such intellect-dependent disasters as Nazism, Hiroshima, and Chernobyl.

25. My project here has more to do with analogy than causality. If pressed, I would posit both that Thoreau has directly influenced contemporary nature poets — Merwin has said that he keeps *Walden* "in the john" for ongoing reading — and that Thoreau has influenced the modern ecological and environmental movements and has therefore indirectly influenced ecological poetry.

III. SOCIALLY CONSTRUCTING PLACE

Culture and Nature

Ten Ways of Seeing Landscapes
in *Walden* and Beyond

JAMES G. McGRATH

The very first vote I cast after being elected to the Missoula City Council in 1995 was to spend $2 million to purchase 1,600 acres of hillside bordering the city to preserve it as open space. An open space bond had passed by a large margin, and the purchase had widespread support. A year later, however, when the city proposed closing access to the land during winter months in order to protect elk, we saw that support splinter. Wildlife advocates, including state and federal authorities, supported the closure. Recreation advocates, on the other hand, used to hiking, riding, and sledding on the hill, bristled at the irony of "closing" access to public "open" space. Clearly the broad support for acquiring the land came from groups of people who held substantially different values about why the city should own it.

In 1976, D. W. Meinig wrote in his landmark essay, "The Beholding Eye: Ten Versions of the Same Scene": "Even though we gather together and look in the same direction at the same instant we will not — we cannot — see the same landscape. We may certainly agree that we all see the same elements — houses, roads, trees, hills — in terms of such denotations as number, form, dimension, and color, but such facts take on meaning only through association; they must be fitted together according to some coherent body of ideas."[1] He set forth ten different ways people see landscapes (acknowledging that there are more): landscape as Nature, Habitat, Artifact, System, Problem, Wealth, Ideology, History, Place, and Aesthetic.

A cultural geographer, Meinig posits the ten ways of seeing as the various American cultural constructs people use to perceive (or even imagine) places. We can find these ways strongly present in our culture and our nature writing. Obviously, nature writing and these cultural assumptions have a dynamic interaction, with important writers or perspectives having strong cultural influence on the one hand, and widely held cultural assumptions pervasively influencing writers on the other.

In *Walden*, Henry David Thoreau makes use at various times of most of these cultural assumptions. It is well understood that he is a founder of American environmental writing, and therefore Thoreau develops most of the ways our culture approaches landscapes. In fact, in order to immerse himself thoroughly in his place, he sets out methodically to explore Walden Pond from as many "ways of seeing" as he can conceive.

Thoreau's multiple approaches are his deliberate strategy to be thorough. He writes in his Journal, "It is wise to write on many subjects to try many themes that so you may find the right & inspiring one. . . . There are innumerable avenues to a perception of the truth. . . . Probe the universe in a myriad points. Be avaricious of these impulses. You must try a thousand themes before you find the right one."[2] These multiple viewpoints are, rather than another example of his self-contradictions, a technique for resolving them. Further, his environmental vision falls short of contemporary views to the degree that he cannot conceive of several ways of seeing that emerge after his time.

The Ways in *Walden*

One of the ways of seeing that Meinig articulates is landscape as place. This involves seeing that "every landscape is a locality, an individual piece in the infinitely varied mosaic of the earth. . . . Such a viewer attempts to penetrate common generalizations to appreciate the unique flavor of whatever he encounters" (53–54). Meinig uses the example of serious travel writers, who understand that "one may discover an implicit ideology that the individuality of places is a fundamental characteristic of subtle and immense importance to life on earth, that all human events *take place*, all problems are anchored in place, and ultimately can only be understood in such terms" (54).

Fundamentally, the entire project of *Walden* is to present it as a place. Thoreau best zeros in on that in the final passage of "Where I Lived, and What I Lived For," wherein he declares his intent to burrow into that one location with his mind to best come to know it: "here I will begin to mine."[3]

In his attempt to depict the place, Walden, and its meaning, Thoreau chooses to view it from as many ways of seeing as he can imagine — even those he dislikes or outright opposes. Only by leaving out none can he truly know (and let the reader know) Walden. In other words, his self-contradictions were part of a strategy, more like viewing an object from the north at one time and later from the south.

Nature

Meinig describes those who see landscape as nature in the following way: "For them all the works of man are paltry in comparison with nature, which is primary, fundamental, dominant, enduring. . . . Such a viewer is ever tempted in his mind's eye to remove man from the scene, to restore nature to her pristine condition, to reclothe the hills with the primeval forest, clear off the settlements, heal the wounds and mend the natural fabric — to imagine what the area is *really* like. It is an old view which separates man and nature. Ideologically it had its greatest vogue in eighteenth century Romanticism, in that longing for wilderness, in the view of nature as pure, fine, good, truly beautiful" (47–48). This is one of the most common ways of seeing landscapes used by environmental writers, from Thoreau on down to the present. (I've never had difficulty explaining this one to undergraduates.)

Clearly, Thoreau first and foremost sees landscape as Nature. Far and above it is his most frequent way of seeing landscape, and presumably his dominant way. For instance, the entire chapters "Solitude" and "The Ponds" approach landscape from this perspective. This is most clearly represented in his valuing of isolation — that his adventures into the woods isolate him from the village. He frequently mentions nature being profaned (e.g., by himself [197] or by boats [199]), and he states, "I discovered that my house actually had its site in such a withdrawn, but forever new and unprofaned, part of the universe" (88). Other typical expressions from this perspective include "No yard! but unfenced nature reaching up to your very sills" (128) and "There are few traces of man's hand to be seen. The water laves the shore as it did a thousand years ago" (186). He writes of nature's power exceeding man's: "Nature continually repairs; no storms, no dust, can dim its surface ever fresh" (188).

In the passage which refers to the "tonic of the wild," he goes on: "At the same time that we are earnest to explore and learn all things, we require that all things be mysterious and unexplorable, that land and sea be infinitely wild, unsurveyed and unfathomed by us because unfathomable. We can never get enough of nature" (317–18).

Obviously, Thoreau frequently approaches landscape as Nature, preferring untrammeled, isolated, and wild landscapes. Often this view for him is enmeshed in a version of romanticism which sees landscapes as both religious or mythological and aesthetic. His largest legacy — the way most readers recall him — is as the first and most representative writer in this vein. He did not approach Walden from this way of seeing alone, however.

Wealth

Seeing landscape as wealth, or, as Meinig puts it, to "look upon every scene with the eyes of an appraiser" (51), is one we all too easily understand — and one too easily dismissed by environmental and other writers as evil. While that opinion goes back much further than Thoreau — he was writing from a long tradition — our present articulation of that opinion does have roots in *Walden*. Meinig notes that, "Like that of science, it is a penetrating view which looks beyond the facade to peer within and to organize what it finds in abstractions" (51). Thoreau also wants to peer within and organize with abstractions. He comments, "I perceive that we inhabitants of New England live this mean life that we do because our vision does not penetrate the surface of things" (96).[4]

Because, as Meinig notes, "This view of landscape as wealth is of course strongly-rooted in American ideology and reflective of our cultural values" (52), Thoreau has to consider landscape as wealth, if only to dismiss it, because he knows his readers will, at least sometimes, see landscapes in this way. He comments, "Economy is a subject which admits of being treated with levity, but cannot so be disposed of" (29). He even selects as his first chapter "Economy." It is for the most part an ancient opponent to his preference for "Nature" and the ideology of purity in nature.

He takes up the task of seeing Walden as wealth in three ways. First, he treats nature as wealth ironically: in several places, for example, he lists ridiculously detailed accounts of his cash earnings down to the halfpenny. Also, in "Where I Lived, and What I Lived For" he spends some time pretending to buy farms. This humorous narrative does allow for his sense of the somewhat legitimate or at any rate normal human practice — "At a certain season of our life we are accustomed to consider every spot as a possible site of a house" (81) — which he himself carries out, selecting a site and building a house and farming.

His second technique, sprinkled throughout, is to lambast avarice, to wail against the Philistines so to speak, as in his tirade on commerce in "Sounds" and against the avaricious ice-cutters in "The Pond in Winter," and even against the greedy farmers at the end of "The Bean Field." In many ways, for Thoreau and many environmentalists since, seeing land-scape as wealth is the exact opposite of an environmental or positive viewpoint, so in that sense it is actually a part of seeing landscape as nature (or as aesthetic or other positive ways of seeing). So, in "Baker Farm," after a disturbing visit to an impoverished Irish family, Thoreau runs down to the pond to fish and advises the reader to "Grow wild according to thy nature, like these sedges and brakes, which will never become English hay. Let the thunder rumble; what if it threaten ruin to farmers' crops? that is not its errand to thee" (207). Here his prefer-ence for nature leads him to utter disregard of human economy, false or otherwise.

His third approach to landscape as wealth, however, is a positive one. He describes an alternative vision of value, of true wealth, which includes spiritual purity, simplicity, leisure, and so on. He states that Walden is a good place for business (of that sort) (21). And at the end of his accounts for house building in "Economy," he adds that he has "on the other hand, beside the leisure and independence and health thus secured, a comfortable house for me as long as I choose to occupy it" (60). In that sense, he does approach Walden as a source of wealth.

Aesthetic

Meinig describes seeing landscape as aesthetic as the "subordination of any interest in the identity and function of specific features to a pre-occupation with their artistic qualities" (54). He says, "The very idea of landscape as scenery is a surprisingly late development in Western cul-ture, requiring as it does a special conscious detachment by the observer. Within the realm of landscape painting we will find examples which ex-press many of the views of landscape discussed" (54). Examples occur in writing as well, as it is a conscious, reflective art form. Meinig notes fur-ther, "This too is a penetrating view. It seeks a meaning which is not explicit in the ordinary forms. It rests upon the belief that there is some thing close to the essence, to beauty and truth, in the landscape" (54).

Obviously, this idea had developed by Thoreau's time. Thoreau breaks into aesthetic description often throughout *Walden*. Sometimes it is an example of romantic sensibility, as in parts of "Spring" (e.g., 312) and in his description of the pickerel: "Ah, the pickerel of Walden! when I see them lying on the ice . . . I am always surprised by their rare beauty . . . dazzling and transcendent beauty. . . . They are not green like the pines, nor gray like the stones, nor blue like the sky; but they have, to my eyes, if possible, yet rarer colors, like flowers and precious stones, as if they were the pearls, the animalized *nuclei* or crystals of the Walden water." Truly seeing them as something close to the essence (as Meinig calls it), Thoreau adds that they are "small Waldens . . . Waldenses" (284).

Usually, these passages emerge in the midst of other ways of seeing, particularly as "nature" and in his scientific descriptions. When initially describing the pond in "Where I Lived, and What I Lived For," he uses the terms "pleasing vista" to refer to peaks that are "true blue coins," and describes the pond as smooth and "full of light" as if he were a painter eyeing the landscape. Notably, that vista results from "where the wood had been recently cut off" (86–87). Later he describes the pond in "The Ponds": "The forest has never so good a setting, nor is so distinctly beautiful, as when seen from the middle of a small lake amid hills which rise from the water's edge; for the water in which it is reflected not only makes the best foreground in such a case, but, with its winding shore, the most natural and agreeable boundary to it. There is no rawness nor imperfection in its edge there, as where the axe has cleared a part, or a cultivated field abuts on it" (185–86). So in one place, hills cut of timber are pleasing, and in another they are not, based not on a respect for natural values but because of the way they look.

History

Another complex but more generally understood way of seeing is landscape as history. Meinig says, "To such a viewer all that lies before his eyes is a complex cumulative record of the work of nature and man in this particular place. In its most inclusive form it sends the mind back through the written record and deep into natural history and geology. . . . The principal organizing system is chronology" (52).

Thoreau realizes that history as a way of seeing is quite common and that he must include it if he is to give his full picture of Walden, though in general he is not much interested in this viewpoint in *Walden* and does not concentrate on it. He often adds historic information to chapters or passages describing other matters. For example, in "The Ponds" he notes the various measured water levels over several years. Later, he launches into a historical anecdote about the yellow pine in White Pond.

His chapter "Former Inhabitants" is his most thorough attempt at the history of his environs. But it is a peculiar history. Whereas many narratives would begin with history (Celia Thaxter's *Among the Isles of Shoals*, for example),[5] Thoreau waits until wintertime, as if he has time for it only then. In fact, he specifically says this history is instead of or in place of human society (256). He prefers a scientific observation in which chronology is an adjunct, as he is doing in "The Ponds." Similarly, he inserts a little hunting history into his description of winter animals, even after his dissertation against eating meat in "Brute Neighbors" — again placing history as a wintertime pursuit.

Meinig notes of seeing landscape as history: "This can be a view of landscape as process, but with a different emphasis from that of the scientist. Where the latter sees an association of classes of things being affected by generalized processes to form a general pattern of predictable events, the historian sees the particular cumulative effects of processes working upon the particular elements of this locality" (53). Thoreau clearly is more the scientist than the historian in *Walden*. Even more, he is a philosopher, asking, "What at such a time are histories, chronologies, traditions and all written revelations?" (310). He is interested in direct and immediate revelation, not written accounts from and of the past.

Habitat

One of the ways of seeing that is more specifically environmental is seeing landscape as habitat. "What we see before us is man continuously working at a viable relationship with nature, adapting to major features, altering in productive ways, creating resources out of nature's materials; in short, man domesticating the earth. . . . Every landscape is therefore basically a blend of man and nature. . . . It is the ideology of the harmony of man and nature, of earth as the garden of mankind, of man as the steward, the caretaker, the cultivator" (48). Importantly, each of these ways of seeing represents a range of views, intensities, and so on, such that "habitat," for instance, can be domestication at one end and cohabitation at the other. Meinig notes that "It lurks in various disguises within much of the recent literature on ecology and environment" (48).

We expect to encounter ways of seeing we consider environmental in Thoreau's writing, such as seeking harmonious relationship with the land. In "Former Inhabitants" (suggestively titled), Thoreau says of older farmers: "Might not the basket, stable-broom, mat-making, corn-parching, linen-spinning, and pottery business have thrived here, making the wilderness to blossom like the rose, and a numerous posterity have inherited the land of their fathers? The sterile soil would at least have been proof against a lowland degeneracy. Alas! how little does the memory of these human inhabitants enhance the beauty of the landscape! Again, perhaps, Nature will try, with me for a first settler, and my house raised last spring to be the oldest in the hamlet" (264). This passage is startlingly not "removing man from the scene," as Meinig describes the perspective of landscape as nature.

Significantly, Thoreau homesteads: builds a house and begins farming. His efforts are at odds with his contemporaries in that he is trying to "live lightly" and be more environmentally friendly in those practices. His house is very environmentally friendly, using recycled materials and local resources (246). But living "close to nature" mostly involves Thoreau adapting to it rather than domesticating it. For example, in "Winter Animals," local fauna live under his house. Metaphorically "domesticated" because they inhabit a human structure, they really make Thoreau's house seem wilder.

At the beginning of "Housewarming," he evokes the Native American practices of inhabiting the land, describing berrypicking and finding "the potato of the aborigines," which he says "seemed like a faint promise of Nature to rear her own children and feed them simply here at some future period" — in other words, that humans could return to eating wild rather than domesticated plants for subsistence. He concludes that if cultivation were to stop and "wild nature" left to reign, "the tender and luxurious [always a negative term for Thoreau] English grains will probably disappear before a myriad of foes" and the "now almost extinct" tuber will revive (239). This is what Meinig refers to when he comments that the concept of habitat "lurks in various disguises within much of the recent literature on ecology and environment." However, most of that literature is contemporary: Thoreau does not make extensive use of this way of seeing.

System

Meinig describes seeing landscape as system in this way: "The land, the trees, roads, buildings, and man are regarded not as individual objects, ensembles of varied elements, or classes of phenomena, but as surficial clues of underlying processes" (49), such as hydrology, energy flows, and so on. "Houses, garages, barns, offices, stores, factories are all 'service stations' and 'transformers,' and may be regarded as crude, imperfect, outward expressions of abstract social and economic systems.... Such a view is wholly the product of science, a means of looking inside matter to understand things not apparent to the naked untrained eye," Meinig notes. "It is an ideology that implies a faith in man as essentially omniscient" (49).

For the most part, Thoreau does not make use of "system" as a way of seeing. He does not hold that humans are essentially omniscient, and he certainly does not view landscapes as "service stations." However, Meinig equates systems thinking with a scientific viewpoint overall, leaving out the "individual objects, ensembles of varied elements, or classes of phenomena" that constitute scientific description in natural history, biology, and zoology. Thoreau finds quite appealing and useful the description of individual objects and classes of phenomena.

In passage after passage of description — and in many ways all of *Walden* is one large holographic portrait — Thoreau identifies, catalogs, measures, surveys, and in other ways uses scientific or objective techniques to describe things. In "Sounds" we get a complete list of the flora surrounding his house (113–14) — botany. In "The Bean Field" we get agronomy (163). In "The Village" he does the village as zoology. In "The Ponds" he details every aspect, size, shape, color, the cycle of rising and falling water, and the temperature, as well as comparing Walden to other ponds. In fact, in "The Ponds," there is a systematic description of ponds, which includes history, myths, or tales — that is, anthropology. In "Housewarming" we get the longitudinal study of freeze dates, paralleled in "Spring" by thaw dates (303) and ranges of water temperatures (299). We get a catalog of animals in "Winter Animals." In "The Pond in Winter" we get geology, as well as the development of a formula for measuring lakes (288–91) — a truly scientific project of formulating hypotheses and laws. And so on.

He often compares scientific observation with old wives' tales and speculation, as in the case of the stones surrounding Walden. He notes that "My townsmen have all heard the tradition" of one story, another story "has been conjectured," and "this Indian fable" is a third version of how they came to be. Thoreau follows with a speculation based on simple and clear observation (182–83). He observes that "The surrounding hills are remarkably full of the same kind of stones . . . and, moreover, there are most stones where the shore is most abrupt, so that, unfortunately, it is no longer a mystery to me. . . . one might suppose that it was called originally *Walled-in* Pond" (183). Obviously, this is part of Thoreau's philosophical strategy of "paring away" so that he can see "reality." But just as clearly, Thoreau himself likes to see landscape as a scientist would.

His science, however, predates the development of ecology, which is what Meinig means by "system." Thoreau's twentieth-century successors often use the ecological way of seeing. In *Walden*, however, Thoreau offers up a few instances that might be seen as heading in that direction. In

"The Pond in Winter," Thoreau says, "If we knew all the laws of Nature, we should need only one fact, or the description of one actual phenomenon, to infer all the particular results at that point" (291). This is not new thinking — Newton offered similar concepts — but it does eventually lead to ecological thinking. At some point, the Enlightenment project of cataloging all species for the great encyclopedia, combined with this approach to understanding the grammar of the world, especially after the theory of evolution emerges, will suggest the logic of linking together various observations into systems. It also "implies a faith in man as essentially omniscient."

Thoreau perhaps is beginning to think that way. At the end of "The Bean Field," in a passage intended to raise wilderness in value by leveling human cultivation as a value, he states, "We are wont to forget that the sun looks on our cultivated fields and on the prairie and forests without distinction. They all reflect and absorb his rays alike" (166). While he "sees" solar energy at work here, his main point is that the heavens care as much about wild plants as the plants we tend and hope are blessed.

In his famous railroad bank epiphany in "Spring," Thoreau uses language in strikingly modern terms. He observes sand and clay thawing and flowing down the embankment and describes the pattern it forms. He equates the sand with leaf, coral, lichen, lungs, leopard's paws, brains, and so on — all similar patterns, just as from the air, river drainages look like leaf or branch patterns. His desire to cross the boundaries between not only species but between organic and inorganic pushes his language further. Thus we get "sand foliage" as "an anticipation of the vegetable leaf" and etymology of the words "lobe," "leaves," "labor," and so on, leading to a comparison: the "feathers and wings of birds are still drier and thinner leaves." That is, we get a snapshot of the evolution of earth from volcanic primordial times to vegetation to birds and, by implication, to humans. His connections continue: "The very globe transcends and translates itself" and ice is seen to have leaves, while "the whole tree is but one leaf, and rivers are still vaster leaves whose pulp is intervening earth, and towns and cities are the ova of insects." The operation of solar energy causes the starting and stopping of the (at this point evolutionary) flow. Blood vessels, lightning, and fingers are all seen in this pattern. He realizes that "the sand organizes itself," which ultimately leads to, "Thus it seemed that this one hillside illustrated the principle of all the operations of Nature." He asks who "will decipher this hieroglyphic for us?" And that question leads to the further statement that "there is nothing inorganic." Finally, nearing a Gaian sensibility, he says, "The earth is not a mere fragment of dead history" for geologists, "but living poetry" (304–9).

A reader today can see the most modern of sciences in this passage. Particularly we see fractal geometry in the persistence of patterns across formations, and chaos theory in the unity of inorganic and organic in evolution and its self-organization and in the possibility that the earth itself is a living being. Through this one particular phenomenon, to paraphrase his earlier statement, he is able to infer all by recognizing the pattern — just as contemporary scientists do using computers, advanced mathematics, and systems thinking. But the similarity to chaos theory and fractals does not equate to ecological thinking. As Valentine Coverly, the mathematician in Tom Stoppard's *Arcadia* might say, he doesn't have the maths. Ecology had not been invented yet, and it is only in recent years, after the computerization of technology, that these sorts of analyses can be performed, that a human faith in actually understanding how these relationships operate simultaneously emerges within that faith's own critique.

Thoreau is not revealing or forecasting the late twentieth century. He draws a clear picture in which we can see, looking backward from the present, a system. However, he does not share our view. A sweeping description of such an inference is well within his contemporary, more static, cultural framework. While seeing at last beneath the surface of things, he sees that underneathness is not so much a system as a unity. He does *glimpse* the system: what he sees is the trace of a process, and that process is a system at work. In any case, this particular insight is confined to the thawing earth — "This is the frost coming out of the ground," he says (308). He goes on past this far from final passage to describe the oncoming spring in more religious and ethical analogies: "the creation of the Cosmos out of Chaos" might seem like negative entropy, but "the realization of the Golden Age" (313) is more his real perspective.

After Thoreau

The ways of seeing that Meinig lists which Thoreau fails to explore are notable. Although he writes in a very scientific way at points, as in "The Ponds," Thoreau does not see landscape as a system in the contemporary ecological sense. Nor does he use landscape as problem — the environ mental planner or designer's perspective — or as artifact. The former view was emerging in landscape architecture around that time, but the latter is a twentieth-century development.

The term "ecology" was coined in 1866, years after *Walden*, but it is not really until the mid-twentieth century that we see the full flowering of ecology or the systems approach to seeing landscapes. In the late 1940s, two writers reached popularity writing from this perspective: in fiction, John Steinbeck (*Cannery Row*), and in nonfiction, Aldo Leopold. In fact, to follow my distinction between natural history and systems thinking, as Thoreau inaugurates American environmental writing overall, Leopold inaugurates ecological writing.

Another development after *Walden* was the emergence and intensification of the ways of seeing landscape as problem and as artifact. Humans have always intervened in their environment, but after industrialization the extent of impact increased exponentially. Around the time of Thoreau, two important figures emerge that exemplify those ways of seeing: Frederick Law Olmsted and George Perkins Marsh.

Meinig explains that for those seeing landscape as problem, "every landscape evokes wrath and alarm, it is a mirror of the ills of our society and cries out for drastic change. Nevertheless, this view of landscape through the eyes of the social actionist may incorporate something from all these other views: it evokes a reverence for nature, a deeply felt concern for earth as habitat, and a conviction that we have the scientific ability to right these wrongs" (50). He refers to Rachel Carson; any number of modern writers fall into that category as well. Olmsted is an early example.

In 1857, Olmsted began work on New York City's Central Park. This launched a new approach to landscape: design. Meinig notes, "There is another set [who sees landscape as problem] which is not so much a shrill citizenry as an interrelated group of professions for whom every landscape is a *design problem*" (50). Olmsted was beginning to found landscape architecture as a profession in the United States shortly before Thoreau's death. Obviously, landscaping of large estates, for example, had a long history. But now as the United States became a more urbanized as well as industrialized landscape, the profession took on a specifically problem-solving approach. Olmsted saw nature as therapeutic, an important safety valve for urban workers. He advocated for places such as Yosemite as well as Central Park. As we advance into the twentieth century, environmental problem solving rises, and with it the proliferation of landscape architects and planners. We see writers like Ian McHarg, whose 1969 classic, *Design with Nature*, and whose distinguished teaching career founded a line of contemporary discourse that is quite broad. We see in *Walden* none at all. Thoreau was not an eco-reformer.

Meinig describes seeing the landscape as artifact in this way: "Such a person sees first of all and everywhere the mark of man in everything. . . . In this view it is idle sentiment to talk of man adapting to nature in modern America. . . . So comprehensive and powerful has been man's role in changing the face of the earth that the whole landscape has become an artifact" (48). It becomes more and more a viewpoint, however. "The twentieth-century concept of man as technocrat in charge of remolding the earth to suit his desires marks the more radical shift. It is concomitant with the growth in the pervasive power of the engineer to alter the physical earth and the biologist to alter organic life" (49).

That there are increasing environmental problems to be solved presumes there is an increasing awareness of human impact on nature. George Perkins Marsh's 1864 *Man and Nature* sets out for the first time the sense of "first of all and everywhere the mark of man in everything" — Meinig's description of seeing as artifact. Marsh himself writes, "But man is everywhere a disturbing agent. Wherever he plants his foot, the harmonies of nature are turned to discords."[6] Marsh's book (quite influential on Muir and John Burroughs) examines the human-caused changes in the environment, contrasting them with what he understood to be ecosystems in equilibrium (a term he uses). "The wandering savage grows no cultivated vegetable, fells no forest, and extirpates no useful plant, no noxious weed. . . . But with stationary life, or rather with the pastoral state, man at once commences an almost indiscriminate warfare upon all the forms of animal and vegetable existence around him, and as he advances in civilization, he gradually eradicates or transforms every spontaneous product of the soil he occupies" (40). Nature thus imbalanced will strive to "avenge herself," resulting in desertification or, Marsh says, "even extinction of the species" (42–43).

We look in vain for much of this in *Walden*, though we might expect it. Thoreau notices in "Sounds," for example, the railroad hauling away resources. "Here comes the cattle-train bearing the cattle of a thousand hills, sheepcots, stables, and cowyards in the air, drovers with their sticks, and the shepherd boys in the midst of their flocks, all but the mountain pastures, whirled along like leaves blown from the mountains by the September gales. The air is filled with the bleating of calves and sheep, and the hustling of oxen, as if a pastoral valley were going by" (122). But even here he seems mostly concerned with *social* rather than *environmental* destruction: the "pastoral life" is "whirled away" as much as the pastoral valley.

Landscape as artifact becomes more and more a viewpoint as human impact increases, however. Meinig comments in 1976 that "Even the weather . . . has been altered." So in the end, we see writers like Bill McKibben, whose 1989 bestseller, *The End of Nature*, describes the human-caused climatic changes from increasing "greenhouse" gases and depletion of the ozone layer as bringing on a new era expressed in his title, where only by ongoing human intervention can the natural order continue.

One final way of seeing landscape that Meinig notes is as ideology. "Just as the scientist looks through the facade of obvious elements and sees processes in operation, so others may see those same elements as clues and the whole scene as a symbol of values, the governing ideas, the underlying philosophies of a culture" (52). Specifically, "those who see it as ideology may see distinct manifestations of American interpretations of freedom, individualism, competition, utility, power, modernity, expansion, progress. That does not mean they cannot see the problems, but they are more concerned to look more deeply to see how the landscape represents a translation of philosophy into tangible features" (52). Seeing landscape as Ideology is done by social geographers like Meinig (or critics like me), but Thoreau rarely if ever is interested in that in *Walden*. In the twentieth century, ideology as a way of seeing is apparent in writers such as Leo Marx and Tom Stoppard.[7]

In the recent flowering of environmental writing, we also see an expanded sense of seeing landscape as habitat and as history. Obviously, some of Thoreau's contemporaries (e.g., Susan Fenimore Cooper and Celia Thaxter) were able and willing to look at landscapes as history. But as the extent of environmental impact becomes more obvious, and as the new sciences of ecology become available as tools, new kinds of history emerge (well represented by writers like Richard White, William Cronon, and Donald Worster). John Steinbeck uses landscape history similarly to how realistic novelists always have. However, Steinbeck brings to that a sharper understanding of ecology and incorporates it thematically.

More recently, bioregionalists have attempted historic depictions in an effort to flesh out specific places of inhabitation. For example, Thomas Berry sketches a history of his Hudson River Valley in which the narrative pivots on the arrival of Europeans and their change in relationship to the land.[8] His overall project is to use this history to instill a hope of a new sensibility of habitat, or the harmonious relationship of humans in their landscapes. More interesting are some Native American writers who articulate a history of habitation itself. The best example is Leslie Marmon Silko's "Landscape, History, and the Pueblo Imagination," in which she describes how the Pueblo people invest in their landscape the oral history and cultural information of their society.[9]

Many writers bring several of these ways of seeing to bear on their material or in their narratives, as Thoreau did. In *Sand County Almanac*, for example, Leopold not only utilizes system, but also at various points history, place, aesthetic, problem, habitat, and ideology. Tom Stoppard's recent *Arcadia* (the only piece of environmental drama I'm aware of) explores aesthetic, problem, ideology, system, and history.

There is an increasing need for such dialogic narratives involving multiple ways of seeing. For example, a contemporary environmental viewpoint often sees landscapes as nature, science, and aesthetic, mixed or in succession — or in alliance. Folks may come together, as they have in my community, to save "open space" with those three differing agendas (and all opposed to landscape as wealth). A substantial portion of the day-to-day business of local government deals with landscapes. Folks see the management of open space differently — protecting natural values, protecting views, enjoying hiking or biking or horseback riding, or preserving historic features. However, even when considering the use of public land for housing versus parks, the provision of sewers, uses of parks (e.g., alcohol), and so on, we encounter different people looking at the same landscapes in different ways.

Meinig writes in his essay: "Identification of these different bases for the variations in interpretations of what we see is a step toward more effective communication. For those of us who are convinced that landscapes mirror and landscapes matter, that they tell us about the values we hold and at the same time affect the quality of lives we lead, there is ever the need for wider conversations about ideas and impressions and concerns relating to the landscapes we share" (54). We can look to Thoreau's *Walden* as an initial attempt, if not to identify and converse in different ways, at least to explore one place from the broadest array of perspectives available to him at his time. And to some not insignificant degree, the very ways we see landscapes today have been shaped by his seminal work.

NOTES

1. Meinig, "The Beholding Eye," *Landscape Architecture*, 47. Subsequent page references are cited parenthetically in the text.

2. Thoreau, *Journal, Vol. 4: 1851–1852*, 41.

3. Thoreau, *Walden*, 68. Subsequent page references are cited parenthetically in the text.

4. Probably the best example of an environmentalist who approaches landscape as wealth is Gifford Pinchot.

5. In *The Environmental Imagination*, Lawrence Buell characterizes the four parts serialized in the *Atlantic* as geographic, historical, autumn to winter, winter to summer (235).

6. Marsh, *Man and Nature*, 36. Subsequent page references are cited parenthetically in the text.

7. See Marx, *The Machine in the Garden*, and Stoppard, *Arcadia*.

8. Thomas Berry, *The Dream of the Earth*, esp. chap. 13, "The Hudson River Valley: A Bioregional Story," 171–79.

9. Leslie Marmon Silko, "Landscape, History, and the Pueblo Imagination," *Antaeus* 7 (Autumn 1986): 83–94.

Sauntering in the Industrial Wilderness

BERNARD W. QUETCHENBACH

On New Year's Day, 1997, the following prediction appeared in a "crystal ball" article in the *Bangor Daily News*: "The paper companies will come together to propose the creation of an 1850s theme park in northern Maine, a place where Thoreau will be the hero and we'll all travel by canoe."[1]

The prognosticator was Stephen Wight, chairman of the Land Use Regulatory Commission known, of course, as LURC, the agency that oversees the vast and sparsely populated forests of Maine. Granted, it is difficult to tell how seriously he intended his prediction to be taken. But Chairman Wight's prophecy captures succinctly a great contradiction in the traditional role of the wilderness as both the land of the radical individual in search of spiritual truth and knowledge and the place ripe for large-scale exploitation, in each case because the land is "open" or away from the restrictions and scrutiny of "the settlements."

Whether we crave "reality" or windfall profits, we find them in the wildlands. Wight's prediction hints at a kind of unholy and, hopefully, unconscious alliance between Thoreau and the paper barons. That Thoreau's ghost should be working for Boise Cascade and Georgia Pacific is unthinkable, isn't it? Maybe not in Maine.

When Thoreau came to the Maine woods in the 1840s and 1850s, the lumber industry was already established. Among Thoreau's information sources is *Forest Life and Forest Trees*, John Springer's 1851 classic, which is occasionally held in Maine to be better than *The Maine Woods*, precisely because it was written by a real logger rather than a tourist. Thoreau acknowledges Springer's authority by citing him several times in "Ktaadn" and in "The Allegash and East Branch."[2]

Since Maine separated from Massachusetts in 1820, the state has maintained two conflicting images of the northern woods. Here, in Thoreau's words, "waves the virgin forest of the New World,"[3] a dense, impenetrable, fundamentally uncivilized wildland, virgin at least in the total effect of the unbroken forest if not in the size and cathedralesque stature of the individual trees. This image of the Maine woods as wilderness persists today in the tradition of the guided adventure, a watery safari into the largest statistically uninhabited area in the lower forty-eight.

But for generations the Maine woods has been a "working forest," the home to large-scale industrialized extraction of natural resources. Many observers, from Springer and Thoreau to Helen Hamlin, have commented on the speed with which the original giant "mast pines" and "pumpkin pines" were eliminated. William Cronon dates the removal of white pine from Maine as beginning in the 1630s.[4] Helen Hamlin, in *Pine, Potatoes, and People*, her informal history of Maine's Aroostook County, documents the industry's shifts to smaller trees and different species over time. Edward Hoagland attributes the pattern of landownership in Maine to a speculation boom designed to benefit Massachusetts interests when Maine became an independent state. This event "froze the patterns of settlement much as they were at the time. The population remained concentrated near the coast, and the large timber companies formed from these nineteenth-century holdings still continue to own two-thirds of Maine."[5]

More precisely, says forest activist Mitch Lansky, nine out-of-state paper corporations control two-thirds of what are variously known as "the unorganized territories" or "wildlands"; 90 percent of the wildlands belongs to twenty companies.[6] In *The Uncensored Guide to Maine*, Mark Melnicove and Kendall Merriam quote a United States Forest Service source as saying that "in no other state does industry ownership account for such a high percentage of forest land."[7] Individual landowners are often dependent on corporate markets and expertise, as in the case of writer-naturalist Bernd Heinrich, who contracts with Boise Cascade to selectively cut his woods. Companies producing forest products practice a variety of harvest techniques, but only a few, including Seven Islands, which considers itself a land management firm, are widely recognized as environmentally responsible. If, to use the popular metaphor of the woods as an agricultural crop, the forest is a farm, then corporate forestry in Maine is agribusiness, complete with monoculture row-cropping and chemical inputs.

These two visions of the Maine woods can be seen coexisting in the publications of the landowners' group known as North Maine Woods. The landowners adhere to the Maine tradition of public access; at their checkpoints, you can buy a permit to pass along private roads into the woods, where you are free to roam, provided you do not interfere with logging operations. Literature provided by the group is replete with pictures of unspoiled scenery, wildlife, hunters, and fishermen. Similar images surround the log truck at the center of the North Maine Woods seal (not the woodcutter's axe, mind you, but the truck). You are told that you are on your own, that rules are few and space uncrowded. And, though North Maine Woods is a place where "past and present; man and nature meet," it is "not a wilderness" but "a giant tree farm."[8] In essence, the two images occupy the same place; they are superimposed on the landscape, which is asked to support both of them simultaneously. This is how it has been since the days of Springer and Thoreau.

It must be noted first that "wilderness" in the 1850s was not generally defined as it is today. The wilderness was simply the "unsettled" country, and, while its potential as a source of spiritual fulfillment was not totally unrecognized, it was ripe for industry precisely because it was the wilderness, and not the habitations. Thoreau even recognizes a kind of fellow feeling with the timber pioneers whose search deep into the wilderness parallels his own. He notes the correspondence at several points in *The Maine Woods*. In encountering timber prospectors, he is drawn to the romance of their search, and compares it to his own quest for a different kind of treasure. He may take pains to establish the difference between what he seeks and what the industry seeks, but he recognizes the analogous nature of their searches. When his companions note their marks of ownership on some timber to be delivered to market in the spring, he muses, "methinks that must be where all my property lies, cast up on the rocks on some distant and unexplored stream, and waiting for an unheard-of freshet to fetch it down" (52–53).

It was generally assumed that the state of wilderness was temporary, as new lands gradually evolved toward a state unsuitable both for spiritual seeking à la Thoreau and for large-scale industrial exploitation. Both Springer and Thoreau foresee a time when the Maine woods would be villages and farms. In a passage redolent of early American concepts regarding the relationship between the "virgin land" and the march of American civilization, Springer notes that,

Not many years since, an unbroken forest stretched abroad over a vast area of country. . . . The pervading silence, which rested like night over this vast wilderness, was only broken by the voice of the savage, and the discordant howlings of wild beasts. But within a few years the ax of the pioneer has leveled large tracts of forest, and thus opened the virgin soil to the sun's germinating rays, so that now may be seen skirting the shores of the lake, north and northwest, cultivated fields, relieving the solitude which once reigned there.[9]

The lumber mills, according to Springer, "build up many beautiful villages" which "serve as so many little hearts in the great system, whose pulsations vibrate with general intelligence, education, and improved manners throughout the interior" (245).

Thoreau's famous predilection for the wild shows when he comments that "the mission of men there seems to be, like so many busy demons, to drive the forest all out of the country, from every solitary beaver-swamp and mountain-side, as soon as possible" (*MW* 5), but he views the clearings and homesteads he passes so frequently as Springer does, as brave leading edges of civilization. He sees in the pioneer home site "the germ of a town" (108), and notes that the placing of oxen on stumps to measure the size of the stumps serves as "a symbol of the fact that the pastoral comes next in order to the sylvan or hunter life" (229). Thoreau's immersion in this sense of inevitable progress conflicts with his love for wild things, and his awareness of the threat posed by American ambition. "The Anglo American," he remarks, "can indeed cut down and grub up all this waving forest and make a stump speech and vote for Buchanan on its ruins, but he cannot converse with the spirit of the tree he fells — he cannot read the poetry and mythology which retire as he advances" (229). And, even if a farm at Chamberlain Lake is "a cheerful opening in the woods" demonstrating that "the influx of light merely is civilizing," still the inhabitants "walked about on Sundays in their clearing somewhat as in a prison-yard" (240). This image is beautifully ambiguous. On the one hand, the settlers are "imprisoned" because of the isolation of their civilized spot surrounded by forest. Yet there is also the suggestion that it is the civilized spot that makes the prison in the boundless freedom of the woods. And Thoreau rarely identifies with the settlers as he does with the timber pioneers. His distance from the nascent Chamberlain Lake community is similar in character to his distance from his farmer neighbors in *Walden*'s Concord. When his guide suggests traveling down the Saint John River instead of the east branch of the Penobscot because the former was more settled, his response is to ask "which course would take us through the wildest country" (233).

Both Springer and Thoreau reflect on the "holiness" of the wilderness. Thoreau's unsettling but profound insight on Mount Katahdin is paralleled by Springer's tamer but uplifting "sketch of a visit to this mountain by a party of gentlemen," in which "our travelers" (193) report that, after experiencing a sunset over "a boundless wilderness in all directions . . . that holy [Sabbath] morning found us refreshed, and somewhat prepared to appreciate our peculiar circumstances," which included "the exercises of a religious conference" (200–201). Thoreau's memorable "contact, contact" passage is less comforting, depicting a kind of biblical desert experience, his soul harrowed through exposure to "forever untameable *Nature*" (69).

As a spiritual saunterer in search of what came to be known as "wilderness values," Thoreau is followed by William O. Douglas, who devotes two chapters of *My Wilderness* to Maine, and by two writers associated with the *New Yorker*, Edward Hoagland and John McPhee. McPhee comes equipped with an "alter ego," the "other" John McPhee, a local game warden. The two McPhees find their way around with an eye to avoiding the loggers, seeking out solitude much as Thoreau's "timber pioneers" sought out stands of pine that had been passed over by their predecessors. Douglas and Hoagland also, in concluding that the New England wilderness is gone forever, take solace in their ability to find a few places where an illusion of its presence remains. It is revealing to contrast the attitudes of these wilderness-seeking "saunterers" with those of a different kind of Maine woods writer. Maine has produced a substantial amount of what has been called retreat literature. Titles like Dorothy Boone Kidney's *A Home in the Wilderness* and *Away from It All* and Louise Dickinson Rich's *We Took to the Woods* are typical. The "retreat writers" are not without regard for or belief in the spiritual attributes of wild land. Kidney is particularly conscious of the religious sensibility fostered by immersion in what to her is God's handiwork. And Rich's description of the failed settlement at Grafton Notch is reminiscent of Thoreau's "contact passage":

> How can I make you see and feel those lofty ledges, imponderable against the sky? They always shine, being always wet or glazed with ice, for somehow from the bowels of the earth, springs leap to the mountaintop and perpetually water the infertile rock. They are cold, those ledges, and implacable, the sworn enemies of anything warm and human and vulnerable. Seeing them, feeling their weight upon the spirit, you understand why no one any longer lives in Grafton Notch.[10]

In general, though, the spiritual value of life in the woods for Rich and others like her consists in the purification of the quotidian. They emphasize everyday interactions with their neighbors, with the animals and plants, and with the landscape. They are not, like the timber prospectors or spiritual saunterers, after something to take back to the "outside." With cabins and camps scattered along paths blazed by industry exploitation and followed by wilderness saunterers, they are more akin to the settlers encountered by Springer and Thoreau.

This retreat literature seems to have reached a pinnacle of popularity in the 1940s, when writers such as Rich and Hamlin were published by major firms like Lippincott (Rich) and Norton (Hamlin). Later works that could be included in this tradition include several books by Kidney and Bernd Heinrich's recent *A Year in the Maine Woods*. Despite its title, Heinrich's book owes much more to *Walden*, which it echoes in its seasonal structure and blending of natural history observations with depictions of everyday activities, than to the three accounts that make up Thoreau's *The Maine Woods*. All of the retreat books include a share of wilderness-related rhetorical flourishes. Yet, despite the wilderness evocations, the writers approach the forest not as pilgrims but rather as homesteaders. Like Thoreau at Walden Pond, they seek to reduce their dependence on "society" and to purify their everyday affairs through simplicity. But they are not overly concerned with wilderness as such, and it is easy to see that to a saunterer in search of the pristine — a Thoreau, a Douglas, or, more recently, an Edward Hoagland or John McPhee — they would appear, for better or worse, as agents of encroaching civilization. In his Maine travels, Thoreau imagines himself among the timber pioneers; Rich, on the other hand, pretends repeatedly as she travels by canoe to be a settler looking for a homestead site.

Like Thoreau in *Walden*, Rich, Hamlin, and Kidney seek to redefine human as well as natural connections in the woods. Thoreau elevates the social call at Walden Pond where people could visit "under more favorable circumstances than . . . any where else." [11] And when Rich declares "happy the land, someone has said, that has no history" (*Happy the Land* 38), she carefully and self-consciously outlines her distinction between textbook history, the story of great events, and the personal history open only to those who have established residency. Heinrich asserts his residency through his family and childhood ties to his region of the woods. A surprising amount of space in the retreat books is dedicated to neighbors, who, despite being as much as ten miles away, are visited regularly. Familiarity is essential to the retreat writers' portrayals of life in the woods, and they tend to distance themselves from the footloose "sports" — including latter-day Thoreaus like Hoagland and McPhee, for whom the unfamiliar "virgin" quality of the surroundings is paramount. Rich, in fact, is embarrassed by her "sneaking desire" to explore the remote "upper lakes" with their "lovely resounding names," since her practical neighbors "never, never, *never* take canoe trips for the fun of it" (81–82).

In *Walden*, though, Thoreau pays close attention to neighbors, and to the local history of Walden Pond and its environs, perhaps most notably in the "Former Inhabitants; and Winter Visitors" chapter. As with Rich's Maine, the history of Walden Pond is alive for the inhabitant with a close and long-standing association with the area. For example, the "half-obliterated cellar hole" of Cato Ingraham is "known to few, being concealed from the traveller by a fringe of pines" (257). Similarly, the poignancy of the luckless Hugh Quoil's story is discovered through Thoreau's visits to Quoil's "unlucky castle," which "his comrades avoided" (262).

Like a homesteader, Thoreau champions a kind of squatter's right to his place in Concord. Thus, by virtue of his regular presence and intimate knowledge of the details of field and path, he more truly "owns" his neighbors' farms than they do. Thoreau's pride in his own understanding of things neglected by others often seems smug, but it provides the basis for his staking his own claim as a rightful inhabitant who may have "traveled much," but whose travels have been largely contained in Concord. This establishment of intimacy with Concord contrasts sharply with his portrayal of Maine as a land that, as Rich says, "has no history." Like Springer, Thoreau generally focuses on the present and projected future in *The Maine Woods*. The lives of the Indians, as former inhabitants, belong to a past that is either irrevocably lost already or timeless. And the forest is portrayed as "virgin" even though Thoreau is acutely aware of the human traces that it already bears.

In Maine, Thoreau is sometimes jarred by the incongruous juxtaposition of industry in "holy nature." Both industry and the spirit may flourish in "pre-settled" conditions, but the two do not necessarily coexist easily. Thoreau is troubled by traces left by loggers in the woods, by the disappearance of the large pines, and by the crass attitudes toward nature exhibited even by the timber pioneers, of whom, although he has "often wished since that I was with them" (*MW* 101), he concludes, "the explorers, and lumberers generally are all hirelings, paid so much a day for their labor, and as such, they have no more love for wild nature, than wood-sawyers have for forests" (119). His relationship with the timber industry is essentially competitive; he envies the timber pioneers because they go first into new areas of the forest, while he himself "would have liked to come across a large community of pines, which had never been invaded by the lumbering army" (210). And he asserts that it is the poet, and not the lumberer, who is truly in sympathy with nature (121).

Douglas, McPhee, and Hoagland, partly from consciously following Thoreau and partly as a consequence of seeking the same thing, are troubled by evidence of logging. On the other hand, the retreat writers are much more willing to accept industrial neighbors. They share corporation roads and telephone lines, and, in general, associate as friends. Rich, though she is occasionally critical of abusive logging practices, is particularly effusive toward the loggers themselves. As a wood-camp schoolteacher, Hamlin goes into what she considers wilderness *because* of the loggers, an experience she details in *Nine Mile Bridge*. For these writers, lumber camps are simply part of the wilderness. Even Heinrich, "a card carrying member of the Wilderness Society" (118) writing in 1994, associates logging and wilderness when he observes that "what the loggers had left imparted a look of wilderness to the area" (99). To Douglas and Hoagland, the sound of "saws screeching in the distance" (Douglas 263) is a constant reminder of the destruction of the pristine; for Kidney, the same sound is an integral part of the world "away from it all," her first exposure to which is a lakeside stop where "there was just the high lonesome sound of wind in trees and the noise of a chain saw echoing from some distant place in the woods" (*Away from It All* 16). To get to the wilderness, Kidney and her husband, Milford, who have given up the city life to tend a small dam and Allagash campsite, pass through a gate with the approval of not one but two industries, the Bangor Hydro Electric Company and the Great Northern Paper Company (16).

Don Scheese notes Thoreau's frequent encounters with human artifacts and habitations, each credited as "the last trace of civilization."[12] A recurring motif in writings about Maine is the discovery of some artifact of former use, a machine, or at least a bolt, in the garden, a signal of human presence that "got there first." The discovery of some discarded item deep in the woods often leaves Thoreau unsettled. In "Ktaadn," he observes that "it was always startling to discover so plain a trail of civilized man there. I remember that I was strangely affected, when we were returning, by the sight of a ring-bolt well drilled into a rock, and fastened with lead, at the head of this solitary Ambejejis Lake" (*MW* 42). For the literary "homesteaders," on the other hand, discarded artifacts afford opportunities for salvage. Rich credits her husband with "an absolute mania for junk" (*Happy the Land* 92). Kidney and Heinrich also emphasize the gathering of cast-off material.

Writing in the 1960s, Douglas, Kidney, and Elinor Stevens Walker are more aware that the woods might not last forever than anyone since Thoreau and Springer. As expected, saunterer Douglas sees the danger to such wilderness values as solitude and silence. But Kidney, also, devotes the end of *Away from It All* to a discussion of new roads and increased numbers of canoeists on the Allagash. Walker, a Maine resident who spent childhood vacations in the woods, is situated midway between the perspective of the saunterers and that of the settlers. Writing in 1966, she sees the forces of industry and preservation engaged in a battle for "the last of Maine's virgin forest lands," which "our lumber companies are fast invading to the very last depths." But the link between wilderness and industrial hinterland is still apparent. In a remote region near Chamberlain Lake, "the roadsides still bore the ugly scars of the deadly work of the cruel bulldozers. And here one feels the solitary loneliness of the deep wilderness." [13]

In nearby Baxter Park, purchased largely from Great Northern for the state by Governor Baxter, the same conflict has been resolved differently, as "the lumbering and exploiting are gone forever. The visitors in the area are those who love life in the open" (23). Clearly, Walker can see that there may not be enough forest left to support both large-scale industrial exploitation and wilderness preservation, but her attitude toward historical timbering is mostly nostalgic, in keeping with her attitude toward the vestigial wilderness of Baxter Park. Both the park and the remaining loggers are colorful remnants of a romantic, perhaps a better, past.

Maine, of course, is not the only place where industrial exploitation converges with "wilderness values." In the West, the heirs of mining and ranching families frequently oppose the "civilization" of the "East," which, they believe, is out to convert truly wild country into parks, often seen as little more than maintained recreation areas for the tourists. What is unique to Maine is the extent to which the concept of wild country includes a kind of outdoor factory complete with heavy machinery and regulated water flow, and the long duration of this wilderness/industry convergence. For generations, both the industrial entrepreneur and the spiritual quester have come to Maine in search of riches, and for the most part have been able to put up with each other, and have even grudgingly recognized a kind of kinship. The homesteaders, meanwhile, take what they can use from both. From the saunterers, they take a romantic attitude toward life in the wilderness, while the loggers provide a colorful history, networks of navigation and communication, and a useful selection of leftovers. In general, industrial landownership is accepted with equanimity because of tradition and because rural Mainers have long understood that, as Rich says, the "lumber company is our privacy insurance, our guarantee that we won't wake up some morning and find new neighbors building a pink stucco bungalow down the river from us" (*We Took to the Woods* 22). But acceptance of industrial ownership has limits. Mitch Lansky discusses small industry-dependent towns like Linneus and Stockholm that, despite economic pressure, have passed ordinances restricting industry activity (53), and competing forestry reform referendums on the 1996 state ballot had combined pluralities in all areas of the state.

Maine residents consistently defend the state's rather eccentric idea of private property. Large tracts of land should be privately held, but the public's access to private lands is taken for granted. Like Thoreau in Concord, Maine residents prefer to roam land that is technically owned by others, but that is, in a sense, theirs by right of familiarity and knowledge. They defend the industry's right to own the forest, but are likely to be skeptical of industrial claims regarding forest management. One reason for this skepticism is the long-standing direct knowledge of the land itself. Loggers who have spent their whole lives in the forest can see a difference between today's woods and the woods of their youth. Many Maine people remain in close and frequent contact with, to use John Daniel's phrase, "not the idea of wilderness, but the land itself in its wild immensity,"[14] and they value the woods for its wildness as well as its economic worth.

While the two conflicting images of the Maine forests could be supported simultaneously, they were. But by the 1960s, the woods were under increased pressure from recreational use as well as from the mechanization of logging. A surprising number of disparate people feel that a line was crossed sometime in the 1970s. Forest economist Lloyd C. Irland identifies four factors that converged in the 1970s: an investment boom, land speculation and subdivision, the occurrence of a spruce budworm outbreak and the resulting "salvage" logging, and an increase in fuelwood cutting.[15] The network of roads and clearcuts and the overall small size of the remaining trees have broken the illusion of balance between the factory and the cathedral. If, as John McPhee notes, the overall effect from the air is still of vast unpopulated spaces, the landscape itself looks, "in many places, like an old and badly tanned pelt" (262). The "new look" has its fans; moose, proving that human conceptions mean little to them, have flourished in the more open woodlands, as have moose hunters, deer hunters, and snowmobilers. But there is a decadent quality to the recreational use. Snowmobile fatalities, often involving alcohol, are increasing. McPhee describes moose hunters driving down woods roads, shooting from their pickup trucks.

As Walker's "cruel bulldozers" attest, it is harder to be nostalgic about fellerbunchers and skidders than about the equally industrial, labor-intensive logging of the past. According to Heinrich,

> There are places in the Maine woods where monster machines snip off whole mature trees, and then also strip them of branches, saw them into sections, and haul them out. They are let loose by a man in a Plexiglass bubble controlling everything by pulling levers. The monster machines replace hordes of tough men who left the horse hovel at dawn with their teams of Percherons, and their chain saws and axes. The men were covered with pitch from head to foot, and the pitch dried black, and it formed a hard carapace on their shirts and pants. They sweated and swore and sang, and they came back to camp in the evening with the satisfaction of a day's work well done. The monster machines are taking their jobs, and to give them scope, the lumber companies clearcut huge tracts of old and diverse forests, replace these with single species of conifers, spew Agent-Orange-like herbicides from helicopters, and call it forest "management." (81–82)

The earlier logging, despite large-scale work camps and wholesale water manipulation, seems either compatible with or at least inseparable from the presence of wilderness. Thoreau, like Hoagland, travels on the artificially maintained smooth water of the industry. The retreat writers of the 1940s are so immersed in industrial logging that it is for them a defining characteristic of the wilderness itself. In this, they can be seen as descendants of Springer. Kidney and Walker note modern stresses eroding the territory, but are mostly nostalgic about the blend of corporate exploitation and open space that is slowly diminishing, perhaps ultimately to disappear. Thoreau's ring bolts, Kidney's telephone lines, and even Heinrich's "hordes of tough men" are easier to reconcile with a sense of wilderness than are fellerbunchers, de-limbers, and other "monster machines" of contemporary timber harvesting.

In the aftermath of the increased recreational use of the 1960s and the clear-cutting of the 1970s, for the first time in Maine history there may not be enough of the woods left to maintain the wilderness part of the wilderness/industry dynamic. With the diminishing forest base, Thoreau's anxiety that the woods might eventually be driven from every mountainside is given expression by Elinor Stevens Walker, who finds historical logging compatible with the wild country she values. Heinrich also tries to drive a wedge between past and present logging practices, and, perhaps motivated by the homesteader's tradition of neighborliness toward industry and a pragmatic recognition that the forest products companies control so much of the transportation networks and local economies of Maine, he tempers his distaste for the "monster machines" with a general respect for industry employees. As both wilderness advocate and neighborly homesteader, his loyalties are divided. For example, despite his outspoken criticism of industry methods, Heinrich is upset when he fears that, because he uses metal spikes to climb trees in his raven research, he will be taken for a tree spiker. But Heinrich's position is clearly more skeptical of industrial logging than Hamlin's, or even Walker's. This does not, however, mean that current rural Mainers are likely to identify with the followers of Thoreau. As a university biologist whose experience includes time spent as a refugee in a German forest reserve, Heinrich is in some ways very different from the other retreat writers. But even Fred King, Edward Hoagland's Allagash guide, who "admires the lumbermen and has little use for the Johnny-come-lately conservationists,"[16] acknowledges the constriction of the woods. As Hoagland illustrates when he notes that "the government-owned wild area ends at Twin Brooks, and soon we saw log trucks alongside the banks" (105), environmentalists and industry have followed Thoreau and the timber prospectors as competitors. Mitch Lansky finds this competitive relationship in a suggestion made by "some of the industrial landowners" in the 1980s to change the official designation of the unorganized territories from "wildlands" to "industrial forest" (6). But as Lansky also notices and critiques, industry and environmentalists have come to know that both rely on the same "unsettled" conditions, and one of the ironies of northeastern environmentalism is the alliance between environmental groups and forest products industries on issues pertaining to subdivision and development.

Perhaps the late twentieth-century works most in keeping with Thoreau's *Maine Woods* accounts are the essays pertaining to Maine in Hoagland's 1973 book, *Walking the Dead Diamond River*. Hoagland's essays, like Thoreau's, were produced as travel pieces for magazine readers. Like Thoreau also, Hoagland studies his river guide and keeps his distance from the more settled elements of the local population. Hoagland regrets the impending loss of human, as well as natural, wildness. In his essay on "The New England Wilderness," he finds that "there is no wilderness as such left in New England, nor any wilderness people of the sort who might miss it either," and concludes that "despite all the fuss about wilderness, people nowadays don't really want to be in the woods all alone. . . . Even faster than the woods go, people are losing their taste for the woods" (257–58). Hoagland foresees a time when Thoreau's descendants in New England will "lose that mysterious sense of felicity and exuberance they once had in the presence of natural grandeur — the feeling of having known it before, of being linked to it via thousands of centuries before they were born — and simply stop caring" (193). If this happens, perhaps the paper companies will succeed in taking over the only part of the Maine woods that they haven't been able to control, the sense that somewhere in the slash piles and paper plantations "waves the virgin forest of the New World." At that point there will be little choice left, and Wight's prediction, which began this essay, will begin to make sense. If the competition between Thoreauvian sauntering and industrial exploitation becomes moot and the pursuit of wildness is reduced to nostalgia, then the paper companies might be tempted to enlist the considerable appeal of Thoreau's image to fend off subdivision and "settlement," the real and insidious enemy of both saunterers and industrialists. As North Maine Woods makes clear, as long as industrial production remains central, the large landowners do not generally oppose recreational use of their lands, especially if that use generates extra income. It isn't all that difficult to imagine a future development in which the corporations would cater to tourists from "away," selling the experience of following Thoreau through the industrial wilderness, while the descendants of homesteaders glean a living alongside. Paddle right over here, folks, and have the kids photographed with Henry.

NOTES

1. Andrew Kekacs, "Mainers' Crystal Ball," *Bangor Daily News*, 1 January 1997, sec. A, p. 7.

2. Thoreau, *Maine Woods*. Thoreau's references to Springer occur on p. 44 of "Ktaadn" and in notes on pp. 20, 43–44, and 68–69; on p. 245 of "The Allegash and East Branch"; and on p. 321 of the appendix.

3. Thoreau, *Maine Woods*, 83. The quoted phrase marks the end of "Ktaadn." Subsequent page numbers are cited parenthetically in the text with *MW*.

4. Cronon, *Changes in the Land*, 109.

5. Hoagland, "The New England Wilderness," in *Walking the Dead Diamond River*, 173.

6. Lansky, *Beyond the Beauty Strip*, 5.

7. Melnicove and Merriam, *Uncensored Guide to Maine*, 87.

8. North Maine Woods, "Sportsman's Map" (n.p., n.d.).

9. Springer, *Forest Life and Forest Trees*, 181.

10. Rich, *Happy the Land,* 66. Subsequent page numbers are cited parenthetically in the text.

11. Thoreau, *Walden,* 211.

12. Scheese, *Nature Writing,* 51.

13. Walker, *Our Great Northern Wilderness,* 69.

14. Daniel, *The Trail Home,* 246.

15. Lloyd C. Irland discusses New England forest history, including the 1970s, in *Wildlands and Woodlots.*

16. Hoagland, "Fred King on the Allagash," in *Walking the Dead Diamond River,* 84.

Walden, Rural Hours, and
the Dilemma of Representation

ROCHELLE JOHNSON

Mere facts & names & dates communicate more than we suspect.
— *Henry David Thoreau's* Journal

When Barry Lopez, surely one of this century's most gifted nature writers, posed the question, "What is a dignified response to the land?," he raised an issue that has been central to nature writers for well over a century.[1] How best to represent a physical place, its various and interdependent life forms, and an individual human's response to this place are crucial and central issues for many. Place-based nature writing necessitates representing observation, perception, and experience, and while language has served as a solution of sorts to this dilemma of representation, the effectiveness of language to respond to a place — let alone in a "dignified" manner — has been called into question by writers even as they have relied on language as a means to that representation. We recall the now-famous words from Henry David Thoreau's *Walden* which reflect this very issue: "I desire to speak somewhere *without* bounds," he writes, "for I am convinced that I cannot exaggerate enough even to lay the foundation of a true expression." For Thoreau, the "truth" of words "is instantly *translated*," and so the dilemma of representing place deepens.[2] This is, then, not only a problem of developing a dignified response to the land, but also a problem of conveying observation and perception, and of cultivating an effective means of representation. Indeed, for many nature writers — and certainly for many of us familiar with the dictums of poststructural theory — the pronounced and problematic divisions between self, language, and place pose fundamental challenges to a satisfying union of human perception and physical reality.

It is, perhaps, partly because Susan Fenimore Cooper's *Rural Hours* (1850), the first book of nature writing published by an American woman, does not reveal its author's struggle with these issues that Cooper's text has been largely dismissed in the twentieth century. While *Rural Hours* was praised in the nineteenth century for the "simple earnestness" of Cooper's "style" and as "delightful reading,"[3] critics in the twentieth century have, until quite recently, found the very simplicity of *Rural Hours* to be indicative of its literary weakness.[4] Just one manner in which Cooper's prose may seem simpler than Thoreau's is its absence of direct attention to the inadequacies of language to represent perception of the natural world. Of course, there are other differences between these two mid–nineteenth-century authors, and I will discuss some of them further, but this one seems especially important since many critics have come to privilege just this dimension of place-based nature writing. In *Rural Hours*, Cooper avoids the reliance on figurative language that characterizes Thoreau's *Walden* prose and through which he most clearly struggles with the dilemma of representation. As she records in journal form the seasonal changes and varieties of life that she witnesses in her Lake Otsego region of New York state, Cooper creates a record of her place that suggests her faith in literal description. That is, she casts her observations in a style that suggests she sees no disparity between her perception, her object of description, and her linguistic representation. Whereas Thoreau exhibits many times in *Walden* his recognition of the potential ineffectiveness of language and his awareness of the difficulties inherent in representing his experience of place in words, Cooper's prose reflects her trust that her language will result in a dignified response to the land. Thus, the very quality that Peter Fritzell has attributed to the "best American nature writers" — an overt interest in the relationship between the self and language — does not appear in one of the most widely read works of nature writing in the nineteenth century.[5]

And yet, despite their differences, *Walden* and *Rural Hours* have similar purposes. Each author sought to present a specific place to readers, and each described his or her surroundings with the hopes of affecting readers' environmental sensibilities. These are projects not only of perception and observation, but also of connection. Cooper and Thoreau both sought cultural change, and they hoped that their literary projects would perform the cultural work of leading people to consider more seriously their connections to natural places.

That these two volumes of nature writing appeared within four years of each other, pursued similar goals, and met with markedly different responses from American readers suggests that their authors' styles and methods affected the reading public in quite distinct ways. Robert Kuhn McGregor has said of Thoreau's contemporaries and of their lack of enthusiasm for *Walden* upon its publication in 1854, "America was not prepared to find spirit in rocks and trees."[6] And yet, *Rural Hours* had faced a similar audience, having been published just four years before, and the nine nineteenth-century editions of Cooper's book suggest that her conveyance of the "spirit" in nature found many ready readers. Of special interest to us here, then, both for explaining the different receptions of these books and, more importantly, for exploring the dilemma of representation seemingly inherent in nature writing, are the contrasting methods Cooper and Thoreau employ in hopes of reaching their goals — specifically, how they represent their perception and experiences in order to bridge the gap between word and place and as a means of leading readers to a subtler recognition of the physical environment.

In this essay, I analyze these authors' differing means of encouraging cultural change, and demonstrate that by considering *Walden* in relation to *Rural Hours* we achieve a fuller understanding of the ways in which mid–nineteenth-century writers employed language on behalf of nature. Through these contemporaneous representations of place, we gain insight into the different theories of representation that circulated in this period, and we thereby acquire a more accurate understanding of Thoreau's place in the history of American nature writing. We also come to recognize that to judge a work of nature writing by the degree to which it exhibits its author's concern about issues of representation is to impose anachronistically a specific conception of language — one which may demonstrate our own complicity in an ideology privileging the metaphysical over the literal, or the philosophical over the material. Finally, this understanding of our own predicament may enable us to address the dilemma of representation still very much alive in our own environmental crisis.

The radical difference between Thoreau's and Cooper's descriptions of their narrative selves offers a quick and telling look at their distinctive narrative postures and methods. Clearly, place-based nature writing offers to some degree an anthropocentric view of its subject, simply because a writer brings a human perspective to the project; yet Thoreau's celebration of his "brag[ging] as lustily as Chanticleer in the morning . . . if only to wake my neighbors up" (84) seems markedly more self-assured and self-centered than Cooper's description of herself, sans metaphor, as a "rustic bird-fancier" who has completed a "simple record" of "trifling observations" on "the seasons in rural life."[7] Thoreau's use of metaphor here typifies his rhetorical strategies throughout *Walden*, where he often relies on metaphor not only to communicate his purposes in representing his Walden experiment but also to convey many aspects of his physical surroundings. Cooper, on the other hand, points critically to the use of this rhetorical device in describing her place. Whereas Thoreau claims of Walden Pond that he is "thankful that this pond was made deep and pure for a symbol" (287), Cooper, when admiring her village's Lake Otsego, remarks, "we are *all but cheated* into the belief that the waters know something . . . of our own hearts" (69, emphasis added). By drawing attention to the symbolic interpretation that Americans conventionally apply to a body of water, Cooper reminds readers of the human tendency to conceive of natural things metaphorically and thus anthropocentrically. For we may imagine the lake's sympathy, but the lake knows nothing "of our own hearts." Nature exists independently of human conceptions of it. Cooper thus appears intent on encouraging and maintaining a cautious awareness of the appropriative tendencies of the human imagination.

One result of Cooper's preference in this regard is that she seems to employ a more "objective" rhetoric; by avoiding symbolism or allegory, she maintains a distinction of sorts between her imagination and nature. While her lack of figurative language and philosophical debates may make her prose appear simple, Cooper's writing nonetheless enables a humble approach to place.[8] Cooper's reliance on a journal format augments this effect by connecting her observations to specific times and locales, thereby suggesting the prominence of the objects of her literary attention — most often natural objects and phenomena — over both her persona and her necessarily human orientation toward place. Her rhetorical posture seems thus designed to represent a nonappropriative environmental ethic.

In his Journal, Thoreau wrote increasingly in an "objective" style; this, along with his attention to the dilemmas of composition in his Journal, suggests that he came to believe that to represent place most effectively, and in the least appropriative manner, one must move beyond a metanarrative of representation — a prose overtly conscious of its inevitable inability to convey natural phenomena, individual perception, and experience — and toward a prose that represents these things as accurately — and as literally — as possible. Despite Thoreau's apparent discovery in this regard, however, readers and critics in the twentieth century are drawn to *Walden's* depiction of place — despite the abstract qualities of that depiction. *Walden* exhibits the slipperiness of representing perception, for even while it attempts to discourage an anthropocentric view of place, Thoreau seems to get caught up in a style that seems, by its very nature, appropriative. In *Walden,* Thoreau engages the dilemma of representation in two particularly clear ways: by reworking his Journal writings in order to present his related thoughts in a form more unified, coherent, and polished than they appear in the Journal, and by using metaphor as a means of granting the Concord wilds a meaning more accessible to those readers living citified lives of quiet desperation. Yet even as Thoreau reworked his *Walden* manuscript for publication, we find in his Journal his concern precisely with these methods of conveying his experience and perception. Even as he increasingly metaphorized his prose, for example, he speculated in 1852, "Mere facts & names & dates communicate more than we suspect." [9] And as he argued even amid *Walden's* copious figurative language, "we are in danger of forgetting the language which all things and events speak without metaphor" (111). Further, as he mined his Journal entries, taking episodes and thoughts out of their original contexts, Thoreau mused, "Perhaps I can never find so good a setting for my thoughts as I shall thus have taken them out of" (*PJ* 4:296).

What these approaches to representing perception risk, Thoreau seems to recognize, is further encouraging an anthropocentric view of one's place in the natural world, one implication of which was the appropriative and utilitarian ethic that the majority of Thoreau's neighbors embraced and against which he wrote. However, the famous loon passage in *Walden* provides one instance in which Thoreau's use of metaphor implicitly encourages the appropriative perspective of nature and wilderness that he worked so hard elsewhere to discourage. Further, through an examination of the construction of this passage, we realize that Thoreau's revision process could — in wrenching his observations out of context — diminish significantly his recognition of nature's otherness.

The loon passage has two fairly distinct parts: preceding Thoreau's two-and-a-half-page account of chasing the loon appears a one-paragraph commentary on the Concord hunters' predations. This published, two-part passage merges two distinct episodes in Thoreau's writings: the first portion, commenting on the Concord hunters' pursuit of loons in autumn, Thoreau wrote in the fall of 1845, and it appears in the original manuscript version of *Walden* (*PJ* 2:213–14).[10] The second and major portion of the passage, however, is a reworded Journal entry from October 8, 1852, a passage which records his actual encounter with a loon on the surface of the pond (*PJ* 5:367–69). Combining the passages in *Walden*, however, makes Thoreau's loon chase appear as a metaphoric rendering of the hunters' pursuit, especially since the two parts of the passage have similar structures and repeat key phrases and images. The "Mill-dam sportsmen," like Thoreau on his pond, "are on the alert" to the loon's "wild laughter" (233). Whereas the hunters arrive at the pond "with patent rifles and conical balls and spy-glasses" (233), Thoreau's chase of the loon on the water begins with his arming himself with oars: "I pursued with a paddle" (234). While Thoreau's tools for pursuit clearly pose less danger to the bird, he nonetheless emphasizes the parallel aspects of the hunt and his own pursuit, and thereby suggests the consumptive dimension of his pursuit of his "adversary" (235).

This passage has been interpreted as one of Thoreau's most effective representations of his simultaneous yearning for the wild and feeling of ultimate separation from the world of nature. Indeed, while Thoreau's literal characterizations of the loon's wild voice and skilled diving emphasize his distinction from it,[11] his rendering of the loon as symbolic of pure wildness allows readers to interpret his chase of the loon as a quest for wildness itself. Through his complex rhetorical maneuvers, he underscores both his own struggle for accurate perception of the wild and the very difficulty of representing an aspect of nature in language. And yet, even while Thoreau communicates his distance from the loon and hence, implicitly, his humility in the face of the natural world, his consumptive desire for the loon rivals his humility. That is, while Thoreau's passage demonstrates his separateness from the loon, the passage also — especially through its reliance on the metaphor of hunting — risks promoting an anthropocentric perception of place, or of nature more generally. Certainly while this may not have been Thoreau's intent, what emerges from his published encounter with the loon is a representation of an encounter with wildness that is guilty of diminishing the very wildness *Walden* seeks to represent. Thus, Thoreau's use of metaphor — as a means of representing and advocating his perception of natural phenomena and his less appropriative environmental ethic — fails him.

In addition to ascribing the metaphor of the hunt to his encounter with the loon, Thoreau alters the tone of his earlier 1845 passage on the hunting of loons and waterfowl generally by removing from the published version a key passage. In the 1845 Journal, Thoreau had written of a waterfowl who had lost its mate to hunters: "And the silent hunter emerges into the carriage road with ruffled feathers at his belt. . . . And for a week you hear the circling clamor clangor of some solitary goose through the fog — seeking its mate — peopling the woods with a larger life there than they can hold" (*PJ* 2:214). When this passage does appear in slightly revised form in *Walden*, it rests in an entirely different context, quite far removed from Thoreau's original clear condemnation of hunting. Originally it conveyed both Thoreau's and the goose's disorienting and wrenching sense of loss, emphasizing both humans' disregard for natural life and their inability to recognize or conceive of nature's distinctly nonhuman version of loss and passion. In its reincarnation in the "Spring" chapter of *Walden*, amid signs of spring's birth, it becomes much more a celebratory statement of the powers of the wild — a symbol of both the force of life and of nature's will to regeneracy (313). Thus, the *Walden* paragraph on the loon hunters originates in a passage centered on and powerfully lamenting the varieties of hunting in autumn; the published version, however, greatly diminishes this mourning tone.

These revisions effectively demonstrate the problematic rupturing of perception involved in Thoreau's re-presentation of his original experience. In fact, the famous loon passage could be said — somewhat paradoxically — to be as much about the difficulty of representing the natural as it is an enactment of that difficult representation. As Daniel Peck notes, "the loon insists upon its separateness from its observer" and thus illustrates for both reader and Thoreau the intractable distance between human and nonhuman.[12] And yet Thoreau's hunting metaphor conveys and mimics the process by which he appropriates the loon in his linguistic representation. Ultimately, then, his representation may be seen to have failed, in that his "hunt" for the loon fails, but as a lesson in consumptive perception, it may be seen to succeed, emphasizing in its final, published version individual transcendence over any call for an end to the destruction of loons or over a celebration of the uninhibited wildness of an individual loon.

Finally, Thoreau's prevalent use of metaphor in *Walden* suggests not only the limitations of human language, but also the limitations of Thoreau's own perception of place. SueEllen Campbell writes, "As [Aldo] Leopold says, 'The outstanding characteristic of perception is that it entails no consumption and no dilution of any resource.' Of course, how we see will often direct what we do."[13] Thoreau's view reflects his own struggle with his culture's appropriative ethic. While "Thoreau's refusal to organize the Walden landscape tidily for his readers may be one sign of his intent to get us lost in it,"[14] Thoreau's method emphasizes the

"getting lost" over the literal "landscape" and, as such, further complicates the already slippery and complex task of representing one's perception of place. The landscape at Walden Pond is finally, for most readers,
an abstract and philosophical landscape. As Thoreau claims in his "Conclusion," "The universe is wider than our views of it" (320); Thoreau's
record of his place and life at Walden Pond perhaps ironically reveals that
the dilemma of representing place concerns waking human perception
to an awareness of its tendency toward a narrow view.

Like *Walden*, Susan Cooper's *Rural Hours* engages the cultural work
of reshaping readers' perception of place; however, in a complex way,
Cooper's critique of her culture is much more understated than Thoreau's, and this complexity results as much from Cooper's humble narrative stance as it does from her lack of overt attention to matters of
representation. Cooper's prose is characterized by a somewhat paradoxical, humble assertiveness. Given the near absence of discussions of her
purpose in recording her observations, Cooper appears to assume an inherent value to her descriptions. While she offers readers brief mentions
of the varieties of birds returning to Cooperstown as spring settles in, for
instance, she offers no developed discussion of their significance — neither to herself nor to the place; she merely notes their return (e.g., 11).
She similarly notes the plants appearing and blooming (e.g., 12, 28–29);
and she mentions the seasonal return of insects: "The fire-flies are gleaming about the village gardens this evening — the first we have seen this
year" (70). In addition, she notes the presence of food on the table that
reflects the changes in season: on Tuesday, June 19, for example, she
writes, "Fine strawberries from the fields this evening for tea" (75). Her
narrative's distinction stems from its absence of self-consciousness, as it
were; Cooper's use of language suggests her assurance that readers would
discern a purpose for such straightforward representation. Her essential
disregard for the gap that Thoreau so clearly regarded as persisting between object and subject implies her belief that readers could share in
her place and its life forms merely through reading her record of them.

From Cooper's essay "Small Family Memories," which she wrote in
1883, well after the publication of *Rural Hours*, we may discern a clue
to how she intended *Rural Hours* to affect readers. For Cooper, *Rural
Hours* represented an outgrowth of her devotion to nature, which had
its origins in her childhood experiences with her maternal grandfather:
"Grandfather [De Lancey] soon commenced my botanical education —
being the eldest of the little troop, I often drove with him, in the gig,

about his farms and into his woods, and it was my duty to jump out and open all the gates. In these drives he taught me to distinguish the different trees by their growth, and bark, and foliage. . . . He would point out a tree and ask me to name it, going through a regular lesson in a very pleasant way. Such was the beginning of my *Rural Hours* ideas." [15] While this passage presents a number of intriguing insights into the development of Cooper's nature study, its emphasis on naming provides a particularly significant context for Cooper's "*Rural Hours* ideas." In much of *Rural Hours,* Cooper dedicates herself to naming her surroundings, that is, to recording the natural life forms and seasonal changes; and she does so in a prose so removed from metaphysical and representational concerns that it seems — to modern readers — simple. However, Cooper's interest in "naming" her surroundings suggests her adherence to an eighteenth-century understanding of natural history.[16] Her faith in language's ability to represent nature reflects the natural historian's faith in the "relation between things and the human eye," a relation which Michel Foucault explains "defines [eighteenth-century] natural history." [17] The simplicity and naïveté that readers have found in Cooper's prose are best understood not as evidence of her poor writing, but as evidence of Cooper's adherence to a fast-fading conception of language. Foucault has explained that the "apparent simplicity, and that air of naïveté [that natural history] has from a distance" belie the complexity of its underlying philosophy of representation, and we can, by extension, say the same of Cooper's nature writing.[18] The "apparent simplicity" of *Rural Hours* proves to be its complex bridging of subject and object and its confidence in representing perception. As Foucault explains, eighteenth-century natural history *is* the "fundamental articulation of the visible." Its purpose, method, and emphasis are *naming:* "its construction requires only words applied, without intermediary, to things themselves." Whereas today — and this was increasingly so throughout the nineteenth century — we recognize "not the sovereignty of a primal discourse, but the fact that we are already, before the very least of our words, governed and paralysed by language," in the eighteenth and early nineteenth centuries, "Natural history [found] its locus in the gap that is now opened up between things and words." [19]

Cooper thus held a faith not so much in language as in representation — that is, she believed that "things and words . . . communicate in a representation," to borrow Foucault's words.[20] And given her unwavering Protestant faith, which she exhibits in *Rural Hours* and which was clearly informed by the tenets of natural theology, Cooper likely believed that giving language to her place was tantamount to spreading the word of God. Through her project of naming her surroundings and the seasonal changes, her "science" and religion would collaborate. By devoting a volume to descriptions of the life and natural phenomena of her village environs, Cooper thus shared with readers both the wonders of the creation and a model, offered through herself, of an individual closer to God through her very attentiveness to her environment. Through this understanding of Cooper's faith in representation, we realize that she had lofty goals indeed for *Rural Hours*; by means of her apparently simple descriptions, she reconstituted the natural environment before her readers' eyes. Moreover, this understanding of the cultural context of *Rural Hours* further explains her humble narrative posture. To be anything but humble in approaching the natural environment — God's domain — would be nothing less than blasphemous. Finally, for Cooper to concern herself with the efficacy of language was as unnecessary as it would be distracting.

Interestingly, Cooper's reliance on this understanding of representation serves partly to enable her to call attention to the changes she witnesses in her surrounding landscape. Many passages in *Rural Hours* suggest that Cooper realized that as the physical environment was altered, Americans' sense of history would change as well. And this concerned Cooper, because she believed that a failure to perceive nature's alteration would result in both an ill-conceived sense of American history and blind adherence to an ethic of "progress," which would inevitably damage the physical environment. Since Cooper recognized the negative effects of this ethic of progress, however, she hoped to convey her belief that cultural memory, or a sense of history, is tied to perception, and that America's prevailing inattentiveness to the natural environment would result in a misrepresentation of the environment in the cultural memory. One obvious result of this would be a history that failed to account fully for the changes in the land. But a more disturbing implication of this distortion in cultural memory was that it would enable and encourage a disregard and even an apathy for environmental destruction. If Americans could not notice the perceptible changes in their environments, they could not represent these changes or their results in the national consciousness. Cooper sought to reverse this tendency by representing in *Rural Hours* the remnants of natural and cultural history she observed in her surroundings. Through her attention to the history revealed in landscape, she seeks both to enlarge her readers' capacities for perception and to call attention to the dangers of destroying nature — and, thereby, history. Cooper's faith that language adequately represents place aids this project.

Two passages in *Rural Hours* particularly manifest this potential of Cooper's faith in literal description. In the midst of a passage in which she describes her local forests — their aesthetic values, their support of diverse life forms, and the varieties of trees found therein — Cooper notes, "The forest lands of America preserve to the present hour something that is characteristic of their wild condition, undisturbed for ages" (128). Her detailed representation of old-growth forests, when placed alongside this remark, indicates that Cooper values the forests for their historical significance. They testify, she explains, to a history fading from her culture's memory. This remark could serve merely to remind readers of their quick and impressive "improvements" to the American landscape; however, Cooper points out to readers that while the forests provide "a sweet quiet, a noble harmony, [and] a calm repose, which we seek in vain elsewhere" (127), they are rapidly disappearing. Her impassioned call for preservation, which appears amid her discussion of forests (131–35), thus emphasizes that Americans risk losing this aspect of the "wild" in their cultural memory. She therefore shares her perception of the forest in order to suggest that the trees "are connected in many ways with the civilization of [the] country" (133), and that one crucial way in which they are connected to America's civilization is that they stand as a testament to a history that will be forever altered should the trees disappear. The American landscape now tells its own history, and this history must remain available to observation. Without the old-growth trees, we lose this sign of change, this evidence of the land's life preceding European colonization. Without the trees, Americans lose a reminder of the American wilderness.

Given the lamentative tone of passages like this one, Cooper's remark in *Rural Hours* that "a stranger moving along the highway looks in vain for any striking signs of a new country" (88) — that is, of a wilderness condition — takes on new weight. If Americans cannot discern the history of the land from the land itself — that is, if alterations to the environment prevent its revelation of its history of development — then Americans cannot perceive their destruction of nature. And with this lack of perception comes, of course, a lack of representation. Americans cannot know what they have displaced if their environment offers no record of the displacement. Thus, not only will America's natural environment suffer from large-scale development, but American culture will, as well, because of both its ignorance and its perceptual distance from the environment.

Cooper therefore instructs her readers in how to "read" the landscape, teaching them to develop as keenly as possible their perceptive powers. As she looks out over a "few miles of country in sight at the moment," she describes her view; and, typically, using the plural pronoun, she reveals that a scrupulous eye can perceive many stages of cultivation in the area: "we amused ourselves by following upon the hill-sides the steps of the husbandman, from the first rude clearing, through every successive stage of tillage, all within range of the eye at the same instant" (89). She points to the "pine stumps" as evidence of recent cultivation; to other signs of some "fallen forest"; and to "traces of water-work" (90, 92). She further differentiates areas, explaining that "those wild pastures upon hill-sides, where the soil has never been ploughed, look very differently from other fallows" (91). And she points to the "softer touches" that "[tell] the same story of recent cultivation": "It frequently happens, that walking about our farms, among rich fields, smooth and well worked, one comes to a low bank, or some little nook, a strip of land never yet cultivated, though surrounded on all sides by ripening crops of eastern grains and grasses." She foregrounds her close knowledge of botany as she explains, "One always knows such places by the pretty native plants growing there," as opposed to the nonindigenous plants that she finds frequently elsewhere (91). Here, then, Cooper encourages a finely tuned perception even as she expands cultural memory by surveying the evidences of natural history available even from one point of observation.

Thus, Cooper saw clear and deep value in "mere" description. In addition to bringing her readers as close as she could to her place, she employed descriptive language as a means of preserving her landscape and of preserving the history that her continent had undergone prior to — and during the early stages of — European settlement. Cooper's particular conception of language thus enabled her to recognize an important new purpose for the genre of nature writing. By recording her place in language, she might literally preserve it for readers; she might also, however, encourage her culture toward a much more acute environmental sensibility by calling attention to her country's path of widespread natural destruction. In relying on language to convey both place and history, she hoped to encourage a humbler ethic in her culture.

Cooper's emphasis on description granted her prose an important quality in a nature writer — humility. Lawrence Buell reminds readers that this is a quality that Thoreau seems to have sought later in his career;

whereas in *Rural Hours* Cooper "managed to cultivate a nonegoistic, eco-centric sensibility," this was a narrative posture "toward which Thoreau had to grope his way laboriously."[21] In Robert Kuhn McGregor's view, we see this change begin during Thoreau's first spring at Walden Pond, as he records spring's arrival in his Journal: "No morals, no transcen-dental lessons accompany the journal entries describing these visions. Simply a lump in the throat in watching nature's overawing beauty."[22] As McGregor demonstrates, we arrive at a very different view of Thoreau's environmental sensibility if we consider *Walden* not the culmination of Thoreau's environmental career, but rather a mere "progress report"[23] in the development of Thoreau's environmental consciousness, a mere step in his long-term quest to convey what Barry Lopez calls "a dignified re-sponse to the land." However, our picture of environmental literary his-tory is further complicated if we consider his quest alongside Cooper's 1850 record of her "ecocentric sensibility."

McGregor's demonstration that Thoreau moved toward a more bio-centric view of the world during the 1850s suggests clearly that as Thoreau became increasingly familiar with his natural environment, his own hu-mility in the presence of nature increased. Yet even in 1854, Thoreau asserts, "There is no such thing as pure *objective* observation. Your ob-servation, to be interesting, *i.e.* to be significant," and — he might have added — to be possible at all, "must be *subjective*."[24] In 1852, he questions his method of mining the Journal for passages and thus presenting ma-terials somewhat out of context, as he did with the lone goose crying out in his "Spring" chapter: "I do not know but thoughts written down thus in a journal might be printed in the same form with greater ad-vantage — than if the related ones were brought together into separate essays. They are now allied to life — & are seen by the reader not to be far fetched — It is more simple — less artful" (*PJ* 4:296). Simplicity, as Thoreau realized, allowed for the written word to be more closely "allied to life," and less allied to art — or, we might say, more closely allied to nature and less so to human reformulating. As Thoreau had written in 1851, "We see too soon to ally the perceptions of the mind to the experi-ence of the hand — to prove our gossamer truths practical — to show their connexion [*sic*] with our every day life (better show their distance from our every day life)" (*PJ* 4:223). This is clearly what Thoreau worked toward in his later years; indeed, as Frank Stewart notes, Thoreau's life work can be interpreted as a "process of perpetually seeking a truth in nature and a way to render it that would betray neither nature nor lan-guage."[25] Thus, while he was clearly cognizant and leery of the problems inherent in representation, the form he worked toward was one in which he humbled himself as narrator and recorded more deliberately "mere facts & names & dates." This is not to say, of course, that Thoreau embraced the conceptions of representation or of natural history that Cooper held, but rather to suggest that even with his more "modern" concerns about perception and representation, he recognized that the most powerful means of understanding his place was to focus more on it, and less on problematizing his means of representation: language. In his later writings, Thoreau worked to create nature's narrative.

Cooper, through her acceptance of a fading theory of language, achieves through her text a representation of her place's natural phenomena. In the perceptive words of one mid–nineteenth-century reviewer, the only story of *Rural Hours* is "the story of the earth." [26] Today, readers in Cooperstown consult this book in order to check in on the progress or cycle of this story, comparing Cooper's descriptions of a day's natural phenomena against the phenomena they witness around them. We might say, then, that in spite of its weak presence in literary history throughout much of the twentieth century, *Rural Hours* has achieved its ultimate goal by leading readers to notice the natural surroundings of a specific place. Clearly, Cooper preserved not herself through her prose, but the passage of time and her environment in Cooperstown. Paradoxically, then, her inability to conceive of a failure of language allowed her to create the story that encouraged "a dignified response to the land."

This mid–nineteenth-century struggle over the issue of representation becomes especially significant when we consider recent theorists' insights into the relation between narrative representation and our environmental predicament. According to Richard Kerridge, the environmental crisis results in part from a dilemma of representation: "The real, material ecological crisis," he argues, "is also a cultural crisis, a crisis of representation. The inability of political cultures to address environmentalism is in part a failure of narrative." [27] We simply do not have narrative structures that can convey or contain the depth and degree of our predicament. Clearly, the shape of narratives available to a given culture largely determines the range of its potential responses to nature, the kinds of nature people can imagine, and the choices for representation available to writers. Exploring the history of nature writers' representations might enable us to expose the ways in which our own narrative forms repeat and endorse an aesthetics of representation which has, in this century, dangerously privileged the philosophical and theoretical at the expense of the literal and material world.

1. Lopez and Wilson, "Ecology and the Human Imagination," 29.

2. Thoreau, *Walden*, 324, 325. Subsequent page references are cited parenthetically in the text.

3. Downing, review [of *Rural Hours*], 232; Sanborn, *Abandoning an Adopted Farm*, 110.

4. See David Jones, introduction to *Rural Hours*, by Susan Fenimore Cooper, esp. xxxvii–xxxviii; and Edward Halsey Foster, *The Civilized Wilderness: Backgrounds to American Romantic Literature, 1817–1860*, 100.

5. Fritzell, *Nature Writing*, 11.

6. McGregor, *A Wider View of the Universe*, 119.

7. Cooper, *Rural Hours*, 72, 3. Subsequent page references are cited parenthetically in the text.

8. Lawrence Buell has also made this observation in *The Environmental Imagination: Thoreau, Nature Writing, and the Formation of American Culture*, 177.

9. Thoreau, *Journal, Vol. 4: 1851–1852*, 296. Subsequent volume and page references to the Princeton edition of the Journal are cited parenthetically with *PJ*.

10. See also "The First Version of *Walden*," in J. Lyndon Shanley, *The Making of Walden*, 193.

11. H. Daniel Peck observes, "The entire scene emphasizes the independence of object from subject" (*Thoreau's Morning Work*, 120).

12. Ibid., 120.

13. Campbell, "The Land and Language of Desire," 130.

14. Buell, *Environmental Imagination*, 135.

15. Cooper, "Small Family Memories," 32–33.

16. For discussions of relevant changes in natural history, see Michel Foucault, *The Order of Things: An Archaeology of the Human Sciences*, and Ernst Mayr, *The Growth of Biological Thought: Diversity, Evolution, and Inheritance*. *Rural Hours* provides ample evidence of Cooper's familiarity with the natural history writings of John James Audubon, Georges Cuvier, Alexander von Humboldt, Charles Lyell, Thomas Nuttall, John Torrey, and Alexander Wilson, among others.

17. Foucault, *Order of Things*, 133.

18. Ibid., 132.

19. Ibid., 134, 131, 298, 129–30.

20. Ibid., 130.

21. Buell, *Environmental Imagination*, 177.

22. McGregor, *Wider View of the Universe*, 68.

23. Ibid., 120.

24. Thoreau, *Journal of Henry David Thoreau*, ed. Torrey and Allen, vol. VI, 236–37.

25. Stewart, *Natural History of Nature Writing*, 11.

26. Downing, review, 231.

27. Kerridge, introduction to *Writing the Environment*, 4.

Wordsworth and Thoreau
Two Versions of Pastoral

GREG GARRARD

Crossings

On the very first page of the first edition of *Walden*, Thoreau issued a challenge: "*I do not propose to write an ode to dejection, but to brag as lustily as Chanticleer in the morning, standing on his roost, if only to wake my neighbors up.*"[1] Not for him the sad, meditative — perhaps rather effeminate — insomnia of Coleridge, but instead a manly and disruptive announcement; a shout for the dawn rather than ambivalent nocturnal thoughts. To drive the point home, he repeated it in "Where I Lived, and What I Lived For." *Walden* announces itself with a dramatic renunciation of English romanticism, suggesting a decided "anxiety of influence." Why might Thoreau, "accidentally" embarking upon his experiment on "Independence Day, on the 4th of July 1845" (84), feel an urgent need to dissociate this work from the English; more specifically, from the English romantic poets; and most specifically, I will argue, from the work of William Wordsworth? The reasons soon become clear.

Walden Pond, the apparent center of Thoreau's New World, is properly introduced to us only well into the book, after a lengthy first chapter. Here we discover that it "impressed [him] like a tarn high up on the one side of a mountain" (86). "Tarn" derives from the Old Norse *tjörn*; Thoreau's vocabulary here comes from the northern dialect of Cumberland, via the most famous poets of that region. Despite the dissociative gesture aimed at Coleridge, the true "precursor" of *Walden* is a Cumbrian native: "It is the figure of Wordsworth . . . beyond any single poem, that engages Thoreau."[2] In this essay I want to look at the "crossing" of Wordsworth by Thoreau — the anxious rejection, the undermining and even betrayal, and the hybridization — in terms of some versions of pastoral, georgic, and the sublime. Although in part a textual exercise, the present experiment must in the main be an experiment in and of the present, because these two figures have assumed a special significance for contemporary environmentalism. Wordsworth's suggestion in his popular *Guide to the Lakes* that the Lake District was seen as "a sort of national property, in which every man has a right and interest who has an eye to perceive and a heart to enjoy," [3] led to the formation of the National Trust in 1895 and later to the designation of the Lake District as a national park. Thoreau, for his part, makes a plea in *The Maine Woods* for the establishment of wildlife reserves: "Why should not we . . . have . . . national preserves . . . in which the bear and the panther, and some even of the hunter race, may still exist." [4]

Furthermore, several of the key works of ecocriticism published in the 1990s have testified to the importance of Wordsworth and Thoreau: Jonathan Bate's *Romantic Ecology* and Karl Kroeber's *Ecological Literary Criticism* focus on Wordsworth; Lawrence Buell's *The Environmental Imagination* uses Thoreau as the center of its argument; Simon Schama's *Landscape and Memory* concludes with a section on Thoreau; and Robert Pogue Harrison's *Forests* has a section on each of them. Without wishing to rehearse their arguments, I might suggest an initial, biographical sense of "crossing" to guide and orient the other senses: Buell argues that "Appearances of self-contradiction notwithstanding, the development of Thoreau's thinking about nature seems pretty clearly to move along a path from homocentrism toward biocentrism," [5] and the period 1845–1854, during which *Walden* was written, revised, and published, must cover a considerable part of that path. Self-conscious artistry and design, according to Buell, coexist in the revision process, with an increasing attention to ecological detail. Wordsworth's path, despite Bate's cautious attempt to revalue *The Excursion*, must still be seen as the reverse of this, as his increasingly complacent and conventional piety and nationalism overwrote — in the fifty-one-year process of rewriting *The Prelude* especially — the youthful republicanism and pantheistic sense of nature's precious vitality Wordsworth worked through in his most productive period from 1795 to 1807. In their respective "great decades," we might say — to simplify a good deal — Wordsworth and Thoreau "crossed" each other in environmentalist terms, heading in opposite directions.

Mountains

One key crossing point is the experience of "the sublime," explored most famously by Thoreau in *The Maine Woods* and by Wordsworth in his literal crossing of the Alps at the Simplon Pass in *The Prelude*. The 1805 *Prelude* saw the poet approach Mont Blanc from Chartreuse full of republican hope, but by 1850 the ejection of the monks had, in defiance of historical fact, been projected back into the account, effectively aligning nature with reaction: "'Stay, stay your sacrilegious hands!' — The voice / Was Nature's, uttered from her Alpine throne" (1850 VI.430–31).[6] This gives a rather different political framing to the anticlimactic, accidental crossing itself, which the climbers discover only in retrospect (1850 VI.577–91). The famous articulation of sublimity therefore occurs as the poet *descends*, somewhat crestfallen, into Switzerland. An increasing tumult of contradictory, bewildering natural phenomena culminates in the poet's sense that the

> Black drizzling crags that spake by the way-side
> As if a voice were in them, the sick sight
> And giddy prospect of the raving stream,
> The unfettered clouds and region of the Heavens,
> Tumult and peace, the darkness and the light —
> Were all like workings of one mind, the features
> Of the same face, blossoms upon one tree;
> Characters of the great Apocalypse,
> The types and symbols of Eternity,
> Of first, and last, and midst, and without end.
> (1850, VI.631–40)

This is not "Mother Nature" by any means. The Alps here become stern instructors, almost overwhelming the poet with their awful splendor (and concomitantly, his own human littleness), but paradoxically only in order to reassure him of the place of both man and mountain in a great Christian drama of fall and redemption. Alienation is merely tactical, the sickening fear at nature's power soon turning to humble acceptance that even the strangely "stationary blasts of waterfalls" might be appropriated as mere *signs* of the fallen state of both humanity and — through humanity's sin — nature. Sublimity confirms what imagination has already suggested: that "Our destiny, our nature, and our home, / Is with infinitude — and only there" (1805 VI.538–39). It brings us not nearer to wild nature, but finally gestures toward an intuition of transcendent divinity, in the context of a radically anthropocentric cosmogony. We might need to add a category to D. W. Meinig's typology of ways of perceiving landscape to accommodate it:[7] landscape as monotheistic *theophany.* As we shall see, this view differs strikingly from a view of earlier date and lower altitude.

Thoreau's encounter with sublime nature, in *The Maine Woods*, tops and in some ways contradicts a genial travel narrative that had tended to stress the pastoral, despite the rugged terrain and thick vegetation. Thus, taking a draft of local beer at Tom Fowler's house at the mouth of the Millinocket, Thoreau asserts that "It was as if we sucked at the very teats of Nature's pine-clad bosom in these parts . . . the topmost most fantastic and spiciest sprays of the primitive wood and whatever invigorating and stringent gum or essence it afforded, steeped and dissolved in it" (27-28). On the top of Mount Katahdin, however, this beneficent mom turns nasty:

> Vast, Titanic, inhuman Nature has got him at a disadvantage, caught him alone, and pilfers him of some of his divine faculty. She does not smile on him as in the plains. She seems to say sternly, why came ye here before your time? This ground is not prepared for you. Is it not enough that I smile in the valleys? . . . Why seek me where I have not called thee, and then complain because you find me but a stepmother? (64)

Clearly there is a "crossing" here: sublimity for Thoreau, while sharing an essential bewilderment with Wordsworth's experience, does not promote intimations of transcendence. Indeed, after descending the mountain, Thoreau is hit by emotions that seem the exact opposite of Wordsworth's — a kind of sublimity of the *flesh*, of matter: "What is this Titan that has possession of me? Talk of mysteries! — Think of our life in nature, — daily to be shown matter, to come in contact with it, — rocks, trees, wind on our cheeks! the *solid* earth! the *actual* world! the *common sense*! *Contact! Contact! Who* are we? *where* are we?" (71). For Max Oelschlaeger, "Ktaadn rekindles for Thoreau a primal or Paleolithic coming-to-consciousness of humankind's naked rootedness in and absolute dependence on nature."[8] In the stirring vigor of Thoreau's exclamations, moreover, we might sense the emergence of "an organic language that combines words of granitic truth ['*Contact!*'] in perfectly natural sentences" (160). Yet just as Wordsworth's sublimity is mediated by the Bible and by Milton, Thoreau's is mediated by Aeschylus: the sublime "stepmother" is really an irate Prometheus, taking back man's "divine faculty." This is the "Titan that has possession" of him. *Contact* must therefore somehow be made through a classical haze, an inevitable irony that must defeat any hope of achieving a "Paleolithic" consciousness. This is not primarily a slight against Thoreau, but against the environmentalist confusion of an illusory "authentic" relation to nature (organic, biocentric, Paleolithic, Indian, or whatever) and a *responsible* one.

Lakes

Thoreau's "anxiety of influence" is most evident when he comes to describe Walden and its surrounding ponds. "This is my lake country," he proclaims (197), but only after issuing this disclaimer: "The scenery of Walden is on a humble scale, and, though very beautiful, does not approach to grandeur, nor can it much concern one who has not long frequented it or lived by its shore" (175). (Walden and environs may not beat the Lake District, but, as Thoreau snidely observed in *The Maine Woods*, "What were the 'forests' of England to these?" [152].) *Walden* begins not with pastoral but with "Economy," a sustained and often brilliant exercise in answering the "pertinent" questions regarding his sojourn at Walden Pond, somewhat impertinently. "Where I Lived, and What I Lived For" however, distinctly invokes pastoral convention: the writer's withdrawal is to a place "as far off as many a region viewed nightly by astronomers," but he is still "a shepherd" even if his thoughts pasture in the heavens (88). He tells us that "Every morning was a cheerful invitation to make my life of equal simplicity, and I may say innocence, with Nature herself" (88). He derides "civilized" accoutrements such as politics, newspapers (though significantly not *publishing* generally), modern forms of labor, and even the postal system as pointless distractions from the real work: the Spartan discipline of the self.

In *Thoreau's Nature*, Jane Bennett has given an excellent account of these techniques of ecological self-craft, but also an honest rendering of his problematic status in a world where *political* environmentalism is a necessity: "Group activism was but busy-ness, a habit of mind inimical to sojourning; action-in-concert, even on behalf of the public good, was a crucible of normalization."[9] Thoreau's ornery rejection of politics and power amounts to a rejection of *history*, a familiar pastoral move; according to Simon Schama, it "was based on the fierce conviction that [history] was irreconcilable with nature. Civilization's habitual way with the natural world, he thought, was to make it meek and compliant, a thing of herbaceous borders and bedding annuals rather than the 'impervious and quaking swamp'."[10] Yet as "Former Inhabitants; and Winter Visitors" seems to show, the pastoral idealization of the landscape of "home" as unsullied *nature* is perplexed and overturned by the reality of landscape as a palimpsest of cultures and natures — in Meinig's terms, as *history* and *habitat*. On the one hand, Thoreau's act of settlement perceives itself, in line with the "morning philosophy" announced in "Where I Lived, and What I Lived For" as the *earliest*: "Alas! how little does the memory of these human inhabitants enhance the beauty of the landscape! Again, perhaps, Nature will try, with me for a first settler" (264). On the other, if the project of Walden is *Walden*, its author its hero, the drama of the "former inhabitants" has a key, though problematic, role to play in its pastoral vision, as H. Daniel Peck argues: it "ties Thoreau and his experiment to his predecessors, and points to *Walden*'s buried themes: the writer's attachment to the human community, and the sense of loss and failure that he shares with that community." [11] This is, then, *ironic* pastoral, and all the more powerful and relevant for it.

The center of Thoreau's pastoral, of course, is the pond itself, "the landscape's most beautiful and expressive feature" (186), and it is here that the "crossing" with Wordsworth is most striking. In the 1850 *Prelude*, the poet remembers as a child "drinking in a pure / organic pleasure . . . from the level plain / Of waters coloured by impending clouds" (I.563–66); in the 1799 version, which is less distorted by pious reflection, Wordsworth acknowledges "the sentiment of being spread / O'er all that moves . . . in the wave itself / And mighty depth of waters" (II.450–58). More importantly, in book VIII (1805), Wordsworth rejects pastoral idealization for a clear-eyed love of "rural ways" that are

> . . . severe and unadorned,
> The unluxuriant produce of a life
> Intent on little but substantial needs,
> Yet beautiful, and beauty that was felt.
> (1805, VIII.207–10)

As the title of the chapter — "Love of Nature Leading to Love of Mankind" (1805) — suggests, amid the lakes, "pastoral life begets republicanism, and . . . pastoral poetry as redefined by Wordsworth begets both reverence for nature and political emancipation." [12] Thoreau's is only a remembered community, but it is one in which he actively participates, whereas Wordsworth's is a "pastoral" world of danger and hard work, but not for the poet himself. The element of counterpastoral in Wordsworth's poetry, nevertheless, has been highly productive in terms of later

English nature poetry, leading, in this century, to the brutal deidealizations of Irish poets Patrick Kavanagh and Seamus Heaney, and Welsh poet R. S. Thomas:

> Too far for you to see
> The fluke and the foot-rot and the fat maggot
> Gnawing the skin from the small bones,
> The sheep are grazing at Bwlch-y-Fedwen,
> Arranged romantically in the usual manner.
> (Thomas, "The Welsh Hill Country")[13]

A couple of other crossings are worth noting. To me, one of the most striking phenomenological exercises in *Walden* is where Thoreau reverses the habitual polarity of land and water: "It is well to have some water in your neighborhood, to give buoyancy to and float the earth. One value even of the smallest well is, that when you look into it you see that earth is not continent but insular" (87). Is it far-fetched to see this perception of insularity as peculiarly "of" the British Isles? It seems especially so when crossed with Dorothy Wordsworth's poem "The Floating Island," published among her brother's poetry in 1842. Here the instability of "dissevered" land (even *Eng*-land perhaps) is nevertheless recuperated, through the lake that temporarily "floats" it, into a larger ecology:

> Buried beneath the glittering Lake,
> Its place no longer to be found;
> Yet the lost fragments shall remain
> To fertilise some other ground.[14]

Another lake "crossing" might pertain to "There was a Boy," in which a boy of Winander, standing "by the glimmering lake," would "[blow] mimic hootings to the silent owls, / That they might answer him" (145). This reciprocity is suddenly overwhelmed by a sort of "contact" in which "the visible scene / Would enter unawares into his mind," not least the striking image of "that uncertain heaven received / Into the bosom of the steady lake." Thoreau, captivated by his own still, smooth pond, likewise perceives how "the water, full of light and reflections, becomes a lower heaven itself" (86), but when he indulges himself like the boy of the poem in an echoing "concourse wild / Of jocund din," it is a far more confrontational affair: "I used to raise the echoes by striking with a paddle on the side of my boat, filling the surrounding woods circling and dilating sound, stirring them up as the keeper of a menagerie his wild beasts, until I elicited a growl from every wooded vale and hillside" (174).

There is, then, no simple priority of one version of pastoral over another. Thoreau's is exact, observant but ironic, undoing even as it asserts its earliness, its ahistorical withdrawal. Wordsworth's is openly political and engaged, but the poetic subject remains an observer, progressively more and more alienated from his own ideal human ecology. In these respects, they enact the ambivalence of pastoral for us today, in its capacity both to trouble and confront urban modernity, and to supply that way of life with the harmless, mystified "elsewhere" of pastoral escapism.

Names

Crossing Wordsworth and Thoreau, it is sometimes possible to discern a shared, trans-Atlantic sense of the local — a sense of place — in opposition to the reductively national and economic articulation of space. To be precise, both writers perceive a special role for the names of places in the project of properly dwelling in them. Ironically it is Wordsworth, a native in his land, who assigns names to places in and around Grasmere Vale, whereas Thoreau, a second-generation colonist, is prepared to engage in spirited argument over the received names in his adopted locale.

Jonathan Bate argues that Wordsworth's "Poems on the Naming of Places," published in *Lyrical Ballads*, ought to be seen as "ecolectal" poems: they "speak" place, simultaneously denominating it and enacting the poet's dwelling in it. Whereas the true native, such as the shepherd Michael of the eponymous "Pastoral Poem," inhabits Grasmere carefully but unselfconsciously, the poet must recuperate a civilized ironic distance by giving names to the significant places among which he dwells. "Emma's Dell," for example, is dedicated to the poet's sister, Dorothy (under the pseudonym "Emma"), by the poem "It was an April morning," because there the poet has experienced an overwhelming sense of natural beauty and plenitude; varied sounds combine to make "a song / Which . . . seemed like some wild growth / Or like some natural produce of the air / That could not cease to be" (p. 116). The act of naming at once commemorates the siblings' newly established residence together among the lakes and represents a way of being there that is neither mere aesthetic tourism nor working inhabitation: "Soon did the spot become my other home, / My dwelling, and my out-of-doors abode."

Not all of these poems are as humble and generous, however. "There is an Eminence" records the naming by Dorothy of a lonely peak after the poet himself, which seems a classic instance of the gendering of the distinction of the sublime and the beautiful: the male poet gets a mountain, while the sister gets a pretty dell. In *Walden*, it is this egotistical and even appropriative quality of naming that can make Thoreau seem "cross" with Wordsworth's poetic mode of dwelling, as we can see from the diatribe on the name of a local pond: "Flint's Pond! Such is the poverty of our nomenclature. What right had the unclean and stupid farmer, whose farm abutted on this sky water, whose shores he has ruthlessly laid bare, to give his name to it?" (195). But then the analogy of poet and farmer breaks down, because Thoreau's real target is the isomorphism he sees between the assimilation of place to name, and the assimilation of landscape to a ruthlessly reductive "economy": "Rather let it be named from the fishes that swim in it, the wild fowl or quadrupeds which frequent it, the wild flowers which grow by its shores, or some wild man or child the thread of whose history is interwoven with its own; not from him who could show no title to it but the deed which a like-minded neighbor or legislature gave him" (196). Wordsworth's naming of Emma's Dell rejects any such assumption of title or legal ownership — "Our thoughts at least are ours" — but still loses Thoreau's critical edge in exploring a sense of place limited to family and friends and evades any larger context.

Thoreau's own most important naming is, of course, Walden itself; it is arguably an extended exercise in "ecolectal" prose. Yet the name of the pond is problematic, even perhaps trans-Atlantic! Thoreau considers a local legend concerning the name which derives it from that of an Indian squaw who escaped the act of divine punishment of her people (182). Without wholly rejecting this "Indian fable," he proposes some alternatives: "If the name was not derived from that of some English locality, — Saffron Walden, for instance — one might suppose that it was called, originally, Walled-in Pond." Given the persistent association in Thoreau's work between "England" and the grasping economics of a Farmer Flint, it is perhaps surprising that its part in naming his own pond is not cause for more anxiety. But then if, as I have suggested, this is ironic pastoral, the indiscriminate juxtaposition of Indian fable, English imposition, and wry pun name can be seen as fruitful hybridization with lakeland eco-piety. In *Walden*, naming can be both care-ful and critical.

Tracks

In Leo Marx's *The Machine in the Garden,* the train appears as the classic instance of the penetration of modernity into the pastoral idyll, the "other" against which pastoralism defines itself. So it certainly seemed to Wordsworth, when in 1844 a company was formed to extend the railway from Kendal to Windermere; he wrote a series of letters to the *Morning Post* to oppose it, complaining principally that it would be obviously counterproductive, ruining the very pastoral peace it brought visitors to experience: "What can . . . be more absurd, than that either rich or poor should be spared the trouble of travelling by the high roads over so short a space . . . if the unavoidable consequence must be a great disturbance of the retirement, and in many places a destruction of the beauty of the country, which the parties are come in search of? Would not this be pretty much like the child's cutting up his drum to learn where the sound came from?"[15] In a series of sonnets on the subject, he calls upon nature herself to rebel against the "rash assault": "Speak, passing winds; ye torrents, with your strong / And constant voice, protest against the wrong" (224). Sonnet XLVI even raises the bizarre specter of a mountain "startled" by the whistle of a passing train! A problem arises, however, because the necessary alignment with capitalism attendant upon his support for his local Tory MPs undermines his prospects for effective critique. In "At Furness Abbey," Wordsworth imagines a group of "Railway Labourers" taking lunch amid the ruins, and breaking into spontaneous songs of praise: "from one voice a Hymn with tuneful sound / Hallows once more the long-deserted Quire / And thrills the old sepulchral earth around" (225). The interpretative crux of the poem occurs in the penultimate line, "Profane Despoilers, stand ye not reproved," which seems to offer a rebuke to the workers themselves. Yet the last line turns out to offer a *contrast* between such "Despoilers" and the "simplehearted men" moved by the "spirit of the place." So who are the unnamed objects of the criticism? Wordsworth's own compromises speak most eloquently in his silence at this crux.

In *Walden,* Thoreau too expresses ambivalence about the railway, although his attitudes are more openly contradictory: "The whistle of the locomotive penetrates my woods summer and winter, sounding like the scream of a hawk sailing over some farmer's yard, informing me that many restless city merchants are arriving within the circle of the town, or adventurous country traders from the other side" (115). The sound is at once offensively penetrating, and oddly naturalized by comparison with the cry of the hawk. Having expressed his morning joy, Thoreau says: "I watch the passage of the morning cars with the same feeling that I do the rising of the sun, which is hardly more regular" (116). Having savaged what passes for "economy" with his neighbors in his first chapter, he praises the "enterprise and bravery" of commerce (as symbolized by the railroad) (118), and admits that he is "refreshed and expanded when the freight train rattles past" (119). Perhaps the strangest contradiction concerns the passage of "lumber": "Here goes lumber from the Maine woods, which did not go out to sea on the last freshet, risen four dollars on the thousand because of what did go out or was split up; pine, spruce, cedar, — first, second, third, and fourth qualities, so lately all of one quality, to wave over the bear, and moose, and caribou" (119–20).

Contrast the remarkably *neutral* tone of that passage with the tone of the following passage from *The Maine Woods*: "the pine is no more lumber than man is, and to be made into boards and houses is no more its true and highest use than the truest use of man is to be cut down and made into manure. . . . Every creature is better alive than dead, men and moose and pine-trees, and he who understands it aright will rather preserve its life than destroy it" (121). It seems that the outraged wilderness voice is somewhat attenuated by the ironic pastoral of *Walden*, admitting to all kinds of unlikely enthusiasms. Yet the sense that trees/lumber (or whale/whalebone, elephant/ivory, man/manure) represents a crucial *decision* in the poetics of human relation to and responsibility for nature is one reflected elsewhere in *Walden*, in the quirky georgic of the bean field.

Beans/Grass

What I have been getting around to saying is that pastoral and the sublime — the latter as the central trope in a discourse of "wilderness" — provide too many opportunities for evasions of human responsibility, in their quest for an aboriginally *authentic* relation of humans to the rest of nature. They make possible the question that entitles Richard White's important essay, "Are You an Environmentalist or Do You Work for a Living?" [16] Environmentalism must be a *way* of working for a *living*, and in this sense it is georgic which should provide its poetics. Thoreau is really the figure that counts here, not because he "enacts what Wordsworth contemplates" [17] — the Lake poet had done his share of weeding too — but because he writes that enactment up in *Walden*, exploring the isomorphism of the questions of the *meaning* and the *being* of the earth.

On one level, Thoreau's work in the bean field is merely self-indulgent; he wasn't interested in eating the beans, but did it "to serve a parable-maker one day" (162). If this is what the "poetics of working the earth" amounts to, it's not worth much. What is powerful and compelling is Thoreau's perception of an *analogy* of hoeing and writing, and therefore between the determination of what a place shall *be* and what it shall *mean*: "Removing the weeds, putting fresh soil about the bean stems, and encouraging this weed which I had sown, making the yellow soil express its summer thought in bean leaves and blossoms rather than in worm-wood and piper and millet grass, making the earth say beans instead of grass, this was my daily work" (156–57).

There is a profound sense here that writing and hoeing are processes that demand letting beings *be*, but also that this process implies a responsibility for "inflecting" them one way or another; as Stanley Cavell says, the writer's vocation "depends upon . . . letting [words] come to him from their own region, and then taking that occasion for inflecting them one way instead of another right then and there, or for refraining from them then and there; as one may inflect the earth toward beans instead of grass, or let it alone, as it is before you are there." [18] The Heideggerian idiom here is appropriate to the realization, not only that there is a relationship between *calling* a stand of trees "lumber" (what Heidegger calls *Bestand*, or "standing reserve," a German forestry term) and *treating* it as such, but that in a sense they are the same activity, on different levels, and in different senses, of *culture*. Charles Taylor has suggested on the basis of Heidegger's philosophy of language that "we can think of the demands of language also as a demand that entities put on us to disclose them in a certain way. This amounts in fact to saying that they demand that we acknowledge them as having certain meanings. But this manner of disclosure can in crucial cases be quite incompatible with a stance of pure instrumentality towards them." [19]

By accepting this, we are accepting that culture is always already in-volved in nature at every level — poetic culture or arboriculture — not only at the boundaries described and enforced by "pastoral" and "wil-derness." We are enabled to unmask the arrogant claims of both purify-ing pastoral and economic instrumentalism, and directed toward what I should call "georgic" questions. Shall we make the earth say/be "space" or "place"? "Mine" or "ours"? In which tense shall we speak/be? We can resolve this into the practical, political, poetical question: beans or grass? Our answers must always be *working* answers, in the senses of being provisional, effective, and engaged. We are all implicated in the hard questions. Our responsibility goes all the way down.

NOTES

1. Thoreau, *Walden*. Subsequent page references are cited parenthetically in the text.

2. Weisbuch, "Thoreau's Dawn and the Lake School's Night," 249.

3. Wordsworth, *Selected Prose*, 61.

4. Thoreau, *Maine Woods*, 156.

5. Buell, *The Environmental Imagination*, 138.

6. Hereafter cited by date of draft, book, and line number. Wordsworth, *The Prelude: 1799, 1805, 1850*.

7. Cf. D. W. Meinig, "The Beholding Eye: Ten Versions of the Same Scene."

8. Oelschlaeger, *Idea of Wilderness*, 149.

9. Bennett, *Thoreau's Nature*, 86.

10. Schama, *Landscape and Memory*, 574.

11. Peck, "The Crosscurrents of *Walden*'s Pastoral," 74.

12. Bate, *Romantic Ecology*, 25.

13. R. S. Thomas, *Collected Poems: 1945–1990*, 22.

14. Wordsworth, *Poetical Works*, 416. Subsequent parenthetical page citations of Wordsworth's poems (excluding *The Prelude*) refer to the de Selincourt edition.

15. Wordsworth, *Selected Prose*, 84.

16. White, "Are You an Environmentalist or Do You Work for a Living?"

17. Weisbuch, "Thoreau's Dawn and the Lake School's Night," 252.

18. Cavell, *Senses of Walden*, 28.

19. Taylor, "Heidegger, Language and Deep Ecology," 267.

Humanity as "A Part and Parcel of Nature"

A Comparative Study of Thoreau's and Taoist Concepts of Nature

AIMIN CHENG

A prominent aspect of Thoreau's philosophy of nature, which makes his view different from that of many Americans, is his absorption of the Chinese conception of the relationship between humanity and nature.[1] His belief in humanity as "a part and parcel of Nature" clearly demonstrates his affinity with Chinese philosophical tradition. Lin Yutang once said, "Thoreau is the most Chinese of all American authors in his entire view of life. . . . I could translate passages of Thoreau into my own language and pass them off as original writing by a Chinese poet without raising any suspicion."[2] Gary Simon also remarked that "Thoreau . . . evidenced, in my opinion, a greater affinity for Taoism than for any other Oriental religion."[3]

It is well known that the Western understanding of humanity's relationship with nature is quite different from that of the Chinese. In the West, it is generally held that nature, like humanity, was created by God and should be conquered and used by humanity, whereas in China, humanity is believed to come from nature and will eventually return to it — therefore, humanity is regarded as part of nature. In Western natural philosophy, the relationship between humanity and nature exists often as the confronting "I-Thou" relationship, while in Chinese philosophy it presents a harmonious "part-whole" relationship.

It is difficult to pinpoint exactly when this Western concept of nature began. In the Bible, the Book of Genesis (1:28) relates how God, after creating Adam and Eve in his image, said to them: "Be fruitful, and multiply, and fill the earth and subdue it; and have dominion over the fish of the sea and over the birds of the air and over every living thing that moves upon the earth."[4] Traditionally, it was thought that the confrontation between humanity and nature was the result of the Fall. Because of the Fall, the harmonious state between humanity and nature in the Garden of Eden was broken.

Clarence Glacken points out, "In the *Politics*, Aristotle expresses clearly but in disappointingly crude fashion the idea of purpose in nature, including the relation of plants and animals to the needs of man. . . . Plants must be intended for the use of animals; animals, we can infer, exist for man; the tame for use and food, the wild — if not all — for food, clothing, and various instruments. 'Now if Nature makes nothing incomplete, and nothing in vain, the inference must be that she has made all animals for the sake of man.'"[5] Glacken continues: "In this anthropocentric conception of interrelationship in nature, the distribution of plants and animals is directly related to the needs and uses of man; the idea has been repeated countlessly in modern times, although many writers on natural theology in the seventeenth and eighteenth centuries protested against it as being incompatible with the Christian religion, maintaining that it was but another example of man's pride" (48). Max Oelschlaeger also argues that "Aristotle wanted to gain rational knowledge and thereby control over nature, rather than to maintain harmony with it."[6]

Ralph Waldo Emerson, founder of American transcendentalism, defined nature in this way: "Nature, in its ministry to man, is not only the material, but is also the process and the result. All the parts incessantly work into each other's hands for the profit of man. The wind sows the seed; the sun evaporates the sea; the wind blows the vapor to the field; the ice, on the other side of the planet, condenses rain on this; the rain feeds the plant; the plant feeds the animal; and thus the endless circulations of the divine charity nourish man."[7]

In modern times in the West, according to our Chinese understanding, nature denotes very often the power external to humanity which includes the sky, the earth, the sea, and all that is in them except human beings. There is a fixed great gulf between the natural world and human society, between conscience and science, and between emotion and reason. Nature has alternately been execrated as humanity's cruelest enemy or worshipped and sung as its kindly mistress or benign saint.[8]

In Chinese philosophy, however, nature itself is believed to possess divinity, and humans are born to be part of it. On top is heaven and beneath is the earth, and humanity is in between, thus forming the harmonious oneness. To be one with nature is the highest ideal in Chinese philosophy, especially Taoism,[9] as Calvin S. Brown and others point out:

"As a philosophy, it [Taoism] stands for spiritual freedom, naturalism, simplicity. . . . In spirit it seeks natural harmony and peace."[10]

Taoist philosophy differs from the Confucian in that the latter tends "to read the human social order into nature. This led to the idea that humans possess an 'evaluating mind,' which can detect nature's ethical signals." Taoism rejects "the Confucian natural order and social hierarchy"[11] and believes in Tao as the ultimate principle underlying every thing and every motion in the universe: "Man follows the ways of the earth. The earth follows the way of Heaven. Heaven follows the ways of Tao. Tao follows its own way."[12] The Chinese concept of nature as a whole sees nature as an organic entirety. According to ancient Chinese philosophy, *qi* is considered to be the source of the constitution of the universe. *Qi* is everywhere: inside the human body as well as in the natural world. Hence it is possible for human beings to attain harmony with nature through the correspondence between the internal *qi* and external *qi*.

While dualism in Western philosophy gravitates toward confrontation, as between humanity and nature, body and soul, spirit and matter, and so on, dualism in Chinese philosophy emphasizes the harmony between the two opposites. This is typically expressed in the concept of *Taiji* (the Great Ultimate), one of the essential concepts of ancient Chinese metaphysics. The *Taiji* theory holds that everything in the universe consists of two opposite but complementary aspects, *yin* and *yang*, as is displayed in the *Taiji* diagram, which, known as the "illustration of the motion of the world," shows symbolically the harmony, balance, and coexistence of these two forces. The black fish in the diagram stands for *yin* and the white fish for *yang*. The *yin* fish and the *yang* fish revolve around and chase each other, representing the principle of unceasing motion and change. A black spot in the white fish and a white spot in the black fish stand for the inclusion of *yin* and *yang* within each other; and the coexistence of the two fish in the same circle not only indicates that the *yin* and *yang* forces are present in everything, but also suggests the great oneness which is actually the central idea of ancient Chinese philosophy.[13] Lao Zi said, "From *Tao* came one; from one came two; from two came three; and from three came everything."[14] It is in this oneness that humanity finds harmony with nature.

With a poignant awareness of the question of the place of humanity in the context of organic nature, Thoreau had to differentiate between these two types of philosophical perception: whether humans and nature form a oneness, or whether they lack such a oneness because of their confrontation. Thoreau conceived of the former as different from the latter, although not disconnected from it. In the case of the Chinese concept, humans, perceiving a oneness with nature because already constituted in nature, will remain satisfied with contemplating nature itself. The Western concept, on the other hand, challenges humans to replace the inherent unity between nature and themselves with an intellectual one. In addition, the Western concept postulates a larger totality of which humanity and nature are only a part. Therefore, humans have to bridge the intellectual gulf between nature and themselves in order to reconstitute their unity with nature. Chinese philosophy loosens the sensory boundaries between humans and nature in contemplation and takes humans closer to the sublime and perfect union, the oneness between humanity and the natural surroundings.

Although the idea of the unity of humanity with nature pervaded Anglo-European romanticism and was present, to a large extent, in American transcendentalism, too, the emphasis on the otherness of nature, its separateness from humanity, was something that Thoreau hated to accept. The problem was, as Frederick Garber suggests, that "The self-sufficiency so admired in organic nature turned out sometimes to contain a disconcerting aloofness."[15] The confrontation between nature and humanity came not only from the otherness of nature but also from humanity's own otherness, the separation of the body and the soul. Emerson put the point bluntly at the beginning of *Nature*: "The universe is composed of Nature and the Soul. Strictly speaking, therefore, all that is separate from us, all which Philosophy distinguishes as the NOT ME, that is, both nature and art, all other men and my own body, must be ranked under this name, NATURE."[16] Taking Thoreau's concept of nature as a whole, one can perceive that traditional Western belief in general and the romantic concept in particular do not fit in many ways Thoreau's inner sense of harmony between humanity and nature and his effort to lessen "the distance between the natural and the human."[17] Thoreau might be content with occupying a happy middle ground between the East and the West if he could, but he never concealed his strong interest in the ancient philosophy of China, which reinforced his attraction to the unity, the oneness, of humanity and nature.[18] Here we find the deepest springs of Thoreau's view of humanity as part of nature, an idea which few Americans before him had held, and which he made remarkably clear in the following passage in "Walking": "I wish to speak a word for Nature, for absolute freedom and wildness, as contrasted with a freedom and culture merely civil, — to regard man as an inhabitant, or a part and parcel of Nature, rather than a member of society" (*Writings* V: 205).

A brief analysis of this passage may help illuminate Thoreau's view of nature. First, Thoreau wishes to defend nature for its "absolute freedom and wildness"; second, Thoreau expresses clearly his view of humanity's relationship with nature: man is "an inhabitant, or a part and parcel of Nature" rather than its master. This union, this oneness of humanity and nature, is not only the spiritual perfection which Thoreau pursued himself but also a doctrine that he fervently preached to others; third, Thoreau asserts that humanity belongs to nature rather than society; and in this assertion Thoreau sets a confrontation not only between nature and society but also between Eastern and Western philosophy.

The idea of humanity as part of nature is continued in the following:

> I would have every man so much like a wild antelope, so much a part and parcel of nature, that his very person should thus sweetly advertise our senses of his presence, and remind us of those parts of nature which he most haunts. (*Writings* V: 225–26)

> When most at one with nature I feel supported and propped on all sides by a myriad influences.[19]

> When, as now, in January a south wind melts the snow and the bare ground appears covered with sere grass and occasionally wilted green leaves, which seem in doubt whether to let go their greenness quite or absorb new juices against the coming year — In such a season a perfume seems to exhale from the earth itself and the south wind melts my integuments also. Then is she my mother earth. I derive a real vigor from the scent of the gale wafted over the naked ground as from strong meats — and realize again how man is the pensioner of nature. We are always conciliated and cheered when we are fed by an influence — and our needs are felt to be part of the domestic economy of nature. (*PJ* 1: 360–61)

With regard to humanity's relationship with nature, these passages ally Thoreau more with the Chinese tradition that humanity is part of nature rather than apart from it. The Chinese philosophical tradition of nature satisfied two of his most important needs: to maintain contact with external natural objects, and to experience a spiritual union with nature. But what is even more important in this tradition to make him comfortable in becoming one of its devoted exponents is that the Chinese notion of unity of the natural world was free from worldly concerns or religious significance. Ancient Chinese philosophers did not care whether the harmony they found in nature sprang from any spiritual source; they simply regarded nature as a place of retreat from society when they were disgusted with its corruption or tired of living in it.

As long as Thoreau remained attracted to the pursuits of Chinese philosophers, he was able to carry on the communion between the soul and natural objects and absorb nature's spirit of harmony and growth by living in its serenity and quietude free from worldly concerns: "Sometimes, in a summer morning, having taken my accustomed bath, I sat in my sunny doorway from sunrise till noon, rapt in a reverie, amidst the pines and hickories and sumachs, in undisturbed solitude and stillness, while the birds sang around or flitted noiseless through the house. . . . I grew in those seasons like corn in the night. . . . I realized what the Orientals mean by contemplation and the forsaking of works" (*Walden* 111–12). Again he said: "I should like to keep some book of natural history always by me as a sort of elixir — reading of which would restore the tone of my system — and secure me true and cheerful views of life. . . . To the soul that contemplates some trait of natural beauty no harm nor disappointment can come. The doctrines of despair — of spiritual or political servitude — no priestcraft nor tyranny — was ever taught by such as drank in the harmony of nature" (*PJ* 1:353–54).

From a strong consciousness of his oneness with nature, Thoreau was endowed with the sense of his close relationship to plant and animal life. This sense of relationship, and the love of natural objects which grew out of it, finds frequent expression in Thoreau's works. A. Bronson Alcott said of Thoreau, "He seemed one with things, of nature's essence and core, knit of strong timbers, — like a wood and its inhabitants. There was in him sod and shade, wilds and waters manifold, — the mould and mist of earth and sky."[20] Stanley Cavell also believes that there were "exchanged identities" between Thoreau and the birds and animals and that "the identification is as complete as reason will permit."[21]

Based on this view of humanity and nature, Thoreau went far beyond the traditional Christian idea of humanity's supremacy in the world. He came to believe that humankind was merely one among many natural kinds existing within an interrelated community of life on earth. As Lyman Cady says, "Thoreau's whole stress is on the *kinship* of man and animal."[22] Thoreau wrote interestingly in his Journal, "I have a contemporary in Walden. It has fins where I have legs and arms. I have a friend among the fishes, at least an acquaintance."[23]

The perception that all creatures in nature are manifestations of and one with the Divine and bear the closest relationship to humanity generates reverence for them as interpreters to humanity of the secrets of the infinite, and brings forth naturally the desire not to injure any living creature as well as the idea of abstinence from eating meat, as the Buddhist and the Taoist doctrines preach. In this respect, Thoreau was very Oriental.[24]

The sense of oneness with natural objects and animals is often expressed in Thoreau's writings in the language of human relationship. Thoreau wrote in his Journal: "What cousin of mine is the shrub oak? Rigid as iron, clean as the atmosphere, hardy as virtue, innocent and sweet as a maiden, is the shrub oak. In proportion as I know and love it, I am natural and sound as a partridge" (*J* IX:146), and "There are some strange affinities in this universe — strange ties strange harmonies and relationships, what kin am I to some wildest pond among the mountains" (*PJ* 2:158).

This relationship or kinship between humanity and nature finds expression in *A Week on the Concord and Merrimack Rivers*. As James McIntosh comments, "The likeness between man and nature is reinforced over and over in individual images and metaphors in the *Week*, in the boat painted in nature's colors, in the cabin roofs reflecting the flight of hawks, in the natural men who resemble beasts and trees. The extreme of this tendency is reached when Thoreau manages, by means of imaginative distortion, to think of himself as dissolved in nature, selfless."[25] But it should be added that by "dissolv[ing] in nature," Thoreau not only became "selfless" but also had the immortal blood of nature flow into his veins, thus turning from the finite into the infinite:

Sometimes a mortal feels in himself Nature, — not his Father but his Mother stirs within him, and he becomes immortal with her immortality. From time to time she claims kindredship with us, and some globule from her veins steals up into our own.

> I am the autumnal sun,
> With autumn gales my race is run;
> When will the hazel put forth its flowers,
> Or the grape ripen under my bowers?
> When will the harvest or the hunter's moon,
> Turn my midnight into mid-noon?
> I am all sere and yellow,
> And to my core mellow.

The mast is dropping within my woods,
The winter is lurking within my moods,
And the rustling of the withered leaf
Is the constant music of my grief. (*A Week* 378)

Thoreau's identification of humanity as well as of himself with trees was a pervasive and continuing attempt, partly conscious and partly unconscious, to see humanity as "a part and parcel of nature." In identifying with trees Thoreau thought that humanity could carry on the exploration of nature's abiding unity and take in its vigor and animation of growth, by which to "mould" the body to fit the soul and finally be one with nature: "We should strengthen, and beautify, and industriously mould our bodies to be fit companions of the soul. — Assist them to grow up like tree, and be agreeable and wholesome objects in nature. — I think if I had had the disposal of this soul of man — I should have bestowed it sooner on some antelope of the plains, than upon this sickly and sluggish body" (*PJ* 1:232).

In a letter to H. G. O. Blake on March 13, 1856, Thoreau compares himself to the sugar maple tree: "Shall, then, the maple yield sugar, and not man? . . . While [the farmer] works in his sugar-camp let me work in mine, — for sweetness is in me, and go sugar it shall come, — it shall not all go to leaves and wood. Am I not a sugar maple man then?" (*Writings* VI:278).

Another tree with which Thoreau closely identified was the wild apple.[26] He wrote, "Every wild apple shrub excites our expectation thus, somewhat as every wild child. It is, perhaps, a prince in disguise. What a lesson to man! So are human beings referred to the highest standard, the celestial fruit which they suggest and aspire to bear, browsed on by fate; and only the most persistent and strangest genius prevails, sends a tender scion upward at last, and drops its perfect fruit on the ungrateful earth. Poets and philosophers and statesmen thus spring up in the country pastures, and outlast the hosts of unoriginal men" (*Writings* V:307). Raymond Dante Gozzi argues, "His essay, 'Wild Apples,' becomes deeply moving when it is perceived as one of his last attempts to ward off the demons of stagnation and despair, to assert emphatically against all doubts that he had led a life of productivity and integrity. . . . Like the wild apple tree, Thoreau's 'interior shoot,' his loftiest aspirations, cannot be reached by his 'foes'; though gnarled and homely as the apples and the tree, he 'has not forgotten [his] high calling and bears [his] own peculiar fruit in triumph' (*Writings* V:305). Thoreau cannot resist the temptation to make explicit the connection between tree and man."[27]

To Thoreau, oneness — identity — with natural objects is oneness with the Spirit of Nature:

> I cannot come nearer to God and Heaven
> Than I live to Walden even.
> I am its stony shore,
> And the breeze that passes o'er;
> In the hollow of my hand
> Are its water and its sand,
> And its deepest resort
> Lies high in my thought. (*Walden* 193)

Thoreau expressed his desire for perfect oneness with nature in a letter to Mrs. Brown (July 21, 1841): "I to be nature looking into nature with such easy sympathy as the blue-eyed grass in the meadow looks into the face of the sky. From some such recess I would put forth sublime thoughts daily, as the plant puts forth leaves" (*Correspondence* 45).

From his firm belief in the oneness with nature, Thoreau was imbued with the sense of sympathy between humanity and nature or natural objects. He wrote in his Journal: "Miss Minott says that Dr. Spring told her that when the sap began to come up into trees, i.e. about the middle of February (she says), then the diseases of the human body come out. The idea is that *man's body sympathizes with the rest of nature*, and his pent-up humors burst forth like the sap from wounded trees" (*J* VII:239, emphasis added).

Thoreau expressed this idea more vividly in *Walden*: "The indescribable innocence and beneficence of Nature, — of sun and wind and rain, of summer and winter, — such health, such cheer, they afford forever! And such sympathy have they ever with our race, that all Nature would be affected, and the sun's brightness fade, and the winds would sigh humanely, and the clouds rain tears, and the woods shed their leaves and put on mourning in midsummer, if any man should ever for a just cause grieve. Shall I not have intelligence with the earth? Am I not partly leaves and vegetable mould myself?" (138).

The expression of this sense of sympathy between man and nature finds interesting parallels in numerous Chinese poems of nature, of which "Autumn Leaves" by Lu Lun is an example:

The years that pass
Have brought with them
White hair
Autumn has come
And the trees stand
Bare and cold.

Perplexed,
I ask the yellow leaves:
"Are you, too, sad?
What griefs have you
That you
Are sere and old?"[28]

Like the Chinese poets, Thoreau loved nature and was so much in harmony with it that he could feel the very pulse beating through nature. By living in nature and being one with nature, Thoreau achieved perfection of life:

The life of men will ere long be of such purity and innocence, that it will deserve to have the sun to light it by day and the moon by night. — to be ushered in by the freshness and melody of spring — to be entertained by the luxuriance and vigor of summer — and matured and solaced by the hues and dignity of Autumn. . . .

When we withdraw a little from the village — and perceive how it is embosomed in nature — where perhaps its roofs are gleaming in the setting sun — We wonder if the life of its inhabitants might not also be thus natural and innocent reflecting the aspects of nature. We are apt to view again the life of the haymaker of such simplicity and innocence as his occupation Do not the gleaming crops — the verdant lawns — the springing groves — the flocks and herds — suggest what kind of a man the farmer should be?

In the first place his life must be serene and calm. (*PJ* 1: 458–59)

This passage may well suggest the ideal life of the Chinese scholar, as is described in "Peach-Blossom Springs" by Tao Yuanming:

Their living they gain by tilling the soil and reaping;
When the sun goes down they go to rest together.
Bamboo and mulberry bend to give them shade,
Beans and rice follow at seasons due.
From the spring silkworm they gather long thread,

At the autumn harvest there is no imperial tax.
The only lanes are made by their coming and going,
Cocks are crowing and dogs are barking together.[29]

Thoreau's way of dealing with natural objects in his writings also reveals his sharing in Chinese philosophy and aesthetics. In his works, especially in his Journal, Thoreau devotes considerable attention to natural objects, trying to capture their myriad forms with a scrupulousness that may appear almost obsessive. Although his landscape descriptions are not all of the same quality or design — some well-organized, styled, and philosophic, others casual, disorderly, and appealing to the senses — they all share one feature. By observing and recording the external appearances of the objects, Thoreau sought the undivided unity or oneness in which they subsist.

Faced with a panoramic view of nature, a writer or artist attempts to satisfy two demands: one is to represent each and every object in all its array of diverse appearances; the other is to encompass the whole into which every object fits as a component part. Ideally, one should be able to describe both the particulars of a landscape and its larger frame without damaging either, but in practice this is very difficult to achieve. Thoreau believed that Chinese philosophy and aesthetics gravitated toward the construction of the whole with parts, while Western philosophy and aesthetics tended to dismember the whole into parts. In absorbing Chinese philosophy, Thoreau was also attracted to the Chinese aesthetic perception that stresses intuition and the sense of wholeness. For instance, a Chinese landscape painter, when at work, perceives a whole already constituted in each object that is being painted. In addition, the artist not only makes all the objects in the picture — mountains, waters, humans, and other natural objects — form a whole, but also sets the painted, visible picture in a larger, invisible, but perceivable totality of which the former is a part, thus enlarging the scope of the visual as well as the spiritual. The following passage is from Thoreau's Journal:

In the moonlight night what intervals are created — ! The rising moon is related to the near pine tree which rises above the forest — & we get a juster notion of distance. The moon is only somewhat further off & to one side. There may be only three objects — myself — pine tree & the moon nearly equidist[an]t. (J V: 416)

The depiction may be totally wrong from an epistemological perspective, but Thoreau is more a poet philosopher than a natural scientist here.

He tries to make the description seem objective, because he delineates a picture of only three objects — himself, a pine tree, and the moon — and does not make any comment on their relations. Though the three objects — a man, a tree, and a celestial body — have nothing in common, in the conventional sense, they exist as a geometric construction, each forming a part of the whole. Sharon Cameron comments while discussing another passage from Thoreau, "I suggest that the Journal raises questions of relation, and the representation of relation, in a number of contexts. It asks us to consider the relation between nature and the mind, and, alternatively, between aspects of a so-called single entity — the landscape seen through the birch trees by which it is therefore framed — that is, between one part of nature and another part of nature, to which it is juxtaposed" (16). This kind of juxtaposition certainly gives us the sense of oneness of humanity and nature. Also, the image created by the above passage and the idea of the oneness between humanity and nature represented by this image may well remind Chinese readers of many classic Chinese poems of landscape or nature.

In conclusion we may say that, taken as a whole, Thoreau's concept of nature admittedly exists within the framework of Western philosophy. Therefore, it is bedeviled, like transcendentalism, by a fundamental tension lurking within its epistemological views, because the fundamental ideologies on which Thoreau's philosophy is based — transcendentalism, romanticism, and Chinese and Hindu philosophies — cannot be combined without conflict, so far as the concept of nature is concerned. On the one hand, the Western roots of his philosophy lead it to emphasize the separation of humanity from nature; on the other hand, this emphasis stands in uneasy conflict with Thoreau's equally strong commitment to Oriental philosophies that urge humanity to "contemplat[e] the harmony of nature and striv[e] to become a part of that harmony."[30] Therefore, Thoreau's concept of nature may have something of the structure of an antinomy, produced by his attempt to combine the Western and the Eastern understandings of human relationship with nature (i.e., the "I-Thou" relationship with the "part-whole" relationship). My claim, however, is that in combining the two conflicting concepts of the relationship between humanity and nature, Thoreau not only tried to maintain a balance by changing his perspectives and shifting his stances without affecting his affinity with the Orient and without altering his belief in humanity as "a part and parcel of nature," but he also presented a complex and bicultural concept of nature which is characteristically Thoreauvian.

NOTES

1. Thoreau's contact with the books of Chinese philosophy began with his first stay in Emerson's house in 1841. Among Emerson's private collection of Oriental books were two English translations of the Confucian books: Joshua Marshman's 1809 *The Works of Confucius* and David Collie's 1828 *The Chinese Classical Work, commonly called The Four Books*. From these books, Thoreau selected sixty-four quotations and published them in the *Dial* for April and October 1843. In *Walden*, according to Lyman V. Cady, there are altogether nine quotations from the Confucian books ("Thoreau's Quotations," 21). For more information, see Arthur Christy, ed., *The Asian Legacy and American Life*; Christy, *The Orient in American Transcendentalism*; and Walter Harding and Michael Meyer, *The New Thoreau Handbook*.

2. Harding, *Thoreau Handbook*, 199.

3. Simon, "What Henry David Didn't Know About Lao Tzu," 253.

4. *The Holy Bible*, 2.

5. Glacken, *Traces on the Rhodian Shore*, 47–48.

6. Oelschlaeger, *Idea of Wilderness*, 59.

7 Emerson, *Selections*, 25.

8. Regarding the idea of confrontation between humanity and nature, see also William Leiss, *The Domination of Nature*; John McPhee, *The Control of Nature*; Carolyn Merchant, *The Death of Nature*; and Steven Vogel, *Against Nature*; in addition to Glacken's *Traces on the Rhodian Shore* and Oelschlaeger's *The Idea of Wilderness*.

9. Although most Thoreau scholars and critics believe that Thoreau was unacquainted with Taoist philosophy, it remains a puzzle to the present author as well as to some other critics that many of Thoreau's views should be so similar to those of Lao Zi (Lao Tzu) and Zhuang Zi (Chuang Tzu). As Lyman Cady says, "Teachers and students who read *Walden* and *The Book of Tao* are struck by the affinity of the two writings and the profound similarity of the points of view, their nature mysticism, love of the simple and 'primitive,' distaste for convention and governmental interference, and the repeated use of paradox" ("Thoreau's Quotations," 31–32). For this point, see also Gary Simon, "What Henry David Didn't Know About Lao Tzu: Taoist Parallels in Thoreau."

10. Brown et al., eds., *Reader's Companion to World Literature*, 511.

11. Munro, *Concept of Man in Early China*, 131–32.

12. Zhou and Liang, *Chinese Culture*, 69–70.

13. See my book *Aspects of Chinese Culture*, 60–67 and 165–77.

14. Xu Fancheng, *An Interpretation of Lao Zi*, 61. (The translation is mine.)

15. Garber, "Thoreau and Anglo-European Romanticism," 40.

16. Emerson, *Selections*, 22.

17. Cameron, *Writing Nature*, 24.

18. In *The Orient in American Transcendentalism*, Arthur Christy makes a de-

tailed study of the beginnings and growth of Thoreau's interest in Oriental philosophy and literature. I have used its chapters concerning Chinese philosophy as resources for my argument.

19. Thoreau, *Journal, Vol. 1: 1837–1844*, 204. Subsequent volume and page references to the Princeton edition of the Journal are cited parenthetically in the text with *PJ*.

20. Alcott, *Concord Days*, 12–13.

21. Cavell, *Senses of Walden*, 38.

22. Cady, "Thoreau's Quotations," 29.

23. Thoreau, *Journal of Henry David Thoreau*, ed. Torrey and Allen, vol. XI, 359. Subsequent volume and page references are cited parenthetically in the text with *J*.

24. According to his biographers, Thoreau did not eat meat, and showed concern for living creatures in nature. As Thoreau describes in *Walden*, he even had a mouse as a companion in his cabin during his stay by Walden Pond. In his later years, Thoreau even gave up fishing.

25. McIntosh, *Thoreau as Romantic Naturalist*, 147.

26. See Sherman Paul, *The Shores of America: Thoreau's Inward Exploration*, 407–11.

27. Gozzi, ed., *Thoreau's Psychology*, 42.

28. See Lu, ed., *One Hundred Quatrains by the Tang Poets*, 52.

29. Tao, *Selected Poems*, 91. Tao Yuanming is one of the greatest poets in ancient China, whose "Peach-Blossom Springs," created under the influence of Taoist philosophy then, expresses a utopian ideal of the Chinese scholar as well as the wishes of the working people to live a happy and peaceful life in a secluded but picturesque land.

30. Brown et al., eds., *Reader's Companion to World Literature*, 292.

IV. SAVING PLACE

Writing as Appropriation or Preservation of Nature

Speaking for Nature

Thoreau and the "Problem" of "Nature Writing"

NANCY CRAIG SIMMONS

At the beginning of the essay "Walking," Thoreau announces, "I wish to speak a word for Nature." Typically this is read as speaking "on behalf of" nature — championing nature, speaking for nature as "cause," as Lawrence Buell puts it in *The Environmental Imagination*.[1] But Thoreau also claims to speak "for" nature in the sense of "in the place of" — of enabling nature, whose language is nonhuman, to speak in his texts. How the nature writer might do this without colonizing or appropriating the nonhuman — imposing his own language on nature, controlling and reducing it through language for human "use" and consumption — is the problem I address in this essay.[2]

Ultimately this is an ethical question, introduced by ecocriticism into the once egocentric field of nature writing: how can the nature writer relate ethically to the nature she observes, perceives, "reads," describes, "translates," records, reports, responds to, and interprets?[3] How practice the virtues of "reverence, humility, responsibility, and care" (qtd. in Buell, 425 n. 1) that Timothy O'Riordan seeks in "ecocentrism"? Related to these is yet another problem for the writer: how to perceive nature immediately and on its own terms rather than through the "writerly" mind programmed to translate sensations into human language in predictably useful ways?

Although Henry Thoreau is generally acknowledged to be one of the "progenitors" of modern nature writing[4] and now stands canonized as an "environmental saint" by Buell, my questions are especially applicable here. As Laura Walls makes clear, in the first half of the nineteenth century, both the prevailing scientific paradigm and the "transcendental" influence of Emerson that grew out of this construction of science located the "value" of particular facts in their "use." Whether used instrumentally or symbolically, facts are merely a veil to be penetrated to arrive at "higher," preexisting "laws" or "truth."[5] As Emerson put it in the 1836 *Nature*, "Particular natural facts are symbols of particular spiritual facts" and "Nature is the symbol of spirit" (*CW* 1:17).[6]

Thoreau was never able completely to overcome the habit of using nature "poetically." In 1851 he reproached himself for not being able to get "material for poetry" out of laboring men in the same way he could from "woods & fields and grand aspects of nature."[7] Three years later he wrote, "I make it my business to extract from nature whatever nutriment she can furnish. . . . I milk the sky & the earth" (see *J* V: 478). Almost any page of the Journal will provide examples of the humanizing or spiritualizing habit at work: anthropomorphized descriptions and strained figures of speech, such as spiders standing on the tips of their toes (*J* V: 465), leaves like socks in wrinkles around the ankles of trees (*J* V: 474), birds in blue uniforms like soldiers who have received orders (*J* V: 488); and of the transcendentalizing impulse, such as "I will be thankful that I see so much as one side of a celestial idea — one side of the rain bow & the sunset-sky — the *face* of God alone" (*PJ* 4: 238).

These examples come randomly from the period 1851 to 1854. This is in the period of the "mature" Journal, after Thoreau has found his form and is writing almost daily, lengthy entries, using the Journal less as a workshop for publications than as a storehouse of facts and observations. At the same time, the "poet" of his earlier Journal is giving way to the "naturalist" of the later career — at least partly, as Walls suggests, as a result of Thoreau's discovery of an alternative construction of what science does, exemplified by Alexander von Humboldt. Whereas the "rational holism" that influenced transcendental idealism tended to be dualistic, splitting subject from object, and consuming natural facts in the leap to higher or spiritual truth, Humboldtian "empirical holism" valued facts for their own sake, seeing nature not as a veil, but the reality itself, known only through experience (senses, contact) — without denying that the resultant facts were interrelated, connected, and meaningful. Humboldt's mantra (Walls suggests) was "explore, collect, measure, connect" (98). As she asserts, Thoreau considered himself a transcendentalist to the end, because the "name allied him with the quest for a morally significant universe" (54). But at the same time, increasingly he valued facts in themselves.[8]

What this implies is a different kind of nature writing than Thoreau had learned from Emerson, whose "Poet" "turns the world to glass."[9] He was defining this new role at the time when he was completing his final draft of *Walden*, in February 1854. In the conclusion to his masterpiece, Thoreau expresses this writing goal as a "fear" — that his expression is not sufficiently "*extra-vagant*," that it "may not wander far enough beyond the narrow limits of my daily experience, so as to be adequate to the truth of which I have been convinced" (see *J* VI:100).

But, writing "extra-vagantly" does not mean "proliferation, unpredictability, and excess" as Walls asserts (10) — for these qualities in writing produce the baroque flourishes that call attention to the writer at the expense of the natural subject. Instead, I believe Thoreau knew that the kind of writing which would faithfully record and communicate nature so as to enable it to "speak" would be "more simple, less artful" (as he put it in January 1852; *PJ* 4:296). The phrase comes from a passage in which Thoreau realizes that the best "form" for his Journal thoughts is the running record of his perceptions, not the literary essays he might compose out of them. To write "extra-vagantly" is to resist the power of cultural modes of thinking — the forms, traditions, figures of speech, and habits that trap and deaden experience, limiting and determining what one can say and reducing nature to an object for human consumption (as he was doing at this same time in "packaging" *Walden* for publication).

One way out of this trap is to serve as a sort of mediator or amanuensis, as a passive medium through which nature expresses itself — as Emerson's "transparent eyeball." In a frequently quoted sentence from his Journal for 1851, Thoreau suggests this is possible: "A writer a man writing [*sic*] is the scribe of all nature — he is the corn & the grass & the atmosphere writing" (*PJ* 4:28). But, how successful is Thoreau — or any "nature writer" — in accomplishing this goal? Given that the instrument for "speaking for" is human language, can any writer speak for nature without reducing it to a human construct? As Michael J. McDowell puts it, "Every literary attempt to listen to voices in the landscape or to 'read the book of nature' is necessarily anthropocentric. It's our language, after all, that we're using" (371). Frankly, as Sharon Cameron notes, is it really possible for the writer to "obliterate" his identity when he speaks "for" nature?[10]

Thoreau could not be a "transparent eyeball." His writing constantly betrayed the influence of human culture on his perceptions. Humboldtian science offered a different way out, recognizing the active role of the scientist/writer as observer, perceiver, listener, reporter, and translator. Thoreau's "vocation," as he tried to define it in 1854, was to hunt nature itself: to observe carefully, to track diligently, to be fully prepared by knowledge of what to look for, and fully receptive to the many ways that nature speaks — and to capture his game alive by giving living expression to the perceptions he worked so hard at capturing. "I would fain be a fisherman — hunter — farmer — preacher &c — but fish — hunt — farm — preach other things than usual," he concluded, with the important distinction that the reason for the hunt was not to destroy the life it finds, "but to save our own" (see *J* VI: 45).

This epiphany and statement of his vocation comes at the end of what I consider a failed "religiocentric" exercise (the term comes from Buell, 128), part of a long entry written on January 1, 1854, in which Thoreau draws on his real and recent experience hunting a moose in the Maine woods to figure the notion of hunting for Purity and tracking the "Great Hare" as a higher vocation — a better "use" of nature.[11]

Thoreau had already written extensively about the moose hunt, in his Journal expansion of the Chesuncook trip made in September 1853. This firsthand account used the conventions of the travel adventure while simultaneously undermining the experience by revealing the sordid brutality of the hunt and Thoreau's sympathy for the slaughtered cow-moose. The experience proved deeply disturbing: he called it a "tragedy" and regretted his part in it, "as it affected the innocence — destroyed the pleasure of my adventure." This kind of hunting he compared to going out and "shooting your neighbor's horses" or "assisting at a slaughterhouse. . . . Poor timid creatures." What he learned then was "how base are the motives which commonly carry men into the wilderness"; explorers and lumberers were "hirelings" with no love for wild nature; other white men and Indians are "mostly hunters whose object is to slay as many moose as possible." He contrasts such "coarse & imperfect" uses of nature with "employments perfectly sweet & innocent & ennobling."[12]

But the problem with attempting to raise hunting from a base to a spiritually significant activity is well illustrated in the January 1, 1854, entry. It began with "reading" the snow for the "footprints" of the wind and recognizing the snow as the "great betrayer" of the secret life of wild creatures, but when Thoreau tried to translate this notion into a statement of faith, that "all that we see is the impress" (or footprints) of the spirit of a "higher life," he gets into trouble. The conceits do not cohere. Leaving behind the scientifically precise description of the effects of a snowstorm and his biocentric understanding of the snow as the great betrayer of wild creatures to potential predators, Thoreau drives the entry into a description of a different kind of hunter for whom the snow is more a "revealer" (see *J* VI:40) than a "betrayer," engaged in tracking "a nobler life," higher game than foxes, with more discriminating judgment than the "senses of fox hounds." This hunter rallies to "nobler music" than the hunting horn. But Thoreau seems at this point to realize that his metaphor has carried him in a new direction. His sympathy for natural creatures has been trapped by conventional allegorizing that returns the animal to its cultural role as the object of the hunt and swallows its reality in the effort to figure the human quest for spirit. In this treatment of the subject, the imaginary fox serves both to absolve Thoreau's continued guilt from participating in the slaughter of the moose the past fall and to aid him in formulating a definition of his vocation. Either way, he's using nature symbolically or instrumentally — "riding on nature's back," to borrow Walls's wonderful formulation of the problem (168).

However, Thoreau does not stop there. To ground this ungraspable figure, he draws an analogy: "So the observer — as he who would make the most of his life for discipline must be abroad early & late in spite of cold & wet ⸱upon the trail of such⸱ In pursuit of, nobler game whose traces are then most distinct." But finally, as we realize at the bottom of this same page, Thoreau is defining his own vocation: "I would fain be a fisherman — hunter," etc. — hunting and preaching, etc., "other things than usual." His definition locates his role within the culture at the same time that it takes him beyond its "usual" boundaries. Speaking from this position was speaking "extra-vagantly," "without bounds" — but still within a culture that valued writing as a culturally significant activity.

Thus writing became for Thoreau a justification of his way of living — his vocation or "business" — specifically his role as an observer and recorder of nature in all her forms and "moods." Several scholars (Howarth, Cameron, Neufeldt) have recently entertained the question, who did Thoreau think was his audience for this mammoth text, his Journal? I'm not sure this is a question that worried Thoreau. By this time, writing the Journal was his occupation and a habit, perhaps a compulsion. Delighting in his increasing awareness of the "facts" of the natural world and his own experience, deep inside, Thoreau cannot imagine a world without human consciousness: the ultimate "use" of all this beauty is to affect human thinking and raise it to another plane. "If the elements are not human, if the winds do not sing or sign, as the stars twinkle, my life runs shallow," he writes in 1853 (*J* IV:472). "What is nature unless there is an eventfull human life passing within her?" (see *J* V:472). Ecstatic states, he mused in 1851 — even those which appear to yield little fruit — have value later when they "color our picture" (*PJ* 4:52).

But the record also mattered. Even if we have no "poems to show for them," our experiences count. "No life or experience goes unreported at last" (*PJ* 4:51–52). In fall 1853, he muses on the power of memories encountered in his Journal: "You only need to make a faithful record of an average summer day's experience & summer mood — & read it in the winter" to get the "rarest flavor — the purest melody — of the season" in which it was written (see *J* V:454). He explains his painstaking measuring of the dead moose because then his general claim that she was "very large" "might be of some use to somebody."

Observing and reporting was no mean assignment, since, in Thoreau's epistemology, the unperceived and unreported event might as well not have happened, because it would not have been known. On August 19, 1853, a perfect late summer day with just a hint of fall, he and Ellery Channing made a boat trip to Sudbury and back. "It is a day affecting the spirits of man," he writes, "but there is nobody to enjoy it — but ourselves." He goes on to proclaim, "This day itself . . . the great phenomenon," and then asks, "will it be reported in any journal? as the storm is & the heat? It is like a great & beautiful flower unnamed" (see *J* V:383).

Naming is a way of knowing. What matters is the report. Without it, the experience might as well not have happened: it would be lost because it had fallen on unreceptive or deaf ears or no ears at all. This argument recalls the philosophical conundrum that asks, "if a tree falls in the forest, and no one hears, does it make a sound?" In fact, Thoreau had entertained exactly this question the preceding fall while in Maine. An unearthly, unidentifiable sound heard in the wilderness is subsequently identified by the Indian guide: "tree fall." In his Journal, Thoreau adds, "If we had not been there no mortal had heard it." [13]

"If we had not been there no mortal had heard it"; if we had not experienced the August trip, no mortal would have enjoyed it. When he is able to resist the siren call of transcendental idealism, Thoreau's reporting is precise, fine, detailed, enabling us to see through his eyes and hear through his ears what would otherwise be lost to us. But the Journal for 1851–1854 shows how difficult it was to resist the cultural traps set for the nature writer.

Still, does "reporting" leave room for the "ethical orientation" that Buell, Scheese, and others insist is essential to "environmental" writing? To reframe Buell's "checklist" of ingredients for an "environmentally oriented work" (7–8): rather than using nature merely to provide a backdrop for human events (e.g., Thoreau and Channing's trip to Sudbury), does the text suggest a different kind of relationship between human and natural history? Is the nonhuman seen as a legitimate interest in its own right? (And, if a right "use" of nature in this situation is "enjoyment," does this rob nature of its own interest?) Is there some sense of human accountability to the environment? Does Thoreau give us a sense of nature as process rather than a constant or given?

My answer to most of these questions, in the case of the entry we have been looking at, is a qualified yes. Thoreau's compulsion to record is not just for the human record, for human consumption; it is also a way of enabling nature to speak, to express itself on its own terms. Admittedly, the account of the trip is framed in a culturally specific way, as a quest or hunt: "to cultivate animal spirits — to embark in enterprises which employ & recreate the whole body" (see *J* V:379). But chief among these enterprises is observing, taking in nature through the senses. Most of the nine-page entry is devoted not to philosophical reflection or even personal response, but to detailed reporting of sights, views, particular phenomena. Nature is foregrounded rather than reduced to background: plants, birds, humans, reflections off the water; scents, sounds, the touch of the wind and sun. Human laborers inhabit the landscape — as mowers, reapers, farmers in fields; the only other human intrusions occur when the boat scares up a flock of ducks or herons, rendering some part of nature that was invisible visible. Ultimately, the day itself, in which human and nonhuman equally participate, *is* the phenomenon, rather than the exploits of the two "huntsmen." The progress of the day, the river, the season all suggest process, not stasis; and the proper human role is celebration, acknowledgment, of a perfect day.

It is less obvious how the entry might speak to human "accountability" to the natural environment. The word connotes for me some need for the writer or text to take responsibility for human impact on (or "ab-use" of) the environment. But I think Buell is really interested in how the text might affect human action. As he asserts, the task for environmental writers and critics is to find "better ways of imaging nature and humanity's relation to it" because "how we image a thing . . . affects our conduct toward it" (2, 3). The one place where Thoreau as writer, rather than reporter, speaks out in this entry is to express his distress that others — laboring indoors and out — are missing what he is enjoying, a genuine relationship with nature, a "natural sabbath" that could be better spent "if only all men would accept the hint" (see *J* V:383). The text that acts to transform lives by waking people up to the heaven that was all around them in the natural world is ecocritically "accountable" or "responsible."

But my evaluation is qualified because what Thoreau is doing in writing the entry also appropriates the nature he describes to traditional cultural uses. Whether naming the flower he has found or writing the hymn to nature that it deserves, he serves up the whole in a predictable frame — the classic American "ramble" in Thomas J. Lyon's "taxonomy," complete with mythological and heroic apparatus that traps and fixes this day as a work of art, freezing the moment in the form of a moralistic "picture" or "hymn." The quarry Thoreau and Channing have tracked and bagged is the series of observations served up in the finely crafted entry. It has not managed completely to get "without bounds."

Understanding how difficult it was for Thoreau to negotiate the opposing claims of transcendentalism and empiricism on his thought, I'd like to look more closely at the concept of "extra-vagance," as expressed in *Walden*: "I fear chiefly lest my expression may not be *extra-vagant* enough, may not wander far enough beyond the narrow limits of my daily experience, so as to be adequate to the truth of which I have been convinced. . . . I desire to speak somewhere *without* bounds; like a man in a waking moment, to men in their waking moments." [14]

Thoreau's punning on the root senses of his key words reminds us of how closely the notion of extravagance is tied to limits: that it requires a sense of boundaries that must be transgressed in the effort to achieve true expression. "Without bounds" could mean "lacking any boundaries," but in the context of "*extra-vagance*" (which Thoreau himself defines in the passage as to "wander . . . beyond . . . limits") it comes to mean "outside of" or "beyond" the boundaries. The boundaries are imposed by culture.

"Culture," that complex whole that, in Stephen Greenblatt's formulation, includes "knowledge, belief, art, morals, law, custom, and other capabilities and habits acquired by man as a member of society" means both "constraint" and "mobility," rules and improvisations. [15] Henry Louis Gates Jr. sees the subject as a "participant in an articulated realm of social practices that . . . are its very conditions of possibility" (qtd. in Buell, 372). For Stravinsky, "The more art is controlled, limited, worked over, the more it is free." [16] Thoreau wrote much the same thing: "nothing is so truly bounded & obedient to law as music, yet nothing so surely bursts all petty & narrow bonds. Whenever I hear any music I fear that [I] may have spoken tamely & within bounds" (see *J* VI:100). This statement of the inextricability of law and freedom occurs in the Journal just after Thoreau drafted the first version of his wish to speak "*extravagant[ly]*" — similarly linking notions of freedom and boundaries. The entry shows how strong was the pull of both positions from which Thoreau wrote, "rational" and "empirical," "poet" and "naturalist." But it also shows a better way out of the trap of using nature for predictable human purposes than his use of the entry on the "Great Hare" to define his vocation. In this piece, Thoreau manages to write truly extravagantly by simply recording the experience of tracking a fox.[17]

February 5, 1854, was a snowy Sunday; the Journal record tells us Thoreau spent the morning reading some account books kept by Concord storekeeper Ephraim Jones in the mid–eighteenth century (and imagining the "dreary & ghastly life" led by these early inhabitants of a "rude straggling village" dominated by the burying ground) and working on the last draft of *Walden* (including a passage for the "Housewarming" chapter comparing animals' winter shelter with human improvements). In the afternoon, after the snow resumed, Thoreau went out for a walk but ended up tracking a fox for several miles through the snow by noticing a variety of signs. Yielding to the fox when it entered the Ministerial Swamp, Thoreau returned home and recorded the event. He also reflected at length on the meaning of a muskrat that had gnawed off its "third leg" to escape a trap. By now it is evening, and Thoreau returns to the *Walden* project, drawing not on immediate experience but on memory to write the conclusion to the sand foliage passage for the "Spring" chapter — one of Thoreau's most "extravagant" pieces of writing (see *Walden* 308–9). After this, Thoreau expresses his "fear" that his expressions are not sufficiently extravagant to convey the truths he knows. Then come more notes on the account book; and finally the entry returns to the fox: "How dangerous to the foxes & all wild animals is a light snow . . . betraying their course to the hunters. . . . I followed on this trail so long that my thoughts grew foxy."

The whole entry mixes current and past events and experiences, indoor and outdoor activity, drafts for *Walden*, reading notes — "dead history" and "living poetry." Both in its variety and the questions it leaves us with, it suggests the problem of trying to read Thoreau's Journal as environmentally sensitive or ethically oriented nature writing.

For example, the section on the muskrat that gnawed off its third leg does not derive from immediate experience at all, but from an anecdote Thoreau heard almost a decade earlier (see *PJ* 2:126–27). The result is anything but ecocentric: in a passage heavily larded with language from epic, traditional religion, and sentimental piety, Thoreau attempts to transform the gruesome death of the muskrat (having been trapped for a third time, in its desperate desire for freedom the creature essentially committed suicide) into an inspiration, or at least consolation, by suggesting that human sympathy for the muskrat derives not from its sufferings, but from our "kindred mortality." Seen from a "higher" perspective, such "tragedies" (as with the murdered moose) "make the plaintive strain of the universal harp which elevates us above the trivial." Both the animal's suffering (and any change in human behavior that might be effected if trappers could recognize the suffering they inflict) and Thoreau's avowal of sympathy and brotherhood with the creature are smothered in baroque prose that calls attention to the writer and sublimates the animal's pain.

However, this is clearly not the only "use" of nature available to Thoreau at this time: the sand foliage passage that immediately follows opens with the recognition of the "fact" expressed by this phenomenon: "that the very soil can fabulate as well as you or I." His account attempts to let the soil tell its story. But the section on tracking the fox is most "extra-vagant," moving by the end to a close identification of human and nonhuman.

What does it mean to think like a fox? Identifying with it in its quest for its dinner? (Thoreau assumes that a farmer's chicken died at the end of the fox's hunt.) That to hunt well, one must be able to think like a fox? Or identifying with its feelings of being hunted, betrayed to hunters by the perfidy of the snow that blankets nature? If we could think like wild creatures, would we perhaps not hunt them? Do foxy thoughts have anything to do with writing, especially writing "extravagantly"? Is wild nature truly free — or, as in Thoreau's comparison of crude animal beds to spacious human habitation, does human culture free man from life at the instinctive level?

To have "foxy" thoughts, the report suggests, is thinking in a decidedly nonhuman way, outside the boundaries culture has established between human and "animal" realms. It means crossing the road, not turning into it — following a different track. This is no simple valorizing of the "wild" over the "civilized" or tame. For several hours, Thoreau played hunter, simply following the trail — noting not only the fox's footprints in the snow, but also where it has "watered" to leave its mark, its manure, where its tail has grazed the snow, where it has "nosed" the snow; at times, he's even noticed its scent, as though he were a hunting dog, and felt he was closing in on his prey — paradoxically feeling "nearer" to the fox even as the fox drew literally farther away.

It was not easy to think and write like a fox. Literary language and forms reveal cultural assumptions, trap thinking in ideological forms, betray their subject to writerly appropriation and "use." We might read this betrayal through literary language, the coinage of the day, as the real moral of the story Thoreau tells about tracking the fox on a snowy day. Like the fox, as a writer Thoreau might prefer to leave no tracks, to be "transparent," to escape the hounds of culture. But the fact is, he is the one who has traveled this unusual path and his job is to report it as truthfully as he can so that it can speak.

By 1853, when he turns thirty-six, Thoreau is aware that most humans in contemporary life either cannot or will not attend to nature in the way that he is driven to. For them, these sights and sounds do not exist, and so they cannot enjoy nature's finer fruits, nor feel her hurts. His role, as hunter/observer, receiver, reporter requires preparation, attention, and memory — but it also requires shaping his discoveries in language. The cultural forms he uses have the power both to enable seeing and to capture, limiting further comprehension by reducing nature to human use. Only by resisting the impulse to use nature in conventional ways can he enable her to speak in her own language. This means faithfully reporting what he's perceived through all his senses.

Increasingly at this time, Thoreau was articulating ideas he would use at the end of "Autumnal Tints" five years later. After letting us see the fall leaves through his eyes, Thoreau sends us out on our own adventure, on a hill on the outskirts of our town. There we will see — "well," he admits, "what I have endeavored to describe. All this you surely *will* see, and much more, if you are prepared to see it, — if you *look* for it."[18] From experience, he knows the value of preparation in ensuring a successful hunt. Helping others to see as he did and thus to share his joy is reason enough for Thoreau to write.

Read in this expanded context, Thoreau's tracking the fox looks decidedly different from his attempt to transcendentalize the Great Hare. Here Thoreau liberates the fox by allowing it, rather than any recognizable cultural form, to determine the shape of the entry. As he tracks the fox, he comes to identify with it to the point that distinctions between himself and nature are blurred. Led by the fox rather than the form, Thoreau does not obliterate himself, even while he enables nature to reveal itself; he speaks *for* and foregrounds nature. To think like a fox is to think beyond conventional and societal limitations and address more senses than one. This kind of *"extra-vagance"* is truly biocentric writing.

NOTES

1. Buell, *Environmental Imagination*, 138 and passim.

2. McDowell, "Bakhtinian Road to Ecological Insight." Michael J. McDowell recognizes the problem and suggests how Bakhtinian dialogics can be applied to analysis of landscape literature.

3. See Thomas J. Lyon's classic "A Taxonomy of Nature Writing."

4. Scheese, *Nature Writing*, 22.

5. Walls, *Seeing New Worlds*, 60–61 and passim.

6. *Collected Works of Ralph Waldo Emerson*, vol. 1: *Nature, Addresses, and Lectures*, 17.

7. *Journal, Vol. 4: 1851–1852*, 10. Subsequent quotations from the Princeton edition of the Journal (5 vols. to date) are cited parenthetically in the text as *PJ*. Quotations from *The Journal of Henry D. Thoreau*, 14 vols., ed. Torrey and Allen, are cited in the text as *J*. Many of my quotations come from the unpublished transcription of Thoreau's notebook XVI (Morgan Library MS 1302:22) for 1853–1854, which I am co-editing with Ronald Thomas for the Princeton edition. Where possible, these are cross-referenced to the 1906 *Journal* as "See *J*."

8. Robert Kuhn MacGregor, in *A Wider View of the Universe: Henry Thoreau's Study of Nature*, traces the same shift, after 1849, from a "classically and staidly trained transcendentalist into a radical naturalist" (5).

9. Emerson, "The Poet," *Collected Works*, vol. 3: *Essays: Second Series*, 12.

10. Cameron, *Writing Nature*, 85–87.

11. Quotations in the following discussion of the entry for January 1, 1854, are from the unpublished transcript of Thoreau's notebook XVI; see *J* VI:42–45.

12. From the unpublished transcript of Thoreau's notebook XVI, pp. 107–9; not printed in the 1906 *Journal* because much of this material was later printed in the Maine woods essay "Chesuncook."

13. From the unpublished transcript of Thoreau's notebook XVI, p. 90.

14. *Walden*, 324.

15. Greenblatt, "Culture," 225.

16. Stravinsky, *Poetics of Music*, 63.

17. Quotations from the entry for February 5, 1854, are from the unpublished transcript of Thoreau's notebook XVI; see *J* VI:94–101.

18. *Excursions*, in *Writings of Henry David Thoreau*, vol. V, 285.

Depopulation, Deforestation, and the Actual Walden Pond

ROBERT SATTELMEYER

Like the raft on which Huck Finn and Jim float the Mississippi River, Thoreau's cabin at Walden Pond has come to possess a kind of hyper-canonical status as cultural icon, both temporary homes figuring a con-fluence of self and place that suggests an ideal if unattainable American existence for the individual in harmony with nature. While the raft is clearly a fictional device that ferries its inhabitants from one adventure to another, punctuated by brief intervals of idyllic drift, Walden Pond and its surrounding forests are clearly more rooted in reality. The pond is, after all, an actual place, and the historical Henry Thoreau did live there in a cabin of (mostly) his own making during a fourteen-month period from 1845 to 1847. Every few years someone attempts to duplicate Huck and Jim's raft trip and gets written up in the local papers, but their numbers pale in comparison to the tens of thousands who annually make what Lawrence Buell has aptly termed "The Thoreauvian Pilgrimage" to Walden Pond.[1] This disproportion exists not just because Walden Pond is easily accessible by car (unless you're trying to visit on a warm summer weekend). It exists because Walden is not only a literary shrine but also a cultural site that provides a focal point for a series of environmental concerns and beliefs that continue to be central to our collective social life a hundred and fifty years after Thoreau moved back to town.

Central to these concerns is the image of Walden's pristine and iso-lated nature, an image both fixed and celebrated by Thoreau's book. This image, in turn, has helped define the controversies of recent years over development of areas adjacent to the pond, and also helped define the extension of the idea of the site to include what is called "Walden Woods" — the pond's watershed as well as the pond itself. The image remains fixed even in the name of a prominent local organization devoted to preservation of the pond and its environs, Walden Forever Wild. Powerful (and productive) as this concept is, however, it tends to obscure and distort both the actual nature of Walden Pond and its surrounding land features during the 1840s and 1850s, and Thoreau's actual portrayal of it in *Walden*.

Thanks to Buell's recent study, *The Environmental Imagination*, we have a thoughtful and comprehensive account of the successive possessions and repossessions of Thoreau and Walden Pond by disciples, publishers, literary scholars, environmentalists, and the public. An important corollary to this story is how Thoreau himself engineered the origins of what Buell terms the "will to pastoralize Walden" by transforming a busy commercial and agricultural site with a long and complex history of human settlement into a remote forest lake that impressed him (and later readers) "like a tarn high up on the side of a mountain."[2] This part of the story is rather difficult to tell, for it requires that we try to look at *Walden* without the accumulated weight of nearly a century and a half of reception by critics and general readers alike. We cannot help being influenced by its reputation as a critique of industrializing America and its celebration of the narrator's solitary life in the woods. But we can situate the image of Walden that we have inherited against what we can discover and infer about the actual environs of Walden during this period, and we can also examine some of the unsettling information about the pond and its surroundings that Thoreau himself provides in the text and in his Journal.

The information that Thoreau himself provides should come as no surprise to careful readers of *Walden*, for it is axiomatic that Thoreau almost always qualifies if he does not outrightly subvert what appear to be his clearest formulations. Indeed, the seemingly endless power of semination that the text seems to possess owes a great deal to the fact that its most cherished wisdoms seem to be always already undercut. This feature seems counterintuitive at first, going against the grain not only of *Walden*'s canonization as a scripture of individualism, iconoclasm, and environmental correctness, but also its announced rhetorical drive toward clarity and simplicity ("I went to the woods because I wished to live deliberately," etc.). But, as anyone knows who has tried to teach *Walden* to undergraduates, clarity and simplicity are not really prominent features of the text. "It is a ridiculous demand," Thoreau says in the "Conclusion," "which England and America make, that you shall speak so that they can understand you" (324), and he seems more often than not bent on demonstrating his allegiance to this belief. To take perhaps the most obvious example of his persistent subversion of a simple understanding, Thoreau concludes "Economy," the longest and most polemical chapter of *Walden* and the chapter in which he describes his "less is more" philosophy, with a poem by Thomas Carew titled "The Pretensions of Poverty." This poem begins:

> Thou dost presume too much, poor needy wretch,
> To claim a station in the firmament
> Because thy humble cottage, or thy tub,
> Nurses some lazy or pedantic virtue
> In the cheap sunshine or by shady springs,
> With roots and pot-herbs. (80)

Clearly, if one actually reads this strategically placed counterpoint, it undercuts the mode of life that Thoreau has just described, undermines his claim to authority, and emphasizes that the author, whatever rural virtues he may practice, possesses a highly refined literary sensibility which he exploits in highly self-conscious ways, using both the pastoral and antipastoral traditions to erect his own edifice of words. In a similar vein within "Economy," Thoreau the radical simplifier, after describing in great detail his spartan diet, seems to subvert the entire experiment by concluding, "The reader will perceive that I am treating the subject rather from an economic than a dietetic point of view, and he will not venture to put my abstemiousness to the test unless he has a well-stocked larder" (61). Even within the list of foodstuffs itself, the careful reader will notice that about two-thirds of the items listed are marked by a bracket denoting "All experiments which failed" (59). Throughout the book, readers who take Thoreau's ringing formulations too literally may find themselves in the position of the traveler who is the butt of the boy's joke in the "Conclusion." Assured by the boy that the bog he is about to walk his horse into has a hard bottom, he advances confidently in the direction of his dreams, only to find his horse mired to its girth. "'I thought you said that this bog had a hard bottom.' 'So it has,' answered the latter, 'but you have not got half way to it yet'" (330).

Armed with this cautionary tale, it is not unreasonable to look for evidence in the text itself that the relative remoteness and natural forested beauty of Walden Pond — the overwhelming image that readers and pilgrims carry with them — are perhaps not all that they were cracked up to be. In fact, in the course of his fable, Thoreau both constructs and deconstructs this image of remote beauty, playing on the reader's desire in much the same way that his equally canny New England descendant Robert Frost does in "The Road Not Taken," establishing the unshakable image of a road less traveled when there really was none. ("Though as for that the passing there / Had worn them really about the same, / And both that morning equally lay / In leaves no step had trodden black.") Not surprisingly, much of the evidence about what Walden Pond and Walden Woods were actually like when Thoreau was living there is to be found in one of the shortest and arguably the most anomalous chapter in the book, "Former Inhabitants; and Winter Visitors."

"Former Inhabitants," because its subject and tone seem so out of keeping with the rest of the book, is one of the least noticed sections of *Walden*. Conventionally, it could be said to occupy a place in the book's narrative of triumphal emergence as a kind of meditative lull preceding the rebirth of spring. In like manner, the second half of the chapter, "Winter Visitors," records the paucity of human contact that the narrator experienced at this season, containing flattering portraits of the improvident Bronson Alcott and Ellery Channing, a curt dismissal of Emerson, and concluding with the narrator waiting for "the Visitor who never comes" (270). More importantly, though, "Former Inhabitants" opens a window on aspects of local culture that tend to be bracketed off in the rest of the book. This window is small, and open only briefly, but it can alter one's experience of the book in the same way that a consideration of Carew's poem (rather than the conventional skipping over) alters "Economy."

"Former Inhabitants" provides a glimpse of Walden's social past, the harshness of which is muted by the chapter's oddly discordant elegiac tone — discordant not only because a brusque disregard of the past is more characteristic of the book's tone, but also because there was not much about the lives of the people described to be nostalgic or elegiac about. But what is most surprising about the chapter is that it describes the area around Thoreau's cabin — a mile from any neighbor, as we recall — as prominently marked by the remains of a small, straggling village that had until rather recently occupied the spot, home to a group of people that readers don't tend to associate with Walden Pond. Cato Ingraham, for example, a slave, lived across the road. He had a grove of walnut trees, but "a younger and whiter speculator got them at last." There was also Zilpha, another African American who had a little house and spun linen for the townsfolk: "She led a hard life, and somewhat inhumane," Thoreau says with uncharacteristic understatement. Brister Freeman, yet another slave, tended an apple orchard and lived down the road toward town. Across the road was the Stratton family homestead, their orchards abandoned and reverting to forest. Near this was Breed's location, once the site of a tavern. The Breed family was destroyed by a demon, Thoreau says, a demon "who has acted a prominent and astounding part in our New England Life" — rum. Then there was Wyman the potter, who squatted in the woods quite near Thoreau's cabin, so poor that when the sheriff came to collect unpaid taxes there was nothing even to confiscate. Finally, the most recent occupant of the neighborhood before Thoreau was Hugh Quoil, an Irishman, an ex-soldier who may have fought at Waterloo. He too was an alcoholic. Thoreau sometimes encountered him in the woods, wrapped in a greatcoat in midsummer, shaking with delirium tremens. He died in the middle of the road that runs by Walden during the first year Thoreau lived there. These people were "universally a thirsty race," Thoreau says, and used the pure waters of Walden Pond only to dilute their rum (257–62).

Reminded as we frequently are today of issues of race and class, and of the tendency of previous literary histories to ignore the darker underside of American life and canonical texts, it should not be altogether surprising to find that Thoreau's cabin was constructed amid the remains of what was essentially a rural slum, a small village of outcasts, misfits, and derelicts who were excluded from the more homogenous society of Concord. Even today, the landfill and the trailer park that were until recently in operation across the road from Walden extend this heritage of class exclusion to the area. In Thoreau's day, the residents were slaves, ex-slaves, alcoholics, rum sellers, and the Irish, people who were literally marginalized and pushed out of Concord proper.

Perhaps the reason for readers' and critics' general failure to pay much attention to this aspect of *Walden* comes from Thoreau's practice of cloaking these stories of exploitation, exclusion, self-destruction, and economic failure in a fog of sentimental elegy in the manner of Goldsmith or Gray. Here is the conclusion of his meditation on the cellar holes of these former residents:

> Still grows the vivacious lilac a generation after the door lintel and the sill are gone, unfolding its sweet-scented flowers each spring, to be plucked by the musing traveler, planted and tended once by children's hands, in front-yard plots, — now standing by wall-sides in retired pastures, and giving place to new-rising forests, — the last of that stirp, sole survivor of that family. Little did the dusky children think that the puny slip with its two eyes only, which they stuck in the

ground in the shadow of the house and daily watered, would root itself so, and outlive them, and house itself in the rear that shaded it, and grown man's garden and orchard, and tell their story faintly to the lone wanderer a half century after they had grown up and died, — blossoming as fair, and smelling as sweet, as in that first spring. I mark its still tender, civil, cheerful, lilac colors. (263–64)

Raymond Williams observes, in *The Country and the City*, speaking of one of Thoreau's models here, Gray's "Elegy in a Country Churchyard," that the musing poet cannot really have it both ways: he cannot both praise the luck of those who lived in the "cool, sequestered vale," *and* bemoan the repression of the "chill penury" that stifled their lives.[3] Similarly, Thoreau ought not to be able to have his rhetorical cake and eat it too, both disclosing the conditions that led to the displacement or extermination of these people — racism, economic exploitation, prejudice against immigrants, and the pandemic abuse of alcohol in the early nineteenth century — while at the same time deriving a tender poetic melancholy from the lilacs blooming around their cellar holes. But he does. And that may be one reason why readers generally fail to take in fully the implications of "Former Inhabitants."

Once the recent human history of Walden Pond is established through "Former Inhabitants," other less consecutive bits of information in the text may be adduced to elaborate its social dimensions. For not only was it the site of a village just recently failed, but also the current site of rather intense commercial and agricultural activity. For example, we learn that during the winter of 1846–47 the pond was harvested for ice, not just by local landlords but in a large-scale operation that involved more than a hundred men and heavy equipment who arrived daily by train from Cambridge (294–96). Although Thoreau says that during the winter "no wanderer ventured near my house for a week or a fortnight for a time" (264), reinforcing the portrait of his self-sufficient isolation, the fact that more than a hundred men with heavy equipment were at work every day in front of his house suggests a somewhat different reality, and reinforces the notion that Thoreau's isolation was a virtual and an imaginative rather than an actual one.

Moreover, the fact that these laborers arrived daily by train underscores the fact that the completion of the railroad to Concord in 1844 — the year before Thoreau moved to Walden — brought the village more solidly into the economic orbit and labor market of Boston. The railroad touches the pond just a few hundred yards from the site of Thoreau's cabin, and passes within earshot of the site of the cabin itself; so that living there in the 1840s must have been rather like living near a just-completed freeway today, only with more intermittent noise. The shanties of the Irish laborers who built the railroad still dotted the right-of-way, and could still be found, inhabited, near where the tracks met the pond. Thus, Thoreau's initial claim that he lived "a mile from any neighbor" (3) is true only if we exclude the Irish, who were not only "silent poor" but apparently invisible poor as well. In a Journal entry for July 11, 1851, Thoreau comments on the Irish and the smell of their shanties along the railroad as he walked near the pond, but in the world of *Walden* they are unremarked except for the exemplary shanties of James Collins, which Thoreau tore down for building material, and that of John Field, which he visited in "Baker Farm."

As for the pristine character of Walden Pond and its surroundings, it needs to be recalled that Concord was the first inland town the English established, in 1635. Thus, the area had been subject to pressures of settlement and cultivation and environmental change by Europeans and their descendants for over two hundred years by the time Thoreau moved to the pond. The landscape of Concord in the 1840s and 1850s was an agricultural one, dominated by tillage and pastures and cutover areas, with only about 10 percent of the area in forest. In fact, 1850 was the historic low point of forest coverage in Concord: it had been steadily decreasing since initial settlement, and has been increasing steadily ever since, as agricultural lands were abandoned and gradually reverted to forest.[4] This decline was also true, although to a lesser extent, of the area around Walden Pond. Here and there the text of *Walden* provides clues to this fact, though the overwhelming impression one is left with is of a lake surrounded by forest. But increasingly the actual landscape consisted largely of fields, such as that eleven-acre plot that Thoreau used a part of to grow his beans on, and woodlots, utilized and managed by the farmers and the townspeople for firewood, both for their own consumption and as a cash crop to sell on the Boston market. The site of Thoreau's cabin was a plot of land recently purchased by Emerson for a woodlot, and the "tall arrowy white pines, still in their youth" (40) that he cut for the timbers of his cabin had doubtless seeded there by wind dispersion after the area had been cut over at some earlier time. Much of the wooded land that did exist in Concord was coppice woods, second-growth timber created by allowing trees to resprout from stumps, a practice which yielded a quick growth of wood suitable for fuel. The landscape of Walden in the mind's eye derives from Thoreau's memory: "When I first paddled a boat on Walden, it was completely surrounded by thick and lofty pine and oak woods"; whereas the actuality, grudgingly acknowledged in a late revision, is that "But since I left those shores the woodchoppers have still further laid them waste, and now for many a year there will be no more rambling through the aisles of the wood" (191, 192).

Nor was the prevalence of open lands solely due to the advent of European axes and plows. Native Americans of southern New England had traditionally set fires to create open savannas richer in game and more conducive to successful hunting than old-growth forests, and they used fires to create crop fields, too. The "ashes of unchronicled nations" (158) that Thoreau disturbs with his hoe in "The Bean Field" are reminders of the long history of both fire and agriculture in the area around Walden.

A physical as well as a literary archaeology of the site of Thoreau's experiment — the Walden Pond of the book and the Walden Pond State Reservation of today — discloses a richly varied human and natural environment that closely mirrors economic, agricultural, and demographic developments in Concord. Like all natural environments, it was and is a dynamic and not a static system. It had been used for more than two hundred years by the descendants of European settlers, and before that for thousands of years by Native Americans, perhaps as long ago as its emergence from the retreating ice sheet. At the time of Thoreau's residence there in the 1840s, it was under particularly intense pressures of cultivation and development from the ice trade, the railroad, and the heavy demand for wood for fuel. As elsewhere in New England, agricultural use around Walden was already beginning to decline, and when the demand for firewood waned after the Civil War, the area joined the rest of the region in the gradual reversion of pastures and cropland to forest. Despite today's pressures of urban sprawl and development, the area around the pond is significantly more heavily wooded today than it was when Thoreau was creating its image as a remote forested lake. Thanks both to reforestation and the power of *Walden*'s rhetoric, today's Walden Pond resembles the Walden Pond of the book more than the actual Walden Pond of 1845 did.

At the same time, the area had a rich if problematic human history, one which exposes aspects of Concord culture largely invisible or present only in abstract critiques in the book, things like the legacy of slavery in Massachusetts, the unsettling influx of large numbers of immigrants, and the prevalence of alcoholism in New England.

Walden Pond was not, in short, either a retired or a pristine place; in fact, one could hardly have chosen a more visible and public spot to retire to in the environs of Concord, for the pond had always had a close connection with the town. But this fact merely highlights the publicness if not the publicity of the gesture of moving there in the first place, which Thoreau had discussed with Ellery Channing and perhaps Emerson the previous year. When Thoreau moved to the pond, he already had in mind some literary project based on the experiment, for he started a new journal volume devoted to recording and immediately working up his experiences there right from the beginning.[5] No doubt he conceived his experiment knowing that it would invite comparison with the other experimental communities, such as nearby Brook Farm and Fruitlands, which had sprouted during the 1840s. And it echoed self-consciously the pioneering fever of the country itself, its rush to Oregon and California. The against-the-grain quality of the experiment (Man Builds Log Cabin in Walden Woods) was actually good copy, and led to a brief burst of notoriety when, on the basis of his lectures about life at the pond, he was written about, attacked, and defended in Horace Greeley's *New York Tribune* over a period of several weeks in 1849.[6] It is against all these contexts that Thoreau's paean to solitude and simplicity and nature must be seen. As for Walden itself, it can't really be Walden Forever Wild because it was never really wild to begin with. But despite the pressures of swimmers, picnickers, and pilgrims, its watershed in some ways is less intensively exploited today than it was one hundred and fifty years ago. Finally, the Walden Pond of the book, it must be said, is a carefully constructed literary site, less Thoreau's home than his home page, a virtual space he designed to represent himself and to promote his business, even if it was only listening to what was in the wind.

NOTES

1. *Environmental Imagination*, 311.

2. Ibid., 320; Thoreau, *Walden*, 86. Subsequent page references are cited parenthetically in the text.

3. Williams, *Country and the City*, 74.

4. Whitney and Davis, "From Primitive Woods to Cultivated Woodlots," 73; Gross, "Culture and Cultivation," 53.

5. Thoreau, *Journal, Vol. 2: 1842–1848*, 454–55.

6. Harding, *Days of Henry Thoreau*, 239.

Skirting Lowell

The Exceptional Work of Nature in A Week
on the Concord and Merrimack Rivers

STEPHEN GERMIC

According to Emerson, visions of nature are privileges of the poet. "To speak truly," he submits in the first chapter of *Nature*, "few adult persons can see nature."[1] Emerson goes so far as to name those, his neighbors, who see and own nature's parts, but not nature itself: "Miller owns this field, Locke that, and Manning the woodland beyond. But none of them owns the landscape" (23). Emerson implies, in fact, that their ownership of nature's parts forecloses the possibility of "seeing" nature. Thus Emerson's punning declaration that "There is a *property* in the horizon which no man has but he whose eye can integrate all the parts, that is, the poet" (23, emphasis added). Even as the vision of the poet unifies, or transforms, the woodcutter's "stick of timber" (23) into a forest that is itself an element of an always exalted *landscape*, the poet, analogously, is transformed. Emerson famously testifies: "I become a transparent eyeball; I am nothing; I see all; the currents of the universal being circulate through me; I am part or parcel of God" (24).

Approaching divinity is, no doubt, an extraordinarily affirmative experience, and most critics who have discussed the latter passage rightly acknowledge its expression of the "optative mood," and even its penultimate status in the metaphorics of transcendentalism. Yet the sentences that immediately follow the "transparent eyeball" passage — sentences far less frequently quoted and glossed — relate, curiously, the negative effects of Emerson's transformation. In his transformed and transforming condition — where nature is landscape and the poet a parcel of God — Emerson, or the poet, loses the capacity to distinguish human relations: "The name of the nearest friend sounds then foreign and accidental: to be brothers, to be acquaintances, master or servant, is then a trifle and a disturbance" (24). The vision of nature Emerson pronounces is exceptionally privileged, and, as an *exceptional* privilege, it obscures and even represses the vision and understanding of the woodcutter and the farmer. To the degree that the relation of master and servant becomes "a trifle," the poet's vision of those who labor, and, I submit, the vision of labor itself, becomes marginalized and discredited.

The voyage Thoreau represents in *A Week on the Concord and Merrimack Rivers* is distinctly Emersonian so far as it demonstrates a practical realization and literary extension of Emerson's transcendental effusions. Thoreau's engagements with "Nature," in other words, advance exceptional(ist) transformations, where "exceptional" refers to a kind of hyperbolic interaction with nature, and, as I will explain further below, to an obfuscation of labor and class. Yet furthermore, Thoreau cannily reiterates the productions of voyages — particularly those of Columbus and John Winthrop — principally responsible for the rhetorical and, in one case, social elaboration of American exceptionalism. In *A Week* Thoreau at once rediscovers America, revises and reaffirms the nation's "errand," and, inseparably, marginalizes or "skirts" the sites of labor that offer a source of representational alternative to the cultural production of exceptionalism.

The debate between those who admit exceptionalism as a fact of American social and labor history and those "against exceptionalism" suffers from disciplinarity. For labor historians, American exceptionalism refers to the absence of class consciousness and attendant absence of revolutionary social and political movements that challenge the interests of producers, employers, and the state. Such movements have appeared in other first-order capitalist nations: Germany, France, Britain. The United States disproves the Marxist dictum that capitalist wage relations directly produce a self-conscious proletariat — the class consciousness that manifests capitalism's most threatening contradiction.[2]

In 1984, Sean Wilentz articulated a rising opinion derived from the sound research of many "new" labor historians that suggested European "working-class" movements were compromised by a capitulation to dominant social and economic interests to a degree that made them quite similar to liberal and progressive politics in the United States during capitalism's formative postbellum years.[3] The working class, that is, or at the very least the leadership to which the working class largely conformed, accepted the interests of capital as their own. Thus, there was nothing "exceptional" about the American case. Wilentz's own primary research presumed to deliver another blow to exceptionalism by asserting, "There is a history of class consciousness in the United States comparable to that of working-class movements in Britain and on the Continent."[4] Wilentz fails to acknowledge the contradiction of the two grounds on which he critiques exceptionalism — a common absence of working-class consciousness on the one hand, a common presence on the other — but the contradiction does not necessarily invalidate his argument. There is a consensus, with which I, for one, agree, that particularly during the crucial and chaotic years of capitalist expansion and industrial formation, the United States harbored and systematically, if negatively, nurtured powerful constituencies of class-conscious political actors on either side of the class line. The unwillingness, for instance, of government agencies to pursue cases against trusts and combinations effectively sanctioned monopolies and money barons like Andrew Carnegie, whose persecution of unionizers led to the class "war" at Homestead in 1892 — class violence both resulted from class consciousness and aroused it. "Specters," occasionally, haunted America.

At the same time, European revolutionary and working-class movements *did* variously capitulate or were made to conform to liberal republican ideology.[5] The rapidity with which the French "revolutionaries" abandoned the principles of the "rights of man" when Santo Domingo revolted is possibly the most tragic example. But the collapse of revolutionary cause or principle, was, in fact, general throughout the nineteenth century. As Eric Hobsbawm has noted, the European revolution of 1848 "appears as the one revolution in the modern history of Europe which combines the greatest promise, the widest scope, and the most immediate initial success, with the most unqualified and rapid failure."[6] As the European balance of power shifted from the aristocracy to the bourgeoisie, bourgeois "revolutionaries" — often while claiming to be socialists — repressed the revolutionary "infection" of the "masses."[7]

The value of the research of antiexceptionalist scholars is inestimable, but those who have taken up the question of exceptionalism have failed adequately to describe and to explain the association of American exceptionalism — as it is traditionally understood by labor historians — with cultural hegemony, or, for that matter, with cultural notions of American exceptionalism. This latter understanding — well summarized by Jack P. Green in his recent volume, *The Intellectual Construction of America: Exceptionalism and Identity from 1492 to 1800* — begins with American "discovery" and the appurtenant promotions of the Columbian era that describe the New World as a place of possibility and paradise, and it extends through a Puritanical notion of mission, where America represents a nation of ideal politics and virtue, a "modell" (*sic*) for Britain, and, finally, the world. Cultural constructions of American exceptionalism punctuate natural beauty and bounty, and the possibility of political perfection. America promised "all the conditions — the exceptional conditions — necessary for [European immigrants] to establish control over their own lives, the [political and natural] conditions required to enable them not simply to survive, but to pursue . . . their own personal dreams for themselves and their families."[8]

To bridge various, and often contradictory, understandings of American exceptionalism, I would emphasize that a diverse field of cultural and political agents deploy — through an equally diverse field of institutions and publicly intended articulations — forces, consciously and unconsciously (or ideologically) to repress class-related dissent. At the risk of seeming to want it both ways, I submit that it was precisely America's antiexceptionalism, or the presence and threat of working-class consciousness, that promoted exceptionalist productions, including, not least, the conceptual exceptionalist production of America.[9] Focusing on the aspects of exceptionalism raised by labor historians, while introducing the less controversial understanding of exceptionalism held by scholars of American literature and culture, reveals the complex character of American exceptionalism. Thoreau's engagement, wittingly or not, with American exceptionalism is likewise revealing.

Thoreau's voyage of *A Week on the Concord and Merrimack Rivers* restages and reaffirms the voyages of Columbus and Winthrop; it reiterates the foundational tropes of American exceptionalism. Furthermore, Thoreau, maintaining an especially "exceptional" affiliation with Winthrop, reaffirms American industrial expansion while complexly recognizing and eliding the fundament of labor and class. *A Week*, in short, reveals the cultural terms of the close relation between the two understandings of American exceptionalism, America as Edenic, that is, and America as the place where the perception of class relations becomes confused, this latter to the profound disadvantage of working-class movements.

In the aphoristic conclusion of *Walden*, Thoreau, through the curious rhetoric of transcendental reformism, urges his readers to self-discovery through metaphors of prime imperialist sites and figures: "What does Africa, — what does the West stand for? Is it not our own interior white on the chart? . . . Be . . . the Lewis and Clark and Frobisher, of your own streams and oceans. . . . Nay, be a Columbus to whole new continents and worlds within you, opening new channels, not of trade, but of thought."[10] Several years earlier, when Thoreau was in the midst of his literal voyage on the Concord and Merrimack Rivers, he explicitly (and contradictorily) associated his adventure with the opening of channels of trade. He begins, in one instance, by announcing his solitary position in the wilderness. He makes camp where "there was no other house in sight, nor any cultivated field. To the right and left, as far as the horizon, were straggling pine woods with their plumes against the sky."[11] Thoreau continues:

> When we had pitched our tents on the hill-side, a few rods from the shore, we sat looking through its triangular door in the twilight at our lonely mast on the shore, just seen above the alders, and hardly yet come to a stand-still from the swaying of the stream; the first encroachment of commerce on this land. There was our port, our Ostia. That straight geometrical line against the water and the sky stood for the last refinements of civilized life, and what of sublimity there is in history was there symbolized. (40)

Thoreau's contradiction, albeit *avant la lettre*, of his urging inward exploration in the conclusion of *Walden* can be attributed to the fact of his literal voyaging, to his adventure on an actual river and across actual geography. Yet what is most interesting about this section of *A Week* is not the understandable contraction, but the brief narrative *eruption* — which is Thoreau's own metaphor — of Lowell, Massachusetts, in this paradoxically idyllic and sublime scene. "For the most part," Thoreau writes, "there was no recognition of human life in the night" (40). The natural sounds Thoreau hears periodically create "a sudden pause, and a deeper and more conscious silence" (40). We are not prepared for Thoreau's next sentence: "There was a fire in Lowell, as we judged, this night, and we saw the horizon blazing, and heard the distant alarm bells, as it were a faint tinkling music borne to these woods" (41). The horizon blazes and alarms sound, but by the end of the sentence the eruption can hardly be discriminated from the music of nature.

The blaze in Lowell does function narratively to introduce other sounds associated with human habitation (the barking of house dogs and crowing of cocks), but the passage continues and concludes without further mention of Lowell. In fact, the human sounds paradoxically evidence the *soundness* of nature: "All these sounds, the crowing of cocks, the baying of dogs, and the hum of insects at noon, are the evidence of nature's health, or *sound* state" (41–42, Thoreau's emphasis). Lowell fails to *alarm* Thoreau or to disturb nature. In narrative terms especially appropriate to *A Week*, the sounds of Lowell produce no digression; they do not compel Thoreau to an extensive discourse on, in Leo Marx's terms, the "machine in the garden." In fact, it is precisely the absence of digression on the matter of Lowell, in a volume rightly noted for its many digressions, that may be the most remarkable feature of this passage. An explanation for the apparent absence (the paradoxically present absence) of disruption and narrative digression is suggested at a later point of Thoreau's journey and narrative.

After a brief rest in Chelmsford, where he discovers "a new flower to us, the harebell of the poets," Thoreau "rowed leisurely along" and begins a series of digressions interrupted by brief notations of the landmarks in the progress of the voyage. Subordinate to one landmark, Salmon Brook, is the manufacturing town of Nashua, New Hampshire: "Salmon Brook near its mouth is still a solitary stream, meandering through woods and meadows, while the . . . mouth of the Nashua [River] now resounds with the din of a manufacturing town" (161–62). The industrial character of Nashua receives no further gloss and it inspires no related digression. Several pages later, we learn that "Soon the village of Nashua was out of sight, and the woods were gained again" (171).

Lowell and Nashua are heard, briefly, even musically, but hardly seen; the industrial towns din, but they do not alarm. The narrative digressions for which *A Week* is so famous, even infamous (especially contemporaneously), obscure what Thoreau saw and heard, what he mentions but avoids. Thoreau voyages through but around the locations of industry and *proletarian*, even abject, labor. In 1820, the population at the future site of Lowell was about two hundred, but by 1833, six years before Thoreau's journey, Lowell was a major city of over twelve thousand with a clear record of labor agitation that began around 1828.[12] During the same period the value of homespun manufactured goods dropped by 80 percent, becoming all but worthless.[13] Towns like Lowell and Nashua were *the* locations of rising working-class consciousness and resistance to exploitation in the United States in the 1830s. Furthermore, the Merrimack River had been, by 1839, thoroughly rationalized to suit industrial development, but the symptoms of this rationalization — canals, mills, the mass of laborers — go almost entirely unremarked as subjects of Thoreau's narrative. Of course, Thoreau and his brother, in their heavy rowboat, used Lowell's canals in order to get around Pawtucket Falls. In ironic terms, Thoreau traveled through the very productions of industry to surmount a natural obstacle, while his narrative skirts the industrial site and the very industrialized "path" of transportation as it celebrates nature.

Among the digressions that occupy the narrative space evacuated by the "skirting" of Lowell and Nashua is a discussion of literature and the craft of writing. In this section, Thoreau's metaphors are rich and various, as well as contradictory. Thoreau asserts, on the one hand, that the "most attractive" writing exhibits "a natural emphasis in . . . style, like a man's tread, [with] a breathing space between the sentences. . . . [The] chapters are like English parks, or say rather like a western forest, where the larger growth keeps down the underwood, and one may ride on horseback through the openings" (104). On the other hand, the best writing comes from having felled the forest and is, furthermore, directed to those who perform such labor:

> Surely the writer is to address a world of laborers, and such therefore must be his own discipline. He will not idly dance at his work who has wood to cut and cord before night-fall in the short days of winter. . . . The scholar might frequently emulate . . . the farmer's call to his team, and confess that if that were written it would surpass his labored sentences. Whose are the truly *labored* sentences? . . . A sentence should read as if its author, had he held a plow instead of a pen, could have drawn a furrow deep and straight to the end. The scholar requires hard and serious labor to give an impetus to his thought. He will learn to grasp the pen firmly so, and wield it gracefully and effectively, as an axe or a sword. (106–7)

Thoreau is not compelled to develop his metaphor of great writing as "old growth," the reading of which is like a stroll through "western forests," in large part because the metaphor is at odds with his digressive narrative. Writing is the digression by which industry is evaded; writing about writing *replaces* the narrative obligation of the travelogue to record the geographic encounters of the journey. Ironically, or, if we honor Thoreau's terms, through some unwitting necessity to "speak deliberately" (98), the labor and laborers of a burgeoning mass industry appear, though transformed to independent agrarians whose very ejaculations are a "natural" poetry. Thoreau himself, when the division between physical and intellectual labor disappears, becomes the worker, the worker of and for *nature*, where nature is the cultivated and developed landscape. Thus, in the following instance, where contemporary environmentalists might be compelled to celebrate the reclamations of nature, Thoreau sees nature "running out." Referring to the town of Billerica, in 1839 already undergoing ecological reclamation, Thoreau writes, "See, is not Nature here gone to decay, farms all run out, meeting house grown grey and racked with age?" (50).

Thoreau's nature is affiliated with the "axe" and the "sword." Like Emerson's poet, he transforms materiality — actual geography traversed by humans amid their *social relations* — and *manufactures* landscape, a version of nature from which he and his productions are inseparable and which is itself productive. Taking account of re-vision and re-placement (not *dis*placement), Thoreau's nature *is* industry. Thoreau disclaims the industry he confronts while he reformulates the confrontation *outside* the relations of labor and industry and their appurtenant human relations. The independent laborer is the idealized product of Thoreau's journey through but around the sounds and sites of dependent labor.

In the Journal entry of January 4, 1851, Thoreau writes that the "longest silence is the most pertinent question most pertinently put. Emphatically silent."[14] This cryptic declaration appears immediately after an extended passage that is, for Thoreau, at once formally characteristic but rather atypical with regard to content. The content is atypical because, in volumes devoted primarily to "natural" observations, it concerns a description of "actual" industry, specifically, the "Gingham mills" at Clinton, Massachusetts. The passage is characteristic because in it Thoreau maintains the tone of the reporting naturalist that dominates other Journal entries. In a sense, industry becomes the narrative, or formal, equivalent of "nature." This equivalence explains why Thoreau provides such a deft, even admiring description of the mill works, but does so with only the vaguest reference to the mill's laborers (he mentions only "operators"). Even where industry is an explicit subject, the subjects, or the human relations that occupy and characterize industry, disappear — on the matter of labor, in short, Thoreau is "emphatically silent."

According to the ideological demands of American exceptionalism, class, the complex relations of dependent and independent labor, must necessarily both function and disappear. Thoreau begins most fully to associate his own journey with Winthrop's extraordinarily "exceptionalist" voyage where Thoreau "encounters" Lowell. Thoreau removes himself from the encounter by narrating the experience of place through the perspective of an historian who sees or "passes through" the layers of history:

It is a rapid story the historian will have put together. Miantonimo,-Winthrop,-Webster. Soon he comes from Mount Hope to Bunker Hill, from bearskins, parched corn, bows and arrows, to tiled roofs, wheat fields, guns, and swords. Pawtucket and Wamesit, where the Indians resorted in the fishing season, are now Lowell, the city of spindles and Manchester of America, which sends its cotton cloth round the globe. (82–83)

In Thoreau's own metaphoric terms, his labor has cleared the space for Lowell and globalized American industry, and, in a sense, it has. The narrative of his voyage is a digression into the *landscape* of nature that at once complexly and intermittently records the industry he encounters while skirting and/or reformulating the encounter. In a strange reversal of a prime economic, even Marxist, dictum, nature (or nature writing) is industry transformed, and an idealized, or Emersonian, relationship with nature obscures and reformulates the social relationships that industry elaborates and on which it depends: "I see, smell, taste, hear, feel, that everlasting Something to which we are allied, at once our maker, or abode, our destiny, our very Selves" (173).

Aboard the *Arabella*, John Winthrop similarly employed divinity to contend with the "problem" of social relations. "A Modell of Christian Charity" begins with an anxious assertion of the need to preserve social differences along the lines of class division in the New World: "God Almigtie in his most wise and holy providence hath soe disposed of the Condicion of mankind, as in all times some must be rich some poore, some high and eminent in power and dignitie; others mean and in subjection."[15] Winthrop aims to preserve an essentially monarchical social order, fully aware that its literal existence will be a conspicuous absence in America. With no royal figure to mediate God's divine plan in the New World, Winthrop skillfully confuses divine ordinance and class division: "All men being thus (by divine providence) ranked into two sortes, rich an poore; under the first are comprehended all such as are able to live comfortable by their own means duly improved; all others are poore according to the former distribution."[16] Winthrop's anxiety about the poor rising up and "shaking off their yoake" reveals that the understanding of class difference as *socially* constituted may have been operative before the proper rise of industrialism, as the term *class* is glossed and dated by Raymond Williams.[17] It is precisely such a social understanding that Winthrop seeks to suppress; he would have it take the form of a transcendent edict. It is in this sense that class, or more exactly, a particular knowledge or understanding of class, one that might motivate a revolutionary sense of injustice, "disappears," or is obscured by the ideological machinations of American exceptionalism.

The best books, Thoreau announces, "contain pure discoveries, glimpses of *terra firma*" (98). As terra firma approached, Winthrop was compelled to pronouncements of the divine regulation of human relations; he directed the attention of would-be American colonists to God that they might not scrutinize the foundations and legitimacy of the social relations that traveled with them from the Old World. Thoreau, in the account of his voyage as an "earnest seeker and hopeful discoverer of this New World" (263), provides no more than glimpses of the industrial terra firma he negotiated. Obscured by a kind of Emersonian divine nature, in Thoreau's case, or by divine ordinance, as with Winthrop, American exceptionalism — the manifold cultural obfuscations of class and labor — persists.

NOTES

1. Emerson, *Nature*, in *Selections*, 23. Subsequent page references are cited parenthetically in the text.

2. See Mike Davis, "Why Is the U.S. Working Class Different?"; Eric Foner, "Why Is There No Socialism in America?"; Byron E. Shafer, *Is America Different? A New Look at American Exceptionalism.*

3. Wilentz, "Against Exceptionalism."

4. Ibid., 18.

5. For a recent overview of the "exceptionalism" debate among historians, see Michael Kammen, "The Problem of American Exceptionalism: A Reconsideration."

6. Hobsbawm, *The Age of Capital: 1848–1875*, 15.

7. Ibid., 98–115.

8. Greene, *The Intellectual Construction of America*, 88–89.

9. Ibid., 1–7.

10. Thoreau, *Walden*, 321.

11. Thoreau, *A Week*, 39. Subsequent page references will be cited parenthetically in the text.

12. Steinberg, *Nature Incorporated*, 217.

13. Ibid., 120.

14. Thoreau, *Journal, Vol. 3: 1848–1851*, 173.

15. Winthrop, "A Modell of Christian Charity," 108.

16. Ibid.

17. Williams, *Keywords*, 51–59.

Rustling Thoreau's Cattle
Wildness and Domesticity in "Walking"

BARBARA "BARNEY" NELSON

A cultural parallax, then, might be considered to be the difference in views between those who are actively participating in the dynamics of the habitats within their home range and those who view those habitats as "landscapes" from the outside.
— Gary Paul Nabhan, "Cultural Parallax in Viewing North American Habitats"

While teaching a new class called "Environmental Literature" at small, rural Sul Ross State University in Alpine, Texas, I was about to assign Henry David Thoreau's 1862 classic essay "Walking." One of the textbooks I had chosen for the class, *American Environmentalism: Readings in Conservation History* edited by Roderick Frazier Nash, contained a shortened version of Thoreau's essay which Nash had renamed "The Value of Wildness."[1] At first glance, Nash's version seemed to adequately summarize what he claimed was the heart of Thoreau's essay: wilderness preservation. But there were many innocent-looking little ellipsis dots where passages had been removed. Curious about what was missing and uncomfortable with his interpretation of Thoreau's meaning, I carefully compared Nash's edited version with Thoreau's original.

Perhaps because of my rural background and affiliation, I noticed that Nash, a highly respected history scholar at the University of California, was carefully omitting almost all of Thoreau's references to horses, cows, farming, and pastures. Missing are Thoreau's statements that he loves to see "domestic animals reassert their native rights — any evidence that t their original wild habits and vigor," that watching cows swimming the river is like watching the buffalo crossing the Mississippi, and that the "seeds of instinct are preserved under the thick hides of cattle and horses, like seeds in the bowels of the earth, an indefinite period."[2] Nash's deletions and his decision to delete one key paragraph and replace it with another change the essay's focus from wildness as a saving grace lurking beneath the surface of all things domestic to wilderness preservation propaganda. But the problem isn't new.

The wild/domestic dichotomy in American literature begins as early as *Mayflower* Pilgrim William Bradford (1589/90–1657). His published journal, *Of Plimoth Plantation*, written between 1630 and 1647, is an account of early Plymouth history. Modern anthologies, biographies, or journal articles dutifully quote Bradford's description of the Pilgrims' fearful first sight of the New England coast as "a hideous and desolate wilderness, full of wild beasts and wild men."[3] With no friends to greet them and the wide Atlantic behind them, the Pilgrim Separatists had indeed finally separated themselves from the corruptive influences of society. Although granting that "Bradford was no romantic," critic David Laurence finds in Bradford's words "the queer music and peculiar visionary irony of the American sublime."[4] Laurence observes that Bradford accomplishes here "in a sudden and singular leap what American writing in general must wait to achieve after a long period of provincialism." Laurence argues further that if we "search the record of American writing between Bradford and Emerson for the like of Bradford's 'Americanness,' we search in vain" (56).

The sublime emotion contained in Bradford's famous passage comes not from his literal description of the Pilgrims' vulnerable position, but from our twenty-first-century perspective of knowing, as Paul Harvey would say, the rest of the story. We know how the story ended. We know that half of the Pilgrims died and half survived that first winter. What many scholars have failed to note seriously enough is that Bradford also knew how the story ended when he wrote those lines. The passage was written not at the moment the Pilgrims sighted land, but ten years later. Contrast the *Plimoth* quotation with the following lines, written on the *Mayflower* during the actual sighting: "After many difficulties in boisterous storms, at length, by God's providence . . . we espied land. . . . And the appearance of it much comforted us, especially seeing so goodly a land, and wooded to the brink of the sea."[5] This *Mourt's Relation* quotation has a hopeful, almost childlike faith in the new land and God's benevolence. At the time, trees represented life-saving firewood and material for homes, not wilderness. But after only ten years on Massachusetts soil, Bradford already adopts the strangely American phenomenon of "remembering" or imagining a howling wilderness which never in fact existed. A great deal of the coastal plain from the Saco River to Narragansett Bay had already been cleared for Wampanoag cornfields before the Pilgrims ever arrived. The indigenous people had also continually burned the forest to improve grazing, leaving it "for the most part open and without underwood, fit either to go or ride in" (*Mourt's* 18–19). According to Bradford's own journal, Pilgrims settled on cleared Indian farmlands which had been vacated by an epidemic in 1616 (Laurence 63). The first Indian they had contact with walked into their camp speaking broken English[6] and taught the newcomers to use fish as fertilizer in order to raise corn. New England was a home, not a wilderness, when the Pilgrims landed, and the Wampanoags were hardworking farmers and pastoralists, not romantic hunter/gatherers.

Gary Paul Nabhan, in his excellent essay "Cultural Parallax in Viewing North American Habitats," recounts the many ways "four to twelve million" Native American people, "speaking two hundred languages variously burned, pruned, hunted, hacked, cleared, irrigated, and planted in an astonishing diversity of habitats for centuries." He also notes that when these "newly arrived 'colonists' came down from the Bering Strait into ice-free country, they played a role in Pleistocene extinctions which amounted to a loss of 73 percent of the North American animals weighing 100 pounds or more."[7] Yet our literature and history have led us to believe that Native Americans lived in an Edenic harmony with a "natural" landscape. Rebecca Solnit finds that "the gap between our view of landscape and of history is full of lost stories, ravaged cultures, obliterated names."[8] This gap is also full of a lost domestic history. Although a staunch advocate of wilderness preservation, even Gary Snyder reminds us that the "wilderness" was actually a "home" full of people and trails.[9] We are slowly realizing that even in the wildest parts of the Amazon rain forest, the flora is not natural but planted, harvested, moved, and managed by the people who live there.[10]

In *Wilderness and the American Mind*, Nash makes another interesting observation: that the "central turning point in the human relationship to the natural world [coincided with] the advent of herding and agriculture some 15,000 years ago. Prior to that time human beings hunted and gathered."[11] Somehow, although the most ancient oral history culture would never claim to know or remember, historians *know* that hunting and gathering linearly preceded herding and agriculture — especially in America. So, although *Mayflower* Pilgrims settled on cleared Indian farmlands, although Native Americans had constantly burned both grasslands and forests in order to improve pasture for and direct the migration of grazing animals, although modern Arizona irrigators follow miles and miles of ancient Hohokam irrigation ditches, and although even ants keep herds of milking aphids — we hold fast to the idea that at some Edenic point in time, land flowed with milk and honey and sinless people hunted and gathered it without effort or harm.[12] Ignoring the heritage of indigenous farmers and pastoralists, Americans still today prefer to imagine their ancestors as simply reborn into a preagricultural Eden that had been created especially for them.

Because the fledgling nation wrongly (or possibly racially) imagined itself without a heritage, ruins, or long traditions like those which stimulated European authors, early transcendentalists searched for something inherently American from which to gain inspiration. If intuition and a metaphysical sense of God or higher laws were inspired through observing wild nature, as European romantics believed, then the spectacular mountains and forests of the new country should have an exhilarating influence on the writing produced by American transcendentalists. Thus, scenic landscape was the logical choice as a source for sublime and superior inspiration with which to compete with European authors. The wilder the landscape, the more romantically superior the writing would be.

So, beginning as early as William Bradford, American authors were continually at work imagining the American continent as empty, wild, and pristine, newly delivered from the creating hand of God to His chosen people. Recognizing this tendency, agreeing with the idea that a "wild" land should inspire exhilarating writing, but disapproving of the racial bias which erased the existence of the continent's former inhabitants and land managers, Henry David Thoreau was trying to imagine a more realistic definition for a wild American heritage in his 1862 essay "Walking." It is in this essay that Thoreau's famous line "In Wildness is the preservation of the world" appears (224). He does not say wildness needs our condescending protection, but that wildness will protect us.[13] However, he is often misquoted as having said, "In wilderness is the preservation of the world." Nash adds to this mistaken interpretation in the introduction to his version of Thoreau's essay when he writes, "Thoreau spoke a half-century before most Americans were prepared to listen sympathetically to his message. Nevertheless, his philosophy survived to become the intellectual foundation of the wilderness preservation movement and of aesthetic conservation" (36). Although Thoreau definitely values wild places, wildness and wilderness are not interchangeable signifiers in his mind. On the subject of wildness/wilderness, Lawrence Buell says that although Thoreau "celebrated wildness, his was the wildness not of the moose but of the imported, cultivated escapee from the orchard that he celebrated in his late essay 'Wild Apples.'"[14] Thoreau's essay "Wild Apples" even describes the way domestic cows can actually help domestic apple trees return to a state of wildness, yet Nash's introduction to the "Walking" essay misleads the reader into interpreting Thoreau's message as a call for wilderness preservation.

Instead, Thoreau explains that while wildness can be found in the forests and in what we call wilderness, he also finds it in domestic animals, in "tawny" grammar, in both "civilized" and "uncivilized" cultures, in libraries, in architecture, underneath calluses, in the migratory instincts of birds, in the simplest and obscurest of men, in "Useful Ignorance," in soil, in the smell on a trapper's coat, in both bogs and spades, in the sound of a bugle on a summer night, and in the humble act of walking. He observes that "wildness" is imported by the cities and that men plow and sail for it, but he doesn't believe all that exotic searching is necessary. Wildness, he argues, can be found everywhere: in the library, beneath skin color, even in cows.

Numerous humanities scholars have recently been investigating this typically American dichotomy between home as a place where people live and nature as a place where humans have been excluded. Donald Meinig's 1976 essay "The Beholding Eye" began the discussion by describing the various ways we imagine landscape: as nature, habitat, artifact, system, problem, wealth, ideology, history, place, and aesthetic. He explains how each view has its own biases, advantages, and disadvantages. Adding another important idea, Annette Kolodny (1984) pointed out that relationships to land were often expressed using female gendered metaphors (mother earth, virgin land) and verbs of sexual conquest (penetration, rape). She claims that "at the deepest psychological level, the move to America was experienced as the daily reality of what has become its single dominating metaphor: regression from the cares of adult life and a return to the primal warmth of womb or breast in a feminine [preferably virginal] landscape."[15] Just as women are often valued primarily as a "visual spectacle," wilderness as imagined by preservationists has a highly aesthetic visual bias as well. Art critic Rebecca Solnit explains that when the landscape is defined as a "visual spectacle," tourism becomes the only "normal and proper" human relationship.[16] Nature reduced to visual spectacle rather than unpredictable, powerful, and cyclic system promotes the idea that nature is a safe, nurturing, and passive — maybe even helpless — place. This is almost opposite to Thoreau's view of a beautifully sublime and dangerous nature, which he compares to a howling mother leopard (237).

In 1989, Buell tentatively began to apply the idea of wilderness as an imaginary construct to Thoreau's work when he argued that nature pilgrims desiring a retreat into Thoreau's "wilderness" had become an "American cult." Trying to follow Thoreau's example, he says, they were flocking to Walden Pond, thinking they had "left the profane metropolis to find solace in the sacred grove," where they worshiped in spite of the fact that in reality the "grove" was actually part of the greater Boston area. This cult, as he calls it, had become almost a form of religion, complete with disciples, evangelists, and saint.[17]

Numerous humanities scholars quickly began agreeing, at some level, that the dichotomy between wildness and home was not only imaginary but harmful. Cultural geographers began talking more and more about the role of imagination in constructing nature when Max Oelschlaeger (1991) argued that wilderness was an idea governed by economic and political ideology,[18] and Neil Evernden (1992) pronounced nature itself a social creation.[19] Recently, William Cronon, in his controversial collection *Uncommon Ground: Toward Reinventing Nature* (1995), succinctly brought together the ideas that had been floating through the humanities for almost two decades. His collection of essays, produced by a group of scholars who sequestered themselves in Southern California for an academic seminar on the topic, uses deconstruction to challenge the whole idea of wilderness, explaining that the North American continent was never a wilderness. A professor of history, geography, and environmental studies, Cronon argued that wilderness had become a powerful but imagined human construct which was preventing a realistic evaluation of ecosystems and providing an unstable foundation for the environmental movement.[20] The book caused a furor of heated responses.[21]

In Cronon's collection, Richard White, a professor of history at the University of Washington, argued that nature as wilderness had become a sacred place where humans not only could not live, but could not work. He said, "Most environmentalists disdain and distrust those who obviously work in nature, and . . . have come to associate work — particularly heavy bodily labor, blue collar work — with environmental degradation."[22] Seemingly in answer to the challenge, Buell admitted in 1995 that although Thoreau did not embrace the wilderness of the moose, he must take some responsibility for "abetting the memorialization of what he stood for as a leisure time activity." "At least ostensibly," said Buell, "precious little work gets done at *Walden* once he builds the cabin" (389). Thoreau does, however, spend a great deal of energy metaphorically and allegorically trying to defend his unemployment as an unpublished saunterer as serious "work."

As a direct descendant of *Mayflower* Pilgrim William Bradford, I am a thirteenth-generation working-class rural American. Educated in a one-room Iowa school, my early childhood was spent fishing the Mississippi River, hunting, and exploring my family's wild Jackson County farm. Later, I spent thirty years living and working on Arizona and Texas ranches. Because of this background, I have always been interested in "nature writing" and the importance of plants, animals, and land in American literature. In the introduction to *The Ecocriticism Reader: Landmarks in Literary Ecology* (1996), Cheryll Glotfelty defines ecocriticism as "the study of the relationship between literature and the physical environment. . . . As a critical stance, it has one foot in literature and the other on land; as a theoretical discourse, it negotiates between the human and the nonhuman."[23] As an ecocritic, I have one foot in literature, the other in rural work, and I am continually trying to negotiate between agriculture and my fellow environmentalists. I believe serious research should matter to the world outside academia, and the most important current environmental problem involving rural people is the grazing issue — the one point, and often the only point, at which I disagree hotly with environmental politics. The idea that domestic animals are somehow more destructive, less intelligent, and less valuable than wild animals seems to be rooted in the wild/domestic dichotomy rampant in American literature. This dichotomy influences public opinion and is currently hampering modern scientific research through funding, publication, and publicity pressures. Thoreau receives blame for inspiring this dichotomy, but that idea is based on misinterpretation of his meaning.

One vivid example of the way Nash changes Thoreau's meaning in "Walking" occurs in the following paired passages. Thoreau's version champions a "wildness" he finds in dark skin color, claiming that perhaps "olive is a fitter color than white" for a "denizen" of the woods. He is attempting to use the American love of all things wild to give not only respect but perhaps even a little advantage to dark skin. Writing about eliminating racism was one of Thoreau's favorite subjects. The passage also exposes a subtle racism contained in Ben Jonson's sentence and Thoreau's suggested revision:

A tanned skin is something more than respectable, and perhaps olive is a fitter color than white for a man — a denizen of the woods. "The pale white man!" I do not wonder that the African pitied him. Darwin the naturalist says, "A white man bathing by the side of a Tahitian was like a plant bleached by the gardener's art, compared with a fine, dark green one, growing vigorously in the open fields."

Ben Jonson exclaims,

"How near to good is what is fair!"

So I would say,

"How near to good is what is *wild*!" (226)

Nash, however, deletes Thoreau's original paragraph and inserts a sentence which actually appears several pages later in the essay. Through this manipulation, Nash gives his own version a preservationist, antiagricultural, and racially whitewashed flavor that totally changes Thoreau's original meaning. Nash's version:

I would not have every man nor every part of a man cultivated, any more than I would have every acre of earth cultivated: part will be tillage, but the greater part will be meadow and forest, not only serving an immediate use, but preparing a mold against a distant future, by the annual decay of the vegetation which it supports. . . .

Ben Jonson exclaims,

"How near to good is what is fair!"

So I would say,

"How near to good is what is *wild*!" (39)

The inserted and moved paragraph originally appears right after Thoreau's sentence, "Not even does the moon shine every night, but gives place to darkness" (238). Thoreau has been discussing the importance of maintaining a balance in one's life between intellectualism and sloth. Metaphorically he compares intellectual enlightenment to sunshine and says there "may be an excess even of informing light." He goes on to explain how the sun's rays produce a destructive chemical effect on granite rock but that at night the rock had the power to restore itself. He goes on to argue that even grammar rules should sometimes be broken in order to allow for freedom of expression. Through his metaphoric comparisons between sunlight and darkness, forests and cultivated fields, proper grammar and lingo, swamps and gardens, Thoreau explains how he believes the world needs, should value, and already contains some sort of balance between this "wildness" he is attempting to define and the constraints placed upon it by society, education, government, and religion. He is defining the human spirit which rises to rebellion when power structures become oppressive. As Buell points out, Thoreau is often appropriated by those with an agenda. He has "been acclaimed as the first hippie by a nudist magazine, recommended as a model for disturbed teenagers, cited by the Viet Cong in broadcasts urging American GI's to desert, celebrated by environmental activists as 'one of our first preservationists' and embraced by a contributor to the John Birch society magazine as 'our greatest reactionary'" (314). Thoreau has become such an inspirational "saint" that adopting him to trumpet one's cause has become quite popular. However, he is not advocating a wilderness preserve, nor is he demonizing agriculture.[24] Through metaphor, Thoreau is emphasizing the importance of maintaining an equal balance when making judgments between the desirable and undesirable.

Thoreau attempts to define the word "wildness" and to show how important it is to the sanity and happiness not only of humans but of animals. In "Walking," Thoreau reminds us the cow was not born domestic, but is in fact descended, like all people, from the savage. Missing from Nash's version is Thoreau's observation that "Any sportiveness in cattle is unexpected. I saw one day a herd of a dozen bullocks and cows running about and frisking in unwieldy sport . . . and perceived by their horns as well as by their activity, their relation to the deer tribe" (235). The modern cow descended from extinct wild ungulates like the African, Asian, and European aurochs (*Bos taurus primigenius*). Scotland's legendary, long extinct, wild white cattle were also ancestors, as are India's endangered beautiful red Gaur (*Bos gaurus*). The cow's family tree includes Caesar's urus, Indonesia's banteng, and the hairy wild yak (*Bos grunniens*). Even the European and Asian wisent (*Bison bonasus*), a small, light-colored buffalo, contributed to the wild gene pool.[25] Thoreau is rejoicing in the fact that the cow has not lost this wildness. Looking to nature for ways to understand human problems, he observes that in each generation "horses and steers have to be broken before they can be made the slaves of men" (235). Although Thoreau's comment could be interpreted as meaning that eventually horses and steers are "broken" mentally, I would say he is using an older meaning, one more familiar to people who depended daily upon horses for transportation and work.[26] "Broken," in this sense, does not mean an animal's spirit is broken, but that the animal has lost its fear of humans and has decided to become cooperative in exchange for regular meals. If a situation becomes stressful enough, the most well "broken" horse or steer will fight back or run away and display the hidden "wildness" Thoreau is looking for and defining. He argues that "The seeds of instinct are preserved under the thick hides of cattle and horses, like seeds in the bowels of the earth, an indefinite period," and he loves "to see the domestic animals reassert their native rights — any evidence that they have not wholly lost their original wild habits and vigor" (234). Domestic animals have been used symbolically to represent oppressed people and the common masses since our earliest literature, yet all of these statements about the wildness in domestic animals were edited out of Nash's new version of "Walking."

Although Thoreau also uses the word "pasture" to encompass wild nature,[27] as Jack Turner points out, Thoreau "did not claim that in ranching is the preservation of the world"[28] — but neither did he say in wilderness is the preservation of the world. His word was *wildness*. Thoreau does not define the domestic and the wild as polar opposites, nor does he devalue or erase the domestic from our history. Through metaphor and a celebration of nature's willingness to bestow wild beauty on all, regardless of race and class, Thoreau is arguing that his neighbors should also learn to recognize beauty in diversity by studying nature. Challenging class, he makes observations like, "When the trapper's coat emits the odor of musquash even; it is a sweeter scent to me than that which commonly exhales from the merchant's or the scholar's garments" (226). Challenging race, he says the white pine produces blossoms "over the heads of Nature's red children as of her white ones" and that the cock crowing in the morning reminds us that where the birds live "no fugitive slave laws are passed" (245, 246).

To Thoreau, taking a walk in nature is more than a form of exercise, more than a relaxing escape from the stress of civilization, more than a simple return to a pristine Garden of Eden or arcadian pasture. He defines sauntering early in the essay as both a real and a religious experience and in the closing paragraph connects it to "a great awakening light" (205–6, 248). He receives this enlightened state of mind simply by sauntering — by walking and observing with a respectful eye. His walk represents a pilgrimage into the transcendental world of nature, a way to see deeply into human problems by looking for answers in a larger system. Nature gives Thoreau a soaring hope that perhaps people can develop a "philosophy and poetry and religion" to equal the American continent's inspiring grandeur (222), and can live up to the ideals of democracy. He repeats a question supposedly posed to all newcomers: "From what part of the world have you come?" The question naturally assumes "these vast and fertile regions" would be a common meeting place for people from around the globe (221). In nature, Thoreau sees a model for pure democracy. Metaphorically, through swamps, he asks the reader to appreciate the natural diversity of our world and to learn to see beauty in the deep black muck of the uncultivated and uncontrived. Nature shows no preference for color, class, creed, gender, but sublimely embraces (or destroys) all equally — like democracy. He does not claim that the process of becoming truly free will always be without pain, mistakes, and frustration, and says a similar wild situation in Australia "has not yet proved a successful experiment" (218). Thoreau also believes in the necessity of civilization to improve the state of natural wildness through choosing one's own direction and path, choosing one's own religion by blending admirable traits from around the world, and choosing to obey just laws voluntarily.

Throughout the essay, Thoreau pulls agreement for his thoughts from world religions and cultures: Spain, Dahomey, the Hottentots, Chaldeans, Arabs, Poles, Russians, and Hindus. He quotes Confucius as saying, "The skins of the tiger and the leopard, when they are tanned, are as the skins of the dog and the sheep tanned" (236). In short, the "wildness" which Thoreau struggles to define is not the wildness of a protected wilderness preserve, but something that cannot be bred out, beat out, preached out, educated out, or domesticated out of any place, plant, or animal, including the human slave. Thoreau argues that wildness is not unique to any nation, government, or race, and is something that cannot be lost, something that should be both valued and feared. He makes clear that civilization can hide it, oppression can stifle it, education and religion can subdue it, but scratch the surface deep enough to draw blood and wildness springs eternal. This is the kind of grand thinking which inspired Lev Tolstoy, Martin Luther King Jr., and Mahatma Gandhi. Thoreau was exploring much bigger ideas than simply advocating preservation of pleasuring grounds for a leisure class. Thoreau's original "Walking" essay is crucial for valuing our natural world and understanding our most problematic human issues. Thoreau said, "In wildness is the preservation of the world." He did not say wilderness, and he did not say it needed our help.

NOTES

1. Nash, *American Environmentalism*. Page references are cited parenthetically in the text.

2. Thoreau, "Walking," *Writings of Henry David Thoreau*, ed. Torrey, vol. V, 234. Subsequent page references are cited parenthetically in the text.

3. Bradford, *Of Plimouth Plantation*, 61.

4. Laurence, "William Bradford's American Sublime," 64, 56. Subsequent page references are cited parenthetically in the text.

5. *Mourt's Relation*, 15. Subsequent page references are cited parenthetically in the text.

6. Holzer, "Strangers and Pilgrims," 32.

7. Nabhan, "Cultural Parallax," 92, 97. Subsequent page references are cited parenthetically in the text.

8. Solnit, *Savage Dreams*, 222.

9. Snyder, *The Practice of the Wild*, 7.

10. Posey, "The Science of the Mebêngôkre."

11. Nash, *Wilderness and the American Mind*, xiii.

12. Pyne, "History with Fire in Its Eye"; Blackburn and Anderson, *Before the Wilderness*; Hurt, *Indian Agriculture in America*.

13. Fritzell, *Nature Writing and America*, 105.

14. Buell, *Environmental Imagination*, 314, 116. Subsequent page references are cited parenthetically in the text.

15. Kolodny, *The Lay of the Land*, 6.

16. Solnit, "Reclaiming History."

17. Buell, "Thoreauvian Pilgrimage," 183, 188–89.

18. Oelschlaeger, *Idea of Wilderness*.

19. Evernden, *Social Creation of Nature*.

20. Cronon, ed., *Uncommon Ground*.

21. Cohen, "The Trouble with Wilderness"; O'Grady, "Thinking Is False Happiness"; Sessions, "Reinventing Nature"; Soule and Lease, eds., *Reinventing Nature?*

22. White, "'Are You an Environmentalist or Do You Work for a Living?'"

23. Glotfelty and Fromm, eds., *The Ecocriticism Reader*, xviii–xix.

24. Gilmore, "Walden and the 'Curse of Trade'"; Gross, "The Great Bean Field Hoax."

25. Nelson, "Edward Abbey's Cow."

26. Dorrance, *True Unity*; Hunt, *Think Harmony with Horses*.

27. Marx, *Machine in the Garden*, 246.

28. Turner, *The Abstract Wild*, 111.

Counter Frictions

Writing and Activism in the Work of Abbey and Thoreau

SUSAN M. LUCAS

Words on a page do not accomplish anything by themselves; but words taken to heart, words carried in mind, may lead to action.
— *Alison Hawthorne Deming, Richard Nelson, Scott Russell Sanders,*
  "Letter to Orion *Readers"*

In American nature writing, two of the most vehement, influential voices to inspire environmental activism belong to Henry David Thoreau and Edward Abbey. Though writing a century apart and about different regions, Abbey and Thoreau openly advocate individual resistance to institutional oppression through jeremiadic rhetoric and acts of civil disobedience. Environmental groups have adopted them as ideological leaders or figureheads for their organizations and have used their words as indictments against land developers, miners, politicians, and others who would injure the environment. The images of Thoreau as hermit of Walden Pond and of Abbey as ecoranger of Arches National Monument continue to dominate their literary legacies and fuel the perceptions of Thoreau as wilderness advocate and Abbey as expert monkey wrencher. While these "green" portraits celebrate the importance of these men to the modern environmental movement, they also misrepresent Abbey and Thoreau as environmental leaders. For both of these writers, the site of resistance occurs primarily on the page, contrary to their glorified images as environmental crusaders in the field. My discussion examines how these portraits distort the actual physical and literary activism of Thoreau and Abbey and how these writers' opposition emerges from the pen rather than through collective protests, petitions, laws, or acts of sabotage.

Writer Wendell Berry compares Abbey with Thoreau, particularly regarding their dubious roles as environmental leaders. Berry explains that "Thoreau was an environmentalist in exactly the same sense that Edward Abbey is: he was for some things that environmentalists are for. And in his own time he was just as much an embarrassment to movements, just as uncongenial to the group spirit, as Edward Abbey is. . . . As a political activist [Thoreau] was a poor excuse."[1] Berry questions the political value of Thoreau's reform writings and suggests that we need not take them seriously. Berry quotes several lines and leaves others out of Thoreau's poem "Great God, I Ask for No Meaner Pelf," attempting to convince us that Thoreau is too self-absorbed to be politically diplomatic. His criticism of Thoreau follows the familiar pattern of those who also criticize Abbey, choosing lines out of context and using them to undermine any of his serious statements. Thoreau's poem actually anticipates themes he will continually revisit in his prose: namely, living according to principle, following one's calling, and rejecting others' expectations of him. In particular, Thoreau's writings on slavery and John Brown are important and enlarge our view of him as a literary figure beyond his environmental writing to include his ideas on social reform. Environmentalists and ecocritics often disregard these works since they have less to do with nature and more to do with society — a position that assumes the social (human) world does not affect our perceptions of the natural world. Thoreau's own political position is difficult to pin down, but it remains important to acknowledge that he was a man involved in his culture, not simply self-absorbed and living in solitude. Many of his literary projects overlapped with his involvement in social issues: his incarceration described in "Civil Disobedience" occurred while he was living at Walden Pond, and during the time he was revising proofs of *Walden*, he delivered one of his most caustic speeches against slavery on July 4, 1854.

Berry's criticism of Thoreau's political activism also applies to Abbey's environmental activism. In "Monkey Wrenching, Environmental Extremism, and the Problematical Edward Abbey," Daniel Payne examines Abbey's efficacy as an environmental polemicist, observing that while Abbey's literary devices of paradox and ambiguity may enhance his literary work for students, scholars, and critics, they ultimately undercut the effectiveness of his environmental rhetoric. Further, Payne observes that Abbey's combative tone and "non-liberal stances on immigration, gun control, and other social issues" have aroused antagonism from the public and criticism from the environmental movement.[2] In "A Writer's

Credo," Abbey explains that a writer should be political and "speak the truth — especially unpopular truth . . . truth that offends."[3] Moreover, he says the role of the writer in a free society is "to be a critic of his own community, his own country, his own government, his own culture."[4] Both Thoreau and Abbey exercise this political duty as writers; both argue for less government control and lament a culture that accepts laws without question and supports unlimited growth disguised as progress. Neither Abbey nor Thoreau was known for collective resistance, preferring individual action instead, and neither was opposed to using aggressive language or violence to defend his convictions.

James A. Papa, Jr., acknowledges a direct influence of Thoreau on Abbey but argues that "what Abbey does, however futile, goes beyond anything ever thought or done by Thoreau."[5] While bolstering Abbey's persona as radical ecowarrior, Papa, like Berry, oversimplifies Thoreau's own involvement in major issues of the mid–nineteenth century, contending that "Thoreau's fervent opposition to society's mad thirst for material wealth and comfort never developed into anything beyond literary rhetoric or a somewhat eccentric lifestyle."[6] His analysis focuses only on *Walden*, where he finds no evidence of activism on Thoreau's part. He fails to consider Thoreau's own ideas of monkey wrenching Billerica Dam with a crowbar in *A Week on the Concord and Merrimack Rivers* and neglects to mention "Civil Disobedience," Thoreau's most famous demonstration of resistance that influenced Mahatma Gandhi, Leo Tolstoy, Martin Luther King Jr., and Edward Abbey. Despite his threat, Thoreau never took any action against Billerica Dam when he saw it on his river trip in 1839; however, his interest was renewed twenty years later when he was "hired to make a study of the depths of the Concord River and its dams and bridge abutments" for a court case involving the "flooding, caused by the raising of dams, of the haying land in the river meadows."[7] Thoreau worked tirelessly on this project.[8] In his Journal on June 24, 1859, Thoreau mentions the process of surveying the area and talking with residents about the environmental changes, and later on February 17, 1860, he refers to people's responses to the controversial trial, one saying that the Concord River "'is dammed at both ends and cursed in the middle.'"[9] J. Ronald Engel finds great power in Thoreau's "parable" of the dam because stories of ecojustice have "the capacity to communicate the meaning of our love for the earth and for people as citizens."[10] Engel believes Thoreau's words are as compelling as any physical action because they sustain our enthusiasm to fight for "the people and the land we love."[11] Without such stories, action would cease. Walter Harding notes Thoreau's physical work reforesting the woods around Walden Pond: "with two men, a horse, and a cart, he set out four hundred pines, fifteen feet apart, on two acres of the Walden property. While one man dug up the trees, another dug new holes and Thoreau himself did the planting."[12] Later, Thoreau planted "a hundred two-year-old larch trees imported from England[,] . . . some birch trees," and some white pine trees.[13]

Regardless of Thoreau's planting efforts in Walden Woods, Papa criticizes him for not taking action in support of wilderness preservation, a critique that seems to be the result of Thoreau's erroneous image as wilderness advocate. Papa concedes that, perhaps, Thoreau's time did not demand any aggressive environmental acts: "given the fact that wilderness may have yet seemed an inexhaustible commodity in mid–nineteenth-century America."[14] Wilderness preservation, as an environmental movement, was not the concern of the 1850s, but abolition, slavery, and the Mexican War were, and Thoreau ardently responded to these issues.

Since the 1960s, Thoreau has been deliberately co-opted as wilderness advocate. In 1962, David Brower used one of the most often quoted sentences from Thoreau's essay "Walking" as the title of a Sierra Club book: "in Wildness is the preservation of the world."[15] Again and again, we see this statement extracted from the essay and wildness used to promote wilderness preservation. Jack Turner points out that Thoreau's statement is misquoted on a hanging plaque at the visitors' center at Point Reyes National Seashore, and that the statement surfaced in its faulty form in a "recent *Newsweek* article on wolf reintroduction."[16] Turner doesn't try to explain what Thoreau meant by wildness, but he does examine the lack of wildness in our wilderness areas in his own essay entitled "In Wildness Is the Preservation of the World." But Turner's questions overlook an important element in Thoreau's concept of the wild — wildness exists not only in remote areas but locally. Thoreau's life and work demonstrate that the two terms are not synonymous. He made contact with the wild in the woods surrounding Concord and on the summit of Mount Katahdin. If *Walden* and "Walking" reveal anything, it is the presence of wild nature in immediate environments, not only in "pristine" areas where humans are merely visitors. At the end of *Walden*, Thoreau retells a story of a "strong and beautiful bug" that emerges from "the dry leaf of an old table" that had been in a kitchen for sixty years.[17] This image of the wild latent in the domestic also occurs in "Walking" when he speaks of the wild seed inherent in domesticated cattle and horses and how farms he has surveyed in the past look quite different when his mind, body, and spirit are attuned to the wild. Thoreau declares himself spokesman for wildness, not wilderness: "I wish to speak a word for Nature, for absolute freedom and wildness, as contrasted with a freedom and culture merely civil, — to regard man as an inhabitant, or a part and parcel of Nature, rather than a member of society."[18] Part of Thoreau's work on behalf of nature exists in the late natural history essays collected in *Faith in a Seed*. His records of the natural world reveal how much time he spent outside to write over 4,000 pages of natural history, which was left unpublished at his death. This vast amount of information clearly represents a figure who lived a life in service to the wild natural world. Neil Evernden finds Thoreau's emphasis on the wild a "prerequisite to any serious defense of life on Earth."[19] Thoreau's immersion in wildness, as evident from these late essays, illustrates a vision of nature that expands the meaning and mode of activism beyond monkey wrenching and political advocacy. These texts exhibit a language-based activism that combines reading, writing, and field research.

While Thoreau was used as wilderness advocate in the 1960s, this same decade of literary criticism primarily lauded him for "Resistance to Civil Government" or "Civil Disobedience," perpetuating his reputation as the voice of passive resistance. This essay does not concern wilderness issues but radically addresses some of the major sociopolitical issues of his day — the U.S. war with Mexico and the abolition of slavery. Thoreau was arrested and incarcerated for refusing to pay a poll tax to support the war, and though he spent only a single night in jail, his articulation of the experience serves as an influential document for justice. "Civil Disobedience" challenges the conventions of what is just and unjust. As a citizen in a democracy, he exercises his right — his responsibility — to criticize the government and the unjust practices it condones: "All men recognize the right of revolution; that is, the right to refuse allegiance to, and to resist, the government, when its tyranny or its inefficiency are great and unendurable."[20] For Thoreau, resistance begins by living a life according to principles, then taking action on behalf of these principles. He believes that "Action from principle, the perception and the performance of right, changes things and relations; it is essentially revolutionary, and does not consist wholly with anything which was."[21] His economic protest of the Mexican-American war occurs without any physical violence, yet as a call to action, he urges readers to resist unjust governments by breaking the law, a call Abbey will hear. Thoreau writes, "If the injustice has a spring, or a pulley, or a rope, or a crank, exclusively for itself, then perhaps you may consider whether the remedy will not be worse than the evil; but if it is of such a nature that it requires you to be the agent of injustice to another, then, I say, break the law. Let your life be a counter friction to stop the machine" (233). If government or any other force demands that one act unjustly, then breaking the law becomes imperative — a necessary resistance. "Civil Disobedience" lays out important ideas of resistance that anticipate his later writings on slavery and John Brown, whose extreme measures in combating slavery exemplify Thoreau's ideal of action from principle, of one's life as a counter friction, whether violent or not.

Thoreau's Framingham address, "Slavery in Massachusetts," complicates his well-known pacifist image. Len Gougeon views this speech as Thoreau's most "acerbic," since it openly advocates militant action to resist the oppressive forces of slavery.[22] No doubt the inflammatory rhetoric appealed to his audience of abolitionists and recalls some of the political events that occurred earlier that year: the Kansas-Nebraska Act became law in May, reversing the Missouri Compromise of 1820 which prohibited the expansion of slavery in the territories; and fugitive slave Anthony Burns had been arrested and returned to his owner despite abolitionists' attempts to free him.[23] In his address, Thoreau admits that he would fight to preserve "a free State, and a court truly of justice."[24] Moreover, he excoriates the people of Massachusetts for supporting a government that enacts unjust laws. His militancy reaches its zenith when he threatens to blow up a government system that supports commerce over humanity: Thoreau avows, "Rather than do thus, I need not say what match I would touch, what system endeavor to blow up, — as I love my life, I would side with the light, and let the dark earth roll from under me, calling my mother and my brother to follow."[25] Truman Nelson says that Thoreau's is "one of the most violent statements ever written, or spoken before a mass audience,"[26] and his willingness to destroy an unjust system for denying independent thought or action anticipates Abbey's rage against Glen Canyon Dam for restricting the rights of the Colorado River. Responding to the crisis of slavery and unjust government, Thoreau declares, "It is not an era of repose. We have used up all our inherited freedom. If we would save our lives, we must fight for them."[27] Thoreau calls for action throughout this address, and he envisions the kind of men needed to combat the social plague of slavery: "What is wanted is men not of policy, but of probity — who recognize a higher law than the Constitution, or the decision of the majority."[28] John Brown exactly fits this criteria; he believed fighting against slavery was his moral mission sanctioned by God.

Within two weeks of the Harper's Ferry raid, Thoreau called a public meeting in which he delivered "A Plea for Captain John Brown." His quick response came when most people were still reeling from the shocking events. Not all Northern abolitionists supported Brown's actions, and certainly white Southerners were alarmed by the bloody attack on Harper's Ferry. In "Thoreau and His Audience: 'A Plea for Captain John Brown,'" Robert Albrecht analyzes Thoreau's preparation for his public address and his careful consideration of the audience. Thoreau had to "defend a notorious man before an unfriendly audience. He had to convince his audience of the rightness of John Brown's principles and the act proceeding from those principles."[29] Consciously crafting this address, Thoreau criticizes unjust government, but levels his harshest criticism at the press, for perpetuating the image of Brown as insane. He refers to his own meetings with Brown and represents him as a personal friend and a true patriot. For Thoreau, Brown was different from other reformers: he was a "man of rare common sense and directness of speech, as of action; a transcendentalist above all, a man of ideas and principles, — that was what distinguished him. Not yielding to a whim or transient impulse, but carrying out the purpose of a life."[30] Thoreau admired Brown for responding to his calling and for living his life according to principle even though it meant death. Thoreau engages in activism, setting himself in opposition to popular opinion by publicly defending Brown.

Thoreau admires Brown's "directness of speech as of action" and finds the two modes of resistance interconnected: "Truth is his inspirer, and earnestness the polisher of his sentences. He could afford to lose his Sharps' rifles, while he retained his faculty of speech, a Sharps' rifle of infinitely surer and longer range."[31] With this statement, Thoreau clearly expresses his opinion on the power of words: they are more accurate and longer lasting than a rifle shot. A similar idea occurs in "Civil Disobedience" when Thoreau explains how he maintained his freedom in jail and how the very institution fails to confine the true source of subversion — the mind. He expresses his amusement at "how industriously they locked the door on my meditations, which followed them out again without let or hindrance, and *they* were really all that was dangerous."[32] Although his body is confined, his mind remains free. The ability to think, speak, and write are the tools of freedom and revolution. Thoreau also participated in the Underground Railroad, and though he never took any direct, violent action against slavery, he was not opposed to doing so, admitting, "A man may have other affairs to attend to. I do not wish to kill nor to be killed, but I can foresee circumstances in which both these things would be by me unavoidable."[33] He hopes Brown's words and acts will stimulate a "revival," and believes John Brown and Harper's Ferry are "the best news that America has ever heard."[34]

Despite the subversive nature of Thoreau's reform writings, many eco-critics and radical activists find Edward Abbey a more daring, effective environmentalist and celebrate him for introducing "full-blown rage" into conservation literature.[35] In his book *Pioneer Conservationists of Western America*, Peter Wild mentions Thoreau as one of the "noble voices" from the East who wrote of "saner approaches to our natural heritage."[36] Wild's impression of Thoreau as a "sane" voice for the environment ignores his involvement and rage against slavery in his reform writings. In contrast, Don Scheese positions Thoreau as radical forefather of Abbey. Acknowledging the zeal of the antislavery writings, Scheese also aligns Thoreau and Abbey in their respective wars against the state.[37] Scheese describes Abbey as heeding Thoreau's call in "Civil Disobedience": "Abbey's life and work have become a counter-friction against those forces that would destroy wilderness."[38] In *Desert Solitaire*, Abbey depicts Ranger Ed dismantling five miles of survey stakes that mark plans for a paved road into Arches National Park. He admits that his action is a "futile effort, in the long run, but it made [him] feel good."[39] Earlier, he portrays Ed as an ecowarrior on winter hiatus, living in some "grimy, cheap . . . decayed, hopelessly corrupt" place and dreaming of "nights of desperate laughter with brave young comrades, burning billboards, and defacing public institutions. . . . Romantic dreams, romantic dreams."[40] Later on in the book, in the chapter "Down the River," he fantasizes about the destruction of Glen Canyon Dam by "some unknown hero with a rucksack full of dynamite strapped to his back."[41] Abbey continues the imaginary sequence, describing the explosion of the dam at the opening ceremony, and later calls his mental games "idle, foolish, futile day dreams" (188). While Abbey's romantic ideals of ecotage may inspire readers to take action, his insistence on them as "futile" and "foolish" sustains his ambivalence as a radical activist.

Abbey, however, fulfills these "futile day dreams" in his most famous novel *The Monkey Wrench Gang*, which takes as its subject four characters (Doc Sarvis, Bonnie Abbzug, George Washington Hayduke, and Seldom Seen Smith) and their resistance to the industrial machine destroying the Southwest. In the first chapter, Abbey describes the destruction of the Glen Canyon Bridge spanning the Colorado River, using images similar to the "day dreams" in *Desert Solitaire*. The novel recounts numerous examples of monkey wrenching: from leveling billboards and pulling up survey stakes to destroying industrial equipment by mutilating engine wires and pouring sand in crankcases and karo syrup in fuel tanks. On another mission, the gang blows up a railroad bridge leading to Peabody Coal Company, destroying a train and overturning a load of coal in the process. The destruction of Glen Canyon Dam looms as a goal throughout their exploits. Abbey published twenty-one books in his lifetime, but *The Monkey Wrench Gang* and *Desert Solitaire* remain his most popular and have made him most famous as a western environmental writer and radical environmentalist, two labels he refuses to fully accept.

Unlike *The Monkey Wrench Gang*, *Desert Solitaire* refuses to be pinned down by genre. This book is structured much like *Walden*, in that several years' experience are condensed into a single seamless account. Moreover, readers have a difficult, perhaps even impossible, time separating the narrator of the book from the author, a distinction that contributes to the problems of valorizing Abbey for a single ideological view of environmental protection. In a 1977 interview with James Hepworth, Abbey discusses the disparity between the persona in his books and his real self, explaining that the person "who writes these articles and books and so on is just another fictional creation, not much resemblance to the real one, to the one I think I know. The real Edward Abbey — whoever the hell that is — is a real shy, timid fellow, but the character I create in my journalism is perhaps a person I would like to be: bold, brash, daring. . . . I guess some people mistake the creation for the author but that's their problem."[42] Is Edward Abbey the wily, offensive narrator who graces the pages of his personal narratives, or is he the husband and father who makes a living by writing and cares about wilderness? His persona is just as difficult to discern as his views on resistance: one moment he poses as expert monkey wrencher and the next as a writer with an interest in wilderness preservation.

In "Eco-Defense," he advocates tree spiking and encourages breaking the law to save wilderness: "Eco-defense is risky but sporting; unauthorized but fun; illegal but ethically imperative."[43] He instructs readers how to act: "Next time you enter a public forest scheduled for chainsaw massacre . . . carry a hammer and a few pounds of 60-penny nails in your creel, saddlebag, game bag, backpack, or picnic basket. Spike those trees; you won't hurt them; they'll be grateful for the protection; and you may save the forest. . . . It's good for the trees, it's good for the woods, and it's good for the human soul. Spread the word."[44] The final words of this essay, "Spread the word," illustrate the most common form of his own mode of activism, despite his reputation as mastermind of monkey wrenching. Abbey views ecodefense as a form of self-defense, identical to the right of defending one's home, one's property, by any means necessary: "if the wilderness is our true home, and if it is threatened with invasion, pillage, and destruction — as it certainly is — then we have the right to defend that home, as we would our private quarters, by whatever means are necessary" (31). Like Thoreau, Abbey is willing to take extreme measures to preserve the environment and to preserve justice; likewise, most of his activism emerges from the pen, with a mission to inspire action and raise consciousness.

In an interview with close friend Jack Loeffler, Abbey reveals himself as an activist through his writing, more than saboteur. He separates himself from activists like David Brower, Dave Foreman, and others who do the tedious work to organize public resistance, lobby, litigate, petition, and run for office, and he respects these people more than those like himself "who merely sit behind a desk and write about it."[45] Abbey admits, "Actually, I've done most of my defending of the West with a typewriter, which is an easy and cowardly way to go about it."[46] In this interview, however, he repeats his willingness to resort to sabotage when political means fail to defend the land he loves (8). The documentary *Edward Abbey: A Voice Crying in the Wilderness* portrays him primarily as an environmental writer and activist. In interviews with close friends, some who inspired the characters in *The Monkey Wrench Gang*, the film continually suggests, though never fully acknowledges, the degree of Abbey's monkey wrenching. It records his participation in an Earth First! demonstration of ecotheater that symbolically cracked Glen Canyon Dam, and refers to various "field studies" Abbey undertook in researching *The Monkey Wrench Gang*, but gives no definitive answer about his involvement in ecosabotage. The image of Abbey from this documentary fuels the perception of him as a radical environmental crusader — an image he both embraces and refuses.

In the essay "Of Protest," Abbey tells the story of an inspiring act of civil disobedience that occurs after proper political channels have failed to defend the environment in Rocky Flats, Colorado. For six months, activists protested the manufacturing of thermonuclear devices by putting their bodies in front of the trains that delivered radioactive materials to the plant weekly. Abbey distinguishes his own ideas of activism — sabotage — from those of the protesters. Examining their home base of operations, a canvas teepee blocking the railroad spur leading to the plant, Abbey notices electric power lines on wooden poles running parallel with the tracks and thinks "that one resolute man with a chain saw could put that place out of business for a short while, easily and quickly."[47] But he acknowledges that sabotage is not the preferred method of these activists, who "were opposed both in principle and in practice to violence in any form. Even to moderate violence, technically restrained, tactically precise, against mere inanimate property."[48] Abbey's short-term solution is an individual effort, whereas the protesters engage collectively and non-violently and end up arrested and charged with trespassing.

Abbey records the trial of the railway trespassers, and while the jury deliberates, he talks with the defendants, who remain uplifted and strengthened through their resistance: "They are happy people, these crusaders, at ease with themselves and with others, radiant with conviction, liberated by their own volition from the tedious routine of passive acquiescence in which most of us endure. . . . One single act of defiance against power, against the State that seems omnipotent but is not, transforms and transfigures the human personality. . . . Perhaps that is enough" (108). This demonstration of civil disobedience restores the protesters' enthusiasm for their cause and Abbey's belief in justice and the importance of resistance. He self-consciously examines his own attitude prior to witnessing these events, recalling that he was "vaguely sympathetic with the protesters, but basically skeptical" (108). He admits sometimes falling into cynicism "that our most serious problems are finding a place to park the car, the ever-rising costs of gasoline and beefsteak, and the nagging demands of the poor, the old, the disinherited" (108). Setting himself apart from the activists, Abbey confesses "a guilty envy of the protesters, of those who actually act, and a little faint glow of hope — perhaps something fundamental might yet be changed in the nature of our lives" (108). Contrary to his own opinion, I believe Abbey engages in activism by recording the events of Rocky Flats and the trial, retelling the story of those courageous enough to defend their principles and suffer the consequences. His activism through writing remains an individual rather than a collective effort.

Though Abbey tells Loeffler that writing is an easier, more cowardly way to defend the West, in classic Abbey fashion he contradicts this statement in "A Writer's Credo," asserting, "I believe that words count, that writing matters, that poems, essays and novels — in the long run — make a difference."[49] Looking in other works, however, one can find other versions of Abbey's conflicting views between acting and writing.

In the preface to *Beyond the Wall*, he addresses the need for action rather than "more words on the matter" of wilderness preservation: "What we need now are heroes. And heroines. About a million of them. One brave deed is worth a thousand books. Sentiment without action is the ruin of the soul. Or as an old friend of mine once said, *If I regret anything, it is my good behavior: What demon possessed me that I behaved so well?*"[50] The "old friend" Abbey invokes is Thoreau, his literary forebear who ardently took action from principles, albeit in writing. Abbey repeats this passage later with some alteration in a letter to Earth First! members, yet interprets Thoreau's statement as one of regret from an "overly-bookish man."[51] Thoreau's statement comes from *Walden* and, rather than indicating regret, it indicates his defiance of society's definition of "good behavior." In the preceding lines of the quote from *Walden*, Thoreau writes, "The greater part of what my neighbors call good, I believe in my soul to be bad, and if I repent of anything, it is very likely to be my good behavior."[52] Thoreau sets himself in opposition to cultural conventions — a position, it seems, Abbey would admire, though he misquotes Thoreau's statement and uses it out of context. Perhaps Abbey is trying to demonstrate how easily words can be manipulated, whereas direct action, once taken, is more difficult to control or reverse.

In a sense, Thoreau's late natural history essays resist this sort of manipulation, as they are based on empirical research, and expand the literary image of him from an overly bookish man to a figure in the field. To record so much information, Thoreau had to spend time walking the land, observing nature, and reading scientific texts. The dominant argument within "The Dispersion of Seeds" refutes the popular idea of spontaneous generation: that a plant can grow from nothing — without a seed, root, or cutting. It is important to acknowledge that Thoreau and Abbey did engage in physical activism, though to a lesser degree than many environmentalists like to imagine. Their activism remains rooted more in language than in physical acts of defiance; yet without their words the modern environmental movement would be unrecognizable. Thoreau and Abbey have sown the seeds of activism in their writing, producing words that continue to stir our hearts and inspire us to envision paths of activism for ourselves.

NOTES

1. Berry, "A Few Words in Favor of Edward Abbey," 6.

2. Payne, "Monkey Wrenching, Environmental Extremism, and the Problematical Edward Abbey," 195–96.

3. Abbey, "A Writer's Credo," in *One Life at a Time, Please*, 163.

4. Ibid., 161.

5. Papa, "The Politics of Leisure," 321.

6. Ibid.

7. Harding, *Days of Henry Thoreau*, 410–11.

8. Harding cites Emerson, who comments on Thoreau's "energetic enthusiasm," 411.

9. Thoreau, *Journal of Henry David Thoreau*, ed. Torrey and Allen, vols. XII, 211–14, and XIII, 149. In *The Days of Henry Thoreau*, Harding attributes this emphatic quote to Thoreau, though in his Journal Thoreau quotes someone else: "Minott says that he hears that Heard's testimony in regard to Concord River in the meadow case was that 'it is dammed at both ends and cursed in the middle'" (149).

10. Engel, "Teaching the Eco-Justice Ethic," 467.

11. Ibid.

12. Harding, *Days of Henry Thoreau*, 410.

13. Ibid.

14. Papa, "The Politics of Leisure," 321.

15. Thoreau, "Walking," in *Writings of Henry David Thoreau*, ed. Torrey, vol. V, 224.

16. Turner, "In Wildness Is the Preservation of the World," 617.

17. Thoreau, *Walden*, 222.

18. Thoreau, "Walking," 205.

19. Evernden, *Social Creation of Nature*, 132.

20. Thoreau, "Resistance to Civil Government," 67.

21. Ibid., 72.

22. Gougeon, "Thoreau and Reform," 204.

23. Ibid.

24. Thoreau, "Slavery in Massachusetts," in *Reform Papers*, 106.

25. Ibid., 102.

26. Nelson, "Thoreau and John Brown," 143.

27. Thoreau, "Slavery in Massachusetts," 108.

28. Ibid., 104.

29. Albrecht, "Thoreau and His Audience," 393.

30. Thoreau, "A Plea for Captain John Brown," in *Reform Papers*, 115.

31. Ibid., 127.

32. Thoreau, "Resistance to Civil Government," 238.

33. Thoreau, "A Plea for Captain John Brown," 133.

34. Ibid., 134–35.

35. Wild, *Pioneer Conservationists of Western America*, 186.

36. Ibid., xiii.

37. Scheese, "*Desert Solitaire*: Counter-Friction to the Machine in the Garden," 223.

38. Ibid., 213.

39. Abbey, *Desert Solitaire*, 67.

40. Ibid., 48.

41. Ibid., 188.

42. Hepworth, "The Poetry Center Interview," 44.

43. Abbey, "Eco-Defense," in *One Life at a Time, Please*, 31.

44. Ibid., 31–32.

45. Loeffler, "Edward Abbey," 9.

46. Ibid., 8.

47. Abbey, "Of Protest," in *Down the River*, 99.

48. Ibid.

49. Abbey, "A Writer's Credo," 162.

50. Abbey, *Beyond the Wall*, xvi.

51. Abbey, "Ed Abbey to Earth First! Mabon 1983," in *The Earth First! Reader*, ed. John Davis, 248.

52. Thoreau, *Walden*, 6.

CONTRIBUTORS

Peter Blakemore lives in the top of the Willamette Valley in Eugene, Oregon, where he teaches literature, environmental studies, and writing at the University of Oregon. He has published essays on inhabitation, western literature, and composition and is currently revising a manuscript, "Writing Home: Inhabitation and Imagination in American Literature." He is also transcribing Thoreau's handwritten Journal for the Princeton University Press's revised scholarly edition of *The Writings of Henry D. Thoreau.*

J. Scott Bryson is an assistant professor of English at Sul Ross State University, Rio Grande College. His publications include work on W. S. Merwin and Thomas Pynchon, and he has just completed his dissertation, "Place and Space in Contemporary Ecological Poetry: Wendell Berry, Joy Harjo, and Mary Oliver," at the University of Kentucky.

Aimin Cheng is a professor at Nanjing Normal University, China. He was awarded a United Board fellowship to study Thoreau at Harvard University. He has published several books, more than 30 scholarly articles, and has translated Joseph Heller's *Catch 22* and D. H. Lawrence's *The Trespasser.*

Greg Garrard is a lecturer in English at Bath Spa University College in the United Kingdom. He has published essays on "green" romanticism and Northern Irish writing, and is currently working on a monograph on "ecocriticism."

Stephen Germic teaches in the Department of American Thought and Language at Michigan State University. He has published on Hawthorne and has two essays forthcoming on class in nineteenth-century American nature writing. Germic's completed book manuscript is titled *First Parks: Central Park, Yosemite, Yellowstone, and the Nature of American Exceptionalism.*

Rochelle Johnson is an assistant professor of English at Albertson College of Idaho, where she teaches courses in American literature and environmental studies. With Daniel Patterson, she completed an edition of Susan Fenimore Cooper's *Rural Hours.*

Susan M. Lucas is a Ph.D. candidate in the Literature and Environment program at the University of Nevada, Reno. Her research examines the intersections between nature writing and travel writing. She is currently managing editor of *ISLE: Interdisciplinary Studies in Literature and Environment.*

James G. McGrath, when not writing or teaching environmental literature, divides his time between work as an alderman on the Missoula City Council and as a community garden organizer for Garden City Harvest, managing a neighborhood community garden and growing 3,500 pounds of organic produce for the local food bank and other food programs, including over 260 pounds of beans.

Barbara "Barney" Nelson is an assistant professor of English at Sul Ross State University in Alpine, Texas. Her publications include three books: *Voices and Visions of the American West*, *The Last Campfire: The Life Story of Ted Gray, A West Texas Rancher*, and *Here's to the Vinegarroon!* A scholarly investigation of the dichotomy between wild and domestic animals in American literature is forthcoming.

Ted Olson is an assistant professor of English and director of Appalachian-Scottish-Irish Studies at East Tennessee State University in Johnson City, Tennessee. His book *Blue Ridge Folklife* was published in 1998.

James A. Papa, Jr., a poet and essayist, is an assistant professor of English at York College, CUNY. He has published critical essays on Henry Thoreau, Jack London, Annie Dillard, and Edward Abbey.

Bernard W. Quetchenbach is an assistant professor of English and chair of Arts and Humanities at the University of Maine at Fort Kent. His book concerning contemporary environmental poetry is forthcoming. He has published poetry and articles in many journals.

David M. Robinson is Oregon Professor of English and Distinguished Professor of American Literature at Oregon State University. He is serving as president of the Ralph

Waldo Emerson Society. His publications include *Emerson and the Conduct of Life* (1993) and *World of Relations: The Achievement of Peter Taylor*.

William Rossi is an associate professor at the University of Oregon, where he teaches American literature and environmental studies. He is author of essays on Emerson, Thoreau, and others and co-editor most recently of Thoreau's *Journal, Volume 6: 1853* (forthcoming).

Robert Sattelmeyer is chair and professor of English at Georgia State University. He has edited and published numerous works on Thoreau, including *Thoreau's Reading: A Study in Intellectual History with Bibliographical Catalogue*.

Richard J. Schneider is professor of English and Slife Professor in the Humanities at Wartburg College. He has written and edited various books and essays on Thoreau, including *Henry David Thoreau* in the Twayne United States Authors Series and *Approaches to Teaching Thoreau's "Walden" and Other Works*.

Nancy Craig Simmons is professor of humanities and English in the Center for Interdisciplinary Studies at Virginia Polytechnic Institute and State University. She has co-edited two volumes of Thoreau's Journal for the Princeton edition of the Journal. Currently she is working on a book on Emerson's lecture career.

Isaiah Smithson is a professor in the Department of English and Women's Studies program at Southern Illinois University at Edwardsville. His publications include co-editing *Gender in the Classroom: Power and Pedagogy* and *English Studies/Culture Studies: Institutionalizing Dissent.* He has published articles on American responses to the land, and he is currently writing a book on American conceptions of the forest.

Laura Dassow Walls is an associate professor of English at Lafayette College in Easton, Pennsylvania. She is the author of *Seeing New Worlds: Henry David Thoreau and Nineteenth-Century Natural Science,* as well as articles on Thoreau, Emerson, and others involved in the intersections of literature and science, in such journals as *American Quarterly, Configurations,* and the *Concord Saunterer.*

WORKS CITED

Abbey, Edward. *Abbey's Road.* New York: E. P. Dutton, 1979.

———. *Beyond the Wall.* New York: Henry Holt & Co., 1984.

———. *Desert Solitaire: A Season in the Wilderness.* New York: Ballantine, 1968.

———. *Down the River.* New York: Plume, 1982.

———. "Ed Abbey to Earth First! Mabon 1983." In *The Earth First! Reader: Ten Years of Radical Environmentalism,* edited by John Davis, 247–49. Salt Lake City: Peregrine Smith, 1991.

———. *The Monkey Wrench Gang.* New York: Avon, 1975.

———. *One Life at a Time, Please.* New York: Henry Holt & Co., 1988.

Abram, David. *The Spell of the Sensuous: Perception and Language in a More-Than-Human World.* New York: Pantheon, 1996.

Abrams, M. H., et al., eds. *The Norton Anthology of English Literature.* 6th ed. Vol. 2. New York: W. W. Norton, 1993.

Adams, Stephen, and Donald Ross Jr. *Revising Mythologies: The Composition of Thoreau's Major Works.* Charlottesville: University of Virginia Press, 1988.

Albrecht, Robert C. "Thoreau and His Audience: 'A Plea for Captain John Brown.'" *American Literature* 32 (1961): 393–402.

Alcott, A. Bronson. *Concord Days.* Boston: Roberts Brothers, 1872.

Andrews, Malcolm. *The Search for the Picturesque: Landscape Aesthetics and Tourism in Britain, 1760–1800.* Stanford: Stanford University Press, 1989.

Appel, Toby A. "Jefferies Wyman, Philosophical Anatomy, and the Scientific Reception of Darwin in America." *Journal of the History of Biology* 21 (1988): 69–94.

Aton, James. "'Sons and Daughters of Thoreau': The Spiritual Quest in Three Contemporary American Nature Writers." Ph.D. diss., Ohio University, 1981.

Austin, Mary. *The Land of Little Rain.* Albuquerque: University of New Mexico Press, 1974.

Bacon, Francis. *The Great Instauration,* in *The Works of Francis Bacon,* edited by James Spedding, Robert Leslie Ellis, and Douglas Denon Heath. Cambridge, Mass.: Riverside Press, 1870.

Baigell, Matthew. *A Concise History of American Painting and Sculpture.* New York: Harper & Row, 1984.

———. *Thomas Cole.* New York: Watson-Guptill, 1981.

Bate, Jonathan. *Romantic Ecology: Wordsworth and the Environmental Tradition.* London: Routledge, 1991.

Becker, John E. "Science and the Sacred: From *Walden* to *Tinker Creek.*" *Thought: A Review of Culture and Idea* 62 (1987): 400–413.

Beer, Gillian. *Darwin's Plots: Evolutionary Narrative in Darwin, George Eliot, and Nineteenth-Century Fiction.* London: Routledge & Kegan Paul, 1983.

Bennett, Jane. *Thoreau's Nature: Ethics, Politics and the Wild.* London: Sage, 1994.

Berry, Thomas. *The Dream of the Earth.* San Francisco: Sierra Club Books, 1988.

Berry, Wendell. *Collected Poems: 1957–1982.* New York: North Point Press, 1984.

———. "A Few Words in Favor of Edward Abbey." In *Resist Much, Obey Little: Some Notes on Edward Abbey,* edited by James Hepworth and Gregory McNamee, 1–14. Tucson: Harbinger House, 1989.

———. *Harlan Hubbard: Life and Work.* Lexington: University Press of Kentucky, 1990.

———. *Recollected Essays: 1965–1980.* San Francisco: North Point Press, 1981.

———. *What Are People For?* San Francisco: North Point Press, 1990.

Beston, Henry. *The Outermost House.* New York: Doubleday, 1928.

Blackburn, Thomas C., and Kat Anderson. *Before the Wilderness: Environmental Management by Native Californians.* Menlo Park, Calif.: Ballena Press, 1993.

Blue Cloud, Peter. "For Rattlesnake: a dialogue of creatures." In *The Remembered Earth: An Anthology of Contemporary Native American Literature,* edited by Geary Hobson, 21–24. Albuquerque: University of New Mexico Press, 1980.

Bode, Carl. Introduction to *Collected Poems of Henry Thoreau,* edited by Carl Bode. Baltimore: Johns Hopkins University Press, 1964.

Boudreau, Gordon. "H. D. Thoreau, William Gilpin, and the Metaphysical Ground of the Picturesque." *American Literature* 45 (1973): 357–69.

Bowler, Peter J. *The Invention of Progress: Victorians and the Past.* London: Basil Blackwell, 1989.

———. *Life's Splendid Drama: Evolutionary Biology and the Reconstruction of Life's Ancestry, 1860–1940.* Chicago: University of Chicago Press, 1996.

———. *The Non-Darwinian Revolution: Reinterpreting a Historical Myth.* Baltimore: Johns Hopkins University Press, 1988.

———. *The Norton History of the Environmental Sciences.* New York: W. W. Norton, 1993.

———. *Theories of Human Evolution: A Century of Debate, 1844–1944.* Baltimore: Johns Hopkins University Press, 1986.

Bradford, William. *Of Plimouth Plantation.* 1856. Reprint edited by Samuel Eliot Morison. New York: Random, 1952.

Brooke, John Hedley. *Science and Religion: Some Historical Perspectives.* Cambridge: Cambridge University Press, 1991.

Brown, Calvin S., et al., eds. *The Reader's Companion to World Literature.* New York: New American Library, 1973.

Buell, Lawrence. "Emerson in His Cultural Context." In *Ralph Waldo Emerson: A Collection of Essays,* edited by Lawrence Buell, 48–60. Englewood Cliffs, N.J.: Prentice-Hall, 1993.

———. *The Environmental Imagination: Thoreau, Nature*

Writing, and the Formation of American Culture. Cambridge, Mass.: Harvard University Press, 1995.

———. Literary Transcendentalism: Style and Vision in the American Renaissance. Ithaca: Cornell University Press, 1973.

———. "The Thoreauvian Pilgrimage: The Structure of an American Cult." American Literature 61 (1989): 175–99.

Cady, Lyman V. "Thoreau's Quotations from the Confucian Books in Walden." American Literature 33 (1961): 20–32.

Cameron, Sharon. Writing Nature: Henry Thoreau's Journal. New York: Oxford University Press, 1985.

Campbell, SueEllen. "The Land and Language of Desire: Where Deep Ecology and Post-Structuralism Meet." Western American Literature 24, 3 (November 1989): 199–211.

Carlyle, Thomas. Sartor Resartus. London: J. M. Dent, 1875.

———. "Signs of the Times." In The Works of Thomas Carlyle. Vol. 27, 56–82. London: Chapman and Hall, 1905.

Catlin, George. "Buffalo Country." In The Wilderness Reader, edited by Frank Bergon, 61–73. New York: New American Library, 1980.

Cavell, Stanley. The Senses of Walden. Chicago: Chicago University Press, 1992.

[Chambers, Robert]. Explanations: A Sequel. In Vestiges of the Natural History of Creation and Other Evolutionary Writings, edited by James A. Secord. Chicago: University of Chicago Press, 1994.

———. Vestiges of the Natural History of Creation. 2nd ed. New York: Wiley and Putnam, 1845.

Cheever, George B. "Coleridge." North American Review 40 (April 1835): 338.

Cheng, Aimin. Aspects of Chinese Culture. Nanjing: Yilin Press, 1994.

Christy, Arthur, ed. The Asian Legacy and American Life. New York: John Day Company, 1945.

———. The Orient in American Transcendentalism. New York: Columbia University Press, 1932.

Coatsworth, Elizabeth. Especially Maine: The Natural World of Henry Beston from Cape Cod to the St. Lawrence. Selected and with an introduction by Elizabeth Coatsworth. Brattleboro, Vt.: S. Greene Press, 1970.

Cobb, Edith. The Ecology of Imagination in Childhood. New York: Columbia University Press, 1977.

Cohen, Michael P. "The Trouble with Wilderness, Comment: Resistance to Wilderness." Environmental History 1, 1 (1996): 33–42.

Cole, Thomas. "Lecture on American Scenery." In The Collected Essays and Prose Sketches, edited by Marshall Tymn, 3–17. The John Colet Archive of American Literature, 1620–1920, no. 7. St. Paul: John Colet Press, 1980.

Collie, David. The Chinese Classical Work, commonly called The Four Books. Malacca: N.p., 1828.

Conrad, Joseph. The Portable Conrad, edited by Morton Dauwen Zabel. New York: Penguin, 1976.

Cooper, Susan Fenimore. Rural Hours. 1850. Reprint edited by Rochelle Johnson and Daniel Patterson. Athens: University of Georgia Press, 1998.

———. "Small Family Memories." In *Correspondence of James Fenimore Cooper*, edited by James Fenimore Cooper. Vol. 1, 32–33. New Haven: Yale University Press, 1922.

Cronon, William, ed. *Changes in the Land: Indians, Colonists, and the Ecology of New England.* New York: Hill and Wang/Farrar, Straus & Giroux, 1983.

———, ed. *Uncommon Ground: Rethinking the Human Place in Nature.* New York: W. W. Norton, 1995.

Cunningham, Andrew, and Nicholas Jardine, eds. *Romanticism and the Sciences.* Cambridge: Cambridge University Press, 1990.

Daniel, John. *The Trail Home: Nature, Imagination, and the American West.* Expanded edition. New York: Pantheon, 1994.

Darwin, Charles. *On the Origin of Species.* 1859. Reprint, Cambridge, Mass.: Harvard University Press, 1964.

Davis, John, ed. *The Earth First! Reader: Ten Years of Radical Environmentalism.* Salt Lake City: Peregrine Smith, 1991.

Davis, Mike. "Why Is the U.S. Working Class Different?" *New Left Review* 123 (1980): 5–44.

Deming, Alison Hawthorne, Richard Nelson, and Scott Russell Sanders. "Letter to *Orion* Readers." *Orion* 14, 4 (autumn 1995): 5.

Dillard, Annie. *Pilgrim at Tinker Creek.* New York: Bantam, 1974.

———. *Living by Fiction.* New York: Harper & Row, 1982.

Dorrance, Tom. *True Unity: Willing Communication between Horse and Human.* Edited by Milly Hunt Porter. Tuscarora, Nev.: Give-It-A-Go Enterprises, 1987.

Douglas, William O. *My Wilderness: East to Katahdin.* Garden City, N.Y.: Doubleday, 1961.

Downing, Andrew Jackson. Review [of *Rural Hours*]. *Horticulturalist* 5, 5 (November 1850): 232.

Dupree, A. Hunter. *Asa Gray, 1810–1888.* Cambridge, Mass.: Harvard University Press, 1959.

Durand, Asher. "Letters on Landscape Painting." *Crayon* (1855), I: 1–2, 34–35, 66–67, 97–98, 145–46, 209–11, 273–75, 354–55; II: 16–17.

Edward Abbey: A Voice Crying in the Wilderness. Produced and directed by Eric Temple. 1 hour. Eric Temple Productions, 1993. Videocassette.

Egerton, Frank N., and Laura Dassow Walls. "Rethinking Thoreau and the History of American Ecology." *Concord Saunterer*, n.s., 5 (fall 1997): 4–20.

Emerson, Ralph Waldo. *The Collected Works.* 4 vols. to date. Edited by Alfred R. Ferguson et al. Cambridge, Mass.: Harvard University Press, 1971–.

———. *Journals and Miscellaneous Notebooks of Ralph Waldo Emerson.* Vol. 4. Edited by Alfred R. Ferguson. Cambridge, Mass.: Harvard University Press, 1964.

———. *Nature, Addresses, and Lectures.* Edited by Robert E. Spiller and Alfred R. Ferguson. Cambridge, Mass.: Harvard University Press, 1979.

———. *Selections from Ralph Waldo Emerson.* Edited by Stephen E. Whicher. Boston: Houghton Mifflin, 1957.

Engel, J. Ronald. "Teaching the Eco-Justice Ethic: The Parable of Billerica Dam." *Christian Century* 104 (1987): 466–69.

Evernden, Neil. *The Natural Alien: Humankind and Environment.* Toronto: University of Toronto Press, 1985.

———. *The Social Creation of Nature.* Baltimore: Johns Hopkins University Press, 1992.

Fancheng, Xu. *An Interpretation of Lao Zi.* Beijing: Zhonghua Shuju, 1988.

Fink, Steven. *Prophet in the Marketplace: Thoreau's Development as a Professional Writer.* Princeton: Princeton University Press, 1992.

Folsom, Ed, and Cary Nelson. "'Fact Has Two Faces': An Interview with W. S. Merwin." *Iowa Review* 13 (1982): 30–66.

Foner, Eric. "Why Is There No Socialism in America?" *History Workshop* 17 (1984): 57–80.

Foster, David R. *Thoreau's Country: Journey through a Transformed Landscape.* Cambridge, Mass.: Harvard University Press, 1999.

Foster, Edward Halsey. *The Civilized Wilderness: Backgrounds to American Romantic Literature, 1817–1860.* New York: Free Press, 1975.

Foucault, Michel. *The Order of Things: An Archeology of the Human Sciences.* Translation of *Les Mots et les choses.* New York: Vintage, 1970.

Fritzell, Peter A. *Nature Writing and America: Essays upon a Cultural Type.* Ames: Iowa State University Press, 1990.

Frost, Robert. *Selected Poems of Robert Frost.* New York: Holt, Rinehart & Winston, 1963.

Fuller, Margaret. *Woman in the Nineteenth Century: A Facsimile of the 1845 Edition.* Edited by Joel Myerson. Columbia: University of South Carolina Press, 1980.

Garber, Frederick. "Thoreau and Anglo-European Romanticism." In *Approaches to Teaching Thoreau's Walden and Other Works,* edited by Richard J. Schneider, 39–47. New York: Modern Language Association, 1996.

———. *Thoreau's Redemptive Imagination.* New York: New York University Press, 1977.

Gelpi, Albert. *A Coherent Splendor: The American Poetic Renaissance, 1910–1950.* Cambridge: Cambridge University Press, 1987.

Gilmore, Michael T. "Walden and the 'Curse of Trade.'" In *Henry David Thoreau,* edited by Harold Bloom, 101–16. New York: Chelsea House, 1987.

Gilpin, William. *Observations on the River Wye.* 1782. Reprint, Richmond, Surrey: Richmond Publishing, 1973.

———. *Observations on the Western Parts of England.* 1798. Reprint, Richmond, Surrey: Richmond Publishing, 1973.

Glacken, Clarence J. *Traces from the Rhodian Shore: Nature and Culture in Western Thought from Ancient Times to the End of the Eighteenth Century.* Berkeley: University of California Press, 1967.

Glotfelty, Cheryl, and Harold Fromm, eds. *The Ecocriticism Reader: Landmarks in Literary Ecology.*

Athens: University of Georgia Press, 1996.

Gougeon, Len. "Thoreau and Reform." In *The Cambridge Companion to Thoreau*, edited by Joel Myerson, 194–214. London: Cambridge University Press, 1995.

Gould, Stephen J. *Ontogeny and Phylogeny.* Cambridge, Mass.: Harvard University Press, 1977.

Gozzi, Raymond Dante, ed. *Thoreau's Psychology: Eight Essays.* Lanham, Md.: University Press of America, 1983.

Gray, Asa. *The Botanical Text-Book: An Introduction to Scientific Botany, Both Structural and Systematic.* 4th ed. New York: George P. Putnam & Co., 1853.

———. "Explanations of *Vestiges.*" *North American Review* 62 (April 1846): 465–506.

———. *A Manual of the Botany of the Northern United States.* Boston: J. Munroe and Co., 1848.

Greenblatt, Stephen. "Culture." In *Critical Terms for Literary Study,* edited by Frank Lentricchia and Thomas McLaughlin, 225–32. Chicago: University of Chicago Press, 1990.

Greene, Jack P. *The Intellectual Construction of America: Exceptionalism and Identity, from 1492 to 1800.* Chapel Hill: University of North Carolina Press, 1993.

Gross, Robert A. "Culture and Cultivation: Agriculture and Society in Thoreau's Concord." *Journal of American History* 69 (1982): 42–61.

———. "The Great Bean Field Hoax: Thoreau and the Agricultural Reformers." *Virginia Quarterly Review* 61, 3 (1985): 483–97.

Grumbine, R. Edward. "Image and Reality: Culture and Biology in the National Parks." *Orion* 16, 2 (spring 1997): 16–23.

Guyot, Arnold. *The Earth and Man: Lectures on Comparative Physical Geography, in Its Relation to the History of Mankind.* Translated by C. C. Felton. Boston: Gould and Lincoln, 1851.

Hall, Donald. *A Roof of Tiger Lilies.* New York: Viking Press, 1964.

Hamlin, Helen. *Nine Mile Bridge.* New York: Norton, 1945.

———. *Pine, Potatoes, and People.* New York: Norton, 1948.

Harding, Walter. *The Days of Henry Thoreau: A Biography.* New York: Dover, 1962.

———. *Emerson's Library.* Charlottesville: University of Virginia Press, 1967.

———. *The Thoreau Handbook.* New York: New York University Press, 1961.

Harding, Walter, and Michael Meyer. *The New Thoreau Handbook.* New York: New York University Press, 1980.

Harjo, Joy. *She Had Some Horses.* New York: Thunder's Mouth Press, 1997.

Heinrich, Bernd. *A Year in the Maine Woods.* Reading, Mass.: Addison-Wesley, 1994.

Hepworth, James. "The Poetry Center Interview." In *Resist Much, Obey Little: Some Notes on Edward Abbey,* edited by James Hepworth and Gregory McNamee, 33–44. Tucson, Ariz.: Harbinger House, 1989.

Hildebidle, John. *Thoreau: A Naturalist's Liberty.* Cambridge: Harvard University Press, 1983.

Hoagland, Edward. *Walking the*

Dead Diamond River. New York: Random House, 1973.

Hobsbawm, Eric. *The Age of Capital: 1848–1875.* New York: Weidenfeld & Nicolson, 1975.

The Holy Bible. New Revised Standard Version. New York: Oxford University Press, 1989.

Holzer, Harold. "Strangers and Pilgrims." *American History Illustrated* 20 (November 1985): 24–32.

Hubbard, Harlan. *Shantyboat: A River Way of Life.* Foreword by Wendell Berry. Lexington: University Press of Kentucky, 1977.

Humboldt, Alexander von. *Cosmos.* 1850. Translated by E. C. Otte. Reprint, Baltimore: Johns Hopkins University Press, 1997.

Hunt, Ray. *Think Harmony with Horses: An In-Depth Study of Horse/Man Relationship.* Edited by Milly Hunt. Fresno, Calif.: Pioneer, 1982.

Hurt, R. Douglas. *Indian Agriculture in America: Prehistory to the Present.* Lawrence: Kansas University Press, 1987.

Husserl, Edmund. *Phenomenology and the Crisis of Philosophy.* Translated by Quentin Lauer. New York: Harper & Row, 1965.

Hussey, Christopher. *The Picturesque: Studies in a Point of View.* Hamden, Conn.: Archon, 1967.

Irland, Lloyd C. *Wildlands and Woodlots: The Story of New England's Forests.* Hanover, Mass.: University Press of New England, 1982.

Jeffers, Robinson. *Selected Poems.* New York: Vintage Press, 1965.

Jewett, Sarah Orne. *The Country of the Pointed Firs.* New York: W. W. Norton, 1994.

Johnson, Linck C. *Thoreau's Complex Weave: The Writing of "A Week on the Concord and Merrimack Rivers."* Charlottesville: University Press of Virginia, 1986.

Jones, David. Introduction to *Rural Hours,* by Susan Fenimore Cooper. Syracuse, N.Y.: Syracuse University Press, 1968.

Kammen, Michael. "The Problem of American Exceptionalism: A Reconsideration." In *In the Past Lane: Historical Perspectives on American Culture,* 169–98. New York: Oxford University Press, 1997.

Kant, Immanuel. *Metaphysical Foundations of Natural Science.* 1786. Translated by James Ellington. Reprint, Indianapolis and New York: Bobbs-Merrill, 1970.

Kerridge, Richard. Introduction to *Writing the Environment: Ecocriticism and Literature,* edited by Richard Kerridge and Neil Sammells. New York: Zed Books, 1998.

Kidney, Dorothy Boone. *Away from It All.* South Brunswick, N.J.: A. S. Barnes, 1969.

———. *A Home in the Wilderness.* South Brunswick, N.J.: A. S. Barnes, 1969.

Killingworth, Jimmie M., and Jacqueline S. Palmer, eds. *Ecospeak: Rhetoric and Environmental Politics in America.* Carbondale: Southern Illinois University Press, 1992.

Kolodny, Annette. *The Lay of the Land: Metaphor as Experience and History in American Life and Letters.* Chapel Hill: University of North Carolina Press, 1975.

Kroeber, Karl. *Ecological Literary Criticism: Romantic Imagining and the Biology of Mind.* New York: Columbia University Press, 1994.

———. "Ecology and American Literature: Thoreau and Un-Thoreau." *American Literary History* 9 (1997): 309–28.

Langbaum, Robert. *The Modern Spirit: Essays on the Continuity of Nineteenth- and Twentieth-Century Literature.* New York: Oxford University Press, 1970.

———. "The New Nature Poetry." *American Scholar* 28, 3 (summer 1959): 323–40. Reprinted in Langbaum, *The Modern Spirit.*

Lansky, Mitch. *Beyond the Beauty Strip.* Gardiner, Maine: Tilbury House, 1992.

LaRusso, Carol Spenard, ed. *The Green Thoreau.* San Rafael, Calif.: New World Library, 1992.

Laurence, David. "William Bradford's American Sublime." *PMLA* 102, 1 (1987): 55–65.

Lawrence, D. H. *Studies in Classic American Literature.* New York: T. Seltzer, 1923.

Leiss, William. *The Domination of Nature.* Boston: Beacon Press, 1974.

Leopold, Aldo. *A Sand County Almanac.* New York: Sierra Club / Ballantine, 1974.

Levertov, Denise. *The Life Around Us: Selected Poems on Nature.* New York: New Directions, 1997.

Loeffler, Jack. "Edward Abbey." In *Headed Upstream: Interviews with Iconoclasts,* 3–19. Tucson, Ariz.: Harbinger House, 1989.

Lopez, Barry, and Edward O. Wilson. "Ecology and the Human Imagination." In *Writing Natural History: Dialogues with Authors,* edited by Edward Lueders, 7–35.

Salt Lake City: University of Utah Press, 1989.

Lu, Shuxiang, ed. *One Hundred Quatrains by the Tang Poets.* Changsha: Hunan Education Press, 1980.

Lyon, Thomas J. "A Taxonomy of Nature Writing." In *This Incomperable Lande: A Book of American Nature Writing,* edited by Thomas J. Lyon, 3–7. New York: Penguin, 1989. Reprinted in *The Ecocriticism Reader,* edited by Cheryl Glotfelty and Harold Fromm, 276–81. Athens: University of Georgia Press, 1996.

———, ed. *This Incomperable Lande.* New York: Penguin, 1989.

Marsh, George Perkins. *Man and Nature or, Physical Geography as Modified by Human Action.* 1864. Reprint edited by David Lowenthal. Cambridge: Belknap Press of Harvard University Press, 1995.

Marshman, Joshua. *The Works of Confucius.* Serampore: N.p., 1809.

Marx, Leo. *The Machine in the Garden: Technology and the Pastoral Ideal in America.* New York: Oxford University Press, 1964.

Mayr, Ernst. *The Growth of Biological Thought: Diversity, Evolution, and Inheritance.* Cambridge, Mass.: Belknap Press of Harvard University Press, 1982.

McDowell, Michael J. "The Bakhtinian Road to Ecological Insight." In *The Ecocriticism Reader: Landmarks in Literary Ecology,* edited by Cheryl Glotfelty and Harold Fromm, 371–91. Athens: University of Georgia Press, 1996.

McGregor, Robert Kuhn. *A Wider View of the Universe: Henry Thoreau's Study of Nature*. Urbana: University of Illinois Press, 1997.

McIntosh, James. *Thoreau as Romantic Naturalist: His Shifting Stance toward Nature*. Ithaca: Cornell University Press, 1974.

McKibben, Bill. *The End of Nature*. New York: Random House, 1989.

McPhee, John. *The Control of Nature*. New York: Farrar, Straus & Giroux, 1989.

————. "North of the C. P. Line." In *Table of Contents*. New York: Farrar, Straus & Giroux, 1985.

Meine, Curt. *Aldo Leopold*. Madison: University of Wisconsin Press, 1988.

Meinig, D. W. "The Beholding Eye: Ten Versions of the Same Scene." *Landscape Architecture* (January 1976): 47–54. Reprinted in *The Interpretation of Ordinary Landscapes*, edited by D. W. Meinig, 33–48. Oxford: Oxford University Press, 1979.

Melnicove, Mark, and Kendall Merriam. *The Uncensored Guide to Maine*. Augusta, Maine: Tapley, 1984.

Merchant, Carolyn. *The Death of Nature: Women, Ecology, and the Scientific Revolution*. New York: Harper, 1990.

Merleau-Ponty, Maurice. *The Phenomenology of Perception*. Translated by Colin Smith. New York: Routledge, 1996.

Merritt, Howard. "Appendix I: Correspondence between Thomas Cole and Robert Gilmor, Jr." In *Annual II: Studies in Thomas Cole, an American Romanticist*. Baltimore: Baltimore Museum of Art, 1967.

Merwin, W. S. *The Second Four Books of Poems*: "*The Moving Target,*" "*The Lice,*" "*The Carrier of Ladders,*" "*Writings to an Unfinished Accompaniment.*" Port Townsend, Wash.: Copper Canyon Press, 1993.

Milder, Robert. *Reimagining Thoreau*. New York: Cambridge University Press, 1995.

Miller, Hugh. *The Foot-Prints of the Creator: or, The Asterolepis of Stromness*. Boston: Gould & Lincoln, 1850.

Moldenhauer, Joseph J. "*Walden* and Wordsworth's *Guide to the Lake District.*" In *Studies in the American Renaissance 1990*, edited by Joel Myerson, 261–92. Charlottesville: University of Virginia Press, 1990.

Mourt's Relation: A Journal of the Pilgrims at Plymouth. 1622. Bedford, Mass.: Applewood Books, 1963.

Muir, John. *My First Summer in the Sierra*. New York: Penguin, 1987.

Munro, Donald J. *The Concept of Man in Early China*. Stanford, Calif.: Stanford University Press, 1969.

Myerson, Joel, ed. *The Cambridge Companion to Thoreau*. London: Cambridge University Press, 1995.

Nabhan, Gary Paul. "Cultural Parallax in Viewing North American Habitats." In *Reinventing Nature? Responses to Postmodern Deconstruction*, edited by Michael E. Soule and Gary Lease, 87–101. Washington, D.C.: Island Press, 1995.

Nash, Roderick, ed. *American*

Environmentalism: Readings in Conservation History. 3rd ed. New York: McGraw, 1990.

———. *Wilderness and the American Mind.* Rev. ed. New Haven, Conn.: Yale University Press, 1973.

Nelson, Barbara "Barney." "Edward Abbey's Cow." In *Coyote in the Maze: Tracking Edward Abbey in a World of Words,* edited by Peter Quigley, 206–25. Salt Lake City: University of Utah Press, 1998.

Nelson, Truman. "Thoreau and John Brown." In *Thoreau in Our Season,* edited by John Hicks, 134–44. Amherst: University of Massachusetts Press, 1962.

Nibbelink, Herman. "Thoreau and Wendell Berry: Bachelor and Husband of Nature." In *Wendell Berry,* edited by Paul Merchant, 135–51. Lewiston, Idaho: Confluence Press, 1991. First published in *South Atlantic Quarterly* 84 (1985): 127–40.

Noble, Louis. *The Life and Works of Thomas Cole.* Edited by Elliot Vesell. 1853. Reprint, Hansonville, N.Y.: Black Dome, 1997.

Norwood, Vera. "Mary Austin's Acequia Madre." In *The Desert Is No Lady: Southwestern Landscapes in Women's Writing and Art,* edited by Vera Norwood and Janice Monk, 223–34. New Haven, Conn.: Yale University Press, 1987.

Novak, Barbara. *American Painting of the Nineteenth Century: Realism, Idealism, and the American Experience.* 2nd ed. New York: Harper & Row, 1979.

———. "Influences and Affinities: The Interplay between America and Europe in Landscape Painting before 1860." In *The Shaping of Art and Architecture in Nineteenth-Century America,* 27–41. New York: Metropolitan Museum of Art, 1972.

———. *Nature and Culture: American Landscape Painting, 1825–1875.* Rev. ed. New York: Oxford University Press, 1995.

O'Grady, John P. "Thinking Is False Happiness." *Terra Nova* 1, 3 (1996): 121–29.

Oelschlaeger, Max. *The Idea of Wilderness: From Prehistory to the Age of Ecology.* London: Yale University Press, 1991.

Ospovat, Dov. *The Development of Darwin's Theory: Natural History, Natural Theology, and Natural Selection, 1838–1859.* Cambridge: Cambridge University Press, 1981.

Papa, James A., Jr. "The Politics of Leisure: Industrial Tourism in Edward Abbey's *Desert Solitaire.*" In *Coyote in the Maze: Tracking Edward Abbey in a World of Words,* edited by Peter Quigley, 316–34. Salt Lake City: University of Utah Press, 1998.

Paradis, James G. *T. H. Huxley: Man's Place in Nature.* Lincoln: University of Nebraska Press, 1978.

Parry, Ellwood, III. *The Art of Thomas Cole: Ambition and Imagination.* London: Associated University Presses, 1988.

Paul, Sherman. *The Shores of America: Thoreau's Inward Exploration.* Urbana: University of Illinois Press, 1972.

Payne, Daniel G. "Monkey Wrenching, Environmental Extremism, and the Problematical Edward Abbey." *Southwestern American Literature* 21 (Fall 1995): 195–208.

Peck, H. Daniel. "Better Mythology: Perception and Emergence in

Thoreau's Journal." *North Dakota Quarterly* 59 (1991): 33–44.

———. "The Crosscurrents of *Walden*'s Pastoral." In *New Essays on Walden*, edited by Robert B. Sayre, 73–94. Cambridge: Cambridge University Press, 1992.

———. *Thoreau's Morning Work: Memory and Perception in "A Week on the Concord and Merrimack Rivers," the Journal, and "Walden."* New Haven, Conn.: Yale University Press, 1990.

Pickering, Charles. *The Races of Man; and Their Geographical Distribution.* London: H. G. Bohn, 1851.

Playfair, John. *Illustrations of the Huttonian Theory of the Earth.* Edinburgh. Cadell and Davies, 1802.

Posey, Darrell Addison. "The Science of the Mebêngôkre." In *Finding Home: Writing on Nature and Culture from* Orion *Magazine*, edited by Peter Sauer, 135–48. Boston: Beacon Press, 1992.

Pyne, Stephen J. "History with Fire in Its Eye." In *That Awesome Space: Human Interaction with the Intermountain Landscape*, edited by Richard E. Hart, 105–12. Salt Lake City: Westwater Press, 1981.

Rehbock, Philip. *The Philosophical Naturalists: Themes in Early Nineteenth-Century British Biology.* Madison: University of Wisconsin Press, 1983.

———. "Transcendental Anatomy." In *Romanticism and the Sciences*, edited by Andrew Cunningham and Nicholas Jardine, 144–60. Cambridge: Cambridge University Press, 1990.

Relph, Edward. *Place and Placelessness.* London: Pion, 1980.

Rich, Louise Dickinson. *Happy the Land.* Philadelphia: Lippincott, 1946.

———. *We Took to the Woods.* New York: Grosset & Dunlap, 1942.

Richards, Evelleen. "'Metaphorical Mystifications': The Romantic Gestation of Nature." In *Romanticism and the Sciences*, edited by Andrew Cunningham and Nicholas Jardine, 130–43. Cambridge: Cambridge University Press, 1990.

———. "A Question of Property Rights: Richard Owen's Evolutionism Reassessed." *British Journal for the History of Science* 20 (June 1987): 129–71.

Richards, Robert. *The Meaning of Evolution: The Morphological Construction and the Ideological Reconstruction of Darwin's Theory.* Chicago: University of Chicago Press, 1992.

Richardson, Robert D., Jr. *Henry Thoreau: A Life of the Mind.* Berkeley: University of California Press, 1986.

———. Introduction to *Faith in a Seed*, by Henry David Thoreau. Washington, D.C.: Island Press, 1993.

Robinson, David M. *Apostle of Culture: Emerson as Preacher and Lecturer.* Philadelphia: University of Pennsylvania Press, 1982.

———. "Margaret Fuller and the Transcendental Ethos: *Woman in the Nineteenth Century.*" *PMLA* 97 (1982): 83–98.

———. "Thoreau's 'Walking' and the Ecological Imperative." In *Approaches to Teaching Thoreau's "Walden" and Other Works*, edited

by Richard J. Schneider, 169–74.
New York: Modern Language
Association of America, 1996.

Roget, Peter. *Animal and Vegetable
Physiology, Considered with
Reference to Natural Theology.*
London: William Pickering, 1834.

Rossi, William. "Emerson, Nature,
and Natural Science." In *Ralph
Waldo Emerson: An Historical
Guide,* edited by Joel Myerson.
New York: Oxford University
Press, in press.

———. "The Journal, Self-Culture,
and the Genesis of 'Walking.'"
Thoreau Quarterly 16 (1984):
137–55.

———. "'The Limits of an
Afternoon Walk': Coleridgean
Polarity in Thoreau's 'Walking.'"
ESQ 34 (1987): 94–109.

———. "Thoreau and the *Vestiges*
Controversy." Paper presented at
the Modern Language Association
Convention, Chicago, December
1995.

Rudnick, Lois. "Re-naming the Land:
Anglo Expatriate Women in the
Southwest." In *The Desert Is No
Lady: Southwestern Landscapes in
Women's Writing and Art,* edited
by Vera Norwood and Janice
Monk, 10–26. New Haven, Conn.:
Yale University Press, 1987.

Sanborn, Kate. *Abandoning an
Adopted Farm.* New York:
D. Appleton & Co., 1894.

Sattelmeyer, Robert. "The Remaking
of *Walden.*" In *Writing the
American Classics,* edited by James
Barbour and Tom Quirk, 53–78.
Chapel Hill: University of North
Carolina Press, 1990.

———. *Thoreau's Reading: A Study
in Intellectual History with
Bibliographical Catalogue.*

Princeton, N.J.: Princeton
University Press, 1988.

———. "A Walk to More Than
Wachusett." *Thoreau Society
Bulletin,* no. 202 (1992): 1–4.

Sayre, Robert. *Thoreau and the
American Indians.* Princeton, N.J.:
Princeton University Press, 1977.

Schama, Simon. *Landscape and
Memory.* London: HarperCollins,
1995.

Scheese, Don. "*Desert Solitaire*:
Counter-Friction to the Machine
in the Garden." *North Dakota
Quarterly* 59 (spring 1991):
211–27.

———. *Nature Writing: The Pastoral
Impulse in America.* New York:
Twayne, 1996.

———. "Thoreau's Journal: The
Creation of a Sacred Place." In
Mapping American Culture, edited
by Wayne Franklin and Michael
Steiner, 139–51. Iowa City:
University of Iowa Press, 1992.

Schneider, Richard J. *Henry David
Thoreau.* Boston: Twayne
Publishers, 1987.

———. "Reflections in Walden Pond:
Thoreau's Optics." *ESQ* 21 (second
quarter 1975): 65–75.

———. "Thoreau and Nineteenth-
Century American Landscape
Painting." *ESQ* 31 (second quarter
1985): 67–88.

Seamon, David. *A Geography of the
Lifeworld: Movement, Rest and
Encounter.* New York: St. Martin's
Press, 1979.

Secord, James A. "Behind the Veil:
Robert Chambers and *Vestiges.*" In
*History, Humanity, and Evolution:
Essays for John C. Greene,* edited
by James R. Moore, 165–94.
Cambridge: Cambridge University
Press, 1989.

[Sedgwick, Adam]. Review of *Vestiges of the Natural History of Creation.* *Edinburgh Review* 82 (July 1845): 1–85.

Sessions, George. "Reinventing Nature: The End of Wilderness? A Response to William Cronon's *Uncommon Ground.*" *Wild Duck Review* (November 1995): 13–16.

Shafer, Byron E. *Is America Different? A New Look at American Exceptionalism.* Oxford: Clarendon, 1991.

Shanley, J. Lyndon. *The Making of Walden.* Chicago: University of Chicago Press, 1957.

Silko, Leslie Marmon. "Landscape, History, and the Pueblo Imagination." In *On Nature: Nature, Landscape, and Natural History,* edited by Daniel Halpern, 83–94. San Francisco: North Point Press, 1986.

Simon, Gary. "What Henry David Didn't Know about Lao Tzu: Taoist Parallels in Thoreau." *Literature: East and West* 17 (1973): 253–74.

Snyder, Gary. *The Practice of the Wild.* San Francisco: North Point Press, 1990.

———. *Turtle Island.* Boston: Shambhala Press, 1993.

Solnit, Rebecca. "Reclaiming History: Richard Misrach and the Politics of Landscape Photography." *Aperture* (midsummer 1990): 30–36.

———. *Savage Dreams: A Journey into the Landscape Wars of the American West.* New York: Vintage, 1994.

Soule, Michael E., and Gary Lease, eds. *Reinventing Nature? Responses to Postmodern Deconstruction.*

Washington, D.C.: Island Press, 1995.

Southworth, James. "Thoreau, Moralist of the Picturesque." *PMLA* 49 (1934): 971–74.

Springer, John S. *Forest Life and Forest Trees.* 1851. Reprint edited by F. M. O'Brien. Somersworth: New Hampshire Publishing, 1975.

Steinberg, Theodore. *Nature Incorporated: Industrialization and the Waters of New England.* Amherst: University of Massachusetts Press, 1991.

Sterrenburg, Lee. "A Narrative Overview: The Making of the Concept of the Global 'Environment' in Literature and Science." Unpublished manuscript.

———. "Romanticism, Technology, and the Ecology of Knowledge." Paper delivered at the Midwestern Conference on Literature and Science, Bloomington, Ind., February 7–10, 1991.

Stewart, Frank. *A Natural History of Nature Writing.* Washington, D.C.: Island/Shearwater, 1995.

Stocking, George W., Jr. *Victorian Anthropology.* New York: Free Press, 1987.

Stoppard, Tom. *Arcadia.* London: Faber & Faber, 1993.

Stravinsky, Igor. *The Poetics of Music.* Translated by Arthur Knodel and Ingolf Dahl. New York: Vintage Books, 1956.

Tao, Yuanming. *Selected Poems.* Translated by Gladys Yang and Yang Xianyi. Beijing: Panda Books, 1993.

Taylor, Charles. "Heidegger, Language and Deep Ecology." In *Heidegger: A Critical Reader,* edited by Hubert Dreyfus and H. Hall,

247–69. Oxford: Blackwell,
1992.

Templeman, William. "Thoreau,
Moralist of the Picturesque."
PMLA 47 (1932): 864–89.

Thaxter, Celia. *Among the Isles of
Shoals.* 1873. Reprint, Boston:
Houghton Mifflin, 1888.

Thomas, R. S. *Collected Poems: 1945–
1990.* London: Phoenix, 1993.

Thoreau, Henry David. *Collected
Poems of Henry Thoreau.* Edited
by Carl Bode. Baltimore: Johns
Hopkins University Press, 1964.

———. *The Correspondence of Henry
David Thoreau.* Edited by Walter
Harding and Carl Bode. New
York: New York University Press,
1958.

———. *Faith in a Seed.* Edited by
Bradley P. Dean. Washington,
D.C.: Island Books, 1993.

———. *Journal. Vol. 1: 1837–1844.*
Edited by Elizabeth Hall Witherell
et al. Princeton, N.J.: Princeton
University Press, 1981.

———. *Journal. Vol. 2: 1842–1848.*
Edited by Robert Sattelmeyer.
Princeton, N.J.: Princeton
University Press, 1984.

———. *Journal. Vol. 3: 1848–1851.*
Edited by Robert Sattelmeyer,
Mark R. Patterson, and William
Rossi. Princeton, N.J.: Princeton
University Press, 1990.

———. *Journal. Vol. 4: 1851–1852.*
Edited by Leonard N. Neufeldt
and Nancy Craig Simmons.
Princeton, N.J.: Princeton
University Press, 1992.

———. *Journal. Vol. 5: 1852–1853.*
Edited by Patrick O'Connell.
Princeton, N.J.: Princeton
University Press, 1997.

———. *The Journal of Henry David
Thoreau.* 14 vols. Edited by
Bradford Torrey and Francis H.
Allen. Boston: Houghton Mifflin,
1906.

———. *The Maine Woods.* Edited by
Joseph Moldenhauer. Princeton,
N.J.: Princeton University Press,
1972.

———. *The Natural History Essays.*
Introduction and notes by Robert
Sattelmeyer. Salt Lake City:
Peregrine Smith, 1980.

———. Notebook XVI (Morgan
Library MS 1302:22). Unpublished
transcription.

———. *Reform Papers.* Edited by
Wendell Glick. Princeton, N.J.:
Princeton University Press, 1973.

———. *Walden.* Edited by J. Lyndon
Shanley. Princeton, N.J.: Princeton
University Press, 1971.

———. *Walden and Civil
Disobedience.* Edited by Owen
Thomas. Reprint, New York:
Norton, 1966.

———. *A Week on the Concord and
Merrimack Rivers.* Edited by Carl
F. Hovde, William L. Howarth,
and Elizabeth Hall Witherell.
Princeton, N.J.: Princeton
University Press, 1980.

———. *Wild Apples.* 1862. Bedford,
Mass.: Applewood Books, n.d.

———. *The Writings of Henry David
Thoreau.* 20 vols. Edited by
Bradford Torrey. Boston:
Houghton Mifflin, 1906.

Topham, Jonathan R. "Beyond
the 'Common Context': The
Production and Reading of the
Bridgewater Treatises." *Isis* 89
(June 1998): 233–62.

Tuan, Yi-Fu. "American Space,
Chinese Place." *Harper's Magazine*
249 (July 1974): 8.

———. *Topophilia.* New York:
Columbia University Press, 1990.

Turner, Frederick Jackson. *The Frontier in American History.* 1920. Reprint, New York: Holt, Rinehart & Winston, 1962.

Turner, Jack. *The Abstract Wild.* Tucson: University of Arizona Press, 1996.

———. "In Wildness Is the Preservation of the World." In *The Great New Wilderness Debate: An Expansive Collection of Writings Defining Wilderness from John Muir to Gary Snyder,* edited by J. Baird Callicott and Michael P. Nelson, 617–27. Athens: University of Georgia Press, 1998.

Vessel, Elliot. Introduction to *The Life and Works of Thomas Cole,* by Louis Noble. Edited by Elliot Vessel. 1853. Reprint, Hensonville, N.Y.: Black Dome Press.

Vogel, Steven. *Against Nature.* Albany: State University of New York Press, 1996.

Von Frank, Albert J. "The Composition of *Nature*: Writing and Self in the Launching of a Career." In *Biographies of Books: The Compositional Histories of Notable American Writings,* edited by James Barbour and Tom Quirk, 11–40. Columbia: University of Missouri Press, 1996.

Wagenknecht, Edward. *Henry David Thoreau: What Manner of Man?* Amherst: University of Massachusetts Press, 1981.

Walker, Elinor Stevens. *Our Great Northern Wilderness.* Lewiston: Central Maine Press, 1966.

Wallach, Alan. "Making a Picture of the View from Mount Holyoke." In *American Iconology,* edited by David Miller, 80–111. New Haven, Conn.: Yale University Press, 1993.

Walls, Laura Dassow. *Seeing New Worlds: Henry David Thoreau and Nineteenth-Century Natural Science.* Madison: University of Wisconsin Press, 1995.

Weinreb, Mindy. "A Question a Day: A Written Conversation with Wendell Berry." In *Wendell Berry,* edited by Paul Merchant, 27–43. Lewiston, Idaho: Confluence Press, 1991.

Weisbuch, Robert. "Thoreau's Dawn and the Lake School's Night." In *Henry David Thoreau's "Walden" (Modern Critical Interpretations),* edited by Harold Bloom, 117–34. New York: Chelsea House, 1987.

Westling, Louise H. *The Green Breast of the World: Landscape, Gender, and American Fiction.* Athens: University of Georgia Press, 1996.

White, Richard. "Are You an Environmentalist or Do You Work for a Living?" In *Uncommon Ground: Rethinking the Human Place in Nature,* edited by William Cronon, 171–85. New York: W. W. Norton, 1995.

Whitehead, Alfred North. *Science and the Modern World.* New York: Macmillan, 1928.

Whitney, Gordon G., and William C. Davis. "From Primitive Woods to Cultivated Woodlots: Thoreau and the Forest History of Concord, Massachusetts." *Journal of Forest History* 30 (1986): 70–81.

Wild, Peter. *Pioneer Conservationist of Western America.* Missoula, Mont.: Mountain Press, 1979.

Wilentz, Sean. "Against Exceptionalism: Class Consciousness and the American Labor Movement, 1790–1920." *International Labor and Working Class History* 26 (fall 1984): 1–24.

Williams, Raymond. *The Country and the City*. New York: Oxford University Press, 1973.

———. *Keywords: A Vocabulary of Society and Culture*. New York: Oxford University Press, 1976.

Winthrop, John. "A Modell of Christian Charity" (1630). In *Early American Writing*, edited by Giles Gunn, 108–18. New York: Penguin, 1994.

Witherell, Elizabeth Hall. "Thoreau's Watershed Season as a Poet: The Hidden Fruits of the Summer and Fall of 1841." In *Studies in the American Renaissance*, edited by Joel Myerson, 49–106. Charlottesville: University of Virginia Press, 1990.

Wordsworth, William. *A Guide Through the District of the Lakes in the North of England*. 5th ed. Kendal: Hudson and Nicholson, 1835. Reprinted as *Wordsworth's Guide to the Lakes: The Fifth Edition (1835)*. Edited by Ernest de Selincourt. Oxford: Oxford University Press, 1977.

———. *Poetical Works*. Edited by Ernest de Selincourt. Oxford: Oxford University Press, 1987.

———. *The Prelude: 1799, 1805, 1850*. Edited by Jonathan Wordsworth, M. H. Abrams, and Stephen Gill. New York: W. W. Norton, 1979.

———. *Selected Prose*. Edited by John O. Hayden. London: Penguin, 1988.

Worster, Donald. *Nature's Economy: A History of Ecological Ideas*. New York: Cambridge University Press, 1988.

Xu, Fancheng. *An Interpretation of Lao Zi*. Translated by Aimin Cheng. 1988.

Yeo, Richard. "Science and Intellectual Authority in Mid-Nineteenth-Century Britain: Robert Chambers and *Vestiges of the Natural History of Creation*." In *Energy and Entropy: Science and Culture in Victorian Britain*, edited by Patrick Brantlinger, 1–27. Bloomington: Indiana University Press, 1989.

Young, Robert M. *Darwin's Metaphor: Nature's Place in Victorian Culture*. Cambridge: Cambridge University Press, 1991.

Zhou, Yi, and Yihua Liang. *Chinese Culture*. Nanning: Guangxi Education Press, 1993.

INDEX

"Guardian Spirit," 109; "Kaater-skill Falls from Below," 95; "Lecture on American Scenery" (essay), 101, 102, 103; "Portage Falls on the Genesee River," 98; "View from Mount Holyoke," 98, 102; *The Voyage of Life*, 96, 102

Coleridge, Samuel Taylor, 19, 23, 30, 194

Collins, James, 241

Colorado River, 271, 274

Columbus, Christopher, 245, 246, 247

Concord (Mass.), 1, 7, 9, 28, 40, 58, 70, 91, 93, 106, 168, 171, 174, 183, 231, 239, 240–243, 269

Concord River, 11, 248, 268

Concord Woods, 6, 10, 22

Confucius, 209, 264

Conrad, Joseph, 76

Constitution, United States, 272

Cooper, James Fenimore, 110

Cooper, Susan Fenimore, 10, 162, 179–192; *Rural Hours*, 179–192; "Small Family Memories," 186

Cooperstown (N.Y.), 192

Coverly, Valentine, 159

Cronon, William, 25, 162, 259; *Uncommon Ground: Toward Reinventing Nature*, 259

Cumberland, 194

Dahomey, 50, 264

Daniel, John, 174

Darwin, Charles, 18, 21, 30, 32, 33, 34, 37, 76, 135, 261; *The Descent of Man*, 19; *The Origin of the Species*, 18, 30, 32, 36, 115

Deming, Alison Hawthorne, 266

Dillard, Annie, 9, 11, 70–79; *Living by Fiction*, 76; *Pilgrim at Tinker Creek*, compared to *Walden*, 70–79

"The Dispersion of Seeds," 22, 54, 59, 116, 277

Douglas, William O., 169, 170, 172, 173; *My Wilderness*, 169

dualism, 18, 22, 23, 24, 26, 209

Durand, Asher, 9, 93, 94, 96, 97, 98, 99, 100, 103, 104, 105, 106, 109, 110, 111; "Catskill Study," 104; "Early Morning at Cold Spring," 106; "Forest Study," 104; "In the Woods," 104; "Interior of a Wood," 104; "Landscape," 104; "Letters on Landscape Painting" (letters), 94, 103, 108; "The Morning and Evening of Life," 96–97; "Study of Rocks," 104; "Through the Woods," 104; "Woodland Interior," 104

Dustan, Hannah, 91

Earth First! (organization), 275, 277

ecocentric views of nature, *see* biocentric

ecological poetry, 10, 133–144

ecology, 3, 4, 5, 6, 7, 12, 17, 18, 21, 22, 24, 25, 44, 45, 61, 126, 159–160, 162, 198, 200, 201; deep ecology, 7, 8

Eden, 84, 90, 208, 247, 256, 257, 263

Edinburgh Review, 30, 39

Edward Abbey: A Voice Crying in the Wilderness (videotape), 275

embryogenesis, 32–36

Emerson, Ralph Waldo, 19, 29, 30, 86, 116, 134, 142, 208, 210, 223, 224, 225, 238, 241, 243, 244–245, 251, 252, 253, 255; letter to John Muir, 25; *Nature*, 19, 31, 210, 224; "The Transcendentalist," 86

Engel, J. Ronald, 268

England, *see* Great Britain

Enlightenment, 39, 158

environmentalism, 3, 17, 55, 59, 62–63, 198, 204, 250, 259

epistemology, 2, 8, 28, 30, 72, 191, 217–218, 228

Etruria, 84

Europe, 47, 48, 49, 50, 51, 52, 53, 54, 100, 101, 102, 103, 105, 109, 124, 125, 162, 190, 210, 242, 246, 247, 257, 262

Evernden, Neil, 122, 259, 270

evolution, 37, 38, 135

The American Land and Life Series